MORE PRAISE FOR
THE VERSATILITY FACTOR

"The Versatility Factor combines great research with practical suggestions to give you a guidebook to your future. It provides fantastic coaching advice for the leaders of today, and even better coaching for the leaders of tomorrow!"

Marshall Goldsmith, *New York Times* #1 best-selling author of *Triggers* and *What Got You Here Won't Get You There* – two of Amazon.com's 'Top 100 Leadership & Success Books' ever written

"Understanding SOCIAL STYLE and Versatility is one of the single greatest factors in my career success. Having high EQ is critical in making sure that what you communicate is heard, understood, and accepted. It's not what you say, or how you say it, it's how you make people feel. I can honestly say that my career would be in a far different, and worse place today, if I hadn't achieved the skills taught in this book. I live SOCIAL STYLE and Versatility in my personal and professional encounters, and the difference they make is dramatic."

Jim Knauss, Global Vice Chair of Accounts and Business Development, EY

"I have introduced the SOCIAL STYLE Model in 2013 to all the leaders in BASF's *Supply Chain Operations & Information Services* organization. This concept has supported us in increasing leadership performance, building relationships, and working in global teams. SOCIAL STYLE is a practical tool for working well with others who are different from you and to make sure that everybody's strengths are used well."

Dr. Robert Blackburn, President BASF Supply Chain Operations & Information Services, Germany

"Working collaboratively for mutual gain has never been more important as we continually seek advantage in increasingly competitive and dynamic marketplaces around the world. It is now crystal clear that one source of that advantage comes from harnessing the talents of the ever more diverse teams in our organizations. Based on many years of research coupled with practical consulting experience, Myers and Pfaffhausen present a comprehensive, elegant, and coherent set of ideas for how to work better together—a comprehensive and fitting update to Merrill and Reid's original work in field of behaviour in the workplace."

Mike Mister, Practice Group Head, Moller Professional Service Firm Group, Churchill College, University of Cambridge

"Myers and Pfaffhausen have validated the significance of knowing and optimizing your and others' SOCIAL STYLE. *The Versatility Factor* aggregates and integrates the knowledge needed to build high-performing relationships in work and life—a must-read resource. You'll want to continually reinforce your "say and do" behavior by referring back to this exceptional book."

Dr. William Klepper, Professor and Academic Director, Executive Education, Columbia University and author of *The CEO's Boss: Tough Love in the Boardroom.*

"*The Versatility Factor* is a great addition to the constellation of SOCIAL STYLE resources and serves as a valuable companion to the SOCIAL STYLE profile. Most of the leadership development and coaching work that I conduct is founded upon helping leaders improve their relationship-building skills. This deeper dive into the characteristics and application of Versatility provides practical and actionable guidance to build and continually improve interpersonal relationships."

Mark Saine, Senior Director, Client Executive and Leadership Development Strategic Solutions and Institutional Client Engagement, TIAA

"I have used SOCIAL STYLE extensively in teaching and coaching. Working with one client, we increased the competitive win rate by 17 basis points by applying SOCIAL STYLE to meeting preparation and presentation. The client's win rate went from the mid-30s percentage to the high-40s."

Henry McIntosh, President, The McIntosh Method

"*The Versatility Factor* is a 'must read' for all of us who realize we get all the things we want and need from other people. It is bound to be a best seller because it teaches us all how to win cooperation, inspire collaboration, and bring out the very best in others by treating them the way 'they want to be treated'. The practical models, plain language, and detailed how to's in this book are as rock-solid as the extensive research behind them. Kudos to Myers and Pfaffhausen for making clear the path to highly productive relationships."

Bob Heavers, President, Priority Management Colorado

THE VERSATILITY FACTOR

STRATEGIES FOR BUILDING HIGH-PERFORMING RELATIONSHIPS

THE VERSATILITY FACTOR

JOHN R. MYERS
HENNING PFAFFHAUSEN, PH.D.

www.bookpresspublishing.com

Copyright © 2016 by The TRACOM Corporation. All rights reserved.
(303) 470-4900 — (800) 221-2321 (U.S. only)
www.tracomcorp.com

SOCIAL STYLE, The Social Intelligence Company, the Creator of SOCIAL STYLE and TRACOM are registered trademarks of the TRACOM Corporation. SOCIAL STYLE Model is a trademark of the TRACOM Corporation.

No part of this book may be reproduced, transmitted or stored in any form or by any means, electronic or mechanical, without prior written permission from The TRACOM Corporation.

Any requests or questions for the authors should be submitted to them directly at jmyers@tracom.com and henning.pfaffhausen@terenia.de

Published in Des Moines, Iowa, by:
BookPress Publishing
P.O. Box 71532, Des Moines, IA 50325
www.BookPressPublishing.com

Facebook, YouTube, WeChat, LinkedIn, Instagram, FaceTime, Skype, and Twitter are registered trademarks.

Publisher's Cataloging-in-Publication Data

Names: Myers, John R., author. | Pfaffhausen, Henning, author.
Title: The Versatility Factor : strategies for building high-performing relationships / John R. Myers ; Henning Pfaffhausen, Ph.D.
Description: Includes bibliographical references. | Des Moines [Iowa]: BookPress Publishing, 2016.
Identifiers: ISBN 978-0-9964428-5-5 | LCCN 2016940440
Subjects: LCSH Interpersonal communication. | Interpersonal relations. | Communication. | Business communication. | Social skills. | Human behavior. | Self-actualization (Psychology.) | Success--Psychological aspects. | BISAC BUSINESS & ECONOMICS / General.
Classification: LCC HM1111 .M94 2016 | DDC 302 –dc23

First Edition
Printed in the United States of America
10 9 8 7 6 5 4 3 2 1

*The Authors wish to acknowledge the contributions of
TRACOM's Founders, Dr. David Merrill and Roger Reid,
to the field of behavioral science through their original research into
identifying and measuring interpersonal behavior preferences and how
behavioral choices impact performance.*

CONTENTS

Preface ix

1 Introduction 1
    1.1   Behavior vs. Personality 7
    1.2   Observable Behavior 11
    1.3   Predicting Human Behavior 15

2 The SOCIAL STYLE Model™ 18
    2.1   Assertiveness 22
    2.2   Responsiveness 25
    2.3   SOCIAL STYLEs® 28
    2.4   Toxic Relationships 38
    2.5   Versatility 41
    2.6   Reliability & Validity 56

3 SOCIAL STYLEs and Versatility at Work 65
    3.1   Driving Style 76
    3.2   Expressive Style 86
    3.3   Amiable Style 97
    3.4   Analytical Style 109
    3.5   SOCIAL STYLE Identification 119
    3.6   Job Function, Industry, and Gender 124

4 Leading with the Versatility Factor 133
    4.1   Managerial Preferences 137
    4.2   Delegating Tasks 143
    4.3   Changing Directions 152
    4.4   Managing Conflicts 159
    4.5   Motivating People 169
    4.6   Providing Feedback 178

5   The Versatility Factor in Customer Relationships 192

    5.1   Building Customer Relationships .196
    5.2   Conducting Sales Calls 215
    5.3   Asking Productive Questions 227
    5.4   Recognizing Customer Attitudes .239
    5.5   Gaining Customer Commitment 251
    5.6   Negotiating Agreements 263
    5.7   Selling to Purchasing Committees 275

6   The Versatility Factor in Teams 287

    6.1   Teaming Preferences 289
    6.2   Building Relationships 296
    6.3   Welcoming Team Members 301
    6.4   Aligning the Team 305
    6.5   Roles & Responsibilities 310
    6.6   Team Meetings 315
    6.7   Decision-Making 321
    6.8   Motivation & Engagement 325
    6.9   Changing Team Direction 330
    6.10   Virtual Teams 335
    6.11   International Teams 344

7   The Versatility Factor in a Broader World of Relationships 355

    7.1   SOCIAL STYLE and Versatility at Home 357
    7.2   SOCIAL STYLEs in the Family 362
    7.3   Do Opposites Attract? 366
    7.4   Social Media 372

8   Final Thoughts 376

Chapter Notes 380
References and Suggested Readings 382
Appendix A – Multi-Rater SOCIAL STYLE and
                 Enhanced Versatility Profile 392
Appendix B – SOCIAL STYLE and Versatility by Job Function 403
Appendix C – SOCIAL STYLE and Versatility by Industry 439

Preface

As our professional and personal lives require that we constantly interact with other people, you already know the frustrations and rewards that interpersonal relationships can have on your outcomes and well-being. Wouldn't it be great to have a well-researched and effective resource readily available to help you to positively impact your relationships? We have written this book to serve as that tool for you.

Through applying the presented strategies in our careers as business leader, salesperson, human resource executive, community leader, and family member we learned about the powerfulness of *The Versatility Factor* and how it improves all aspects of our lives. We felt it was our duty to share our insights from researching, enhancing, and applying the SOCIAL STYLE Model™ and its Versatility concepts with all interested and those who could benefit from it.

This book is the result of years of intensive research and structuring the knowledge about the advancements of the concepts Dr. David Merrill and Roger Reid developed over 50 years ago. We hope it will become a much-valued tool set relevant for those working extensively with other people. For those who know the Model already, this book is intended to become a valuable resource for refreshing and deepening skills for further improving Versatility. For those for whom this Model is new, the content is very practical and easy to apply in both professional and personal contexts. We also hope that it serves to motivate gaining a deeper understanding of strengths and weaknesses by seeking feedback from others.

When we use the technique of stereotyping in the book, we do this for simplification only. It is not our intention to criticize anyone's habits or to present a methodology to be used to manipulate people! We want to provide guidance for how to build better relationships with your colleagues, customers, friends, and family members based on a sincere respect of behavioral preferences and personal priorities.

We want to thank Dr. David Merrill for giving us the opportunity to advance and apply the concepts he and Roger Reid developed in the 1960s. These early pioneers in the field of applied behavioral science and 360-degree feedback made a major contribution to the success of hundreds of thousands of organizations and individuals throughout the world. To this day, the simplicity yet elegance of their Model has proven to be a major contributor to interpersonal success regardless of industry, job function, geographic, or cultural differences.

We explicitly want to thank Dr. Casey Mulqueen for his insights on the latest research into the application of the Model on a global basis. We are grateful to Sean Essex and Sierra Charter for their critique and support and to Annette Lingerfelt and Kendra Whelchel for getting the book pulled together for our publisher. We also wish to thank the thousands of trainers, coaches, and individuals who have been working with the Model all across the globe for their continued feedback on the validity and relevance of *The Versatility Factor*.

Finally, we wish to thank Roswitha Pfaffhausen and Sandra Myers for their support, patience, critiques, and insights throughout the journey of writing this book.

1 INTRODUCTION

There is no doubt that we are all different individuals who desire to be treated with unique approaches based on who we are. But, how different are we really? On the one hand, we are distinguished by genetics, our culture, education, and the experiences we have throughout our lives. On the other hand, behavioral scientists tell us that we behave in similar patterns when we interact with others as a team member, sales professional, leader, customer, or even as a family member. Accepting the fact that we share common behavioral patterns, there must exist more than one best approach for dealing most effectively with others. This challenge can be overcome with the help of this book—*The Versatility Factor* and the "how-tos" of building high-performing relationships!

Trying to understand the way others prefer to go about getting things done can be a source of frustration and tension for us and frequently the most perplexing challenge we face in our daily lives. Even in the best of our relationships we can experience this type of challenge. In our troubled relationships, these challenges most often lead to poor performance, loss of productivity, lost sales, and weakened teams. For many of us, it leads to increased feelings of stress which negatively affect other relationships at work and at home.

For most of us, the problems we encounter from a task can be energizing. Task challenges stimulate us to be creative, innovative, thoughtful, focused, and engaged. Compare that to what you feel when you encounter a *people problem*! People challenges are the most difficult for us to overcome. They drain our energy and shift our focus away from what we are trying to accomplish. They can overwhelm our emotions, reduce our sense of well-being, and negatively affect our health.

Is there something wrong with us when we encounter problems when working with someone else? The quick answer is a resounding no!

For thousands of years, people from Socrates to Galen to Jung to Isabel Myers speculated that people fell into distinctive "types" and that these "types" held the potential for conflict with non-similar "types." In the past 100 years, behavioral psychologists and researchers have discovered that only 25% of people are like us and the other 75% are significantly different from us in important ways. The majority of people important to your happiness and success are substantially different from you in how they:

- Approach problems
- Approach people
- Deal with feelings
- Come to decisions
- Take risks
- Resolve challenges
- Use time
- Share information
- React to conflict

These differences are not the only sources of our people problems;

however, research shows them to be the most frequent. We can also be challenged by different values, beliefs, and cultural differences, but these differences in behavior are what we first encounter from others and are the most common causes for conflict and misunderstanding. The challenge we face, whether at work or at home, is that our success and happiness ultimately depend on how well we can bridge these differences. If we can do this, our lives become more fulfilling, happier, and successful!

Communication is perhaps the most complex thing humans do. It is arguably the most critical skill for thriving and surviving in almost any situation, short of being stranded alone on a desert island. This is why the work of trying to uncover the secrets and mysteries of effective communication is an industry unto itself. Albert Mehrabian, professor emeritus at the University of California in Los Angeles and the author of *Silent Messages: Implicit Communication of Emotions and Attitudes*, has often been credited for determining that the effectiveness of communication is based on these three factors:

- 7% is based on the meaning of the words we use
- 38% is based on the way we say the words we choose
- 55% is based on nonverbal cues, such as facial expressions

Although Mehrabian's research was done back in the 1970s, this insight about the disproportional importance of tone of voice and nonverbal signals in communication still is incorrectly quoted by many people today. Merhabian's study was too limited and specific to make such broad generalities. He did, however, get across that communication is both what we say and how we say it. A study done by T. Lockwood and published by Fenman Ltd in 2009 demonstrated that 86% of total communication is "tone" and only 14% is content. Communication is far trickier than the mere passage of words from one person's lips to another person's ears. Communication is a key determinant of high-performing relationships!

Regardless of the studies, it is important to keep in mind the following:

- Verbal and nonverbal elements both play an important role in effective communication.

- Verbal communication makes our meaning understood. Nonverbal communication makes our attitude, feelings, and emotions understood.

- If there are inconsistencies between what we say (words) and how we say it (nonverbal), the nonverbal is believed more than the verbal.

The science and technology of communication continue to evolve at a staggering pace. The unending parade of technology allows us to bombard each other with information from an inescapable and growing array of sophisticated methods. Many experts argue, however, that the art of human interaction ultimately plays the most critical role in building relationships capable of reaching high performance.

As you work your way through this book you will learn a research-based framework known as the SOCIAL STYLE Model™, which will give insight into four universal behavioral Styles and how you can use them to understand the implications they have for you and your behavior with others. This is the methodology for applying the Versatility Factor. You will learn about each SOCIAL STYLE® and how it influences your success in establishing and maintaining important relationships. You will learn how to "read" Styles and adapt your behaviors to improve your chances of getting along and performing better. You will gain appreciation for the strengths that each Style offers.

Understanding the critical role of effective communication is the beginning. Whether you are a leader who wants to motivate others, a salesperson who wants to gain more business, or a team member interested in improving how your team works together, the concepts, tools, and techniques in this book can have a profound influence in your life. In the end, you will be better prepared to understand, influence, and collaborate with everyone from co-workers and customers to family and friends.

You do not need to change who you are, what you believe, or how you feel about what is important to you. And, it doesn't mean becoming manipulative or dishonest in your relationships. If you apply what you learn about the Versatility Factor and SOCIAL STYLEs with sincerity, learn a few new behavioral options, and make a real effort to use behavior appropriate for the other person, you will gain amazing results without a major personal overhaul.

The authors make two critical assumptions that you need to keep in mind as you begin to explore SOCIAL STYLEs and the Versatility Factor.

A. SOCIAL STYLE is about observable behavior

The SOCIAL STYLE Model does not assess intelligence or aptitude, nor does it interpret personality or character. It does not evaluate performance or correctness. SOCIAL STYLEs don't help you delve into people's heads or hearts. You can never know for sure what a customer, boss, co-worker, or even a close friend is thinking or feeling. Watch and listen closely; you can see and hear what they're doing and saying. Those actions show you what it will take to earn their trust, confidence, and willingness to build a relationship with you. In doing so, you will be bringing the Versatility Factor to your relationships.

B. Perception is reality

What we see is what we believe. Unfortunately, what we infer from what we see isn't always true. It will take practice using SOCIAL STYLEs for you to increase your awareness, improve your powers of observation, and sharpen your ability to draw accurate conclusions about the significance of other people's behaviors.

Perhaps more important, your perception of yourself and your own SOCIAL STYLE may not match what others see. In fact, research shows that more than 50% of the time, how someone sees themselves is different from how others see them. Although the key people in your life may not know the SOCIAL STYLE Model, they nonetheless are making judgments about, and reacting to, your behaviors with them. Ultimately, your SOCIAL STYLE is how others see you, not how you see yourself. How others see you using your behaviors in relationship to them is what impacts your Versatility Factor.

Learning and using the SOCIAL STYLE Model can open your eyes to new ways of seeing things, help reduce the tension that can threaten relationships, and make you more successful at just about anything you do that involves communication—which is a lot. It will take on-going effort and energy to make the Versatility Factor a personal strength for you. Doing so will give you significant advantages in your relationships and your career. Mastery in Versatility will take patience, practice, persistence, and solid comprehension of the terms and models that come next.

1.1 Behavior vs. Personality

We all find ourselves frustrated by how others behave, and we are driven to figure out why people behave the way they do. After all, people are social by nature and we would much rather find a way to relate comfortably with someone than to find ourselves always facing difficult interactions. To achieve this, we must have an objective and non-judgmental way to understand others.

Before we go on, it is useful to clarify a fundamental construct on which SOCIAL STYLEs and the Versatility Factor rest. Behavior is what we can know about another person; we cannot know their true personality. You can think of a person's behavior and personality like an iceberg. Their behavior is the part of the iceberg we see and describe. Their personality is the part of the iceberg (see Fig. 1-1) below the surface, and we can only make inferences regarding its shape, size, depth, etc.

- *Personality* is a combination of characteristics that uniquely influence a person's thoughts, motivations, and behaviors. It flows from the interplay of our thoughts, beliefs, motivations, values, and actions. Personality is derived from the Latin *persona*, which means mask, or the public face we display. While our world today associates a mask with something that hides the identity of the wearer, in ancient times, the mask was used to represent the character.

- *Behavior* is simply what we say and do, as well as how we say and do things. It is verbal and nonverbal and is seen in each observable act we display. How fast do we speak? Are we loud or quiet? Are we faster or slower paced in our actions? Do we show more or less facial expression? Do we use our hands broadly or only to emphasize specific things? While behavior is but one part of our overall personality, it is what others observe and use to understand us and how they choose to react to us.

Before the beginning of the 20th century, philosophers and psychologists relied on non-empirical theories to identify and explain personality and its associated traits. It wasn't until the middle of the 20th century that focus was placed on using behavior to help us understand people. These two approaches are different and serve different purposes. Personality research is centered on helping

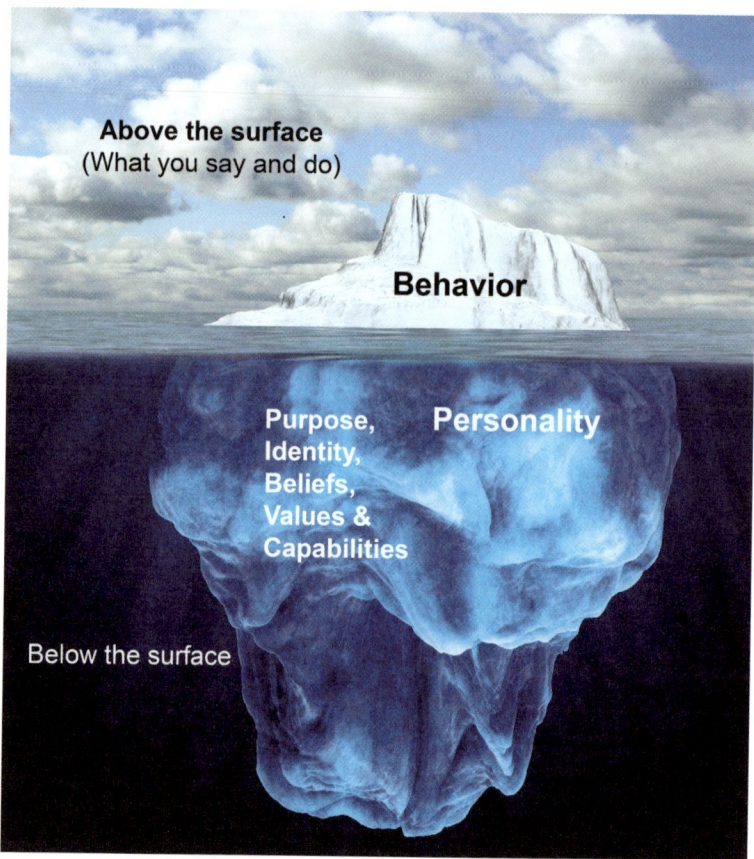

Fig. 1-1: Observable Behavior vs. Personality

individuals understand themselves, their underlying motivations, and temperaments. Personality research is also used by professionals to identify and treat clinical disorders, especially serious mental problems. Research like this is also used in career and education counseling.

It is in everyday life that behavioral research has been proven to be more useful. All of us can observe what others are saying and doing. Research has uncovered models for using those observations to both understand ourselves and others, and then determine how to interact effectively together. These models can be used by each of us in all parts of our everyday lives from the workplace, to the community, to our interactions with family and friends. The empirical research that has led to these models gives real-world proof of their relevance and effectiveness and why understanding behavior is critical for working with others. For decades some scientists have argued that our personalities and behaviors are formed entirely as expressions of our genes. Others have argued the opposite—that we develop as individuals primarily based on our environments and how we are raised. This debate has been very difficult to solve because it requires longitudinal research over the course of individuals' lifetimes, not to mention a great deal of sophisticated measurement.

Thanks to some dedicated scientists, just this type of research is available.[1] Much of this research has been conducted with twins involving those who were raised together and the rare cases of twins who were raised in separate households. Twin studies are necessary because twins are the only people who share both genetics and environment in common.

As most people would guess, this research has determined that both genetics and environment contribute to who we eventually become. Much of this research examined personality attributes, not behavioral styles, but similar results can be assumed. The details of the research are complex, but essentially genetics accounts for only a slight portion of the similarity in personalities among twins. As twins grow into adolescence and young adulthood, their unique experiences (different environments) account for the majority of their individual personality differences.

We can assume that genetics accounts for some of our behavior. For example, some of us are predisposed toward being talkative while others are predisposed toward being quieter. This is a natural expression of our genes. As we grow older and experience the world around us, some behaviors are reinforcing while others are not. Fairly early in life, usually by late adolescence or early adulthood, we stabilize into a behavioral SOCIAL STYLE that works for us, and this SOCIAL STYLE is greatly influenced by our environments.

If your colleagues were to follow you around for a couple of days and record your behavior, they would see some interesting results. First, the observers would say that you engaged in a wide range of behaviors. Next, they would notice that you used some behaviors more than others; some a lot more.

Behavioral psychology has demonstrated that, to a certain degree, we develop behavior patterns based on what is most effective for us. By "most effective" we mean that some behaviors are more likely to get the responses we desire. Also, we engage in behaviors that are most comfortable for our particular make-up.

Simply put, we use some behaviors more than others because they are the behaviors that make us most comfortable in relating to others. These behaviors became comfortable for us early in life. As we used them more often, they became behavioral habits. Since these patterns work over time for each of us, fundamentally changing them becomes less likely as we mature into adulthood.

1.2 Observable Behavior

When people ask, "Do I know myself?" the whole spectrum of psychology opens up in front of them. Many individuals try to answer this question by exploring their innermost feelings and thoughts, and while this is one approach to self-awareness, it is not ours. Instead, we are going to ask you to attempt to understand yourself by seeing yourself as others see you; try to look at yourself objectively, much as a behavioral scientist would. Our SOCIAL STYLE, the "you" on display every day, can be quite independent of what we may believe about ourselves or wish we were. Because others react to and draw conclusions about us mainly from our behavior, whether they know why we act as we do or not, our actions have a significant effect on our success in dealing with others.

Our study of behavior revolves around one key principle: the conclusions that people draw about us are based on what they observe us saying and doing. Other aspects of our personality, including our abilities, dreams, ambitions, beliefs, likes, and dislikes, play no role whatsoever in the discussion of behavior. In this book, the "you" that will be discussed is the "you" that says and does things—the "public you." Your intentions are disregarded, because they belong to the "private you."

This approach to gaining more understanding about ourselves by seeing our behavior as others see it is rather challenging. It's difficult to stand outside ourselves as observers, and then to think about how our actions affect others. This challenge is made all the more difficult when we realize that others cannot feel what we are feeling nor think what we are thinking. They can only observe what we say and do. Learning to see ourselves as others see us can be a very rewarding way of understanding ourselves. As we study how others react to our behavior, these insights about ourselves can become useful almost immediately and allow us to take advantage of the Versatility Factor.

What we say and do, and how we say and do it, is our definition of behavior. It is both verbal and nonverbal. The broad grouping of the things we tend to say and do is most often called behavioral preferences: ways of talking and acting that we feel comfortable doing, and that we come to like in ourselves and in others. Because behaviors associated with our Style are so habitual, they feel natural ("second nature"). We rely on them almost instinctively! They are our automatic responses to those we encounter in the world around us.

Some of our habitual behaviors are linked to other often-recurring behaviors, which form clusters. These clusters of interrelated behaviors are key to understanding others and ourselves. The understanding of behavioral clusters enables us to predict how another person would like to be treated. When you note a person using behaviors associated with a particular cluster, you may speculate that other behaviors linked to that cluster are part of that person's mode of operation. You can predict behavioral characteristics that you haven't observed based on your knowledge of SOCIAL STYLE and behavior clusters.

If we are to observe behavior objectively and understand its impacts, we will have to take the subjective elements out of our observations. To achieve this objectivity, there are two types of words and phrases that we should avoid. The first type are those words and phrases that describe the inner qualities of a person, such as the words honest, intelligent, ambitious, motivated, interested, sincere, hypocritical, etc. These are traits we ascribe to someone rather than what is real. Others may have extremely different views based on how they experience a person.

The second type are those that describe our own reactions, feelings, and judgments about a person, words such as likable, confusing,

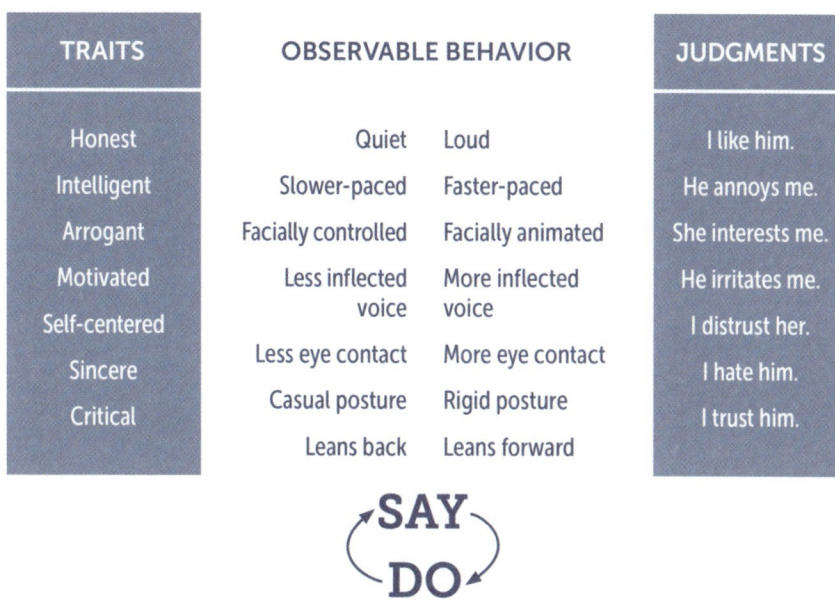

Fig. 1-2: Common ways of describing people

nice, odd, good or bad, etc. These represent our reactions to someone. Again, other people may have a different reaction that results in differing responses, feelings, and judgments.

The words we use to describe someone objectively are those that describe what a person is actually saying or doing in a social situation. Words and phrases such as loud, quiet, facially animated, facially controlled, fast-paced, slower-paced, more eye contact, and less eye contact describe behaviors without attaching value judgments to them (see Fig. 1-2). These descriptions identify (1) an interpersonal situation in which two or more people interact; and (2) observable behavior, which can be described by an observer and verified by observations made by others.

One way to increase this skill is simply to practice observing others. For example, if you are at a party, you might stand away from a group of people and observe the verbal and nonverbal behavior going on around you. Identify the people who tend to dominate the conversation, the ones who speak in a loud, fast-paced manner. In contrast, which people tend to be more reserved and voice their comments in the form of questions or support for someone else's statement? Which people show more animated behavior—smiles, finger-pointing, body movement? Which ones limit the amount of expression they show? By observing people this way, without paying attention to either the content of the conversation or to our like or dislike of the individuals, we can increase our ability to observe behavior more objectively.

We've mentioned that it's important to observe both verbal and nonverbal behavioral clues. In fact, 70-80% of what people learn and believe about others is based on nonverbal communications—on what they see, rather than on the words they hear. For instance, if someone says, "Boy, am I enthusiastic!" and yet at the same time shows no facial expression, very few people will believe the statement. They are much more likely to believe the nonverbal, unenthusiastic behavior that they see.

A cautionary word—as we become people observers, we must constantly remind ourselves that our feelings and attitudes may be getting in the way of our objectivity. For example, if a person sits down beside you at the airport and avoids making eye contact or speaking to you, you might tend to think this is some reflection on you. But if you move away and watch another stranger sit down next to the same person, it's likely the response to the second person will be equally aloof. Although we often can't help having a positive or negative reaction to someone's behavior, we should try to recognize these feelings for what they are—subjective, rather than objective, responses.

An objective observer who is able to apply the Versatility Factor can describe what went on in a situation so that others who were present and saw the same behavior can agree with the description.

1.3 Predicting Human Behavior

Have you ever found yourself confused over how someone has reacted to something you have said or done? Even when trying to help someone, we sometimes end up upsetting them. You think, "What did I do now? I will never understand them." Frustrated, you end up shaking your head and conclude that you'll never be able to know how someone is going to react to you. Sure, all of us can act a bit surprising at times, but that is the exception, not the rule. In fact, although each of us is an individual, our behavior is not as unpredictable as we may think.

Throughout history, philosophers, psychologists, and researchers have attempted to understand and define human traits and behaviors, especially those that lead to effective performance. During WWII, studies moved away from focusing on personality traits and began to focus on behaviors. In 1945, researchers at the Office of Naval Research and Ohio State University began to focus on identifying the behaviors of effective leaders. These studies were significant. For the first time, a scientific study focused on behaviors of leaders and not their personalities. Even more substantial, these studies focused on the perceptions of the leaders' followers and not the leaders themselves.

In the early 1960s, Dr. David Merrill, an industrial and organizational psychologist, built on the previous research from Ohio State University, B.F. Skinner, and others. Dr. Merrill focused on developing a typology that centered on the behavioral differences between people. Rather than developing a theoretical model, Dr. Merrill and his partner, Roger Reid, used an empirical approach to their work. Aided by emerging computer technology, they discovered that people do not perceive as many variables in real-life behavior as fiction and drama might suggest. What they discovered were two strong and independent factors for describing human behavior that, when combined, provided a practical model for understanding and predicting social behavior: Assertiveness and Responsiveness. They called this the SOCIAL STYLE Model.

Like all good models, the SOCIAL STYLE Model simplifies reality so we can manage it, especially when dealing with such a complex creation as another person. The SOCIAL STYLE Model allows us to make predictions about different types of people, how they are likely to behave, and how they like to be treated. It gives us an easy-to-use tool to enhance our understanding of people's behavior, thereby increasing our interpersonal effectiveness by reducing the complexity of relationships to a manageable level. It allows us to unlock the Versatility Factor!

Does it really work? Absolutely! Simply put, our research has shown that people across a wide range of industries and roles who apply the SOCIAL STYLE Model are better able to:

- Identify the significant elements of human behavior.
- Interpret what they observe about the behavior of others.
- Gain a reasonably accurate picture of an individual without trying to know everything about them.
- Predict the likely behavior of a person, which provides the basis for improved communication.
- Adapt their behavior according to others' preferences, leading to more productive relationships.

The SOCIAL STYLE Model provides us with a research-based, proven, and practical tool for simplifying an incredibly complex element—human behavior. It enables us to understand ourselves and others and to predict how someone is likely to behave in the future. This framework allows us to take appropriate actions to keep our relationships moving forward in positive ways and avoid the risk of allowing another person's behavior to become a source of tension for us. Applying the Versatility Factor is how we use our knowledge about behavior to interact with others in the way most likely to build a high-performing relationship with them.

A word of caution before proceeding: behavioral science is a probability science, not an absolute. While the SOCIAL STYLE Model can allow us to predict someone's behavior, it does not mean they will always react that way. People are unique and have all ranges of behavior available to them. SOCIAL STYLEs allow us to understand what behaviors they use most frequently and which behaviors they use with much less frequency. But we need to remember that when working with someone, the best strategy is to meet them where they are currently behaving and not where they are most of the time. Understand that they will return to their typical behavior pattern very quickly as that's what makes them most comfortable, especially as they experience an increase in tension.

2 THE SOCIAL STYLE MODEL

In the 1960's, Dr. David W. Merrill, an organizational psychologist and the founder of TRACOM,[1] undertook research to explore ways to predict success in selling and management careers. He understood that people tend to behave in consistent ways others can observe. He sought to find a method for measuring these behavioral observations through the use of descriptive adjectives. Using a unique technique for that time, Dr. Merrill measured behavior using a multi-rater approach, believing that people can agree about the behavior of a person they know. He utilized an empirical approach, meaning the research was not designed to support any specific theory of behavior and could be tested by other researchers.

The original adjective checklist of the SOCIAL STYLE Model was derived from an initial pool of more than 2,300 words developed by Dr. James W. Taylor[2] in the early 1960s, to which Dr. Merrill acquired the rights. This checklist was used in a study with a major life insurance company that provided a pool of 600 participants. These individuals had their co-workers complete an adjective checklist on them. Participants answered "yes," "no," or "don't know," when asked to describe the person being observed. Statistical analysis found that if a respondent felt a certain adjective described the individual's behavior, the same respondent answered "yes" or "no" to certain other adjectives. In other words, some adjectives clustered together. Hundreds of adjectives were compared to one another to see which words clustered together. Clustered adjectives were considered to measure a dimension of human behavior.

In contrast to research done in everyday clinical settings, Dr. Merrill and his team's approach was to statistically correlate every aspect of the data so all results could be scientifically quantified. The availability of computers was instrumental to this type of research because it enabled them to compare small units of behavior descriptions to one another (factor analysis). If these units statistically "clustered," or fell together in any way, it was probable they measured a specific dimension of human behavior.

A total of 150 adjectives measuring three scales were finalized. The three scales were labeled Assertiveness, Responsiveness, and Versatility.[3]

- *Assertiveness:*

    The way in which a person tries to influence others. In other words, it is the degree to which individuals tend to "ask" or "tell" in interactions with others.

- *Responsiveness:*

    The way in which a person outwardly displays feelings and emotion. It is a measure of the degree to which a person tends to "control" or "emote" when interacting with others.

- *Versatility:*

    A type of support and respect given to a person by others. Versatility is based, in part, on the extent to which others see the individual as interpersonally effective. It can be thought of as the extent to which a person appears to be working to make relationships mutually productive.

The scales that were discovered during this early research were used to develop the SOCIAL STYLE Model. By combining the two dimensions of Assertiveness and Responsiveness, four patterns of behavior, or SOCIAL STYLEs, could be identified. The four SOCIAL STYLEs are:

- **Driving Style** (Tell Assertive + Control Responsive): These individuals are seen as strong-willed, direct, and more emotionally controlled.

- **Expressive Style** (Tell Assertive + Emote Responsive): These individuals are described as outgoing, competitive, and more dramatic.

- **Amiable Style** (Ask Assertive + Emote Responsive): These individuals are seen as easy-going, communicative, and supportive.

- **Analytical Style** (Ask Assertive + Control Responsive): These individuals are described as serious, detail-oriented, and more exacting.

From 1999 through 2003, the way SOCIAL STYLE and Versatility were measured was significantly enhanced for three reasons:

1. The growing multiculturalism of societies and natural language evolution have made some of the original adjectives less frequently used in today's common language. In addition, the popular meanings of some of the adjectives have changed over the years. Since responses to the adjective checklist rely

on a certain level of common vocabulary without the use of a dictionary, newer generations of people may be challenged by some of the items on the original questionnaire. Unlike the original questionnaire, the SOCIAL STYLE Model today utilizes behavioral statements. These statements are responded to on an agreement continuum (a five-point scale ranging from "strongly disagree" to "strongly agree"), and have more inherent meaning than single adjectives. Behavior is a continuum; thus the continuous rating scale is ideal for allowing people to describe behavior.

2. Although the concept of Versatility precedes and parallels many of the concepts of *Emotional Intelligence*, research in the area led to a desire for updated research and expansion of the concept of Versatility. Of the three constructs measured by the SOCIAL STYLE Model, Versatility is the most unfixed and changeable, whereas Assertiveness and Responsiveness tend to be more consistent aspects of SOCIAL STYLE. Versatility can change across time and circumstances. Therefore, Versatility is the most amenable to training and development, and the one that is most important for working effectively with others. Moving to an explicit behavioral approach enabled us to measure and report more specific aspects of the Versatility dimension (Image, Presentation, Competence, and Feedback), in order to leverage a person's overall effectiveness and impact on others.

3. Updating the measurement system allowed for the instrument to be more easily translated into other languages and adapted to other cultures. When translating single adjectives, the original meaning of the words can be lost, affecting the

validity of the profile. This is less of an issue when utilizing behavioral statements. In addition, during the translation process the statements are easily edited to ensure their meaning remains stable across international cultures.

Before separating behaviors into the categories of the SOCIAL STYLE Model, it's important to remember no one behaves in one way all the time. We all exhibit a range of behaviors, and this variability combines with the other elements that constitute personality, such as our abilities, attitudes, and ideas of what we are and of what we would like to be. These elements make each one of us unique. However, when we consider just SOCIAL STYLE—what other people can see us doing and saying—we realize it's possible to generalize about the behavior of other people, and they, in turn, can generalize about ours. We do behave in predictable ways most of the time!

Although each one of us is a unique individual, others rarely get to know our uniqueness. Instead, they generalize about us, and we generalize about them. That's fine, as long as our generalizations are accurate so that we can predict the best way to communicate effectively with the other person. That's where SOCIAL STYLE and Versatility come in and how they can enhance performance.

2.1 Assertiveness

Briefly defined, Assertiveness is the aspect of behavior that measures whether we tend to tell or ask and the degree to which others see us as trying to influence their decisions. Levels of Assertiveness are fairly easy to determine; we quickly recognize the Tell Assertive behavior of an individual who forcefully states their opinions. But Tell Assertiveness, as we define the concept, is not just the amount of "air time" we take. Talking a lot or dominating a conversation may not make our ideas, beliefs, or opinions clear to others. In these cases, our behavior may not be seen as strongly Tell Assertive by others, even though we think we are being forceful.

A person seen as Tell Assertive is someone who takes a stand and makes a position clear to others. It doesn't matter whether we hold strong convictions internally; if we don't publicly use actions to communicate our opinions effectively, we probably will not be described by others as Tell Assertive, no matter how much talking we do.

We might like to think we are flexible enough to vary from shy to bold to quiet to noisy. However, as we've stated before, what may seem variable to us is not perceived that way by others, and they are probably able to place us in a general position on the scale of Ask or Tell Assertiveness.

In the SOCIAL STYLE Model, the dimension of Assertiveness is divided into four ranges. In our diagram of the Assertiveness dimension (see Fig. 2-1) these ranges are labeled "A," "B," "C," and "D." We divided the norm population into four equal groups, or quartiles. Individuals who are seen as more Tell Assertive than 75% of the population are found in the "A" quartile, "D" indicates those seen as having more Ask Assertiveness than 75% of the population; "B" and "C" are in between the two outer quadrants.

Less Tell Assertive individuals, those in the "C" or "D" quartiles, will be seen as more reserved, unaggressive, and easygoing. They rarely appear dominant and tend to keep thoughts to themselves. Their behavior seems tentative, and others see them as individuals who do not communicate their ideas or beliefs without a specific need to do so. Ask Assertive individuals are often seen as cooperative because they tend to listen well and utilize opportunities to support the ideas and attitudes of others.

If we observe individuals who are often silent, express moderate opinions, seldom take charge, let others take the social initiative, seek to avoid risk, and decide slowly, we can place them on the "asking" end of the Assertiveness dimension.

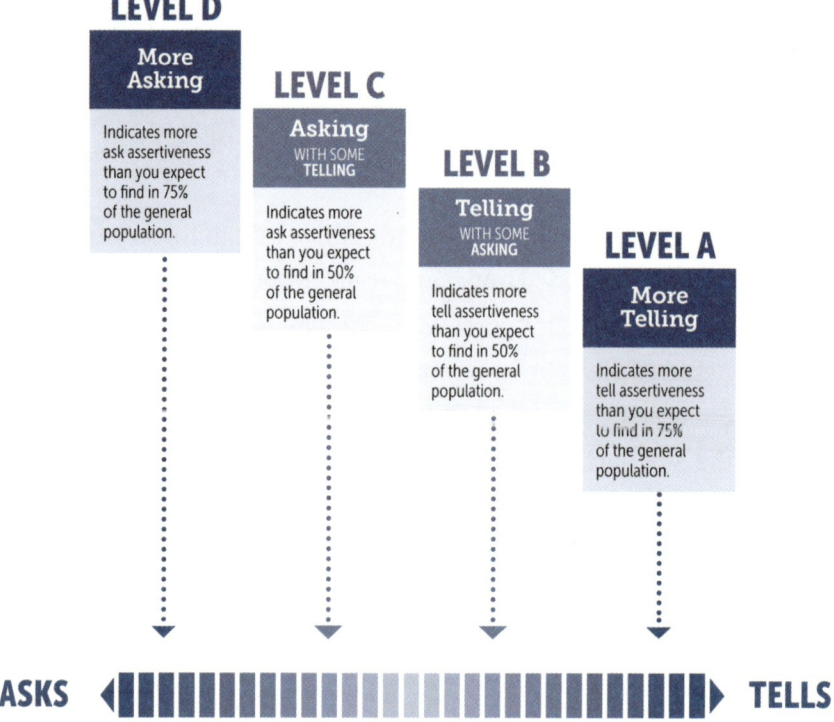

Fig. 2-1: Assertiveness dimension diagram

At the other end of the scale are more Tell Assertive individuals ("A" and "B"). They are often described as active, forceful, aggressive, and ambitious. A Tell Assertive person tends to make their presence known, likes to be in on the action, and tends to tell others what they think. Such a person will often initiate social contacts and communicate with others, even when it may not be appropriate to do so.

If we observe someone who is outgoing, has a take-charge attitude, a willingness to express strong opinions, takes risks, and makes quick decisions, we can place this individual on the "telling" end of the Assertiveness dimension.

To simplify this scale, the more Tell Assertive person tends to make statements rather than ask. When they are under tension, they tend to "fight," or confront the situation, rather than avoid it. The Ask Assertive person tends to ask more than they tell, and when under tension, they prefer "flight," or to avoid the situation, rather than confront it.

2.2 Responsiveness

The second dimension of the SOCIAL STYLE Model is called Responsiveness. In summary, it is the dimension of behavior that indicates whether one tends to emote or to control their feelings and the extent to which others see them as an individual who displays feelings or emotions openly in social situations.

Responsiveness indicates how much feeling a person tends to display. The more responsively people behave, the more they appear to react to influences, appeals, or stimulation, and to openly express their feelings, emotions, and impressions. A more responsive person readily expresses anger, joy, or hurt feelings. If any given part of the population is measured, the level of Responsiveness will range from more responsive or "emoting" behavior to less responsive or "controlling" behavior.

As with the Assertiveness scale, we used norms to divide the population into each of four equal ranges on the scale; these ranges are labeled "1," "2," "3," and "4" (see Fig. 2-2). Those who are seen as more Control Responsive than 75% of the population are placed in the quartile labeled "1." Adjectives often used to describe these individuals are cautious, intellectual, and serious.

Those who display their emotions and feelings more readily

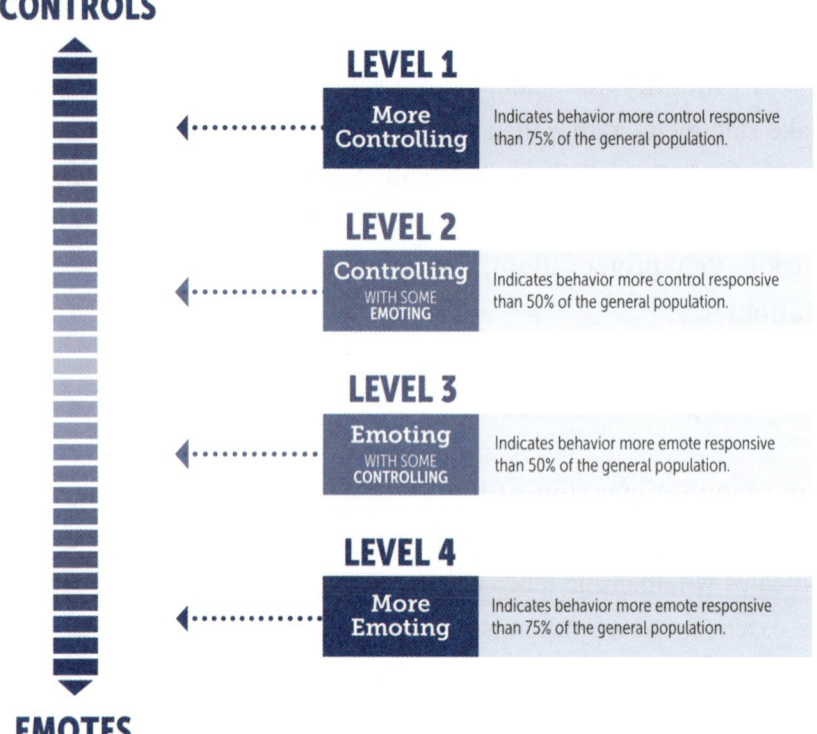

Fig. 2-2: Responsiveness dimension diagram

than 75% of the population are placed in the quartile labeled "4." They are often described with adjectives such as warm, emotional, or lighthearted. Those between the two extremes (placed in quartiles "2" and "3") might be described as sometimes impulsive or private.

Control Responsive individuals, those in the "1" and "2" quartiles, are seen as more independent of, or indifferent to, the feelings of others. They are seen as people who rely on reason and logic when making decisions, who are often formal, proper, or stiff in social relationships, and who tend to avoid personal involvement with others. A more Control Responsive person appears precise, makes specific points, can be critical, has a no-nonsense attitude, and has a high desire to get things done efficiently. Such a person tends to focus on ideas, things, and tasks rather than on people and seeks to gain approval through achievement.

If we observe an individual who dresses and speaks more formally than most, is private and reserved, is a cautious communicator who displays measured, factual opinions, and who has a strict, disciplined attitude, we can place them on the "controlling" end of the Responsiveness dimension. As Control Responsive, these individuals can seem difficult to get to know, are demanding of themselves and others, and are impersonal and businesslike in interpersonal situations.

At the other end of the scale ("3" and "4") are more Emote Responsive individuals. These people are often described as being outgoing, self-indulgent, attention-seeking, and involved with the feelings of others. They appear to be concerned with relationships and act in informal, casual, and playful ways in social situations. Others may see these more emoting individuals as having a tendency to talk in a general and imprecise way, showing a gamut of emotions ranging from frivolous laughter to dark depression. They can appear to be unconcerned about getting things done efficiently.

If we observe a person who dresses and speaks informally, is an open, impulsive communicator, talks and acts dramatically, and who seems to have a casual, easygoing attitude toward life, we can place this person on the emotive end of the scale. As Emote Responsive, they can appear to dramatize their ideas, seem easy to get to know, and are open with themselves and others.

To simplify the Responsiveness scale, Emote Responsive individuals tend to say and do things that show, rather than control, their feelings. These people will display feelings and emotions and work at maintaining relationships to earn social acceptance. Control Responsive people, as we have said, tend to control emotions and tend to focus on ideas, things, data, and tasks—rather than on people—to gain approval through achievement.

2.3 SOCIAL STYLEs

The two dimensions of behavior, Assertiveness and Responsiveness, can be observed in everyone. Whether consciously or unconsciously, we often decide how to deal with our acquaintances and co-workers on the basis of our perceptions of their Responsiveness and Assertiveness.

ASSERTIVENESS + RESPONSIVENESS = SOCIAL STYLE

SOCIAL STYLE is the result of our measurement of how others describe us. It is like a picture or map of what others can see you

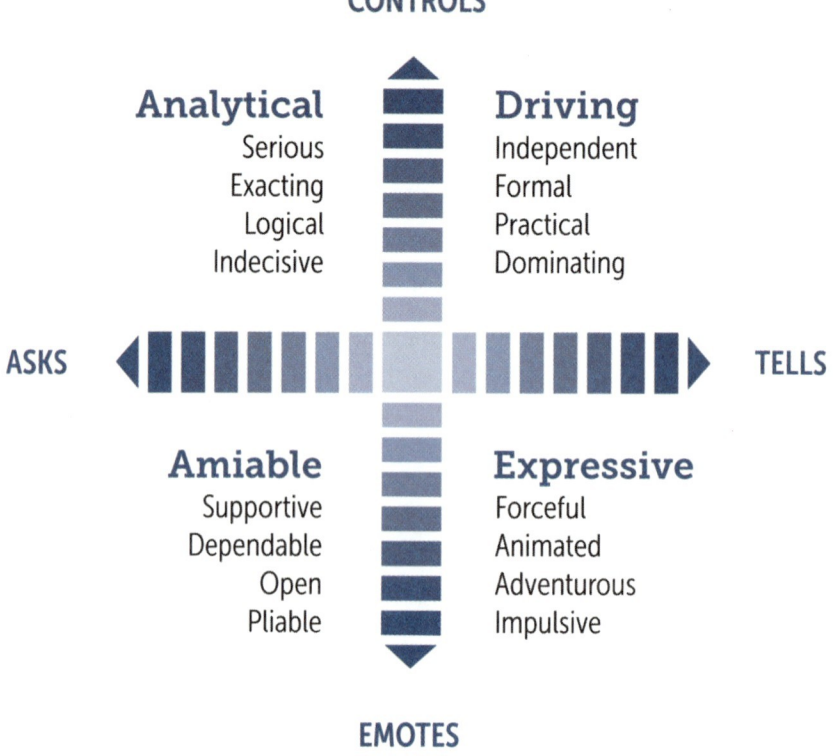

Fig. 2-3: Assertiveness vs. Responsiveness diagram

doing or saying and shows where you most frequently position yourself within the total universe of available actions on Assertiveness and Responsiveness.

Because we all display certain behaviors that can be placed on either the Assertiveness or Responsiveness scales, these two independent scales can be combined (see Fig. 2-3), permitting us to describe the various possible combinations of these qualities in people as a matrix. The horizontal axis shows the range from Ask to Tell Assertive. The vertical axis shows the range from Control to Emote Responsive.

By combining these two independent dimensions, the SOCIAL STYLE Model and its quadrants emerge. Through norming, an equal number of people (25% respectively) in a randomly selected population will fall into each of the four quadrants or squares combining Assertiveness and Responsiveness.

We've labeled these quadrants as follows:

- Upper right-hand quadrant: Control Responsive + Tell Assertive = **Driving Style**

- Upper left-hand quadrant: Control Responsive + Ask Assertive = **Analytical Style**

- Lower left-hand quadrant: Emote Responsive + Asks Assertive = **Amiable Style**

- Lower right-hand quadrant: Emote Responsive + Tell Assertive = **Expressive Style**

In the Model's upper right-hand quadrant, we place individuals whose behavior is usually characterized by both "telling" and "controlling" their feelings. They are primarily direct, serious people. These individuals make an effort to tell people what they think and require, and they can appear severe or formal because they don't display feelings or emotions readily. We call this SOCIAL STYLE the "Driving Style."

In the lower right-hand corner of the profile, we find people who tend to "tell" and to "emote." This Style is also Tell Assertive, like the Driving Style, but these individuals are generally more willing to make their feelings public. Rather than trying to control emotions, someone with this Style will readily show both positive and negative feelings. This SOCIAL STYLE is called the "Expressive Style."

As we move to the lower left-hand corner of the profile, we find a SOCIAL STYLE that "asks" and "emotes." Like someone with an Expressive Style, this individual usually displays feelings openly, but is Ask Assertive and more interested in being agreeable and cooperative. This SOCIAL STYLE is called the "Amiable Style."

Finally, as we look at the upper left-hand corner of the profile, we find a Style that "asks" and "controls." This Style is Ask Assertive, and high in control of emotions. Rather than being quickly decisive or forceful (like the person with the Driving or the Expressive Style), an individual displaying these behaviors will tend to ask questions, gather facts, and study data seriously. This SOCIAL STYLE is called the "Analytical Style."

This leads to the questions: Which quadrant has the good and successful people? What is the best SOCIAL STYLE?

Research indicates that there is no "best" SOCIAL STYLE. Each one has its good and bad points, and we tend to like or dislike individuals displaying a particular Style because of our own personal points of view, value judgments, or needs. Generally, if someone relates well to us, we describe their Style with favorable adjectives; if not, we will tend to use more unfavorable terms. All Styles can be successful, and there are no good or bad Styles.

Our SOCIAL STYLE is determined by a theme or pattern of

typical behaviors. These behaviors are habits we develop over long periods of time to enable us to interact with other people in varying situations and environments. SOCIAL STYLE is built on collecting multiple observations of our behavior and describing this pattern.

SOCIAL STYLE is not a box. You do not always respond in all situations according to your primary SOCIAL STYLE patterns. For instance, an Amiable Style person who finds themselves in an emergency situation may exhibit Driving Style behaviors in response to the situation for a brief period of time.

The descriptions in this book illustrate common patterns of behavior observed among the four SOCIAL STYLEs. However, not all people of one SOCIAL STYLE will exhibit all of the behaviors listed as descriptors for this SOCIAL STYLE. That much specificity could border on a caricature of each SOCIAL STYLE, which is not the intent. The purpose is to give a large sample of the behaviors observed among people of each SOCIAL STYLE, not to describe how all people of that SOCIAL STYLE behave all the time. Below you'll find a few key characteristics of each SOCIAL STYLE.

Driving Style

"Let's get it done now!"

Driving Style people have a strong need for results and they try to satisfy this need by taking action. They usually speak directly and often, letting others know their opinions. Their main challenge, or growth action, is to listen. It is difficult for them to pause and listen to what others are saying and why they are saying it or to actively solicit the input of others.

Others see these people as active, forceful, determined, and direct. They initiate social interactions. They focus their efforts and try to influence the efforts of others toward the goals and objectives they want to get accomplished. They want to achieve their objectives quickly. Others typically describe them as cool, less personable, guarded, and sometimes aloof, as they typically do not openly show their feelings or reveal the depths of their emotions.

Traits of Driving Style people:

- Active, forceful, and sometimes aggressive
- Direct in initiating social contact
- Focused on goals and objectives that need to get done
- Willing to challenge the ideas and views of others
- Willing to take risks and make quick decisions
- Impatient with others if things don't move as quickly as desired
- Cool, distant, guarded, and aloof at times
- Emotionally controlled with others
- Formal, self-sufficient, serious, and usually deal with the reasoning and logic behind actions and decisions
- Competitive when interacting with others
- Focused on the immediate time frame with relatively little concern for the past or future
- May seek control through the use of position or coercive power
- Disciplined in their use of time

Expressive Style

"I have an idea and it's going to be great!"

Expressive Style people have a strong need for personal approval, which results in them behaving in a very outgoing and spontaneous way. Like Driving Style people, they speak directly and frequently, but also loudly and with more emotion. Their behaviors can sometimes go too far and result in the need to take their growth action to check their behavior. Their challenge is to stop and monitor their own behavior, which is sometimes impulsive and potentially inappropriate.

These people tend to be much more willing to make their inner feelings known to others. At times they can appear to react impulsively and openly show both positive and negative feelings. Others typically describe them as personable, spontaneous, talkative, and sometimes opinionated.

Traits of Expressive Style people:

- Direct and seek to be involved in activities with others
- Active, spontaneous, forceful, and make their presence known
- Reactive and impulsive about showing both positive and negative feelings
- Emotionally open in their display of feelings
- Open and communicative with others even when it may not be appropriate to do so
- Quick to decide and make decisions based on intuition
- Assertive in their attempts to influence others

- Casual, general, imprecise, and impulsive
- Dramatic
- Focused on the future with intuitive visions and outspoken spontaneity
- Imaginative and creative
- May make mistakes and have frequent changes in direction and focus because of their desire to act on opinions, hunches, and intuitions, rather than facts and data
- May seek to influence others through the use of charisma
- Undisciplined in their use of time
- Takes risk

Amiable Style

"One for all and all for one!"

Amiable Style people have a strong need for personal security, which means they like to be confident and stable in their relationships with others. Because of this need, they naturally focus on maintaining good relationships. They usually speak less often than Driving or Expressive Style people, are relaxed in their interactions, and are focused on people or stories. Their growth action is to initiate, which means to take more risks by expressing their viewpoints, to share or make a first move in a situation, and to share realistic feedback.

These people openly display their feelings to others. However, they appear less demanding and are generally agreeable. They are interested in achieving a good rapport with others, who often describe them as informal, casual, and easygoing. They tend to be sensitive to keeping relationships with others on a friendly, personal basis.

Traits of Amiable Style people:

- Approachable, concerned, and supportive
- Trusting in their personal relationships
- Unlikely to impose their views on others
- Emotionally open in their display of feelings
- Informal, casual, and easygoing
- Sensitive to keeping relationships on a friendly basis
- Slow to decide and make decisions based on impacts on relationships
- Often less concerned about the efficiency of their actions
- Focused on the present
- Likely to interpret the world on a personal basis by getting involved in the feelings and relationships between people
- Likely to get things done with and through others
- Effective at social networking
- Likely to stick with the comfortable and the known
- Likely to avoid decisions that might involve personal risks and conflict in relationships
- May try to influence others through the use of rewards
- Sometimes undisciplined in their use of time

Analytical Style

"Just the facts!"

Analytical Style people have a strong need to be right, meaning that they want to be correct in terms of their approaches to situations or their use of information when solving problems. Because of this need, they tend to focus on principles, processes, and procedures. They typically speak slowly and deliberately and are emotionally controlled. Their growth action is to declare, meaning they need to assert themselves and share their opinions while resisting the urge to hesitate or be indirect in their statements.

Others typically describe these people as quiet, logical, and sometimes reserved. They sometimes appear distant from others and may not communicate with them unless there is a specific need to do so. They tend to make decisions thoughtfully and act deliberately. Other people usually see them as cautious, careful, and thorough.

Traits of Analytical Style people:

- Reserved, unaggressive, and avoid appearing dominant
- Tentative and may not communicate with others unless there is a specific need to do so
- Slow to make decisions and act thoughtfully
- Likely to make decisions based on reason and logic
- Unlikely to impose on others
- Cautious, careful, thorough, and avoid risk
- Formal, stiff, and proper
- Cautious about becoming personally involved with others

- Precise, specific, and critical
- Cool, distant, and detached
- Focused on the past
- Likely to live life according to facts, principles, processes, logic, and consistency
- Likely to behave in ways that fit into their overall theory and ideas about the world
- Sometimes unenthusiastic
- May try to influence others through the use of personal expertise
- Generally disciplined in their use of time

Some people believe that certain SOCIAL STYLEs are more likely to succeed at certain professions, tasks, or roles. However, our research shows that no SOCIAL STYLE is preferable to another and that SOCIAL STYLE does not predict success at any occupation. Versatility, however, has been found to predict performance. We will explore this further a bit later.

What is often true is that people of a particular SOCIAL STYLE will be attracted to certain occupations and roles. For example, Analytical Style people tend to be strongly represented among accountants, engineers, and information technology workers. Many Driving Style individuals tend to prefer roles where they can influence others, such as management. Expressive Style people are commonly found in marketing and retail occupations. Likewise, Amiable Style people are also attracted to these roles, in addition to human resources and teaching.

To be clear, this does not mean that there are no successful managers or engineers with Amiable or Expressive Styles and no successful marketing and teaching professionals with Driving or Analytical Styles. Our research shows this is absolutely not the case. People are often attracted to roles that require behaviors that are comfortable for them. People whose SOCIAL STYLE behaviors match occupational behavior demands feel more comfortable in those roles. Our research has never found a single occupation where more than 50% of the people have a single SOCIAL STYLE. You will read more on this research in Chapter 3.

2.4 Toxic Relationships

By knowing the four different SOCIAL STYLEs, it is clear that occasionally two people of different SOCIAL STYLEs fall into a pattern of conflict (see Fig. 2-4). Of course, there is nothing new about conflict. It is common in workplaces, and there is a distinction between productive conflict and conflict that leads to a multitude of undesirable consequences.

The type of conflict we are describing results from SOCIAL STYLE-related behaviors that cause two people to fall into a pattern of conflict. This is not about co-workers arguing about the best marketing strategy for a new product or the best solution to a problem, though, SOCIAL STYLE differences can intensify these types of situations. When relationships turn sour because of fundamental differences in SOCIAL STYLE behaviors, we call this a "toxic relationship."

Toxic relationships often result in conflicts. The greatest potential for a toxic relationship occurs on the diagonal of the Model—that is, between Analytical and Expressive and between Amiable and Driving Styles. This is because these SOCIAL STYLE pairs have the most obvious behavioral differences on both the Assertiveness and Responsiveness dimensions. They are mirrored opposites of each other.

THE SOCIAL STYLE MODEL 39

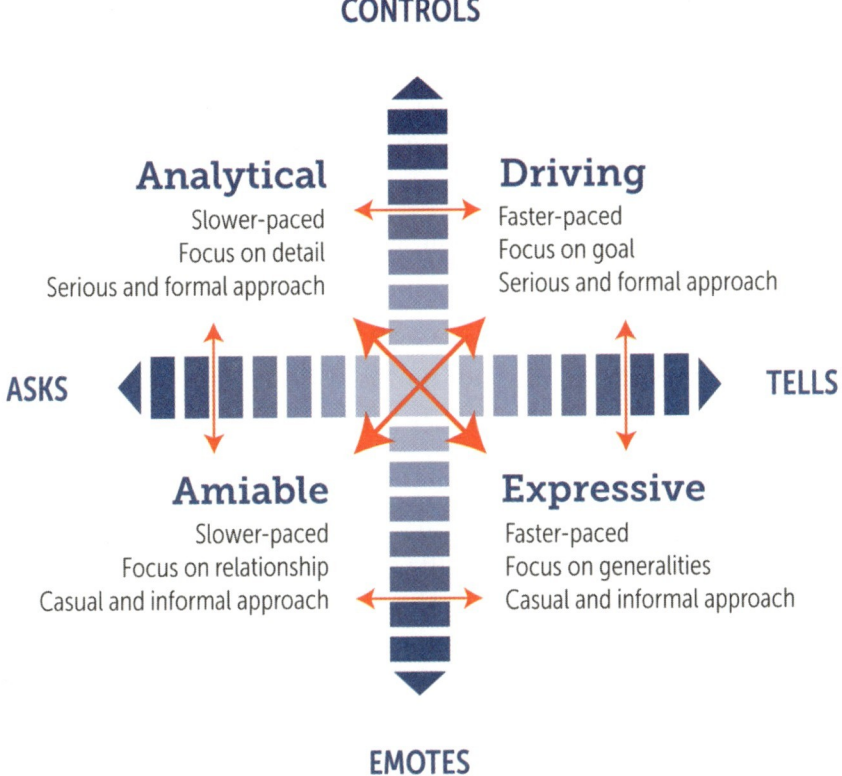

Fig. 2-4: Potentially toxic relationships

For example:

- The Analytical Style is slower-paced while the Expressive Style is faster-paced.
- The Analytical Style focuses on details while the Expressive Style focuses on generalities.
- The Analytical Style has a serious and formal approach while the Expressive Style prefers a casual and informal approach.
- The Driving Style is faster-paced than the Amiable Style.

- The Driving Style focuses on tasks while the Amiable Style focuses on the impacts actions have on people.
- The Driving Style approaches situations seriously while the Amiable Style prefers to be light-hearted with others.

A toxic relationship can also exist between SOCIAL STYLEs that differ on only one dimension. For example, both the Amiable Style and the Expressive Style are on the same end of the Responsiveness scale, but not on the Assertiveness scale. Thus, one is slower-paced and the other is faster-paced. This difference in pace, as well as other Assertiveness-related differences, can cause conflict.

Finally, a toxic relationship can also exist between two individuals with the same SOCIAL STYLE. Conflict can occur in these relationships because of the similarity in SOCIAL STYLE preferences.

For example:

- Two individuals with a Driving Style can have interpersonal tension because of a conflict over differences in the results each wants, as well as over who is in control. Since both don't listen well, this can contribute to tension and conflict.

- Two individuals with an Expressive Style may compete as to who gets the personal approval they both need. They might also clash as a result of each other's optimism and tendency to underestimate how long things may take or how much they will cost.

- Two individuals with an Amiable Style may compete in receiving the personal security they both need. They may also tend to acquiesce to each other to the point where their relationship exhibits passive-aggressive behaviors.

• Two individuals with an Analytical Style may differ in deciding which one has the right approach or the right interpretation of information. They may also argue as a result of each other's desire to avoid making decisions or acting quickly.

2.5 Versatility

We call the ability to handle our behavioral preferences in a skilled way Versatility, the third dimension of human behavior. Just as the other two dimensions of behavior, Assertiveness and Responsiveness, are independent of each other, Versatility is also a separate facet of human behavior. Statistical research demonstrates that people who are seen by others as highly versatile in interpersonal situations can be found along all ranges of the Assertiveness and Responsiveness scales, as can those people who are seen as less versatile. What separates the versatile from the non-versatile is the amount of endorsement, support, and respect they receive from others regardless of Style. This is what we mean by "The Versatility Factor"!

Remember that SOCIAL STYLE is mostly a fixed set of behaviors. It would be hard to change our SOCIAL STYLE, but Versatility is different. Versatility is a set of behaviors that can be learned; these behaviors are not fixed. We can change our appearance and the way we dress. We can learn to present ourselves more effectively in meetings. We can learn to be more flexible, dependable, and innovative, not to mention how to listen more carefully to others and pay attention to their needs. These are behavioral skills that we can add to each of our SOCIAL STYLEs with conscious thought and practice.

Most people are aware of the Golden Rule: treat people the way you would like them to treat you. Versatility employs what David Merrill termed the Platinum Rule: treat people the way they want to be treated! The difference may seem subtle, but it is critical. What it implies is that different people have different ways in which they want people to treat and interact with them. All people are not the same, therefore, you cannot assume that others want to be treated the same way you want to be treated. This is why SOCIAL STYLE awareness is so important and linked to Versatility. By understanding a person's SOCIAL STYLE, you will be able to employ versatile behaviors more effectively and meet the needs of the other person.

Two things typically characterize someone who acts with low Versatility: they display poor SOCIAL STYLE awareness and they focus on meeting their own needs. They do not understand, or appear not to care about, other people's preferences. Therefore, they do not attempt to adjust to those preferences. They focus primarily on meeting their own needs without considering the expectations of others. This is displayed through their behavior.

For example, they abruptly interrupt co-workers and tell them how things should be done. When others try to communicate their viewpoints, they are not allowed to finish sharing their ideas as the low Versatility colleague moves the discussion on to the next topic on their agenda. They barely show an awareness of others' presence, much less their opinions or needs. They are behaving with low Versatility because they are entirely focused on meeting their own needs and are completely unaware of the SOCIAL STYLE preferences of their co-workers.

In contrast, someone who is behaving with high Versatility actively displays two attributes: SOCIAL STYLE awareness and an appropriate focus on other people's expectations or needs. During a meeting, they actively listen to their co-workers and let them know their viewpoints are understood, even if they don't agree with them. Before moving on to other topics, they ensure the expectations of others have been met and it is done in a way that considers their SOCIAL STYLE orientations. For instance, if one of their co-workers has an Analytical Style, they might ask if the discussion is taking all-important information into consideration before coming to a decision.

The support and respect individuals earn from others may increase or decrease. The more support and respect one earns, the more effective one is likely to be. Therefore, a high level of Versatility is virtually always a good thing.

Versatility is scored in a way that is very similar to scores on Assertiveness and Responsiveness. Versatility is normed, meaning that an individual's scores are compared to a large sample that is representative of the population. This sample is divided into four equal quadrants. From low to high scores, these are labeled "W," "X," "Y," and "Z" (see fig. 2-5).

Fig. 2-5: Versatility dimension diagram

A "W" score is the lowest quartile, indicating that the score is lower than 75% of the norm group. The "X" quartile is lower than 50% but higher than 25%. "Y" is the quartile that is higher than half the norm group, and "Z" scores are those in the top 25%.

Four Sources of Versatility

Versatility is comprised of four independent sources: Image, Presentation, Competency, and Feedback. The analysis provides results on the total Versatility, as described previously, and on each of the four sources of Versatility separately. The four sources are scored the same way as overall Versatility using the "W" to "Z" scoring system. This is important because a person may have a high "Z" score on Image but a low "W" score on Feedback.

This information helps people pinpoint specific areas where they can improve. It is most helpful to consider each of the four sources separately instead of focusing on a single overall Versatility score. Results for the four sources are independent. That is, one might score high on Feedback but low on Competence, or vice versa.

As noted previously, Versatility is not related to SOCIAL STYLE. Any SOCIAL STYLE can have higher or lower Versatility. However, there is an exception to this rule. There is a slight relationship between Feedback and Responsiveness, so Amiable and Expressive Style people are naturally advantaged in terms of higher Feedback scores. This natural advantage, however, is slight and does not mean that all Expressive and Amiable Style people will score high on Feedback.

In the following sections we describe the four sources of Versatility, the ways in which SOCIAL STYLE impacts each source of Versatility, and how people of different SOCIAL STYLEs respond to each source of Versatility. Keep in mind that these statements are generalizations about people of each SOCIAL STYLE.

Image

Co-workers assess Image by making judgments, usually subconsciously, about the appropriateness of your dress, demeanor, and the organization of your work area. From what they observe, they make judgments about whether you project an image that is within established norms for your role and responsibilities at work.

An image that others feel is out of the norm tends to get in the way of effective interpersonal communication. For example, consider a person with an Expressive Style who likes to assert their individuality by wearing flamboyant attire when traditional business-casual is the norm. Think about a Driving Style individual who comes across very formal and business-like, even in casual situations. Regardless of SOCIAL STYLE, if your work area continually appears to be in disarray, co-workers will need to overcome the negative impressions created by that image in order to have productive interactions with you.

Image is most important in initial interactions with others. Negative impressions of Image can usually be overcome over time with high Versatility in the areas of Presentation, Competence, and Feedback. However, one can avoid the negative Image problem by "doing something" for others, such as making any necessary adjustments to dress, demeanor, and organization in the work area. Ideally, such adjustments should simultaneously meet one's needs and make others more comfortable when interacting.

As an example of how Image displays itself regardless of SOCIAL STYLE, consider an executive who shows up at the company sponsored soccer match wearing a suit and tie, even though shorts and athletic shoes are the norm. People might be a little uncomfortable interacting with this person, unless the executive shows high Versatility by adjusting to the situation by taking off his or her tie and jacket and rolling up their sleeves.

One other aspect of Image is worth consideration. A part of Image is how a person "carries" himself. In other words, demeanor can impact perceptions of Image. In general, all people, regardless of their SOCIAL STYLE, appreciate a self-confident demeanor.

How Does SOCIAL STYLE *Impact Image?*

Appropriately dressing and presenting yourself for different circumstances and having a functional and comfortable workspace are at the heart of Image. To a certain degree, your Image is a reflection of your own personal SOCIAL STYLE and tastes. Your clothing and the way you decorate (or don't decorate) your personal space is an indication of your SOCIAL STYLE.

Driving Style people tend to be more formal and conservative in their appearance than some of the other SOCIAL STYLEs. They generally will not wear flamboyant clothing in terms of style or color. Even if a dress code is very relaxed, many of these individuals will prefer to dress in a more formal or reserved manner. Their workspaces are often organized with the sole purpose of productivity. They might have some family pictures and personal items, but the primary concern will be getting things done. This does not necessarily mean that their work areas are neat or tidy. In fact, they can appear to be in disarray, but this is usually a reflection of the pace and focus of their work and their tendency to multitask.

Expressive Style people are usually the most likely of all SOCIAL STYLEs to dress in a unique and colorful way. They will often use their clothing and appearance as a way to express their individuality and tastes, and they may be particularly prone to showing name brands and logos. In a similar way, their workspaces often include many indications of their interests and personal lives. They like to surround themselves with pictures of family and friends, and also with memorabilia and even toys. When entering the office or workspace of an Expressive Style person, there are often a lot of unique objects to grab a person's attention.

Amiable Style people are generally more casual in their choice of clothing. They prefer to be comfortable and project an easily approachable Image, and this comes across in their dress and demeanor. They are similar to Expressive Style people in this regard, though they are usually less flashy in their choice of clothing. Their work areas are often treated as an extension of their personal life. They like to display objects that are meaningful to them, such as family photos and memorabilia. They also tend to add personal touches to their areas that make their spaces more comfortable and intimate, such as works of art.

Analytical Style people are similar to Driving Style individuals in that they tend to dress more conservatively. They might not expend much effort on their work clothing, considering it to be just a "uniform" that they wear. In some instances, they can be rigid about their appearance, not wanting to deviate from their own standards of professional attire, even when the company norm is more relaxed. Their work areas tend to be organized for efficiency. They may not be neat, but they are organized in a way that helps them work effectively. Of all the SOCIAL STYLEs, they might be the least likely to display personal photos or objects. However, these individuals will often display items that hint at their personal interests or provide mental challenge, such as works of art.

Presentation

Co-workers assess Presentation by making judgments, mostly subconsciously, about the ability you have to deliver information in different settings at work. Presentation includes the following: their assessment of the comfort level you demonstrate when making a group presentation, your organization and delivery, and how you make them feel about the interaction.

When someone feels uncomfortable when making presentations to co-workers, chances are their co-workers also feel that uneasiness. To increase one's abilities in this area, focus concern on confidence in the topic and materials, on how well it is organized, and on an appropriate choice of words and topics to accommodate the audience. Also, they should consider the pace of the presentation based on the SOCIAL STYLE preferences of the audience.

In addition, think about how the SOCIAL STYLEs of both presenter and recipients may affect the message. For example, someone with an Analytical Style might need to consider whether they have too much detail and not enough big picture descriptions. Those who have an Amiable Style might want to make sure that they are getting to the point quickly enough for their audience and are presenting ideas in a bold enough way to challenge others' thinking.

During presentations to co-workers, one should be sure to continually look for signs of confusion or boredom and periodically ask whether they have questions. This will help to keep them engaged and might lead to a two-way conversation, which inherently has a higher comfort level for most people.

Choice of words, and the audience's ability to understand and relate to those words, are critical. For example, someone who is relatively young compared to their co-workers may be prone to using slang they use with their friends or learned during their college years. Older co-workers might view this person's ability as similar to those of teenagers, rather than those of a business colleague. Similarly, an older presenter trying to engage an audience of younger people must remain aware of differences of not only SOCIAL

STYLE, but of approaches to work and the workplace and how these differ across generations.

How Does **SOCIAL STYLE** *Impact Presentation?*

Driving Style individuals are usually very businesslike, getting to the point quickly. They speak forcefully, but show little emotion in their facial expressions. If the meeting agenda is within their control, they will generally take command of the meeting to make their points and ensure their objectives are met. They can be blunt when sharing their opinions, which is an expression of their direct approach. While they may not be loud talkers, they will generally speak with enough volume that everyone in the room can hear them.

Expressive Style people are generally the most outgoing of the SOCIAL STYLEs during meetings and presentations. They tend to speak loudly and often, especially if they are the ones running the meeting. They will use hand gestures and display a great deal of facial animation. They may sometimes be disorganized in their focus, starting on one topic and quickly moving to new topics. Like Driving Style people, they can often be very frank in the way they express their opinions, and they will act this way when providing both positive and negative comments.

Amiable Style people usually like to be conversational, bringing others into the discussion. Their voices will be more inflected than a Driving Style person's, but they will speak in a relatively quiet tone. They express themselves with hand gestures and facial animation, but this is usually less obvious than with Expressive Style people. They tend to express their opinions in a way that reflects their focus on the team or workgroup and, in particular, the impact their actions will have on their team.

Analytical Style people will usually want to cover all aspects of a topic in detail, often in a linear or time-bound way and with a slower pace. They tend to be deliberate when they speak and have a subdued voice, displaying few obvious hand or body gestures. Their focus is often on processes and procedures, and they generally want to center on these topics during meetings. They prefer to get others' input, so they will ask questions and spend a relatively large amount of time listening to others' viewpoints before responding.

Competence

Co-workers assess Competence based both on how good we are at achieving our individual goals and how much help and support we provide them in achieving theirs. Competence includes a number of abilities, including dependability, perseverance, and flexibility. Competence is also influenced by one's level of optimism and creativity in terms of solving problems and offering unique ideas.

People at work tend to view one another's Competence through the prism of their own SOCIAL STYLE preferences concerning use of time, actions toward others, and approaches to decision-making. For example, a Driving Style co-worker might judge Competence, in part, based on how quickly you can get something done. In contrast, an Amiable Style co-worker might be less concerned with speed and more concerned with how well you work with others while performing a task.

You can increase co-workers' perceptions of Competence by taking a number of actions that reinforce their positive evaluations. Be reliable for getting things done in a reasonable time frame, be flexible in regard to shifting priorities, be open to new perspectives and different ways of doing things, offer creative ideas, and stay optimistic and enthusiastic.

How Does SOCIAL STYLE *Impact Competence?*

Because Driving Style people achieve their need for results through taking action, some of the behaviors that lead to Competence might seem natural for them. For example, they might often be perceived as dependable, since they like to get things done quickly, and as persistent, since they drive toward goals. These individuals usually don't show optimism through exciting speeches or a cheerful presence. Rather, their optimism comes across as confidence that things will turn out alright, and that positive outcomes will happen through taking a course of action. In terms of flexibility, some Driving Style people tend to see changes as challenges that should be met head on. They may actually be faster to respond to changes than is comfortable for people of other SOCIAL STYLEs. As natural risk-takers, these people generally are not afraid of new ideas. They may generate their own ideas and solutions or, if practicing their listening skills, will take the time to solicit others' ideas and work with them.

Expressive Style people have a natural orientation toward spontaneity, so they might display flexibility to new circumstances and adaptability to change more readily than others. Their creativity will sometimes show itself through generating ideas, especially since they are generally big-picture thinkers. When feeling optimistic, these individuals will show it through their enthusiasm and outward energy. Expressive Style people are not as influenced by time constraints as some of the other SOCIAL STYLEs, so they may display dependability somewhat differently. This is not to say that they are incapable of taking responsibility for their work or meeting deadlines; people of all SOCIAL STYLEs do these things. However, they may have different understandings of time frames and expectations of others.

Amiable Style individuals are focused on relationships, and this can often come across in how they display Competence behaviors. For example, they might persevere through problems by involving others and focusing on working as a team rather than trying to tackle every problem on their own. When feeling hopeful about things, they will generally be cheerful toward co-workers and display energy around work activities. Their personal creativity is most apparent when it involves some form of group activity. For example, an Amiable Style person might develop a new process that eases the workloads of fellow team members as well as themselves. The desire to please others is strong for these people and, to the extent that they agree with decisions and processes, they will display their reliability by meeting their responsibilities and deadlines.

Analytical Style individuals tend to be somewhat reserved, and this can come across in their Competence behaviors. Rather than being very vocal and obvious in their actions, they will sometimes show their perseverance by quietly moving forward and working through problems, often by themselves. When change occurs, they will generally want to find some assurance that the change is positive before committing themselves. Rapid transitions from one situation to another can be challenging for them. When coming up with new ideas or solutions to problems, they often want time alone to think before offering their input to the larger group. Because they tend to be emotionally controlled, their displays of optimism might not be as forthright as they are for people of other SOCIAL STYLEs. In fact, their enthusiasm might be so subdued that others don't realize they are actually excited.

Feedback

Strong perceptions of Feedback as a source of Versatility begin with the wisdom of seeking "first to understand and then to be understood." Feedback includes listening carefully and attentively to others and responding in a way that reflects that understanding in order to help build a mutually productive relationship. A critical component of Feedback is empathy, or the ability to understand others' situations and take these into account during interactions.

As a point of clarification, use of the term "Feedback" is distinct from how this term is often used in organizations. Many people automatically associate this concept with giving professional performance feedback, coaching, or advice. Our use of the term is broader than this. Feedback skills are critical for engaging in these activities, but they extend beyond these instances.

You can think of Feedback skills as a personal radar system people use to monitor their interactions with others. By accurately assessing the impact you make based on the verbal and nonverbal feedback others give you, you can adjust your communication as needed. Therefore, Feedback is a critical component of Versatility. By monitoring your impact on others, you can adjust the other Versatility skills—Image, Presentation, and Competence.

The ability to both give and receive Feedback can be affected by SOCIAL STYLE. For example, Amiable Style individuals have a natural orientation toward relationships, which means they are advantaged in terms of building relationships. Our research has confirmed there is a slight statistical correlation between Responsiveness and Feedback. This means that, on average, Amiable and Expressive Style people tend to score slightly higher on Feedback. However, this does not mean that all Expressive and Amiable Style people have good Feedback skills.

By contrast, Driving Style people are oriented toward action, making it more of a challenge for them to listen attentively to others (remember, their growth action is to listen). Likewise, Analytical and Expressive Style people can be challenged in their own ways to listen attentively. For example, a message may be delivered too quickly and with too few details for an Analytical Style person, or too slowly and with too many details for an Expressive Style person.

Ensure that message and feedback fully consider both the sender's SOCIAL STYLE and the SOCIAL STYLE of your co-worker. When listening to co-workers, make a sincere attempt to see things from their points of view, even when there is disagreement. This advice applies to what the co-worker literally says and, of equal importance, to his or her choice of words, tone of voice, facial gestures, and body language.

Solidly giving and receiving feedback, then, involves using the senses both to hear their message and to interpret the accompanying nonverbal clues. When the message and the nonverbal behaviors mismatch, tension is probably increasing. In most situations it is non-verbal behavior that carries the most meaning and has the largest impact on others. Acknowledge others' messages, both in terms of content and in terms of the emotions attached to that message. Finally, make sure your communication to your co-workers conveys you are open to their input. This approach fosters good communication and helps to build stronger interpersonal relationships.

How Does SOCIAL STYLE *Impact Feedback?*

As mentioned earlier, listening is the growth action for Driving Style people, so they will have a natural challenge in this regard. When they listen and understand another person, they will usually state they have heard what was said or give some other indication they understand. These people are often brief in their interactions (and patience), so they tend to communicate using as few words as possible. This can make it difficult for other people to decipher exactly what the person wants or is really saying. The relationships they form with others tend to be formal and professional, yet they can be open to more personal involvement. Their primary need is to get results, so once a person has established his or her competence and abilities, a Driving Style person is more open to forming a personal bond or friendship. This need for results also often drives the skilled use of professional networks for these individuals, since they understand they can get things done by knowing key people.

Expressive Style people are oriented toward personal relationships, so in some regard they are naturally advantaged in their use of Feedback skills. Because they have behaviors that are more Emote Responsive, in combination with Tell Assertiveness, these individuals may be able to communicate their intentions in ways that are apparent to others. In other words, they talk a lot and they are physically animated, which makes their feelings clear. Likewise, these individuals tend to be very outgoing, which may aid them in developing relationships at work. They seek personal approval, so these individuals might use their networking skills to their advantage by getting to know important people within the organization. While their natural tendencies might assist them in these areas, the degree to which they actively listen and understand others might be less apparent. For example, during a conversation an Expressive Style person might do the majority of talking, and this can leave the other person feeling a bit overwhelmed and uncertain as to whether he was heard or understood.

Like Expressive Style people, Amiable Style individuals also display their emotions more than other Styles, and this can naturally help them in their use of Feedback skills. They tend to be good listeners who are attuned to others' feelings and well-being. During interactions they often leave the other person feeling like she has been heard and understood. Since they are naturally friendly, they will usually go out of their way to maintain good relationships with their co-workers. However, they might not always develop deep and personal relationships with a large number of people. Instead, they reserve their more personal sides for a select group of people while maintaining cordial relationships with most other people.

Displaying Feedback skills can be more challenging for Analytical Style people since they tend to be reserved and somewhat hesitant to engage with other people. They tend to be good listeners, so others will often feel they have been heard after an interaction. However, because they are emotionally controlled, it might be difficult for others to determine whether the Analytical Style person truly understands or cares about them or their issues. This does not necessarily mean the person does not care; it is simply that he may not communicate his concern in a way that is obvious to others. These individuals might form personal relationships with only a small number of people within the organization. Being socially cautious and reserved by nature, they might not be inclined to form networks that could inevitably help them in their work and careers.

2.6 Reliability & Validity

The SOCIAL STYLE Model measures behavioral style. But behavior, like all psychological phenomena, is not something that can be easily and accurately measured in the physical world, such as weight and height. How do we know we are accurately measuring behavior?

In order to make this claim, the instrument has to adhere to standards that have been set forth by the scientific community. In particular, research evidence should correspond to criteria set forth in the "Standards for Educational and Psychological Testing,"[4] which provides benchmarks for developing psychological measurement instruments. This evidence comes in two primary forms: *Reliability* and *Validity*.

> 1. Reliability determines whether an instrument measures in a way that is consistent and dependable. For example, imagine a brick stamped with the phrase "50 pounds" on the side. The brick may feel light to you so you decide to verify its weight by weighing it yourself. You put it on a scale and it registers a weight of 50 pounds. Just to be extra sure, you weigh it every day for a week, using the same scale, and every day the brick registers at 50 pounds. Although by now you can be reasonably sure of the brick's weight, you wonder if maybe your scale is faulty. So you weigh the brick on 10 different scales, and every scale tells you the brick weighs 50 pounds. You can now be sure the brick weighs 50 pounds, and your measurement is reliable.
>
> The example of the brick points out two unique but similar aspects of a reliable measurement system. First, is one of the measures dependable? The first scale was dependable because every day it indicated the brick weighed 50 pounds. We can be confident the first scale is a dependable measure of weight. Second, if using more than one measure, are these measures consistent with one another? By using multiple scales, we showed they were consistent in their measures; they all indicated the brick weighed 50 pounds. Therefore,

we can be confident all of these scales are consistently agreeing with one another about the weight of objects.

2. Validity determines whether an instrument measures accurately. In other words, does it measure what it proposes to measure? Let's return to the example of the brick. If, after determining your weight scales were reliable using the procedure above, you placed the same brick on a brand new scale and it told you the brick weighed 30 pounds, you would not be able to place faith in this new scale. In fact, you would conclude this new scale does not measure "weight" accurately at all. It is giving you a measurement in pounds, but it is way off base in terms of its accuracy. Because of its unacceptable lack of accuracy, this new scale is not valid for its intended purpose of measuring weight.

TRACOM regularly assesses the reliability and validity of its SOCIAL STYLE Model. In the following, we provide a general overview of this evidence. Specific information about reliability and validity studies can be found in the SOCIAL STYLE & Versatility Technical Report. The most current Technical Report is available at www.tracomcorp.com.

Reliability

Several types of reliability evidence exist for the SOCIAL STYLE Model. Here we present two of the most important types of reliability evidence: internal consistency and inter-rater reliability.

Internal Consistency:

One of the most common and established methods for establishing the reliability evidence for instruments like the SOCIAL STYLE Model is internal consistency. Internal consistency measures the degree of correlation among survey items that claim to measure the same thing (a survey item is a single behavioral statement on a survey). Just as the 10 weight scales were consistent with one another about the weight of the brick, each item on our measurement scales should be consistent with one another.

Each scale is measured using a set of items. For example, the Assertiveness scale currently consists of 15 items. If all items on the Assertiveness scale are truly measuring the same thing, then they should correlate with one another to a certain degree; they should be internally consistent.

The Model's scales were analyzed for internal consistency reliability using a statistic called coefficient alpha. Alpha values range from 0.0 (no relationship among the scale items) to 1.0 (perfect internal consistency). Scale alpha values on the instrument are all above 0.7, which is the benchmark for acceptability. In the case of alpha, having values that are too high is not a good thing. For example, if alpha were 1.0, this would indicate the scale items are completely redundant with one another, meaning that asking a single item provides as much information as asking 15 items. In the previous example, we don't need 10 weight scales to measure the weight of the brick because they are perfectly consistent with one another. Using one is as good as using another. This is usually the case when it comes to measuring things in the physical world (think of temperature, height, and distance). However, for behavioral measures such as SOCIAL STYLE and Versatility, every item on a scale provides unique information, so they should never be perfectly correlated.

Inter-rater Reliability

The second type of reliability evidence is called inter-rater reliability. The multi-rater profiles of the SOCIAL STYLE Model are generated based on the ratings of at least three feedback providers (the self-score is reported separately). For these profiles, reliability evidence comes from the consistency in judgments among raters. In other words, would all my feedback providers view me as relatively similar, with "ask" assertive and "control" responsive tendencies (Analytical Style), or would some of them view me differently? This question is answered through analysis of inter-rater reliability.

Inter-rater reliability was calculated using the Intraclass Correlation Coefficient (ICC).[5] Like internal consistency, values range from 0.0 to 1.0, with higher values indicating greater consistency among raters.

Two forms of ICC were calculated—an average ICC for a single rater and an average ICC for all raters who evaluated each participant, described below.

- Average ICC for a single rater—Indicates the reliability (or relative consistency) for any given individual rater who is observing someone's behavior across all dimensions of the SOCIAL STYLE Model. In other words, does a given individual evaluate a person consistently as he or she is responding to the questionnaire?

- Average ICC across raters—Indicates the reliability (or relative consistency) for all of the raters who evaluate any single individual. In other words, is there consistency among the individuals who are evaluating a person across all Model dimensions?

These forms of ICC were calculated from a random sample of over 9,000 participants. The average ICC for a single rater was 0.96, while the average ICC across raters was 0.99. These values indicate excellent consistency, both for individual raters and for groups of individuals who evaluate a participant's behavior using the instrument.

Validity

As mentioned previously, validity refers to the extent to which an instrument measures what it is supposed to measure and the interpretation of scores and the appropriateness of inferences drawn from those scores. TRACOM evaluates validity using a rigorous model that includes different types of evidence. Here we discuss just one form of validity, called impact validity. This form of validity determines the Model's usefulness and applicability in the workplace. We highlight this type of evidence because it is the most meaningful for facilitators and others who are using the SOCIAL STYLE Model.

Versatility and Managerial Performance

In 2005, TRACOM partnered with an international publishing company to examine the relationship between Versatility and job performance and conducted a study to answer three primary questions:

1. Is Versatility related to managerial effectiveness?

2. Is there a meaningful difference in performance between managers with lower Versatility and managers with higher Versatility?

3. To what extent can Versatility and SOCIAL STYLE predict managerial performance?

Compared with managers lower in Versatility, we believed that managers higher in Versatility would perform at a higher level of effectiveness across a range of behaviors, from technical skill to coaching ability. We also believed that Versatility would contribute unique variance (or predictability) to job performance, whereas SOCIAL STYLE would not. In the past we've found that SOCIAL STYLE is independent of job performance and that individuals can succeed in their chosen fields regardless of their particular SOCIAL STYLE.

We found evidence for all three of these questions.

Relationship between Versatility and Managerial Effectiveness

This research study found that Versatility is a strong indicator of workplace effectiveness. As Versatility increases, so do evaluations of job performance. Versatility was highly correlated with various important components of managers' jobs—for example, ability to coach others (0.44), ability to work well within a team (0.47), ability to establish effective relationships with direct reports (0.51), and effectiveness as a team leader (0.47), just to name a few.

To put these numbers into context, it's helpful to examine some correlations among variables that are commonly understood by most people: taking aspirin daily and reduced risk of death by heart attack (0.02), antihistamine use and reduced runny nose and sneezing (0.11), SAT scores and subsequent college GPA (0.20), effect of alcohol on aggressive behavior (0.23), and relationship between weight and height among U.S. adults (0.44).[6] The correlations of Versatility with managerial performance are strong and meaningful, indicating that the higher a manager's Versatility, the higher his/her performance will be.

Difference in Effectiveness between Managers with Lower and Higher Versatility

Correlation analysis indicated that Versatility is positively and significantly related to workplace effectiveness. We wanted to specifically examine the differences in performance between managers with lower Versatility and managers with higher Versatility. We hypothesized that managers would differ significantly across job performance measures depending on their Versatility category.

We tested this hypothesis using analysis of variance (ANOVA). We found significant differences in job performance ratings between managers with lower Versatility and those with higher Versatility.

Managers with higher Versatility had significantly higher job performance ratings on 46 of the 47 performance measures.

These findings indicate that managers' levels of Versatility are related to their effectiveness across many key indicators of job performance.

Versatility and SOCIAL STYLE as Predictors of Job Performance

Our third question was whether Versatility can predict job performance. We also wanted to test for the predictive effects of Assertiveness and Responsiveness, the two dimensions that make up SOCIAL STYLE. Our hypothesis was that SOCIAL STYLE is independent of effectiveness, and that a person of any SOCIAL STYLE can be equally effective in a managerial position, whereas Versatility can predict performance to some extent.

Multiple regression analysis was used to test how well each of the three measures predicted overall job performance. Both Assertiveness and Responsiveness were found to be non-significant contributors to variance in job performance. However, Versatility accounted for 15% of the variance in overall job performance, comparable to to the effects of intelligence and personality. This means that overall job performance is independent of a person's Assertiveness and Responsiveness, but is meaningfully affected by Versatility.

3 SOCIAL STYLES AND VERSATILITY AT WORK

So far we've discussed many of the mechanics of the SOCIAL STYLE Model, including how SOCIAL STYLE behaviors are displayed and scored, how the instrument is organized, and some of the evidence for its effectiveness. Now we want to turn to more complete descriptions of each of the SOCIAL STYLEs.

The following sections will provide you with a firm grasp of SOCIAL STYLE behaviors. You will learn how people of each SOCIAL STYLE operate on a day-to-day basis. Each SOCIAL STYLE has its own theme, and there are several elements that make up this SOCIAL STYLE theme. These elements are:

- Style Need
- Style Orientation
- Style Growth Action
- Actions Toward Others
- Use of Time
- Approach to Making Decisions
- Style Backup Behavior
- Versatility

Style Need

Each SOCIAL STYLE has a particular need. People of each SOCIAL STYLE are heavily motivated to meet their SOCIAL STYLE-specific need. It is difficult to describe precisely why these needs are so strong, except to say that they represent a conglomeration of the primary motivations of people within each SOCIAL STYLE. When we don't meet our SOCIAL STYLE-specific need, we feel stress and discomfort.

As an analogy, consider sleep—a fundamental human need. We all need sleep, and to this day scientists are still not certain exactly why we need it. At very deep levels, it serves to regenerate neural connections and even helps to process memory. Still, it serves important functions, many of which we are unaware. If we don't get sleep, we feel not only tired but also stressed. If we are deprived of sleep for long enough, we will do just about anything to get it. Our minds will actually take control of our bodies and essentially shut down, even if our eyes are open and we are standing.

In a similar way, if people are deprived of their SOCIAL STYLE-specific need, they will become increasingly uncomfortable and stressed. We will describe each need in detail, but briefly here are the SOCIAL STYLE needs:

- Driving Style - Need for results
- Expressive Style - Need for personal approval
- Amiable Style - Need for personal security
- Analytical Style - Need to be right

It's important to keep in mind that all Styles have the desire for results, personal approval, security, and to be right. What we are talking about in terms of Style Need is the primary reason a particular

SOCIAL STYLE engages in the core behaviors associated with that SOCIAL STYLE. It is the fundamental motivator of that person's behavior and takes precedence over other needs.

Style Orientation

People of each SOCIAL STYLE have a way that they go about meeting their need. This is called SOCIAL STYLE Orientation. You can think of Style Orientation as a behavioral way in which people meet their fundamental need. These behaviors are the way people seek to meet their needs.

For example, Expressive Style people have a need for personal approval. In order to meet this need, they have to engage in some behavior. These individuals meet their need by being spontaneous. They might attempt to be funny or controversial or creative in order to draw attention to themselves, or might speak about themselves in a group even when others have not given any indication they are interested in what the person has to say. They meet their need for personal approval through an orientation toward spontaneity.

Each SOCIAL STYLE has an Orientation they use to get their needs met. Briefly, here are the SOCIAL STYLE orientations:

- Driving Style - Orientation is to take action
- Expressive Style - Orientation is to be spontaneous
- Amiable Style - Orientation is to maintain relationships
- Analytical Style - Orientation is to think

Style Growth Action

Because needs are so strong, even if we are not conscious of them, we are likely to engage in behavior that has the best chance of helping us meet our needs. Since these behaviors have succeeded for us so

Fig. 3-1: Need, Orientation, and Growth Action

often, we tend to use them frequently. This leaves other sets of behavior that we do not use very often. We might view these less frequently used behaviors as frustrating. This is because they often get in the way of our attempts to meet our needs. For this reason, we tend to disregard these behaviors in favor of our SOCIAL STYLE Orientation behaviors, although others view the absence of these behaviors as a fundamental weakness of our SOCIAL STYLE.

For example, imagine we surveyed the co-workers of a Driving Style person, asking the question, "If this person should do just one thing more often, what would it be?" There is a good chance most co-workers would respond by saying this person should "do a better job of listening." This is because Driving Style people meet their need by taking action, and for them listening gets in the way of taking action. It forces them to stop and take account of what others are saying and doing. Therefore, they do not listen as often or as attentively as they should. It is an infrequent behavior for them.

Each SOCIAL STYLE has a specific Growth Action (see Fig. 3-1), and it represents a primary aspect of behavior that is most frequently ignored or overlooked during interactions with other people. Instead, people prefer to engage in common and comfortable behaviors for their SOCIAL STYLE. Briefly, the Growth Actions are:

- Driving Style - Growth Action is to actively listen to others
- Expressive Style - Growth Action is to check their behavior
- Amiable Style - Growth Action is to initiate their will
- Analytical Style - Growth Action is to declare a stance

Style Action towards Others, Approach to Time, and Decision-Making

We have reviewed how each SOCIAL STYLE has a Need, Orientation, and Growth Action. These are important to understand because they fundamentally impact how people behave at work. In particular, they impact three specific areas of people's work lives: how they act toward others, approach time, and make decisions. How people approach these three aspects of work is influenced directly by their Style Needs and Orientations. During stressful times, they might fall back on an exaggerated form of this basic behavior, which is referred to as Backup Behavior.

At work, each SOCIAL STYLE has particular ways that it acts

toward others. For example, Driving Style people are very direct. Remember, their need is results and they achieve this need by having an orientation toward taking action. This need and orientation propels them to behave in specific ways with others. Most notably, they are fast-paced, action oriented, and can come across to others as insensitive, impersonal, and having unrealistic demands.

Each SOCIAL STYLE also has a specific way in which it approaches time. As you can probably guess, some SOCIAL STYLEs are more rushed than others. To continue our example, Driving Style people are impatient. They like things to be done yesterday. They are also impatient with people who they believe are wasting their time. Once again, this is a direct result of their need and orientation. They want results quickly, and when people seem to waste their time, this is in direct conflict with their need.

Likewise, Need and Orientation impact how people make decisions. For example, Driving Style people tend to make decisions quickly. They are usually logical in their approach but they decide quickly, take risks, and move forward quickly once they have made a decision. Again, this approach is a direct result of their need for results and their orientation for taking action.

Each SOCIAL STYLE has a specific way they prefer to act toward others, how to use time, and to approach decision-making. People engage in these behaviors because they are compatible with their Style Need and Orientation. Briefly, the behaviors characteristic to each SOCIAL STYLE are illustrated in the following graphics (see Fig. 3-2):

Style Backup Behavior

In order to get things done, a certain degree of tension is necessary. For example, if your manager gives you an assignment with no

SOCIAL STYLES AND VERSATILITY AT WORK

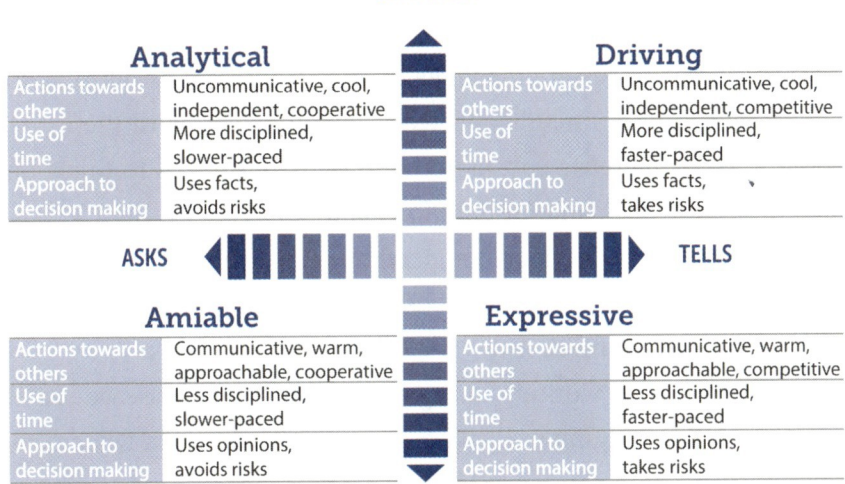

Fig. 3-2: Style Action towards Others, Approach to Time, and Decision-Making

deadline, you will likely feel very little tension. You will not feel motivated to make significant progress on the project. However, if the deadline for the assignment is the end of the week, you will experience enough tension that you will make efforts to complete the project on time. This is an appropriate amount of tension. Sometimes tension can be too high and overwhelming, in which case, it becomes stressful. If your manager tells you that the deadline has been moved up to tomorrow morning, chances are your tension level will rise dramatically. In fact, it will become stressful and you will likely have difficulty completing the task. As long as it is at a reasonable level, tension leads us to act. It is one of the forces that leads us to develop our particular SOCIAL STYLEs. Therefore, tension is not something that needs to be avoided, but it does need to be managed at appropriate levels when possible.

When it comes to behaving with high Versatility, tension plays an important role. When we are working under conditions of low or moderate tension, it is relatively easy to display high Versatility. Because stress levels are manageable, we can go out of our way to meet other people's needs and work productively with them. As tension levels increase substantially, it is harder for us to focus on others' Style Needs and Orientations and behave with high Versatility. We feel overwhelmed and need to escape the tension in some way, and this often results in focusing on our own Style Need and Orientation, resulting in low Versatility.

When we are working in highly stressful situations, we are at greater risk of engaging in Backup Behavior. This occurs when people are unable to meet their SOCIAL STYLE need. In particular, it occurs when they try to meet their SOCIAL STYLE need by engaging in their typical SOCIAL STYLE behaviors but experience tension in this attempt. This leads to more stress and results in an

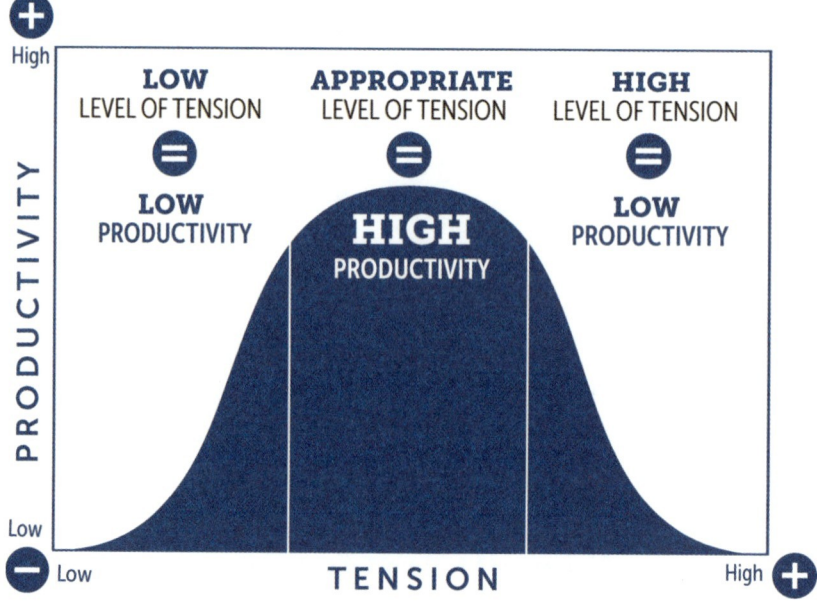

Fig. 3-3: Tension Productivity Curve

exaggerated form of SOCIAL STYLE behavior to reduce their stress. In the graph (see Fig. 3-3), Backup Behavior occurs on the right side in the area of high tension or stress.

You can think of Backup Behavior as being similar to a fight-or-flight mechanism. When animals are threatened, they either find a way to escape or they are forced to fight whatever is threatening them. Humans have developed a less physical form of this same mechanism. Even for Amiable and Analytical Styles, their Backup Behaviors are an attempt to fight off the excess tension they are experiencing in a relationship.

Backup Behavior can be a significant contributing factor in unproductive relationships. When we are in backup mode, we are not concerned with the effects such behavior has on others. Backup Behavior always occurs within the interpersonal relationship that caused the stress, and it is the most ineffective use of SOCIAL STYLE behavior.

Briefly, here is how each SOCIAL STYLE exhibits Backup Behavior (see Fig. 3-4):

> • The Driving Style becomes autocratic, often trying to take charge of situations and force others to act in order to accomplish a task or reach a goal. They will try to dominate situations, including meetings and conversations, sometimes rolling over others or simply acting independently without regard for others.

> • The Expressive Style attacks, often becoming angry and venting their feelings about the situation. They are occasionally abusive in their relationships when they are frustrated with a specific person.

> • The Amiable Style acquiesces, often complying without

actually giving any commitment. They don't want to risk damaging the relationship so they will not state their true opinions. The Amiable Style will subtly attempt to derail the course of action they feel was forced on them and/or others.

• The Analytical Style avoids, often withdrawing from situations. This form of retreat is their way of escaping situations rather than dealing productively with them. This may look like deferring a decision, seeking more data, leaving the situation without commitment, or simply refusing to participate in the meeting or project.

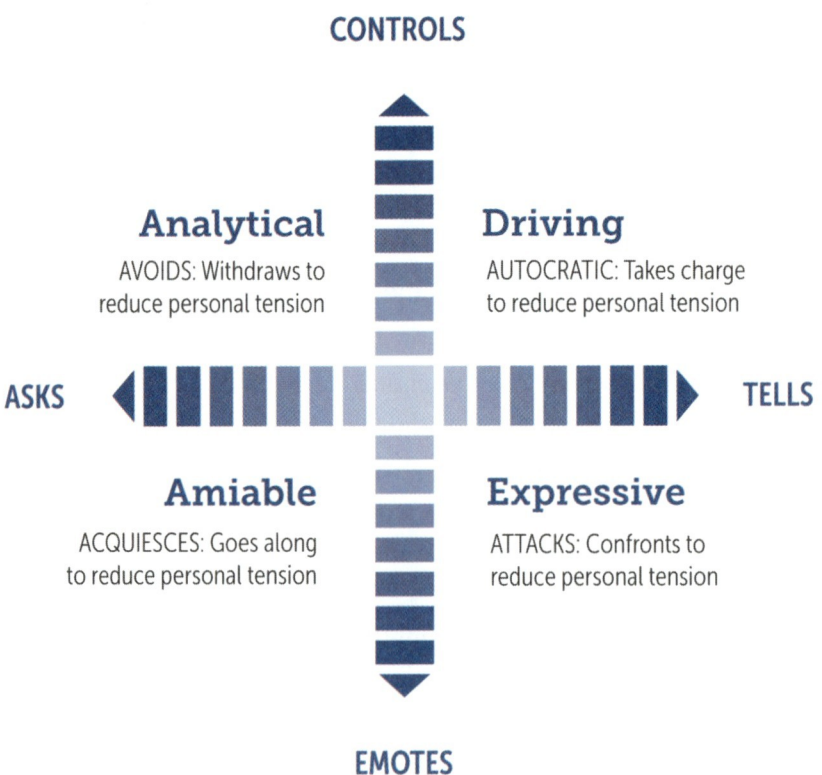

Fig. 3-4: Style Backup Behavior

Versatility

When describing SOCIAL STYLEs, we stated that people's SOCIAL STYLE behaviors tend to be consistent across situations. This is true; we are who we are. However, people behave differently with different groups of people or in different situations. This adaptable behavior tends to be that which is under our control, or Versatility. Most of us will display it differently depending on who we are interacting with. We do not always do this, but we all do it some of the time. For example, a manager may be very aware of her behavior when she is interacting with her supervisors. The manager is attuned to her colleagues' needs and expectations, as well as their SOCIAL STYLEs, and thus is very conscious about how not to behave.

Some aspects of low Versatility will be common across SOCIAL STYLEs. For example, a person who consistently submits low quality work will be described by co-workers as "unreliable" no matter their SOCIAL STYLE. This is a reflection of Competence. Low Versatility often takes on SOCIAL STYLE-related characteristics. You'll find this behavior is often characterized by acting in SOCIAL STYLE-bound ways—rigidly adhering to SOCIAL STYLE behaviors without displaying any acceptance of the behaviors of other SOCIAL STYLEs. Likewise, high Versatility behaviors are often the polar opposites of what is found among people acting with low Versatility. People who act with high Versatility are aware of how they impact others and consciously behave in a way that minimizes stress or tension for people around them. They don't stop being themselves but they do control their behavior so the other person can get their needs met in the relationship.

As you read the descriptions given in the following sections, it is important to remember that SOCIAL STYLE is independent of Versatility. People often wonder how an Amiable Style person can have low Versatility, since their orientation is toward maintaining relationships. As you read the description for Amiable Style people with low Versatility, you will probably be reminded of some people you know. Likewise, some people think that all Driving Style people have low Versatility, and of course this is not true.

3.1 Driving Style

The Driving Style Need can be summed up in one word: results. These people prefer to deal with their issues first, focusing on their desired outcomes. Their Style Orientation is action. In order to meet their Need, they are highly compelled to be active and move toward their goals. Their Growth Action is to listen, as listening forces them to slow down. This is the opposite of their Orientation.

People with a Driving Style have a series of strengths and weaknesses, summarized below.

Strengths

- On teams, they tend to keep the group focused on its purpose and targeted results.
- They thrive on variety and challenges; they will meet a challenge because it is there.
- They are persistent and tenacious.
- They sort information according to what is significant in terms of accomplishing their goal versus spending long periods of time analyzing information.
- They are decisive.
- They are action-oriented.
- They initiate innovation and change.

Weaknesses

- They tend to be poor listeners.
- They are impatient and create anxiety in others.
- "Fire, ready, aim"—they tend to start moving forward without a solid plan.
- Their worst fear is loss of control or that someone will take advantage of them; consequently, they tend to be argumentative and overbearing at times.
- By not fully listening and not listening for meaning, they do not acknowledge others' thoughts, ideas, and feelings.
- They sometimes overrule people, or are blunt and sarcastic.
- They are inattentive to details and can be dissatisfied with routine work.
- They may resist participation as part of a team, preferring to do it themselves.

Actions towards Others

People with a Driving Style are typically more oriented toward results and tasks than they are toward relationships and people. As a result, they may appear uncommunicative, cool, formal, independent, and competitive in relationships with others.

A Driving Style individual tends to initiate clear action. However, the personal reasons for such action may not be obvious to co-workers because this person seldom sees a need to share personal motives or feelings. They tend to focus on efficiency or productivity rather than on taking the time to develop warm interpersonal relationships with co-workers. Thus, co-workers may feel they really don't get to know these individuals on a close, personal basis.

In discussions about people, Driving Style individuals seem to display an attitude that suggests they have learned how to work with others only because they must do so in order to achieve their objectives, and not because they enjoy interacting with people on a personal basis. In their drive for results they often view others as mechanisms for achieving their own needs. However, they often appear very pleasant and even charming—on their terms. These individuals may appear to treat people as objects rather than individuals. Keep in mind that although they may control how they share emotions and feelings, this does not mean they don't have them. They simply prefer not to openly display or to share them.

Driving Style people respond well to co-workers who support their conclusions and the actions needed to implement those conclusions. This is because they view this positive support as a way to move forward in achieving their goals. However, it may sometimes be difficult for them to move forward because they may not openly and fully communicate their objectives and underlying motives, unless doing so is necessary for achieving the goal.

Driving Style individuals respond well when they are asked specific questions about an objective they have identified as important. They want to get a job done and are usually willing to describe what outcomes they are striving to achieve. They appreciate assistance that can help with achieving stated objectives and prefer "what" and "when" questions rather than off-track discussions of "how," "who," or "why."

People with a Driving Style appreciate efforts that support the results they want more than things done for them personally. This SOCIAL STYLE prefers an emphasis on outcomes and goals instead of personal support and encouragement. In addition, these people prefer working with others who help them identify options, indicate how they can contribute to achieving them, and ask which of these actions they would prefer taking.

When someone disagrees with the specifics or objectives of Driving Style individuals, they will tune out personal challenges or philosophical viewpoints. Driving Style individuals tend to listen more carefully to arguments based on facts, logic, and realistic alternatives.

Approach to Time

Driving Style individuals have little tolerance for actions or discussions they deem a waste of time. As pointed out earlier, if they feel their time is being wasted, this prevents them from meeting their need for results. They prefer getting to the point and staying on target. They prefer co-workers who show respect for their time, recognize the importance of sticking to a schedule, and can sense when they want to move on. For example, they like meetings to end on time. When it is necessary to continue beyond the agreed-upon time frame, they prefer to be given a choice of whether to continue the meeting or schedule a second meeting.

A Driving Style individual can find it a misuse of time if co-workers use work time to build personal relationships. These individuals typically prefer co-workers who are disciplined in their use of time, are able to move quickly, and focus on business. The further a co-worker's behavior appears to stray from that objective, the more restless they become. Equally, as co-workers use their time efficiently, their work relationship with the Driving Style person tends to improve. While not becoming as personally warm and approachable as individuals with Expressive or Amiable Styles, co-workers frequently discover signs of a person with a Driving Style thawing out and warming up after real progress has been made toward achieving some goal or objective at work.

Customary Approach to Decision-Making

When making a decision, a Driving Style individual prefers to be provided with facts, useful information, and viable options. These individuals enjoy having power and like making their own decisions. They don't like someone telling them exactly what to do or what not to do.

In addition, when making a decision, a Driving Style person wants to know the probability for the success or effectiveness of the various options. They are likely to choose alternatives with good probabilities of success, but may occasionally select a less-likely-to-succeed alternative. This is because their need for results is more important than accuracy or certainty and, therefore, they are willing to take what they see as calculated risks. While the Driving Style individual can accept risks, they may be considering facts in addition to the ones presented. Thus, those wishing to influence their choices should use solid, salient facts to make their case. The risk is in providing them too many details and facts they consider irrelevant.

Backup Behavior

A Driving Style individual uses Autocratic Backup Behavior. They attempt to take charge of the situation and the people in it, and seek total control in order to achieve their desired objective. Perceived by others as overbearing, this autocratic approach represents a natural, predictable method of behavior when the going gets rough for those with a Driving Style.

Another careful look reveals this is an extension of the typically impersonal, unresponsive, assertive behavior of the Driving Style. Autocratic Backup Behavior seeks two objectives:

1. To reduce the tension of the present circumstance that isn't going well (a need for control)
2. To achieve something in the process (taking action)

The attempt to take over is not perceived as a mature interaction. Rather, it represents a selfish move to have things just the way the individual with a Driving Style wants them. This will make them feel a lower level of tension no matter what it does to the relationship.

Versatility

Driving Style people tend to be formal in their dress and appearance, and depending on the circumstances of your workplace, they might expect you to dress in a similar way, especially if you have interactions with customers. However, they place high value on professional competence, so if you have proven your abilities to them, they may be more open to your own personal tastes in clothing and appearance. These individuals prefer a work area that is organized to help them get things done. They may look for the same in your work area. However, they are likely to be more interested in how well you get work done rather than how you decorate your work area.

When appealing to Driving Style audience members, remember to clearly state the goal and focus of your presentation. This will help them meet their need for results. Be efficient and brief in your presentation, since this will help them feel their time is well spent. In situations where there are multiple SOCIAL STYLEs present, begin your remarks with an overview summarizing the topic to be covered and the action you expect from the audience.

Driving Style people are always in a hurry, so it is important to establish your reliability and credibility early. Until they see this, they may be hesitant to trust you. Follow through on your commitments, and show you can adapt to changing needs. Explicitly state your opinions without automatically deferring to their opinions or demands. Driving Style people don't usually focus on relationships. Therefore, when priorities shift they show a greater focus on the outcome to be achieved rather than on the interpersonal repercussions of the situation. These individuals will appreciate your efforts to articulate bottom line results or benefits of your decisions or actions.

When communicating with Driving Style people, keep the key components of Feedback in mind: active listening, empathy and adaptive communication. Listen for deadlines, specific requests, and actions to be taken. Clarify things as needed to show you understand what they plan to achieve. Show empathy by reflecting their need for results and requests for action. Respond promptly to messages and requests. Show that you understand their frustration when things aren't moving fast enough for them or in the way they desired. Ask direct questions to better understand their motivations, which they may not reveal unless they feel revealing them is necessary for achieving the goal. When communicating, be direct and concise. When they are communicating with you, respond directly and get to the point quickly.

Low Versatility

Driving Style people's Growth Action is to listen, and this deficiency is a key characteristic among those who are behaving with low Versatility. They have a problem with listening because they are in a rush to take action in order to achieve results. They often listen only at a superficial level without understanding the underlying messages that others are communicating.

Related to their poor listening skills, these individuals often come across as insensitive or uncaring. They do not display interest in matters important to others, such as personal issues, career goals, or feelings about work. This is an outcome of their focus on their own need and orientation. Though it may not be their intent, they are perceived as discounting what other people say or want. They often fail to remember personal information about their co-workers, or at least will not bring it up in conversation. It is as if this personal information goes in one ear and out the other for them; they consider it less important than other information. In the short-term, the Driving Style person might get what she needs, but this focus on short-term needs will often result in long-term consequences. For example, remembering and caring about other people's personal interests and lives is critical for building relationships.

These people are often highly impatient. They are constantly moving things along without waiting for others or for information they might need. For example, when leading a new group, a Driving Style person will not allow time for the group to get to know one another or develop rapport before launching into the work. They consider their own priorities to be the most important, and will push to achieve their agendas. Of course, this often backfires because they don't have buy-in or commitment from others. They also might rush into a decision, only to realize later the decision was faulty because they didn't have all the information they needed.

One of the key characteristics of Driving Style people who display low Versatility is their extreme need to control. They will try to control processes, outcomes, and people. For example, during meetings they will dominate discussion so it goes in the direction they desire. They will freely interrupt others without apology. This can have both short- and long-term consequences. In the short-term, people will feel run over and disregarded, while in the long-term they might not support the Driving Style person's agenda or expend any effort to help the person.

These individuals are often very secretive. They keep information to themselves, which frustrates other people because they may need this information in order to succeed at their jobs. They tend to view information as power rather than something to be shared. Related to this, they don't disclose their feelings. This makes it difficult for other people to form meaningful relationships with them. Some Driving Style people struggle to understand their feelings, so in a very real sense they are unable to reveal their emotions to others.

Driving Style people tend to be formal, and this can make others uncomfortable. This is especially true when the person is in a position of power or authority. Their formality makes them hard to read, and since they are reluctant communicators, other people are left feeling as though they don't understand what the person is thinking.

Similar to Analytical Style people, these individuals tend to be very rational, to the point where they discount other ways of approaching issues. They inherently see the logical approach as the most valuable. This can result in two problems. First, the person does not take into account other approaches equally valuable to their own. Second, it leaves others feeling as though their input is not valued.

These individuals sometimes put others through trials in order to evaluate their ability to contribute to a goal. For example, during a meeting a Driving Style person might ask an individual to respond to very difficult questions or to otherwise prove their abilities. They often use public settings to put others on the hot seat. Of course, this can cause resentment among the people who are being put through this treatment.

There are other, more subtle ways that Driving Style people will show low Versatility. For example, when on the phone with someone, the person might read emails or attempt to do some other distracting task that prevents him from paying attention to the conversation. This is another form of impatience. Like some of the other behaviors described above, this can leave other people feeling they are not important or their time is not as valuable as the Driving Style person's time.

High Versatility

When behaving with high Versatility, Driving Style people are real assets to organizations and are helpful for their co-workers. They are able to keep projects moving ahead, but instead of taking all control they get input and buy-in from others. In particular, they display good Feedback skills by actively listening to others, understanding their viewpoints and why they have them, and responding to them. The skilled use of Feedback is particularly noteworthy among individuals of the Driving Style who demonstrate high Versatility because it involves a high degree of listening, which is their Growth Action.

Like all people who are using high Versatility, these individuals are aware of the impact they have on others and consciously monitor their behavior. They make an effort to work on their listening skills, as well as getting to know others on a personal level. This benefits them by helping others be more comfortable, which in turn affects their working relationships and ability to get things done. They display this by slowing down and taking the time to get to know others. Even if they are in a hurry, they ask people how they are. They will ask them about their families, or any other subject that they know the person is interested in. Critically, they show genuine interest in others. Merely asking the questions does not suffice.

Instead of being secretive, these people are upfront in sharing their knowledge and opinions. This is not done in an aggressive manner. Rather, they provide their opinions directly, but not bluntly. They let others know where they stand, and by displaying their openness, they allow others to express themselves and build trust. Further, they make sure to gather input from people prior to making decisions. This helps not only the other people who are involved, but also almost always results in more informed decisions.

While Driving Style people are always oriented toward taking action, when displaying high Versatility, they are able to maintain patience. They keep things moving along without unnecessarily rushing others. They understand the different skills and value their co-workers bring to projects, and they allow them the time and focus they may need to succeed at their tasks.

Challenges and Benefits

In order for Driving Style people to act in ways that lead to high Versatility, they have to diminish many of their natural tendencies. They want to dominate discussions, but they have to make sure to involve others. They want to control things, but they have to give up some of that control. They want to move quickly, but they have to slow down. Inevitably, all of these behaviors help them achieve their need for results, so it can be difficult for them to moderate these tendencies.

Acting in ways that lead to high Versatility has two primary benefits for Driving Style people. First, relationships with co-workers will be much stronger, and this in turn will have ongoing benefits. People will trust the and will be more willing to actively collaborate with them. Second, the person's decisions and work effectiveness will be improved. This happens by taking into account other viewpoints and information, resulting in more informed decisions and higher quality work.

3.2 Expressive Style

The Expressive Style Need is personal approval. These individuals need to be recognized and know others value their contributions. Because of this, they like to relate to others on a personal basis. Their SOCIAL STYLE Orientation is spontaneity. Acting in spontaneous and outgoing ways helps them meet their need for personal approval. This can lead to creativity, imagination, or inspired action. It can also lead to misunderstanding. Spontaneity can come across as impulsiveness at times. These individuals can change directions quickly, moving from one subject or task to another.

The Expressive Style's Growth Action is "to check." This means that they do not check their behavior as often as they should; at times they go overboard in their behavior. For example, they will make inappropriate jokes without stopping to consider these can be offensive to others. In their enthusiasm, they can rush into action without pausing to consider others' viewpoints or needs. They can frequently change direction and allow meetings to run over schedule. They need to manage their impulsiveness. Expressive Style people can earn support and respect from others by taking the extra time to look at—or check—the finer points of an issue or situation.

Strengths

- They build strong, lasting networks with others.
- They can sell ideas and they get cooperation from others.
- On a team, they make good ambassadors to others in the organization and to customers or vendors.
- They can be strong in situations that require building bridges to others.
- They tend to have good judgment about how others are feeling and about their attitudes in a situation.
- They have a strong ability to influence and persuade others.

- They can be creative and innovative.
- They see the big picture and can be visionary.
- They can make work fun.

Weaknesses

- They tend to make overly optimistic estimates of how long things will take or how much they will cost.
- Under pressure, they can become disorganized or disoriented.
- They make decisions on the basis of hunches or intuition, rather than analysis or logic.
- They do not pay attention to details and processes.
- They can waste time for others.
- They are sometimes more concerned with popularity than tangible results.
- They act impulsively and can be unrealistic in appraising people.
- They easily get off topic and on to something they consider more exciting or innovative.

Actions towards Others

People with an Expressive Style appear communicative, fun, exciting, warm, approachable, and competitive. They generally approach situations in a more casual manner than other SOCIAL STYLEs. These individuals often openly share their feelings and thoughts with co-workers. They appear to want others as friends, but in the role of followers or personal supporters of their aspirations rather than as competitors. Again, their actions toward others are a direct result of attempting to meet their need for personal approval. They do this by being spontaneous in the ways mentioned here.

These people consider power and politics important because they can enhance personal recognition and help recruit supporters to the cause. While relationships and people are meaningful to them, these relationships may lack depth and be short-lived.

Expressive Style people tend to get along well with co-workers who provide support for their desires and intuitions. They see this as a show of approval. They willingly share their opinions (on almost everything), future goals, and information about what they think others need to do to achieve objectives. If asked, they will also share what they are doing personally to reach those objectives. In fact, they prefer discussions about people and their future goals to discussions about specific actions that must be taken to achieve an end result.

The Expressive Style individual can, at times, commit to a goal without necessarily agreeing to the processes that lead to the goal. This is because they are generally not detail-oriented. This can lead to problems if co-workers proceed on the belief that everything will somehow work out for the best. Because the individual typically shows little interest in how others plan to reach agreed-upon objectives, they usually have limited interest in details such as *who*, *what*, and *how*. Thus, these individuals appreciate co-workers who take the initiative to handle details and follow up to ensure that necessary things are actually done without burdening them.

Expressive Style individuals like to spend time exploring mutually stimulating ideas and possible solutions. They do not like to be rushed in a conversation that does not allow them to build on the ideas of others. These individuals also like to get credit for their contribution to the effort. Remember, they are creative, fun, and exciting, and they seek support for their aspirations from co-workers.

These individuals feel a strong need to defend personal positions they have taken, so co-workers are advised to use caution when challenging them. Challenging them is in direct contrast to their need for approval. Instead, they prefer to hear about alternative solutions that co-workers can both share and enthusiastically support.

Best Use of Time

Expressive Style individuals tend to move quickly in their actions, have less discipline about time, and rapidly enter social interactions. They appreciate co-workers who try to stimulate them by developing and presenting clear pictures or motivational stories that support ideas in a positive way.

The Expressive Style person acts quickly and can change a course of action rapidly and unexpectedly. Thus, this person appreciates it when others take responsibility for keeping activities on a timetable and focusing on specifics, as long as the relationship is maintained on a friendly and enthusiastic basis. Having the specifics summarized in writing can help the person stay on task and on time.

Because the Expressive Style individual has a less disciplined use of time, a 30-minute meeting is only a guideline from his or her point of view. If this person gets excited about the content of the discussion, a meeting can go on significantly longer than scheduled and flow in many directions. They appreciate it when others do not unnecessarily cut an exciting interaction short just because the clock on the wall says it's time to go.

Customary Approach to Decision-Making

The Expressive Style person tends to take risks based on the opinions of people he or she considers important, prominent, or successful. In fact, the opinions of others can often mean more in this person's decision-making process than mere facts or logic. Thus, the person's decisions can sometimes be swayed to take on additional risk if notable or prominent people support a particular course of action.

Expressive Style people tend to respond to special benefits, immediate rewards, and extra incentives for their willingness to take risks and move rapidly in making a decision. Personal social recognition or prestige sometimes provides the extra incentive necessary for making a decision.

Backup Behavior

Under high tension, the Expressive Style individual tends to become angry, perhaps abusive, and vents his or her feelings. This is called Attack Behavior. It is a natural outlet and a predictable way to behave for these people. If you look carefully, you will recognize this attacking mode as an extension of the Expressive Style. It is emotional and assertive. It includes highly emotional Tell Assertive statements about the other person.

Attack Behavior stems from the desire to eliminate the intolerable tension present in the relationship. It is selfish behavior because the individual no longer seeks to work productively with another person. Attack Behavior damages others, making the relationship less effective. Tension is not directed into effective or productive activities.

Versatility

Expressive Style people look for freedom of personal expression in their work and appearance, and they will generally be open to your own individual preferences in this regard. They might even appreciate it when you wear less formal attire or can create opportunities to do so. These individuals often display achievements and inspirational items, along with humorous ones. They want you to be energetic and, if possible, relax time constraints when you enter their work environment.

Expressive Style people want to be involved in the discussion. They will respond well when the presenter allows them opportunities to express themselves. They generally will not need specific requests, since they naturally assert themselves in groups. Show excitement about your presentation, since this will appeal to their affinity for stimulation. These individuals typically have a need for big-picture thinking and strategic approaches, so provide a broad, visual depiction of the goal of your presentation.

When working with Expressive Style individuals, it is important to show enthusiasm. They appreciate working closely with people, and you can use this as an opportunity to display your abilities. They can move quickly from topic to topic or from priority to priority. You can show your flexibility by keeping pace with them and helping them refocus when necessary. When giving ideas, avoid overemphasizing details and frame your solutions in big picture terms using descriptive language where possible. Show self-confidence with these individuals to inspire their confidence in you.

When communicating with Expressive Style individuals, listen for their feelings, enthusiasm, and ideas. They want you to see their spontaneity and ability to explore possibilities. Avoid appearing to be aloof or too task-focused, and allow time to build a relationship. Show empathy by being attentive. Touch base on a personal level, and avoid starting discussions with work issues or action items. Acknowledge their feelings and share some of yours, for example, by talking about things that are happening for you and others. Understand their frustration when others don't seem to appreciate their input or when they are frustrated by details, routines, and standard procedures.

When communicating with Expressive Style individuals, allow time for conversation and for processing their feelings. Don't concentrate just on specifics and avoid overwhelming them with facts. Show your concern for the human side of issues by expressing warmth and interest. Avoid looking too critical. When they are communicating with you, try to respond in a positive and upbeat way. You may need to help them narrow down options, and plan to follow up with them. If you do not respond in ways that meet their needs, they might react by becoming visibly impatient and vocal.

Low Versatility

The Growth Action for Expressive Style people is to "check their behavior." This casual lack of control is a hallmark of low Versatility behavior among these individuals. They do not take the time to consider what is appropriate for situations and audiences, and this comes across in their mannerisms, dress, the types of stories they tell, and other behaviors. They behave this way because their need for personal approval is so strong they are not interested in evaluating the impact their behavior might be having on others.

A characteristic of these people is their habit for improvisation. They are often unprepared for a given situation and will respond with an impromptu display that relies on charm or humor. They will often display charisma rather than substance. They never hesitate to speak up or share their opinions, but they will often skirt real issues by relying on their personality to cover up their lack of insight or knowledge. They quickly move from smooth to slick. There are both immediate and long-term consequences of this behavior. In the immediate moment it can leave people feeling frustrated, since they might be relying on the person for meaningful input. If this behavior occurs often, others will simply come to believe the person lacks any meaningful ability.

Low Versatility often shows itself through exaggerated SOCIAL STYLE behaviors. Expressive Style people seek recognition, and this often comes across as a strong need to be the center of attention. This can display itself in a number of ways, including publicly pointing out their achievements or efforts, acting as the office comedian, and self-aggrandizement. They are especially prone to disclosing personal information about themselves that is inappropriate or even offensive to others. In moderation, some of these behaviors can be appropriate and even helpful to a given situation. However, when this behavior becomes frequent it is distracting, unproductive, and is seen as a cover for inadequacies.

The Backup Behavior of Expressive Style people is to Attack, and this will be displayed in combination with low Versatility behaviors. The attack can come as a full frontal assault or can be less aggressive. They will bring up issues that are unrelated to the matter at hand, and will criticize others on a personal level. In subtler forms, they might publicly call attention to an issue with the intent to embarrass a co-worker or put them in a difficult spot, even when not actively in confrontation with the person. On occasion, the person is not even aware they are attacking someone. This is an example of a person who is not checking their behavior, since they seem to have no awareness of the consequences they have on others. Of course, the major consequence is that people will not trust them and may be very hesitant to work closely with them.

These individuals typically approach time in a very undisciplined way, and it is difficult to get them to commit to specifics. Related to this, they often fail to follow through on others' expectations. For example, when discussing outcomes and next steps after a meeting, such a person will be ambiguous about their commitments even though others in the meeting will have clear definitions of next steps. When the next meeting comes around, this person will show up but will be unprepared and late. This can result in feelings of resentment among others, who may feel they are carrying an unfair share of the workload.

When displaying low Versatility, Expressive Style people will discount the logic of a course of action. Others may have a real need and rationale for being precise about something, but because these people approach situations in a very loose and free way, they will disregard the more logical approach. This can leave others feeling discounted and frustrated.

High Versatility

A key feature of behaviors that lead to high Versatility for Expressive Style people is their ability to take their Growth Action—checking their behavior. Like all people who act with high Versatility, they are aware of their own behavior and they actively monitor their impact on others. This is especially important for Expressive Style individuals because their expansive behavior can easily become overwhelming and lead to tension for others. When acting with high Versatility, they recognize this and rein in their tendencies in order to meet the needs of others and different situations. This allows them to become more attuned to how others respond. Where appropriate, their contribution of emotions or humor to situations is valuable because it helps to build or solidify relationships. This can help make workgroups more cohesive, fun, and productive.

For example, during a meeting a person with high Versatility will make jokes that are not offensive but charming. The intent of the joke is to make people comfortable, not to embarrass anyone. Instead of trying to dominate the meeting, the person will listen and avoid interrupting others when they are speaking. Critically, the use of these high Versatility behaviors is not meant to draw attention to the Expressive Style person. Remember the need for personal approval is strong for these individuals, and when they act with high Versatility they are not focused on their own need.

When these people display high Versatility, they are showing substance in addition to charisma. Their natural sociability endears them to others. However, they do not rely only on this. They are prepared and actively contribute to projects. This leaves others feeling not only good about the interaction, but also confident in the person's abilities.

Because they show an awareness of other people's strengths, these individuals will often show respect for co-workers who contribute in a more logical manner. This is very valuable for them because by first showing their understanding of a logical approach, they win credibility from their co-workers. This allows them the opportunity to bring emotions and humor into the situation without risking alienating others.

Expressive Style individuals can be excellent for relieving group tension. Their easy use of humor helps put others at ease and allows for fun within work settings. When attuned to people and situations, they are better than any other SOCIAL STYLE at using humor and personal feelings to make others comfortable.

Challenges and Benefits

Expressive Style people like to be outgoing, which can sometimes come across as verbose, self-centered, and offensive. They run into difficulty because in order to behave in ways that lead to higher Versatility, they need to apply their SOCIAL STYLE "brakes." Remember their Growth Action is to check their behavior. They want to be outgoing, creative, exciting, and fun, but they need to understand not everyone responds well to these behaviors, so they have to moderate these tendencies. They want to be spontaneous and funny, but they need to realize blatant humor is not always appropriate or appreciated. They want to be the center of attention, but they need to allow other people to have the spotlight sometimes.

As with all SOCIAL STYLEs, acting in ways that lead to high Versatility will benefit Expressive Style people by improving their working relationships and personal effectiveness. Relationships will be improved because people will be able to interact with them without feeling overwhelmed. Instead of constantly walking on pins and wondering when the person is going to go on the attack, others can interact with the person without being overly cautious or fearful of retribution. Their personal effectiveness will improve because people will see substance behind the dramatic displays. Instead of relying solely on their ability to network with others, they will garner recognition through their skills, team-focus, and competence.

3.3 Amiable Style

An Amiable Style person's need is Personal Security. Before they feel comfortable dealing with the issues at hand, these individuals prefer to establish a comfortable, personal, and safe relationship. The SOCIAL STYLE Orientation of the Amiable Style is Relationships. They meet their need for personal security by building a personal connection and approaching others in a cooperative, friendly, and supportive manner.

This individual's Growth Action is "to initiate." Others would show more support and respect for these individuals if they would take the lead in an appropriate way when the situation calls for it. They need to deal with a situation head on, raise disagreements, and take a personal stand without being swayed by its impact on relationships. This willingness to make an effort to initiate action will help move things forward, even if it involves personal risk. This behavior will most likely result in establishing even stronger relationships over time.

Strengths

- They are loyal and trustworthy.
- They form long-lasting bonds and friendships.
- They execute processes and procedures reliably and consistently.
- They attend to details and protocols.
- They consider others' feelings and needs.
- They build strong and lasting professional networks.
- They build consensus.

Weaknesses

- They can be challenged by innovation and change.
- They tend to avoid direct confrontation, even when personally involved in conflict.
- They resolve conflict by complying or withdrawing too frequently.
- They will go along a mistaken pathway rather than asserting their viewpoint.
- They forgive slights and oversights, though they do not forget.
- They can be undisciplined in how they use time when with others.

Actions towards Others

The Amiable Style is the most people-oriented of the SOCIAL STYLEs. To them, people count as individuals rather than ways to achieve results or recognition. They prefer cooperating and collaborating with others rather than competing with them. This makes sense, as their need is to be on a secure basis with others. They do not seek power over others as an important personal objective. They achieve objectives with people through understanding and mutual respect rather than through force and authority.

These people get along well with co-workers who adopt an interactive approach that supports their feelings and relationships with others. These individuals typically seek the recommendations and personal support of others, and they readily accept advice from friendly, understanding co-workers who take the initiative to treat them genuinely. They are comfortable sharing information about personal subjects, such as family, hobbies, or personal pursuits, and they enjoy exploring areas of common interest that build a personal connection with others.

In order to avoid confrontations, this SOCIAL STYLE can be too quick to reach agreement. The apprehensions and concerns may later become apparent when the person withholds full cooperation and support, despite their earlier agreement. These individuals appreciate the co-worker who takes the initiative to talk through potentially volatile issues before seeking their concurrence.

The Amiable Style individual tends to get along well with co-workers who also work cooperatively. They want to do things on a joint basis as a means of achieving their personal objectives. However, to avoid possible conflict, this person may understate personal goals. Others may need to clarify the specifics in terms of *why, who, how,* and *what* the Amiable Style individual expects to achieve.

The Amiable Style person values co-workers who realistically state what they can do to achieve mutually agreed-upon objectives. This SOCIAL STYLE individual tends to take it personally and is quickly alienated when co-workers overstate what they can do and do not fully deliver on their promises or fulfill their commitments.

In heated discussions, an Amiable Style person prefers focusing on personal opinions and feelings rather than examining facts and data. If co-workers disagree with this person too openly, expect he will have hurt feelings. If the disagreement is loud, he will likely see it as a personal attack.

Best Use of Time

The Amiable Style individual tends to move at a slower pace and with less time discipline. Because this SOCIAL STYLE tends to avoid direct confrontations, others may feel they can exert themselves and quickly achieve their objectives. Because they tend to act with a slower pace during interactions, faster paced co-workers may quickly move forward, believing they have agreed to a course of action when they have not. In such circumstances, people with an Amiable Style may later resist implementation of objectives, even though it might have appeared as if they had agreed to them.

An Amiable Style individual tends to achieve lasting results when others display a willingness to spend some time, listen, and respond. In such circumstances, this individual is more likely to share both positive feelings (such as hopes) as well as negative feelings (such as apprehensions).

The Amiable Style person wants time allowed for small talk, and values co-workers who genuinely want to hear what they have to say. However, these individuals must make an extra effort to ensure talking and socializing does not become so important that it is difficult to get back to the task at hand.

Customary Approach to Decision-Making

The Amiable Style individual values the input of others with whom they have established a personal relationship. Such others can influence this person's decision-making process, even if they are not formally involved in the decision or the outcome. Remember, these individuals are not risk takers and attempt to reduce risk by ensuring any actions taken will not damage ongoing personal relationships.

An Amiable Style individual often wants others with whom they have a trusted relationship to make specific recommendations for safe choices that minimize risk. This person also wants reassurances from others that they will stand behind their recommendations. In contrast to the Driving Style, the Amiable Style individual really doesn't want options and probabilities. Instead, they seek a clear, specific solution with maximum assurances this is the right decision with no need to look at other options. Typically, the need to feel safe in the decision-making process gets very high priority from an Amiable Style person. If this person does not feel secure in acting on a recommendation, they will tend to involve others in the decision process, which can draw out the time it takes to come to a decision.

Backup Behavior

Acquiescence is the Backup Behavior for an Amiable Style individual who does not wish to engage in a conflict-filled or tension-producing relationship. In this acquiescent mode, the person displays a quiet "don't fight, go along with it" attitude that seeks to minimize conflict.

This Backup Behavior makes sense, since these individuals have such a strong need for personal security and are oriented toward maintaining harmonious relationships. You will recognize this Backup Behavior as the Amiable Style in extreme. Unfortunately, there is no real effort to participate in a relationship. You will see Ask Assertive behavior bordering on the noncommittal about almost everything, plus Responsiveness in the form of giving in rather than withdrawing.

Acquiescing meets a selfish need to reduce anxiety. However, it can make an interaction nonproductive. Acquiescence looks like agreement. In reality, it includes neither agreement nor any form of commitment. It provides nothing solid on which others can rely. While everyone can and does give in from time to time, this behavior typifies the Amiable Style when under too much pressure.

Versatility

Amiable Style people prefer a personable and friendly image. To build rapport with them, especially during initial encounters, it may be helpful if you dress less formally. It might be appreciated if you create occasions that allow for casual attire. These individuals often create an inviting and homey environment, which may include pictures of family and friends or significant events with work teams. When you are in their environment, it will be appreciated if you recognize these personal touches and comment on them. Of course, you should not do this merely because you think it's important. These individuals will recognize your lack of sincerity.

Amiable Style people also want to be involved, though they are less likely to want to talk than Expressive and Driving Style people. Instead, they will look for the presenter to invite them to share their opinions. For example, the presenter can directly ask for their opinions by asking them to share their thoughts. This is a comfortable way to involve these individuals. Ask them their opinions about the topic at hand, and demonstrate active listening. Be alert to any non-verbal signals indicating they are experiencing doubt or insecurity about the information you presented. Because they most likely will not be willing to come right out and disagree with your points, you might have to ask them questions to get the concerns out in the open. These individuals will be particularly mindful of how the presenter relates to other colleagues and whether they treat others considerately and with respect.

With Amiable Style co-workers, emphasize your relationship and how you will work together toward common goals. Instead of emphasizing tasks and your process for accomplishing them, underscore the positive impacts your approach will have on people and the organization. They will think more highly of you when you offer ideas to them rather than working out everything on your own. This allows them to be a part of the process, which is an important need. It is very important to follow up on your commitments, particularly since this builds trust. Failure to follow up on your commitments in a timely manner can cause a great deal of tension in your relationship with these people. Finally, show enthusiasm when working with Amiable Style people. They are very personable and group-oriented, so let them know you're a part of the team and want to work with them.

When communicating with Amiable Style people, listen for their feelings, sensitivity, and awareness. They want you to see their helpfulness and cooperation. Avoid behaviors that could be seen as unfeeling, tough-minded, or unnecessarily competitive. Allow time to build a relationship. Show empathy by giving these individuals sincere and genuine personal attention. Starting discussions with work issues or action items can suggest you don't care about them personally, so be sure to take a moment to touch base with them on a personal level.

When communicating, give them time to take their concerns

and feelings into consideration before they respond. Show that you see the human side of things, and not just the bottom line, especially when making a decision or implementing a change. Avoid coming on too strong and overwhelming them. Make suggestions rather than bold statements. Be open for input and negotiation. Amiable Style individuals are typically uncomfortable with conflict; don't expect them to spontaneously give you constructive criticism or corrective feedback.

Low Versatility

Low Versatility is harder to recognize with Amiable Style people because their behaviors are not as active as some of the other SOCIAL STYLEs. As with other SOCIAL STYLEs, much of their low Versatility behavior contains elements of their backup behavior (Acquiescing) and Growth Action (To Initiate). The phrase "going along to get along" applies to these individuals. The root of this behavior is to fulfill their fundamental need to achieve personal security, which they attempt to gain by maintaining good relationships.

These people have such a strong need to maintain relationships that they will go along with others solely because they want to minimize interpersonal conflict. They will not express their opinions or say what they want or need. For example, when asked their preference for a course of action, they'll say, "Whatever is easiest for you," or, "I'm fine with whatever you want." Paradoxically, this habit of not meeting their own needs actually makes it harder for others to interact with them. Their efforts to make things convenient for others can be an inconvenience for both parties. This can result in frustration for others.

The Amiable Style's acquiescence can be a disservice to others who rely on them to be active contributors and state their opinions.

Like many people who behave with low Versatility, it may not be their intent to cause tension for others. They may think their behavior is acceptable because they don't disagree with anyone. However, not only does this behavior fail to contribute to productivity and effectiveness, it can make others feel the Amiable Style person is not open to them. By constantly focusing on the other person and what they think will make that person happy, these individuals send a message their true selves are closed off. This can make other people feel like they aren't worthy of a meaningful relationship, resulting in others feeling distant from the Amiable Style person.

In a more extreme form of this behavior, an Amiable Style person will actively disagree with a point of view, but will not share their disagreement or opinion, instead choosing to go along with the crowd. However, while on the surface they have agreed to something, they have not actually agreed to a course of action. This is a problem because the lack of agreement will continue to surface in this person's behavior. For example, they may be abrupt toward others and respond with brief critical remarks. Also, they might share their critical opinions with others at work who are part of their inner circle, but will not directly confront the source of the disagreement. This results in the conflict continuing indefinitely without any meaningful resolution. In the long-term, this hurts the Amiable Style person because their grievances are never put forth. It also is unhelpful to others who should hear and respond to the issues.

These individuals are sometimes seen as fickle in their relationships and opinions. This might seem surprising since maintaining relationships is such a strong need for them. But it is just this need that creates the tendency to be erratic with others. For example, an Amiable Style person will support and agree with a person who is being critical of something or someone, but will then turn around and criticize them when talking with someone else. In this sense, these individuals tend to "love the ones they're with." This can result in feelings of betrayal and a loss of trust among their associates.

Amiable Style people who display low Versatility often have problems with change, especially when it impacts their working relationships. They may show resistance, especially if they were not involved in making the decision. This type of inflexibility is a part of the Competence component of Versatility. The consequence is that change might occur in spite of their resistance without allowing them the opportunity to have meaningful input. As a longer-term consequence, it's likely the person will continue to feel resentment about the decision.

These people are rather undisciplined in their use of time. They generally are not in a rush to complete tasks, even when the situation requires them to be. They tend to waste quite a bit of time talking with others instead of focusing on what needs to be accomplished. For example, during a meeting they can quickly get off topic and talk about other matters. It can be difficult for people of other SOCIAL STYLEs to refocus the meeting, especially if there are many Amiable Style people in the group. This can result in people feeling like their time is being wasted.

These individuals have a propensity to act based on their emotions, even if something has already been agreed upon. They will want to change course mid-stream if someone or something appeals to their emotions. For example, if criteria have been set that excludes people from participating in a developmental activity, an Amiable Style person who is in charge of the activity might accept those individuals just because they asked if they could participate. In these situations, their intent is usually to do good, but they often push the boundaries of already established limits. This results in a lack of trust when it comes to maintaining agreements or a lack of confidence in relation to tough decisions.

High Versatility

When behaving with high Versatility, Amiable Style people are very skilled at getting people to work together in a productive way. They create a calm and friendly environment but remain industrious. They are consummate at networking and build relationships with a variety of people. This benefits themselves as well as the people they put into contact with one another. They often know the people to turn to for a variety of circumstances.

Since they are naturally focused on relationships, these individuals are skilled mediators. When conflicts arise, Amiable Style people show high Versatility by working through the issues with both parties, including themselves if they are part of the conflict. They remain optimistic during difficult times, and this optimism helps their co-workers persevere and remain focused. These individuals display their optimism in very forward and obvious ways. They are cheerful with others and verbally express their favorable opinions about topics. For example, during meetings they will show their enthusiasm about projects or about good news. This kind of outward cheerfulness is often contagious and results in a friendly and productive work environment.

An aspect of Versatility that is particularly noticeable among these individuals is their use of Feedback skills. They are very good listeners and are able to communicate meaningfully with a variety of people. Further, they are truly concerned with other people's well-being, and this empathy helps others to trust them. In the long-term, this can result in a high degree of trust in the person and their intentions.

As an example of this, Amiable Style people have a very good memory for important facts about others' lives. They will remember something that might be only briefly mentioned in conversation, but is obviously important for the person who mentions it. At appropriate times, they will recall this information and bring it up with the other person. This displays a true empathy and concern for the other individual.

The use of Feedback skills among Amiable Style people is a slight exception to the rule established previously that Versatility is independent of SOCIAL STYLE. Our research shows there is a small but meaningful relationship between high Feedback skills and Responsiveness. On average, those higher in Responsiveness are also slightly higher in Feedback. Therefore, Expressive Style people also have this natural advantage.

Challenges and Benefits

Their focus on maintaining friendly relationships is often what keeps Amiable Style people from behaving in ways that lead to higher Versatility. They want to get along well with everyone, but they need to realize professional disagreements are acceptable and not taken personally by everyone. They may prefer to maintain the status quo, but sometimes change is necessary, and it is better to have some influence on the matter than go along unwillingly. They want to be helpful to others, but there are times when this is not possible. Taking these actions is difficult because they are contrary to some of the fundamental behaviors common for Amiable Style people.

Acting in ways that lead to high Versatility is beneficial for relationships and overall effectiveness. Relationships can be improved because people will actually have greater trust in the Amiable Style person. When these individuals are forthcoming in their opinions, other people will be clear about where they stand and will have a better understanding of how to approach and interact with them. Likewise, their personal effectiveness will increase for many of the same reasons. By appropriately asserting themselves, they will have greater influence within the team or organization. Inevitably, this can increase not only their effectiveness, but also their own personal satisfaction.

3.4 Analytical Style

The Need for the Analytical Style is "to be right." These individuals are most comfortable when they can establish or rely on processes, principals, facts, and methodologies to minimize the potential for an incorrect or unforeseeable outcome. They like hard facts to support their actions and decisions. The Analytical Style's Orientation is thinking. This is how they meet their need to be right. Instead of acting quickly, they would rather think through the details of a situation before moving forward with a plan.

The Growth Action for these people is to "declare." In other words, they generally hesitate to take a firm stand on issues. This makes sense, since being decisive invites the opportunity to be wrong. It is in direct contradiction to their need to be right and their orientation toward a thoughtful approach.

These people have a natural tendency to take time to evaluate and carefully mull things over. By taking their Growth Action to declare, they make an effort to share information appropriately, to take a stand on an issue, and to share their perceptions more readily. They need to keep others' needs in mind and at least provide some preliminary conclusions. Others will usually accept a tentative or imperfect conclusion and show support and respect for their efforts to provide some direction, even if it means later revisions.

Strengths

- They pay attention to details.
- They plan, track, and focus on a set course.
- They have a rational and logical approach.
- They are persistent toward an outcome.
- They anticipate issues, barriers, and problems.
- They are dependable and thorough.
- They are cooperative and not competitive.
- They are disciplined in how they use time.

Weaknesses

- They can be slow to make decisions and commit to a course of action. They avoid risk.
- They have a low sense of urgency; they would rather be 100% right than 90% right and a week early.
- They can be nonresponsive to others' emotions and needs.
- They are sometimes uncomfortable interacting with others in large groups.
- They can be overly reliant on feedback and direction from supervisors.
- They can resist delegating tasks to others.
- They may yield their position in order to avoid controversy, but as a result will not be fully committed.
- They can seem distant and aloof to others.

Actions towards Others

The Analytical Style individual can appear uncommunicative, distant, formal, cool, and independent. They are cooperative in their actions, as long as they have some freedom to organize their own efforts. This is a natural extension of their Need to be right and their Orientation toward thinking.

They tend to be cautious about extending friendships or personal warmth, and initially will be concerned about how to do things without the need for personal involvements. Paradoxically, people and friendships may be very important to them, even though they may not seem to be at first. Analytical Style people don't want to rush into a relationship until they understand how they can manage the relationship. They have a "show me" attitude. They tend to be suspicious of power and will avoid becoming involved with others who have power or leverage until they see a predictable pattern in the way power is used.

The Analytical Style person appreciates co-workers who support their principles and thoughtful approach. This SOCIAL STYLE also appreciates colleagues who help in gathering facts and data. They want to be sure others understand the problem without being too quick with any solution, and they seek assurances their decisions are "right" and based on accurate data.

The Analytical Style person values co-workers who stick with specifics and deliver what they promise. If a co-worker has not provided detail and supporting information, the individual will likely conclude this co-worker is overselling or overstating what they can or will do.

Best Use of Time

The Analytical Style person has a strong time discipline coupled with a slow pace to action. They move with deliberateness and take the time to review carefully all facts and data available, and thus require others to be patient. This SOCIAL STYLE does not respond well to being rushed by co-workers, even when they have established a relationship. A forceful approach or an insistent attitude typically alienates these individuals. However, once this individual has made a commitment, they will do everything stated, as promised.

The Analytical Style individual appreciates co-workers who take the time to prepare well, and can become irritated when co-workers attempt to substitute thinking on their feet, social skills, or personal charm for doing their homework. The Analytical Style person especially appreciates it when co-workers take time before a meeting to make sure they have their facts straight and data to back up what they are saying. They will want to know if a co-worker is truly knowledgeable or just bluffing. Even though the Analytical Style person is likely to be uncommunicative, cool, and distant, they are also likely to be cooperative. If a co-worker moves too quickly, this individual's slow actions may be mistaken for uncooperativeness. However, the problem may be the co-worker simply hasn't given the person sufficient time to "think about it."

The Analytical Style individual appreciates it when co-workers keep their approach realistic and business-oriented. Co-workers' approaches to interacting with this SOCIAL STYLE will work best when well thought-out, based on common sense, and not too flashy. Because the Analytical Style person demonstrates a strong time discipline coupled with a slow pace to action, they appreciate time to reflect and think things through.

Customary Approach to Decision-Making

The Analytical Style person tends to make decisions based on facts and verifiable information. Co-workers must provide proof that what they say can be backed by relevant facts. This SOCIAL STYLE needs this evidence to be tangible, realistic, and convincing—not someone's opinion. In addition, they require assurance any decision made today will be valid in the future. However, because the Analytical Style person tends to avoid risks, they will frequently continue to display caution and deliberateness.

To influence an Analytical Style individual's decision, co-workers need to indicate the specific things they can and will do to support the decision once it is made. The Analytical Style wants co-workers to be methodical about making their "can do" and "will do" contributions on the schedule they mutually establish. Also, they must stay with it or notify the Analytical Style person when and why they are deviating from the schedule. The Analytical Style person expects co-workers to demonstrate actions that assure no surprises down the road. Co-workers' performance and follow-through do more to build the relationships than anything they can say.

An individual with an Analytical Style is not easily swayed by name-dropping or by making personal appeals. Creative approaches, gimmicks or clever manipulations that others might think will help in getting a fast decision quickly alienate this SOCIAL STYLE. People with this SOCIAL STYLE expect co-workers to live with the fact that it may take some time for them to reach a decision. New information may cause them to withdraw support for one path in favor of another. Their options always remain open. However, once the person has made a decision, they will stick with it, which will help to form the basis for more productive interactions in the future.

Backup Behavior

The Backup Behavior for the Analytical Style is to Avoid. Like all Backup Behavior, it represents their way of seeking to reduce tension within a relationship. In essence, it is a withdrawal from conflict and an attempt to handle the problem by being alone and avoiding people. It is also a form of escapism, since these people do not like to deal directly with conflict. This behavior carries the Analytical Style to an extreme. The individual becomes Ask Assertive and Control Responsive to the point of actually avoiding interaction. They can stop participating in the discussion or even physically leave the interaction. The need for more information and the desire to "think it over" can be examples of this SOCIAL STYLE's Backup Behavior, but not always.

Once again, the motivation for this behavior stems from the need for personal release of interpersonal tension. The basic result is frequently an escape from the relationship and a retreat into self-serving solitude. This behavior is not forward moving or interpersonally productive. Avoidance as a form of backup can happen even before others sense the tension. It frequently occurs before others perceive the interaction has become stressful.

Versatility

Analytical Style people often project a formal, conventional, and punctual image. Depending on their position of authority and the norms of their workplace, they might be somewhat judgmental of nontraditional garb. These individuals seek accuracy and thoroughness, and they typically prefer work environments that support solitary and deliberate pursuits for doing their work. They might be generally accepting of other types of workspaces, as long as organization is displayed.

Analytical Style people will expect a presenter to be organized and give enough details to support their position. They generally won't be eager for the presenter to involve them in the discussion, but if they have strong opinions about a topic they will want the opportunity to speak. Similar to the Amiable Style, the presenter can invite them to share their opinions by asking open-ended questions. Provide logical conclusions and step-by-step action plans at the presentation's conclusion to help them understand what will occur next. Doing so will help them be more willing to participate in future efforts.

With Analytical Style people, initially it is important to show your focus and abilities. Let them know you can be trusted and you have meaningful contributions to offer. Tell them how you plan to approach a task or situation. This meets their propensity for influencing processes as well as their need for information. When you have ideas, present them in a logical way. Explain the benefits of your ideas and how they can be implemented.

Because Analytical Style individuals might be uncomfortable with emotional situations or conflicts, maintain a calm and rational demeanor even when crises arise. You can show your optimism by staying positive and letting them know you'll support them as much as possible. It can take a while to get to know these people on a personal basis. Once you have worked with them for a while and proven your abilities, they will usually become more personable and open.

When communicating with Analytical Style people, listen to their details and plans. They want you to see their logical organization, thoroughness, and thoughtfulness. Slow down, talk less, and put things in writing for them to review. Give them time to study and to think. Show empathy by giving them time to be thorough and thoughtful. Understand they need time to think, to review plans, and to check for accuracy. You'll get the best from them by not demanding tight deadlines or quick decisions. When communicating, allow them to respond thoughtfully. Give them enough time to consider your viewpoints. When you request changes, provide a sound rationale to justify your request. Examine and discuss advantages and disadvantages of options. Because they tend to be uncomfortable with conflict, don't take it personally if they withdraw and withhold Feedback. When they are communicating with you, take the time to listen carefully to them and allow them to make all their points before you respond. Approach their input in a rational way.

Low Versatility

Analytical Style people have a need to be "right." This need is often expressed in how they approach time, processes, and principles. Problems occur when these individuals do not share what is on their minds regarding these things. This leaves other people frustrated and without an understanding of what these people need. As a consequence, the person might not get what they need immediately, and they might not have a voice in longer-term or more substantial matters.

When displaying low Versatility behaviors, Analytical Style people are often very slow in how they approach tasks and associated relationships. They are slow to act, but are also slow in conversation, often drawing out explanations or conversations beyond what other people want or need. Their slow pace is often a mechanism to ensure things are done according to their own definition of what is right. This is ultimately self-serving and over time becomes very frustrating for their co-workers and others. This can result in people becoming impatient with them and in trying to work around them rather than with them.

These individuals will often engage in a variety of behaviors indicative of their Backup Behavior, Avoidance. In extreme circumstances they might actually try to walk away from a situation or physically isolate themselves. More commonly, they will disengage by remaining silent and withdrawing in subtle ways. When behaving this way, they will not meaningfully contribute to conversations and can be noncommittal regarding decisions or outcomes. When trying to communicate with them, they might not give timely responses to emails or calls. This mechanism of "going dark" highlights particularly poor use of Feedback skills and is a passive-aggressive form of avoidance. The short-term consequence of these activities is that others will not be able to respond to them because they have been unclear about their opinions. If they behave this way over a period of time, they risk becoming completely disengaged from others and from important decisions or events they might otherwise have some influence on.

Another expression of low Versatility with Analytical Style people is stubbornness. They will cling to their position without appropriately responding to others' ideas or alternatives. Although people of all SOCIAL STYLEs can be stubborn, Analytical Style people can be especially rigid once they have established a position on something. As a consequence, they can alienate others or make them feel their opinions are unworthy.

These individuals are very cautious. They will hesitate to take action on something, many times losing an opportunity because of their indecisiveness. Another way they express caution is by keeping information to themselves. They will not disclose information unless they absolutely have to or will delay disclosing for too long. This can result not only in lost opportunities, but also it can frustrate other people who are expecting them to provide information in a timely way.

Sarcasm is one of the subtler expressions of low Versatility common with Analytical Style people. The person uses biting humor to send a critical message without being overtly hostile. In a similar way, they can be perceived as judgmental, critical, or moralistic in their attitudes. These are often outward manifestations of what they believe is right. Consequently, they leave people feeling offended and alienated.

High Versatility

When acting in ways that lead to high Versatility, Analytical Style people use their organizational skills to influence processes without being rigid. They listen with an open mind and are willing to change their opinions. They actively contribute and support group decisions. Along with this openness, they display a less critical mindset and are not as picky or judgmental about other people or situations. This results in much easier working relationships as well as better decisions.

These individuals are forthright in expressing their opinions. Instead of holding back, they actively state their ideas and are vocal members of group discussions. When situations call for it, they will make decisions in a timely way. Though they tend to act cautiously, they will resist this urge when it is unnecessary and will act decisively. This helps others achieve their goals without having to wait for the Analytical Style person to take action.

Analytical Style people will sometimes use subtle or dry humor to break tension or bring levity to a situation. In such situations their humor is not mocking, but is more of a way to communicate their less serious side with others. In fact, these people often show a personal part of themselves as a way of opening up. In SOCIAL STYLE terms, they add more Emote Responsiveness behaviors to their repertoire in order to counteract their normally controlled exteriors. This helps others to see a more animated side of them, which is often helpful for developing personal relationships.

Challenges and Benefits

In order to act in ways that lead to high Versatility, Analytical Style people have to temper their need to be right. They want to act cautiously and slowly, but they need to take more risks and be quicker to act. They want to take a methodical approach to problems and tasks, but they sometimes need to be less systematic. They prefer to stay in the background, but they need to be more upfront in stating their opinions. These behaviors are all contrary to comfortable behaviors for Analytical Style people, which is why it can be difficult for them to act in ways that lead to high Versatility.

The benefits of enacting high Versatility behaviors are improved relationships and greater effectiveness. These individuals can improve their relationships by allowing others to experience them on a more personal level. By showing the more human side of themselves, others will feel closer to them and have a greater understanding of their needs. This can lead to the many benefits of trusting relationships, both personal and professional. These individuals can increase their personal effectiveness because using more directive behaviors provides others with information they need and also opens up resources that can help Analytical Style people succeed in their jobs. For example, by providing their input directly and making quicker decisions, work can be accomplished more efficiently. This is particularly true if the person involves other people in the process instead of trying to do things alone.

3.5 SOCIAL STYLE Identification

SOCIAL STYLE identification is based on the observation of behavior.

As described, behavior is the observable acts of a person. Behavior includes posture, gestures, facial expressions, the actions we take, and so forth. A person's inner qualities lie beneath the behavioral surface; thoughts, feelings, attitudes, motives, beliefs, or values cannot be observed. One can never be sure what's taking place in someone else's mind. We can only infer what someone else is thinking or feeling.

When it comes to identifying a person's SOCIAL STYLE, discipline yourself to focus strictly on behavior—what the person says or does (see chapter 1.2). Avoid the tendency to jump from observation of behavior to conclusions about the person's thoughts or feelings.

Let the Other Person Take the Lead

Although a person's SOCIAL STYLE is apparent in most situations, it's likely to be most clearly manifested when they take the lead in the conversation. If you come across too strongly with your own SOCIAL STYLE-based behavior, the other person may respond more to your manner of relating rather than behave in ways characteristic of their SOCIAL STYLE. When trying to identify someone's SOCIAL STYLE, temporarily take a back seat in the conversation.

Pay Attention to Body Language

Since the SOCIAL STYLE Model is a set of behavioral measurements, the best clues for identifying someone's SOCIAL STYLE are nonverbal. Regrettably, there's a strong tendency in our society for people to overlook body language clues. To become proficient at SOCIAL STYLE recognition, train yourself to be more observant of people's gestures, posture, facial expressions, rapidity, and voice volume, among other clues. Try watching your favorite TV show or movie without sound to see if you can determine what their nonverbal behavior reveals about their character's SOCIAL STYLE.

Avoid Trying to Define a SOCIAL STYLE Too Quickly

Since we all tend to jump to conclusions, we should try to observe a person in as many situations as possible. If we force SOCIAL STYLE identification too quickly, we might create a self-fulfilling prophecy. Use a suspended reaction to confirm the validity of observations. Avoid taking sides in an interaction. Hang back and get out of the picture as much as possible. Don't grasp onto one bit of observed behavior and ignore others that don't fit. Rather, let the behaviors add up and be willing to add more later if necessary.

Stay Away from Stereotypes

Not all Italians are Expressive. Not all women are Amiable. Not all CEOs are hard-edged, bottom-line Driving Styles who don't like social activities and interacting with others. The data collected about SOCIAL STYLEs for more than 50 years show that some industries, some professions, and some cultures do have slightly higher representation of certain SOCIAL STYLEs, but no SOCIAL STYLE represents the majority of any profession, job role, or career.

Get Out of the Way

Our personal feelings toward the people we are observing can hinder the accuracy of our objective observations. We should attempt to forget how we feel and react and instead concentrate on how the other person is acting. Give people a "second chance" to display behavior. Learn to observe more accurately and describe their actions without making early "good," "bad," or "why" judgments.

Our natural response to others is an early "like" or "dislike" judgment. More often than not, this is a SOCIAL STYLE reaction and gets in the way of objective observation. The test of accurate observation is to describe a person's actions in such a way that others can readily agree. For example, the observation, "John sat quietly during the meeting and had an expressionless face," can be quickly verified or denied by others who attended the meeting. However, the statement, "John wasn't interested," is an interpretation, not an objective description, and it can lead to serious errors in predicting John's future behavior. Concentrate on observing behavior until you can predict someone else's typical action pattern; don't worry about motivations.

Separate Clues from Assigned Authority or Roles

We often jump to conclusions based upon assigned roles. For example, we might say, "He's a soccer player—a competitor—so he must be assertive." This statement is not necessarily true. Assertiveness is how someone says or does things within a relationship, not how well someone competes in a contact sport. Many soccer players are socially unassertive when off the field.

Set the Stage for the Person Being Observed

If someone is busy reacting to you and your SOCIAL STYLE, you will find it very difficult to observe their SOCIAL STYLE. You must give the other person a chance to show their SOCIAL STYLE by effectively "setting the stage." To do this, approach the individual in an open, nonthreatening way. Demonstrate an interest in the person. After the normal greetings, begin the conversation with nondramatic questions rather than statements. In this way, you will be showing interest in the person and giving the individual a chance to display their habitual SOCIAL STYLE.

At the beginning of the process, the key to the technique is to provide as few clues as possible about how you expect, or want, the person to act. This creates an ambiguous situation and mild stress, which causes people to rely on their own SOCIAL STYLEs. The less other people know (or think they know) about what you expect, the more they will rely on their most comfortable behavioral habits—their SOCIAL STYLEs. The more they use those habits, the clearer their SOCIAL STYLEs will become to you.

Moderate Stress Clarifies SOCIAL STYLE

As already mentioned, we often fall back on those patterns of action that have worked well for us in the past in social situations that cause us moderate tension. It's fairly easy to use different, less comfortable behavior patterns when the situation doesn't put us under stress. But watch a person "snap back" to normal habits when the situation is not so comfortable.

Recognize that Knowing a SOCIAL STYLE is Just a Starting Point

Knowledge of someone's SOCIAL STYLE is the beginning of wisdom about a person. We are constantly amazed at how much SOCIAL STYLE has helped us better understand, relate to, live with, sell to, and work with people. When a person's SOCIAL STYLE is accurately identified, it provides a surprising amount of useful information about constructive ways of relating to them. Nevertheless, it's important to remember SOCIAL STYLE only pertains to certain aspects of a person's life. Each of us is far more than our SOCIAL STYLE. Thus, while the identification of a person's SOCIAL STYLE sheds light on many important characteristics, it is just one useful step of what can be a long and exciting journey of understanding and appreciation of another person. If you have a room full of 1000 Expressive Style people, you would still have 1000 individuals. Always treat people of any SOCIAL STYLE as an individual and not a stereotype.

3.6 Job Function, Industry and Gender

We've already mentioned that SOCIAL STYLE does not predict success at work, while Versatility is a predictor of performance. While all SOCIAL STYLEs can be successful, there is no doubt people will be more engaged in jobs and occupations that suit their natural talents and inclinations. This is why people are attracted to some occupations and not others, and why recruiters are so concerned with interviewing people who will "fit" with the roles for which they're hiring.

Of course, not all engineers are Analytical Style and not all marketing people are Expressive Style. Plenty of people, of all SOCIAL STYLEs, succeed in these roles every day. In fact, we have never found an occupation where more than 50% of people are of a single SOCIAL STYLE, and usually it is much less than this. What is true, though, is people often seek out jobs aligned with their natural SOCIAL STYLE preferences, and this is demonstrated in our research.

It is not unusual for people to have a view that leadership is almost the exclusive domain of Tell Assertive Styles within organizations. However, in regards to industry and job function, research shows this is not true. All SOCIAL STYLEs are represented in leadership positions, and having a Tell Assertive SOCIAL STYLE is no indication of success as a leader. Again, success as a leader has much more to do with one's Versatility than with their SOCIAL STYLE.

In the following sections some of the categories used are

identical or similar for both job function and industry. For example, healthcare occurs in both lists. When applied to job function, healthcare indicates a doctor, nurse, or technician working in any type of business such as hospital, school, or a drug company. When applied to industry, healthcare indicates any person working in a healthcare setting regardless of their job role. Thus, you could have accountants, sales people, etc. who work for hospitals.

SOCIAL STYLE and Versatility by Job Function

In an analysis of more than 53,000 North American profiles, we found that certain SOCIAL STYLEs are heavily represented in job functions where those SOCIAL STYLE characteristics would naturally fit. This research shows that many people are naturally drawn to certain occupations aligned with their SOCIAL STYLE preferences. It is likely that the Style distribution in other parts of the world is similar. The table on the next page (see Fig. 3-5) summarizes the SOCIAL STYLE distribution for the analyzed job functions ranked according to their group's average Versatility.

Not surprisingly, Analytical Style individuals are highly prevalent within engineering (38.3%) and information services/technology (35.7%), while many people with Expressive Style are employed in outside sales (37.7%) and marketing (33.9%). The Amiable Style is predominant in teaching (40.1%) and human resources (31.5%), whereas Driving Style people are heavily represented in construction (31.3%) and as general managers (30.0%).

A more detailed analysis of SOCIAL STYLE and Versatility by Job Function is included in Appendix B.

SOCIAL STYLE and Versatility by Industry

While people typically choose their occupations through natural

Rank	JOB FUNCTION	SOCIAL STYLEs			
		Driving Style	Expressive Style	Amiable Style	Analytical Style
1	Teaching	15.1%	28.5%	40.1%	15.9%
2	Healthcare	18.4%	26.1%	24.8%	30.6%
3	Consultant	23.3%	31.5%	16.9%	28.4%
4	Executive	30.2%	35.9%	10.3%	23.6%
5	Outside Sales	18.4%	37.7%	23.7%	20.2%
6	Human Resources	13.3%	29.5%	31.5%	25.7%
7	Training	12.9%	35.5%	30.4%	21.3%
8	Manager	25.6%	28.7%	16.8%	28.9%
9	Marketing	17.7%	33.9%	24.8%	23.6%
10	Finance & Accounting	19.1%	28.6%	20.2%	32.0%
11	General Manager	30.0%	30.1%	14.0%	26.0%
12	Project Manager	25.4%	26.6%	18.6%	29.3%
13	Protective Services	23.8%	21.2%	15.2%	39.7%
14	Legal	22.4%	22.3%	19.0%	36.3%
15	Customer Service	13.2%	32.9%	27.7%	26.2%
16	IS/IT	26.2%	24.0%	14.1%	35.7%
17	Bank Teller	13.2%	32.6%	31.6%	22.6%
18	Research & Development	21.9%	26.2%	16.4%	35.5%
19	Purchasing	23.7%	26.1%	15.4%	34.8%
20	Administrative/Clerical	10.7%	25.2%	31.3%	32.8%
21	Engineering	28.9%	21.6%	11.2%	38.3%
22	Construction	31.3%	29.0%	12.9%	26.9%
23	Manufacturing & Assembly	29.4%	28.9%	11.7%	29.9%
24	Installation & Repair	26.1%	25.5%	11.1%	37.3%

Fig. 3-5: Versatility Factor Ranking by Job Function

interest, talents, and ambitions, they don't always determine the specific industry in which they work. A Human Resources professional might just as easily work in the energy industry as in a retail organization. Interestingly, though, we find some evidence of SOCIAL STYLE trends even within industries. For instance, the aerospace industry is dominated by Control Responsive individuals—35.6% Analytical Style and 26.1% Driving Style. This industry employs many engineers and technical people, which likely leads to this result. Similarly, the marketing and advertising industry is populated mostly by Emote Responsive people—35.0% Expressive Style and 26.9% Amiable Style. Again, this is likely due to the types of occupations heavily represented within these industries.

While this is interesting, what about the Versatility Factor? Are some industries more versatile than others? We stress it is the individuals within companies that are either highly versatile or not, but some industries do display meaningfully higher Versatility than others. Based on our research we are able to create a ranking of industries according to their Versatility Factor (see Fig 3-6).

The healthcare industry has one of the highest average Versatility scores among all occupations with 62% of people scoring "Y" or above. This is not surprising, considering the high level of teamwork, not to mention customer interaction, common in this field. Many people in this industry are highly attuned to the needs and preferences of others and skillfully put this into practice in their daily work lives.

It's worth noting the healthcare field also has a fairly equal distribution of SOCIAL STYLEs. Healthcare professions run the gamut from emergency room surgeons to administrative specialists in records departments. The wide range of occupations in this industry makes room for people of all SOCIAL STYLEs. Each SOCIAL STYLE brings unique strengths to the healthcare field. Analytical Style people

Rank	INDUSTRY	Driving Style	Expressive Style	Amiable Style	Analytical Style
1	Education	15.4%	28.6%	29.7%	26.3%
2	Healthcare	20.4%	26.7%	22.9%	30.0%
3	Telecommunications	24.9%	34.5%	17.4%	23.2%
4	Media	22.2%	27.1%	24.9%	25.8%
5	Legal	20.4%	29.1%	16.5%	34.0%
6	Accounting	16.1%	29.0%	24.2%	30.7%
7	Consulting	22.0%	29.2%	19.1%	29.7%
8	Government	23.3%	24.9%	16.9%	34.9%
9	Entertainment & Leisure	23.7%	32.9%	17.3%	26.1%
10	Hospitality	26.1%	36.7%	11.9%	25.3%
11	Pharmaceuticals	16.4%	34.6%	23.6%	25.4%
12	Business Services	18.6%	26.9%	22.8%	31.7%
13	Computers & Technology	26.4%	26.1%	17.2%	30.3%
14	Marketing & Advertising	15.0%	35.0%	26.9%	23.1%
15	Transportation	18.8%	29.5%	19.2%	32.5%
16	Nonprofit	19.4%	26.3%	24.7%	29.6%
17	Consumer Products	21.5%	33.3%	20.2%	25.0%
18	Banking & Finance	18.8%	31.0%	22.4%	27.8%
19	Insurance	20.3%	26.2%	20.5%	33.0%
20	Chemicals	20.9%	27.1%	19.6%	32.4%
21	Defense	19.3%	23.1%	17.0%	40.6%
22	Retail	20.7%	32.7%	20.3%	26.3%
23	Automotive	27.4%	35.4%	15.4%	21.8%
24	Construction	21.7%	28.3%	18.7%	31.3%
25	Utilities	28.4%	27.6%	10.1%	33.9%
26	Publishing	20.8%	28.3%	16.7%	34.2%
27	Aerospace	26.1%	25.7%	12.6%	35.6%
28	Manufacturing	25.7%	28.0%	15.7%	30.6%
29	Electronics	23.4%	28.1%	12.3%	36.2%
30	Energy	23.2%	23.9%	16.3%	36.6%
31	Extractive	28.0%	20.9%	13.3%	37.8%
32	Research & Development	19.2%	26.6%	15.8%	38.4%

Fig. 3-6: Versatility Factor Ranking by Industry

are skilled at developing and following procedures, which can literally help save lives in medical care. Amiable Style people are natural caretakers, helping patients feel at ease through their empathy and willingness to help. Expressive Style people can bring a sense of optimism and humor to customers who may otherwise struggle with worry and nervousness. Driving Style people can rally employees and provide quick direction in emergency situations.

Consulting is another industry with above average Versatility, with 60% of people scoring "Y" or above. Employees in this industry are highly attuned to the needs and preferences of others, and they have the ability to effectively work with others in a wide variety of situations. This sector also has a large percentage of Analytical (29.7%) and Expressive (29.2%) individuals. This may sound counterintuitive at first, since Analytical and Expressive people fall on the opposite end of both the Assertiveness and Responsiveness scales.

However, digging deeper into the daily challenges consulting businesses face can provide insight into why this dichotomy holds true. Analytical Style people are driven by a need to be right. Since a consultant's job may be to meticulously analyze a segment of clients' businesses and make sure everything is "right," this is a natural fit for them. Consultant positions allow Analytical Style people to exercise their precise knowledge of a particular subject while being able to work independently for a large portion of their time. Expressive Style people are naturally drawn to positions with a great deal of personal liberty, especially in the area of personal expression. Since experienced professionals who wish to continue in their current roles while achieving career independence often create consultancies, this is a natural fit for experienced Expressive Styles.

What about the other end of the spectrum? What industries have lower than average Versatility? Two industries with this distinction are the energy and electronics sectors, with 66% and 65%, respectively, scoring "X" or lower. While there's no glossing over this undesirable result, opportunities can be extrapolated from this data. For example, energy employees working in the field often need to be more concerned with quick results and safety protocols than with good relationships. Similarly, people in the electronics field might rarely have contact with customers and interpersonal effectiveness is simply not a priority. The data also reveal an opportunity for companies in these industries to differentiate themselves from competitors by increasing employees' Versatility scores and the effectiveness of interactions with colleagues and outside stakeholders.

A complete listing of SOCIAL STYLE and Versatility by industry and its analysis is included in Appendix C.

SOCIAL STYLE and Versatility by Gender

To what extent are there SOCIAL STYLE differences based on gender? Are men or women more emoting or controlling when compared to each other? Who prefers to deal more with facts and data than emotions and feelings?

Many people believe that women are more risk and loss averse than men—implying women make safer and more cautious financial decisions. Some research has supported this, suggesting that the gender differences may be biologically rooted or evolutionarily programmed. However, other research shows when the negative stereotype about women was not hinted at, there were no gender differences in financial decision-making. Moreover, when people are cued with stereotypes (e.g., women are more risk averse or less capable in math), they are more likely to behave in accordance with them. This suggests that earlier findings and anecdotes about differences in decision making between the sexes may actually be the result of gender stereotypes (and not the basis for them).

Researchers have only found slight differences between men's and women's approaches to leadership, conflict management, and decision-making. Where differences do exist, they are small (on average), inconsistent, or inconclusive. What about our normal daily lives? Are there really no differences between men and women in how much we display our emotions? If there is a difference, does it show itself in SOCIAL STYLE patterns?

It turns out the answer is yes to a certain degree; more women are seen as Emote Responsive and more men are seen as Control Responsive (see Fig. 3-7). On average, more women (59%) profile as Amiable Style and Expressive Style, the two SOCIAL STYLEs that display their emotions often and without much hesitation. Likewise, more men (59%) profile as Analytical Style and Driving Style, the two SOCIAL STYLEs that are emotionally controlled and don't frequently show their emotions. While these differences aren't extreme, they are noticeable.

Even more interesting is the gender difference regarding the Versatility Factor. On average, women score higher on the Feedback

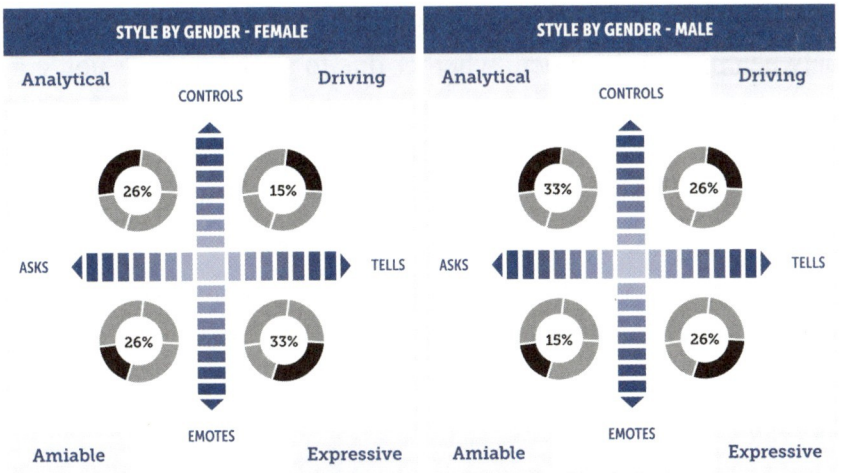

Fig. 3-7: SOCIAL STYLE by Gender

component of Versatility. As this category consists of empathy, interpersonal relationships, and communication, this implies that women are—on average—better at building relationships and showing more empathy than men. Though women score higher, we emphasize that this is not a practically significant difference. As with all group-level research, it applies to large groups but individuals must always be evaluated on their own merits.

The gender differences by SOCIAL STYLE are based on cumulative research through 2014, and there seems to be a shift in behavioral patterns within the last few years. As this evolving trend might just be a temporary effect, we can't say at this point in time what the exact reasoning for this development is. Even if the trend remains, there still will be no simple answer. While people might look to age as a factor, our research shows that it isn't. There are no meaningful differences across age categories of women in how they are evaluated on Responsiveness. However, there are a number of other factors which might be driving the gender differences, like the increasing number of women in leadership positions, which might suggest that the actual distribution is truer than the past numbers. This difference may also result from inherent differences between men and women, whether due to stereotypes or not, e.g. the stereotype that more women are perceived as nurturing and caring than men. This is a perception, not necessarily reality, but this perception may very well influence how women and men are rated on Responsiveness.

Still, keep in mind that all people have emotions. SOCIAL STYLE does not measure how much emotion a person is feeling on the inside; it only measures how much emotion is displayed to others through outward behavior.

4 LEADING WITH THE VERSATILITY FACTOR

Are great leaders born or are they made? Over the years there has been a persistent belief that exceptional leaders are naturally gifted, and that they possess a myriad of abilities beyond the grasp of the rest of us. In fact, many theories around leadership deal with the various competencies, values, and characteristics that affect the success of a leader. To relate all of these to the SOCIAL STYLE Model would require a much longer book, so to illustrate how the Versatility Factor enhances your ability to lead others, we will focus on two of the most widely-used leadership concepts.

The idea that great leaders are born is referred to as the "Great Man" theory of leadership, and it is a myth. In their research on leadership, Jack Zenger and Joe Folkman show leadership not only can be developed, but also essential leadership skills are relatively few in number. Further, virtually no leaders possess all of these skills, nor do they have the same patterns of skills. The researchers found there are different styles of leadership, but they can all be effective.

When Zenger and Folkman set out to write their book on exceptional leadership, they wanted to separate themselves from the crowded field of leadership books by basing their teachings on verifiable empirical research. They realized the most important aspects of leadership can be categorized into five clusters: Character, Personal Capability, Focus on Results, Interpersonal Skills, and Leading Organizational Change. Through their research, one of the key insights the authors discovered is that leaders are made, not born. People can learn and improve their leadership effectiveness through self-development.

Many of the key findings from the Zenger and Folkman research are similar to our insights. We know that people of any SOCIAL STYLE can be great leaders; there is no single best SOCIAL STYLE for leadership. Not only can leadership be developed, but also the best way to develop it is to focus on strengths and to balance these strengths with other abilities. Both models demonstrate that behavior change is the best strategy for changing leadership effectiveness.

The four different SOCIAL STYLEs are naturally suited to specific abilities. While these behaviors might be natural strengths, leaders may lack other critical abilities, and this can prevent them from becoming great leaders. For example, it is not uncommon to encounter Amiable Style leaders who are centered on maintaining good relationships, but who lack a Focus on Results. They have not developed significant skills in this area because they focus on people and relationships, and they simply don't invest time and energy into this skill set.

However, instead of toning down their Interpersonal Skills and being more hard-nosed, Amiable Style leaders should balance this natural skill set by learning and practicing how to focus on results (as well as other abilities as necessary). Once learned, they can demonstrate the skills around results in their Amiable way. By doing this, these leaders will improve their followers' confidence in them by showing they are highly capable leaders who can make things happen, in addition to being personable people who care about their followers as individuals.

Beyond SOCIAL STYLE-specific strategies, the Versatility dimension consists of intelligence competencies that are fundamental for increasing interpersonal skills and managing the fatal flaws that can undermine a leader's effectiveness. By practicing strategies for increasing abilities within the four areas of Versatility (Image, Presentation, Competence, and Feedback), leaders can help ensure they do not fall victim to the career derailers described by Zenger and Folkman.

> Numerous studies on the importance of a network of good interpersonal relationships demonstrate the critical link to a leader's ability to formulate and implement an agenda. The quality of such relationships is a key factor determining managerial effectiveness. Additional studies have shown that the higher the level of Versatility demonstrated by a manager, the higher their compensation and performance ratings.

Working on personal abilities is, of course, fundamental for achieving leadership effectiveness. But there is another very important aspect to the leadership equation: followers. SOCIAL STYLE and Versatility contribute not only to self-awareness and self-management, but also to awareness of followers and how to effectively manage those relationships. The SOCIAL STYLE Model shows leaders how they can enhance the effectiveness of their followers. By understanding their SOCIAL STYLEs, leaders can help them focus on their areas of strength and can develop well-rounded teams of individuals who complement one another.

Representative of the large number of popular leadership development frameworks, the Situational Leadership II® (SLII) model by the Ken Blanchard Companies helps leaders adjust their management style to suit any work behavior. This model describes four unique leadership styles, or strategies, that can be used when interacting with followers depending on the person's development level (readiness and ability) for a specific task or situation. These four leadership strategies (S1 to S4) differ in terms of the amount of direction and support provided by the leader. In order to determine which strategy a leader should implement in any given situation, the model describes a three-step process to be followed for each follower and for each situation.

The true value of SLII is the fact that it recognizes the importance of the situation to leadership, and it provides a mechanism for leaders to adjust their behavior based on situational differences. However, just as different situations affect both leaders and followers, so do their unique SOCIAL STYLEs. Therefore, it is vitally important for leaders to understand their own and their followers' SOCIAL STYLEs, and to act with high Versatility. Without this awareness and accompanying adjustment to behavior, there is a risk the SLII method will be used inaccurately and/or inappropriately, undermining its effectiveness.

In addition, Versatility provides insight and mechanisms for more successfully interacting with others. Thus, the SOCIAL STYLE and SLII models complement each other quite well. When leaders use the SOCIAL STYLE Model as an overarching framework, their efforts to employ situational leadership strategies will have a higher chance of success.

Following this chapter, we will elaborate on how the SOCIAL STYLE and Versatility concepts can be used to develop appropriate interaction strategies with your direct reports that allow your people to meet their Style Needs as you mutually achieve your goals.

4.1 Managerial Preferences

In chapter 3.1-3.4 we introduced you to the major characteristics of each SOCIAL STYLE. In this section we will describe in more detail how team leaders of each SOCIAL STYLE behave at work. In particular, you will understand how each SOCIAL STYLE typically acts towards subordinates, and how each SOCIAL STYLE uses time and approaches decision-making in their daily business life.

By recognizing these behaviors, you can better understand how team leaders prefer to act and interact with their subordinates to get things done at work. At the same time, this knowledge will help you predict your team leader's behavior most of the time.

Driving Style

The people on a team see a Driving Style leader as direct and assertive. This person's need for results and orientation for taking action can help the team focus its efforts on goals and objectives. This person has the ability to summarize information from the team into its most meaningful elements, which helps the team remain oriented toward the things that matter most.

The Driving Style leader's behavioral preferences can have more negative consequences. This person might come across as indifferent and pushy. In team meetings, others might see this person as domineering and unwilling to listen to their ideas. Even worse, they may feel steamrolled. Some people will view Driving Style leaders as speaking too quickly or forcefully, which makes them feel like they cannot join in the discussion. If their focus is solely on results without considering issues that are important to other team members, they may actually slow the team down and delay getting the results they want. Similarly, if they push for a solution or decision too quickly without getting input from others on the team, a Driving Style leader might not get the buy-in the team needs to succeed.

As a leader with a Driving Style, one of the best ways for you to build close bonds with your teams and others is simply to remember to take the time to do it. Although it may be difficult to slow down and focus on people instead of tasks, this is a very important part of organizational life and will ultimately increase your effectiveness with others. Make an effort to understand the people who work for you. When attempting to motivate others, show patience and restraint. Most people will not be as quick to act as you, so approach the art of influence by using a longer-term perspective. Be particularly careful to avoid needlessly confronting or challenging your team members. Help develop your subordinates by approaching them in an open way free from competition. Helping them develop their skills will require they see it as a mutual opportunity rather than a challenge. Also, employ your Growth Action of listening since this is a necessary skill for understanding and mentoring others. And remember, listening is more than just hearing the words; you need to listen to the emotions and feelings of others.

As a Driving Style team leader, you will need to be more patient with other team members. Give them opportunities to talk during meetings, and listen carefully to what they are saying. Some team members with different SOCIAL STYLEs might need to be prompted to express themselves, so it is usually a good idea to ask questions. Show interest in their points of view, and incorporate their perspectives and talents into team solutions. By their nature, team meetings require time to allow for all participants to give their input and come to agreements. If you are scheduling meetings, be sure to allow enough time for this even if you feel time is being wasted.

Expressive Style

The people on a team see Expressive Style leaders as personable and willing to make their inner feelings known to others. They openly show positive and negative feelings rather than controlling or concealing their emotions. Their orientation toward spontaneity can help the team not only have fun, but also solve problems and achieve greater creativity and innovation.

An Expressive Style leader seeks personal approval through a variety of behaviors, some of which can come across as overwhelming for others. Their team members may view them as too talkative and opinionated. They usually don't hesitate to show their enthusiasm and appreciation of others, but during team meetings they might come across as aggressive or overly dramatic. Though an Expressive Style leader may not intend to offend other team members, the team might sometimes feel personally attacked by them. Because Expressive Style people are talkative, some people on the team might find it difficult to join in the discussion. In extreme circumstances in which Expressive Style leaders are dominating a conversation, some people may simply "surrender" and not attempt to state their opinions. Paradoxically, their attempts to gain what they want may backfire and those on the team will not support their opinions and advice.

As an Expressive Style leader, you are likely to build relationships with others and form solid networks, which is a natural advantage for motivating people. Increase your leadership abilities—continue to be open, and make an effort to act on objective information in addition to your intuition. People look to you for inspiration and well-reasoned judgment. While naturally influential, you can increase your abilities by toning down your more aggressive habits. You will have plenty of opportunity to move things along, but will allow your team members to express themselves and take the time they need to act. You can also use your personable nature to develop your subordinates. Pay careful attention to your own feelings about mentoring them to ensure you are not tacitly competing with the people you have committed to help.

To improve as an Expressive Style team leader, you will need to make sure you don't overwhelm your team members. This can happen if you are too talkative or opinionated. Give others the time to speak and opportunities to share their points of view. Recognize that others have a greater need for data and processes, and will move toward decisions at a slower pace. Be open to others and understand they might have information about specific topics you might not necessarily have. During team meetings, you might want to lower your tone of voice since your volume and your intensity can overwhelm some people. Be sure to follow through on your commitments to the team and pay attention to timeframes.

Amiable Style

The people on a team see an Amiable Style leader as someone who openly displays feelings and concern for others. This person seems interested in achieving rapport with the team, and is viewed as informal and easy-going. An Amiable Style team leader tends to be sensitive to keeping relationships on a friendly, personal basis.

Because they have a strong preference for feeling personally secure in their relationships, the behaviors an Amiable Style team leader uses to fulfill this need can have detrimental consequences on teams. While Amiable Style people are normally comfortable displaying their feelings, in team meetings they might be hesitant to fully voice their opinions or state a firm point of view. In such situations, others may be uncertain of the direction of the team. This can result in confusion about priorities and the specific work required to meet goals. While listening to and incorporating the views of others is something leaders should do, the Amiable Style leader should also voice their opinions and make firm decisions when necessary.

Most Amiable Style people are easy to interact with, and you will naturally get along with your team. To be most effective, be direct with your input and ideas. Move more quickly when it is appropriate, and don't be afraid to speak your mind or initiate differences of opinion. The team will appreciate your direction and will also have a clear understanding of where you stand. Remember that disagreements are usually expected within work teams, and people can distinguish between work issues and personal disagreements.

Being an Amiable Style team leader, building bonds, and enhancing team camaraderie are strengths for you. You should leverage these abilities to increase your effectiveness, while maintaining an appropriate emphasis on tasks and professionalism. You have natural interpersonal abilities that can be seen as effective leadership qualities. Build on these strengths by taking a stand on issues, even though on occasion this might have a detrimental impact on others. Being decisive and proactive is just as important for effective leadership as good interpersonal skills. Inevitably, followers will perceive this as a good quality. When coaching or mentoring others, rely on your natural abilities to interact with them and understand their motivations. The best way to improve in this area is to share your true opinions and advice, even if this may pose risk to a harmonious relationship. Most people appreciate honest feedback even if it is difficult to hear, and in the long-term they will respect you for providing the information. Research shows negative feedback given in a positive manner is more effective than positive feedback delivered poorly.

Analytical Style

The people on a team see an Analytical Style leader as logical, reserved, and cautious. Their thoughtful approach can help the team stay organized and on top of important information that may impact team outcomes. Their orientation toward thinking helps both the team leader and the team to be efficient.

The behavior of an Analytical Style team leader can also have negative consequences. Outside of team meetings, they may be uncommunicative with their team, even when team members need their input. When making team decisions, this team leader may come across as obstinate and inflexible, depending on the importance they place on an issue or the approach to it. They may see the Analytical Style leader as needlessly clinging to a position, without taking into account other viewpoints. Alternatively, in some situations they may see them as withdrawn. The Analytical Style leader may simply refuse to take part in an argument or discussion, which others can see as unproductive and even arrogant.

As a leader with an Analytical Style, it may be difficult for you to quickly and easily form bonds with your staff. It will help if you move out of your comfort zone and share more personal aspects of yourself with others. A good sense of humor can be an effective tool for showing a less serious side but be cautious with your sarcasm. To improve your leadership skills, try to be more outgoing and available to your followers. People need to hear their leaders speak and share their views, goals, and insights. Analytical Style people can be reticent to communicate, so it is important that you take this as a growth opportunity.

When coaching or mentoring your team members, rely on your objective and rational methods as strengths. Build on them by getting to know the people you are developing on a more personal basis, since it is important to understand your team's personalities and interests in order to help them succeed.

You can enhance your effectiveness as a team leader by more directly providing your opinions and input. Determine what your point of view is, and make it known. Try to make your main points efficiently, since your team might not need very much detail or information about the history of an issue. When decisions need to be made by the team, agree to take a course of action even though you might feel you don't have all the necessary information to move forward. When difficult situations come up, do not avoid them. Instead, face these situations with an awareness that this approach will ultimately lead to better outcomes.

4.2 Delegating Tasks

Each SOCIAL STYLE has its own tendencies and strengths when approaching work. By recognizing these strengths, you can guide the efforts of direct reports to enable them to become more effective and productive.

First, a few words of caution related to assigning work to your team without consideration of their Styles. In general, task assignments and the associated goals should be clear and well defined. Goals that are vague lead to confusion and are difficult to measure. Deliverables should be defined in terms of quality and timeline, being specific enough that their achievement can be measured. Also, goals should be reasonable and realistically achievable, yet challenging. Setting unattainable goals is a sure way to fail no matter what SOCIAL STYLE a subordinate has.

As appropriate to the situation, consider the following guidelines when delegating work to your direct reports.

Driving Style

Driving Style people are often in a hurry and do not always listen well. When delegating, be clear and to the point. Verify they understand how they are to be accountable for the assignment.

- Assign tasks that have clear objectives and explain how the assignment will contribute to bottom-line results. Describe exactly what needs to be accomplished by discussing how the deliverables will be measured, but do not describe how to approach the task. Focus on outcomes and, where appropriate, allow the person to have control and make decisions about details. Clearly indicate they are accountable and in charge of this task.

- When setting goals with a Driving Style person, make sure you are direct, use the time efficiently, and come prepared with relevant facts and alternatives. Also, look for opportunities to let the person make decisions. Keep in mind they are logical and achievement-motivated. Therefore, stay away from long-term goals that don't have shorter-term results built-in; the person may lose interest and focus.

- Point out the competitive aspects of the goal (e.g., advantages over competitors or career implications). If possible, avoid forcing the person to depend on people they may not have control over, since this may frustrate them and slow them down. If they must depend on others to accomplish this task, be sure they understand that how they interact with those individuals will be an important consideration when evaluating the success of the outcome.

- When giving difficult assignments, be direct and support the necessity of the assignment with enough facts to make your point. Let these people know you have confidence in their abilities. Try to frame the assignment in terms of needed results, and provide options for achieving goals. Don't be afraid to challenge a Driving Style subordinate.

- Within a reasonable timeframe, be direct in asking for a commitment to accomplish the task. In general, don't expect these individuals to provide detailed or frequent progress reports. Periodically check in with them rather than "check on" them. Remember, these individuals like to use time efficiently and work at a faster pace. To keep them motivated, let them stay focused on impending deadlines.

Expressive Style

Expressive Style people are spontaneous, active, and don't always check their work carefully. Show enthusiasm when delegating to them, point out how the assignment can benefit them, and help them stay focused afterwards.

- Find ways the assignment can personally benefit the Expressive Style person. Highlight the exciting or creative possibilities of the assignment. Allow them to speculate on what might be possible, but be prepared to help them be realistic. These individuals like to focus on the big picture, so setting goals is usually not difficult.

- When setting goals with someone with the Expressive Style, keep in mind they are spontaneous and seek recognition. Therefore, develop goals that allow the person to receive acknowledgment. If possible, design the goal so the process of achieving objectives is exciting and enjoyable. If the assignment is limited in this area, tell them their completion of the work will be appreciated and recognized by yourself or others.

- Develop goals that take into account the person's ideas and opinions. It may be necessary to initially focus on the big picture rather than specifics, so prepare to follow up with the person to discuss details. Make sure the person understands how the goal is related to a broader strategy or meaningful outcomes. Even if you know exactly what these people need to do to achieve the goal, they like to be asked for input and given the opportunity to display their creativity.

- Expressive Style people will be most open to a challenging assignment if you show them how it will help them achieve their personal goals. They will want adequate motivation (including job titles, rewards, or bonus payments) to move in the direction you suggest. When setting such goals with an Expressive Style person, plan to present the goal as a stimulating or exciting opportunity. Beware of overwhelming them with too much information right at the start. Start with the big picture and then add details as needed.

- In order to keep an Expressive Style subordinate motivated, provide recognition through such things as offering praise for their input, ideas, and vision for the future. Allow for their continued spontaneity, but be sure to provide regular follow-up to keep them focused on the tasks necessary to move toward the goal. This is particularly important for those tasks that are less challenging and exciting to them. Remember, these individuals prefer you to be future-oriented. Be careful not to ignore their enthusiasm or to be impatient with their creativity. Make sure having fun is part of the goal.

Amiable Style

Amiable Style people are friendly and enjoy working with others, but can be slower to accomplish objectives. When delegating, point out how the assignment can benefit the team or others, and look for ways to include collaboration as part of the assignment.

- When setting goals with Amiable Style subordinates, keep in mind they are friendly and like to collaborate. Consider the possible viewpoints of the person and how the goal setting might impact other people.

- This person is likely to become disengaged during the conversation if he or she feels you are unilaterally setting goals. Make sure the discussion is collaborative. Let the person know you have their interests in mind in addition to the organization's needs and the needs of other team members. As long as the person trusts you, he or she is likely to be cooperative and enthusiastic about setting a goal.

- Be clear about objectives, but allow for some flexibility in how the person achieves the goal. The Amiable Style person may have less time discipline, so be very clear about specific timeframes or deadlines. Give the person written follow-up that describes the goal and provide the person with support during the process of working toward the goal.

- If a disagreeable assignment has to be given to an Amiable Style subordinate, clearly explain the reasons why the assignment is being made. Point out how the assignment will provide opportunities for them to contribute to the team. Do not press too hard for immediate results or come across as impersonal. Verify the person is ready to proceed before forcing a decision.

• Give the person your personal assurance the tasks and corresponding objectives are positive and may even enhance working relationships with others. Give the person sincere compliments about progress on the goal and its importance to the team or organization, but do not expect the person to provide regular progress reports.

• Because these individuals tend to show a less disciplined use of time and move at a slower pace than those with a Driving or Expressive Style, be sure to make regular, friendly checks on their progress. Show awareness of their needs and allow them to be flexible. If they seem to be on the right track, give them verbal assurance they are doing well. You will be more likely to help them achieve goals if you praise their contributions. Amiable Style individuals respond negatively to being pressed for details, written analysis, or homework. Be certain not to come across as autocratic or too demanding when checking on progress.

Analytical Style

Analytical Style people are cooperative and methodical and do not like to be rushed. When delegating assignments give them all the information they will need to succeed and let them organize their own efforts.

• Analytical Style people like to be accurate, so it is important to provide them with evidence and the reasoning behind your assignment. Be clear about the goals, and provide any relevant background information, related details, and supporting information to help the person organize their efforts. Avoid pressing them for an immediate response or action plan. Instead, let them work out the details on their own and present them to you; do not encourage shortcuts.

• Ask questions to ensure the person clearly understands the scope of their responsibilities; let the person voice any concerns. Be very specific about numbers or other quantitative ways the goal will be measured and collaborate with the person to determine how to measure. Once a goal and plan are agreed upon, put them in writing for reference and to aid with progress checks.

• Be very clear about timelines, deadlines, and how the goal might affect other priorities and commitments. Schedule regular checkups, but allow the person to work through the details of achieving the goal without unnecessary interruptions.

• As with Amiable Style individuals, allow for the Analytical Style to move at a slower pace but be reassured by their more disciplined used of time. Start-up is usually the slowest time for these people, since they need to think things through and mentally work through the details before taking action. Avoid pressing for immediate decisions to do something differently. When following up, avoid making emotional or personal appeals, since these individuals are driven more by logic than emotions.

The following chart (see Fig. 4-1) summarizes the recommendations of how to delegate tasks by SOCIAL STYLE.

Analytical Style

- Assign this person tasks where he or she can work with details and use logic and analytical skills
- Explain what needs to be done and why it is necessary or important
- Be business-like
- Provide facts and data necessary for moving the project along with any related backup data
- Give this person enough time to sort through the facts and data
- Be organized and logical in your presentation of assigned tasks

Driving Style

- Give this person tasks that have clear objectives to achieve; start by focusing on the outcomes you are expecting.
- Be business-like and get to the point in explaining what needs to be done
- If there are choices to be made in performing the assigned tasks, let this person participate in making the decision
- Provide the facts and data necessary to get results
- Where appropriate, allow this person to take charge and make decisions related to accomplishing their goal

Fig. 4-1: Delegating Tasks by SOCIAL STYLE

Amiable Style

- Assign this person tasks that will give him or her plenty of opportunities to interact with others
- Make clear what this person's authority and responsibility are in carrying out the tasks
- Allow this person to identify what resources are available to get the job done
- Provide clear instructions on what is required, in writing where possible
- Work cooperatively with this person to establish regular interim check points for him or her to keep track of details and to stay on target to achieve desired outcomes
- Reinforce how accomplishing the assigned tasks will be appreciated by co-workers or how these accomplishments will be important for the goals of the organization

Expressive Style

- Assign this person tasks that he or she will find personally rewarding with the ability to see the big picture
- Start by painting a general picture of what needs to be accomplished
- Explain what makes the tasks you are assigning to them unique or interesting
- Mention how this person might personally benefit by successfully accomplishing the tasks
- Mention any risks or special challenges associated with the assigned tasks
- Invite this person to be creative (within limits, of course) in accomplishing assigned tasks
- Set agreed-upon time-frames and decision points

Fig. 4-1: Delegating Tasks by SOCIAL STYLE (Cont.)

4.3 Changing Directions

Changes in organizational or department strategy are not only inevitable, but also commonplace. Change can be challenging, especially for the leader who has to communicate the necessity of the change and guide its implementation. At the beginning of change efforts, people are often resistant. There is comfort and stability in resistance. Eventually, with appropriate support and influence from the leader, people will become resilient and begin to focus on supporting the change effort. People tend to respond to change in predictable patterns, even when the change is seen as good. However, people of different SOCIAL STYLEs display their behavior in unique ways.

In the following pages we will discuss techniques to support subordinates of each SOCIAL STYLE to adapt to changing directions in an effective and sustainable way.

Driving Style

Driving Style people prefer to handle events as they occur, rather than delaying action or thinking about things for too long. When confronted with change they might react quickly, sometimes too quickly. While others will take time to process the implications of the changes and wait for further direction, these individuals will respond quickly with some form of active behavior.

They may try to assert some form of control or influence over events. Depending on their position of authority, they might try to influence matters within their personal span of control, or they may even try to influence the overall change process or direction. These individuals will view the new direction as either a manageable challenge or an obstacle. Either way, they will respond with some form of active behavior.

It is common for Driving Style subordinates to resist change if they perceive it as an unnecessary impediment to progress or as a threat to their autonomy. No matter what their reasons, they will respond in a similar way to positive change—with action. They will usually be direct with the leader about their beliefs. However, simply expressing their opinions may not be enough; these individuals often feel a strong need to take action in order to maintain control over events. They may even actively oppose and attempt to thwart the course of the change effort, involving individuals outside of the department if they feel it is necessary.

To ease their concerns, show them the benefits the change will have for them, their projects, and their goals. Point out any increases in efficiency, cost savings, or any other area of importance for them. If feasible, involve them in making decisions that influence the change effort. This will help them maintain some form of control over events and will lead them to support the effort. Whenever possible, find ways to keep them involved in the change activities.

Expressive Style

Expressive Style people will respond to change with activity. However, unlike Driving Style people, there will be a strong emotional component to their reactions, which can range from intense excitement to outright hostility. They will verbalize their feelings immediately after it is announced without taking time to reflect on the change or its long-term implications. If they do not express themselves directly to the team as a whole, they will make their feelings known to the leader or other department members.

If they support the change, Expressive Style subordinates will want to be actively involved in the effort. They may view it as an exciting occasion and might look for opportunities for self-promotion or role enlargement. They will show outward enthusiasm and seek out an active role in helping move the change forward.

Expressive Style people will often resist change if they feel personally threatened or in some way disrespected by the change. They are more likely to feel this way if they believe they were not involved in making decisions or their input was not sought. In such situations they are likely to be very forthright with their dissatisfaction. They may act impulsively, venting their feelings before thinking through the situation in a rational way. If they feel a specific person or group is responsible, they might express their dissatisfaction with these people in a highly emotional way.

Time is a necessary ingredient for helping Expressive Style people become more accepting of change. If they need to vent, allow them to do this but do not allow them to dominate or influence the rest of the department. Bring them to a less emotional state by presenting the rationale for change, and highlight any ways that they might benefit from the new situation. When feasible, involve them early on in making decisions about the change, or at least informing them that change is going to occur and sharing as much insight as you can. Once the change has been announced, keep them actively involved in relevant aspects of the change process. Being involved will help meet their need for approval and will also help them to accept the changes.

Amiable Style

Amiable Style people will often be quiet in their reactions to change, at least in the short-term. Their initial inclination will be to support the department in its change efforts, though they may struggle internally with the implications of the change. This is because change can be challenging for them and they will look for some signals that the change is not too threatening.

Though they may imply their support for the change, these individuals are not always outwardly active in their support. They will go along with the change efforts and will appear to support the requirements of the department, but they may be reluctant to take on active roles as do some other SOCIAL STYLEs. However, if they fully support the change they may become highly involved in helping see it through to completion. Change can provide opportunities for these individuals to develop new or better working relationships with others.

Amiable Style people resist change if they perceive it as too threatening to the status quo. These individuals often develop comfort with the people they work with and the processes in place, so anything that affects these things can be disorienting for them. This is not to say they are incapable of change; however, they need time to develop a level of comfort with the implications.

In situations where they are opposed to change, these individuals may display their resistance in passive ways. They might be quietly hostile toward those they feel are responsible, and they may reduce their performance. In some circumstances they might play the role of victim, indicating they feel they have no control over their situation.

To help these individuals be more accepting of change, clearly explain the reasons for the change. If possible, try not to press too hard for immediate changes in their work or circumstances. Instead, institute change gradually and involve them in the process. Point out any opportunities in the new situation for them to contribute.

Analytical Style

Similar to the Amiable Style, Analytical Style people are often quiet and cautious in their reactions to change, at least initially. Particularly when a change is significant and comes as a surprise, they will want some time to consider the implications before offering their full support. They will consider not only the impacts change will have on them personally, but also whether the change represents a logical or strategic step that will benefit the department and organization.

These individuals are cautious to take action. Therefore, when an organization or team suddenly changes direction, they may be slower to embrace the change than others. If they are feeling supportive of the change, they might look for opportunities to have an influence on the details of the change. For example, they may want to be involved in designing new products, strategies, or processes.

Analytical Style subordinates are most likely to resist change if they believe it is the "wrong" thing to do. Usually, this means they do not agree with the strategy or rationale of the decision; they believe a different decision would result in better outcomes. Similar to Amiable Style individuals, they may show resistance in less obvious ways than others. They may procrastinate with their work or commitments, or they may try to withhold important information. In a more active way, they might make demands on the department, such as insisting changes be implemented in a specific way they think is right.

To help these individuals move into a more productive state, show them the rationale and reasoning leading into the decision to make a change. They often prefer to be alone with information before acting, so give them time to process the implications. If possible, provide them with opportunities to influence the way in which change is implemented, or to contribute within their area of expertise.

The following chart (see Fig. 4-2) summarizes recommendations when changing directions by SOCIAL STYLE.

Analytical Style	Driving Style
• Take your time to be accurate by being well prepared and organized • Present relevant information (facts, time frames, and data) • Don't rely on testimonials or opinions to make your strongest points • Present both the pros and cons of your idea to help establish (or maintain) credibility • Approach the situation as though accepting your idea/action was the next logical step in the process • If the Analytical Style person seems hesitant or reluctant, ask, "Do you have enough information?"	• Be direct; use your time to be efficient and keep your case short and to the point • Focus on what will be accomplished by going along with your idea/action • Provide facts and logic as support, but keep your main points simple. Have the details ready, but don't present them unless requested • Look for opportunities to give the Driving Style person choices in how to support you • To gain commitment, give choices by asking questions like, "Which one do you think is best?" • Don't beat around the bush and don't be afraid to ask for a decision

Fig. 4-2: Changing Directions by SOCIAL STYLE

Amiable Style	Expressive Style
• Use a less direct approach, one that does not take on the appearance of confrontation	• Use your time to be stimulating by presenting the "big picture" of your idea (avoid excessive detail)
• Take time to be agreeable by presenting your ideas in a less formal, more personal way	• Refer to respected others who agree with your idea
• Focus on providing assurances that a decision to go along with your ideas/actions is relatively safe	• Be inspiring, but don't try to outshine this subordinate
• Ask if your idea is acceptable to others who are important to your subordinate	• Explain how your ideas/action might personally benefit this person in the future
• If the Amiable Style subordinate seems hesitant, ask, "What other things should we talk about?"	• Press for a decision, but let the Expressive Style subordinate make it
• When an Amiable Style person reaches a decision, "double confirm" to ensure that he or she is not just saying "Yes," (acquiescing) to appease you	• When you get a commitment, follow up with an e-mail or other reminder of the details
	• Do what you said you would do in a timely manner

Fig. 4-2: Changing Directions by SOCIAL STYLE (Cont.)

4.4 Managing Conflicts

Many people try to avoid conflict, but disagreement and debate can be a very positive and effective way for solving problems and coming to agreement. The key is to avoid the type of interpersonal conflict that results in personal attacks and damaged relationships. Instead, effective conflict occurs when people debate about ideas while maintaining or strengthening their interpersonal relationships.

- When conflicts occur, as a Driving Style leader you might try to assert active control over the issue. You might attempt to resolve the conflict by siding with one party over the other, basing your decision on how effective one side is at making their argument. You may also show impatience with the conflicting parties, believing the conflict is getting in the way of progress. In this case you might try to suppress the conflict or force the involved individuals to settle the matter by themselves and on their own time.

  To productively manage conflict, use your Driving Style Growth Action of listening. Before trying to control the argument or make a quick decision about who is right or wrong, give each party a chance to make their points. Be patient with the individuals involved. If you are personally involved in the issue, be careful not to dominate the discussion or force your opinions onto others. Although you might believe you have won the argument, this will leave others alienated and it is unlikely they will truly support your position.

- As an Expressive Style leader you can become animated during difficult discussions, and while this is an aspect of your SOCIAL STYLE, your expressiveness can make others feel tense. When conflict occurs, even if you are not directly involved, you may try to assert your influence over the parties. You generally do not withhold your opinions, so you are likely to tell the conflicting parties exactly what you believe at that moment in time. This can leave people feeling offended and the conflict unresolved.

When managing conflict, first control your natural impulse to immediately involve yourself by sharing your opinions. Take the time to listen to the individuals involved in the conflict. Do not rush to make a judgment or come to a conclusion quickly unless this is absolutely necessary. If you do this, you may alienate at least one of the conflicting parties, and in turn they are not likely to support the outcome of the conflict.

- Conflict can be uncomfortable for many people, and this is likely true for you as an Amiable Style leader. When discussions become heated, you might attempt to stop the involved parties before things get out of hand and relationships are damaged. Alternatively, you might do your best to please all parties by insisting on compromises. While this can seem like an agreeable approach, it is not always the best strategy. By doing this, you might suppress discussion that needs to take place in order to solve problems or determine strategies.

When called upon to manage conflict, make an effort to allow the sides to make their cases without trying to placate either side. Manage the conversation to prevent matters from becoming personal, but let the individuals openly state their full opinions. While it can seem tense, it is better to let people express their opinions than force them to compromise or not express themselves.

- Conflict can be uncomfortable for people, especially for an Analytical Style leader. When individuals become engaged in heated discussions you might try to avoid the situation by redirecting the individuals to a different topic or by postponing the discussion. While this can diminish the conflict in the moment, it risks leaving the situation unresolved and the involved parties unfulfilled and stifled. With this strategy it is likely the conflict will still simmer and come up again, perhaps with even more force and potential for damaged relationships.

When managing conflict, allow the individuals to have their say without trying to keep things comfortable. Though it may feel tense for an Analytical Style person, when debate is healthy and not personal it leads to more informed decisions and greater support for the group's direction. Clearly state your own opinions without holding back; this will add to the effectiveness of the discussion.

In the following pages we will provide some techniques on how to engage in productive conflict management with people of each SOCIAL STYLE.

Driving Style

When conflict arises, expect Driving Style people to be very direct in their behavior. Their Backup Behavior is to become autocratic and take control of situations, so be particularly aware of this type of behavior.

- These individuals enjoy debate, so be direct about surfacing issues that need to be discussed. They will usually be forthright and interact directly with the people with whom they are in conflict. They might become verbally confrontational.

• They may try to take control of the situation in whatever way they can and try to assert formal authority over others. At least until they have made their points, they are likely to dominate the conversation. Therefore, allow them to make their points and encourage them to listen to others. This can be done by redirecting the conversation to involve others and by using active listening skills like clarifying, paraphrasing, and confirming.

• They appear argumentative when making their points, but unless they are obviously frustrated or insistent, this is simply their SOCIAL STYLE. Frame different points of view as options. Instead of competing viewpoints, discuss them as alternatives for solving the issue that can be evaluated in a rational way.

• If feeling a high level of stress, they may raise their voices and will be more animated than usual. This is an indicator they feel high tension. Take time to refocus them on shared goals and results that are important to them.

Expressive Style

When conflict arises, expect Expressive Style people to be animated and to freely share their opinions. As their Backup Behavior is to attack, be vigilant about recognizing this type of behavior.

- These individuals may respond defensively when others disagree with them. This is because they can have difficulty separating disagreements about their ideas from rejection of them as individuals.

- They will be very direct when in conflict and will say things without pausing to consider the implications, not to mention other people's viewpoints. They also may interrupt others before these individuals have had a chance to state their opinions, and they might dominate discussion until they are satisfied they've fully communicated their opinions.

- Keep Expressive Style individuals engaged in the debate but do not allow them to become aggressive toward others. Help them separate their emotions about a topic from the objective facts and viewpoints of others. Summarize or restate their opinions in a calm and straightforward way. As much as possible, include these individuals in the conversation and seek their input for finding solutions. This will appeal to their need for recognition and involvement.

- When feeling stressed they might display hostility toward others, confronting them personally rather than focusing on the topic of the debate. Even though debates can become heated, try to diffuse tension through humor and active listening. This helps in many situations and is particularly effective with these individuals.

Amiable Style

When conflict arises, Amiable Style individuals will usually stay relatively quiet and might not share their true opinions. Their Backup Behavior is to acquiesce, so look for this type of behavior to identify them.

- Amiable Style people will often become less assertive during conflict, hesitating to voice their position. Though they will not always be very vocal during conflict, these individuals often display their discomfort non-verbally through their facial expressions and body movement.

- At times they will appear to acquiesce, going along with the rest of the group or a decision, even when they privately disagree or have concerns. Their feelings will not disappear and may surface later. Instead of openly sharing their beliefs with the team, these individuals might share their feelings with specific individuals outside of meetings.

- An effective way to help these individuals engaged in productive debate is to openly ask for their input. This helps them overcome their natural hesitancy. If you believe these individuals are not engaging in the conversation, you can bring to the surface topics you think might be important for them. This provides them with an entry into the discussion and reassures them others might share their opinions.

- When exchanging arguments, be sure to consider the impacts on people (e.g. outside of the discussion). Amiable Style individuals are focused on such issues more than others. When decisions are being made, it is important to show you have listened and understood their opinions prior to making the decision. This is good practice for everyone, and is especially relevant for Amiable Style individuals.

Analytical Style

When conflict arises, Analytical Style individuals might remain relatively quiet or wait for others to share their opinions before taking part in the debate. Their Backup Behavior is to avoid conflicts, so look for this type of behavior to support them appropriately.

- Analytical Style people will often wait until others have clearly stated their opinions before offering their own viewpoints. This is because they are most comfortable when they have heard different sides of the debate and information they may not have considered.

- When debating the issues, try to summarize the main points and discuss things in a rational way in terms of pros and cons, implications of decisions, and so on. When discussing differing opinions, show that you recognize the Analytical Style person's points of view and have taken those into account. Then discuss the other opinions in a logical and unemotional way.

- These people might want time to think about the issues before the debate is finished. Allow an appropriate amount of time for them to process the issues and fully support the decisions made by the involved parties. Similar to Amiable Style people, an effective way to engage these individuals in the discussion is to ask for their opinions. It is often helpful to ask them about a specific point rather than asking open or vague questions.

- When the discussion around conflicts gets difficult, these people might avoid direct eye contact with others more than usual, and might physically show their discomfort by frequently shifting in their chairs and other nonverbal signals. They display their discomfort by becoming more withdrawn and hesitating to engage in the conversation. Take time to engage them and ask them what you or others may not have considered so you can get their perspective on the change.

The following chart (see Fig. 4-3) summarizes recommendations to manage conflicts by SOCIAL STYLE.

> **Analytical Style**
>
> **Signs:**
>
> - In general, this individual becomes less assertive and shows less emotion
> - Assumes stiff or formal body movements, for instance, tight lipped, "poker face"
> - May insist on doing things in a certain way, withdraw, and can become overly critical
>
> **Your Positive Reaction:**
>
> Isolate the specific problem by asking questions related to preferences for using time, and making decisions based on data. Mention the things this person has gotten right, and take the time to discuss details. Help this individual become comfortable with the process or program, and to get involved with its progress. Encourage him or her to interact with others by identifying them as sources of valuable information.

Fig. 4-3: Managing Conflicts by SOCIAL STYLE

LEADING WITH THE VERSATILITY FACTOR

Driving Style

Signs:

- In general, this person becomes more assertive and shows less emotion
- Has more animated facial and hand gestures
- Becomes visibly impatient, openly and sharply states objections, and may attempt to take charge of or cut off discussion

Your Positive Reaction:

Isolate the specific problem by asking about this individual's concern over use of time (e.g. wasted time), inefficient use of resources, or not being given choices. Pay particular attention to his or her need for results, but earn respect by standing up to him or her, especially when the process results in achieving objectives. Offer this person options on how he or she can best help the team move forward.

Amiable Style

Sign:

- In general, this individual becomes less assertive and shows less emotion
- May seem to go along (acquiesce) but does not give a firm commitment
- Expresses doubt and uncertainty in a questioning way, and may postpone decisions beyond deadlines

Fig. 4-3: Managing Conflicts by SOCIAL STYLE (Cont.)

Amiable Style cont.

Your Positive Reaction:

Ask questions to determine the source of the problem, which might be related to the Amiable Style person's preferred actions toward others (lack of team cohesion), use of time (things are too rushed), and/or approach to decision-making (no opportunity to consult with others). Let this person know that your relationship with him or her is all right, and find a way to allow this person to help build a team effort. Help this individual feel safe in discussing different viewpoints.

Expressive Style

Signs:

- In general, this individual becomes more assertive and shows more emotion
- Openly states what he/she does not like about you, your ideas, your work, or that of others
- Openly criticizes others, but may try to save the relationship through conversation

Your Positive Reaction:

Identify what is troubling this person in terms of preferred actions toward others, use of time, and/or approach to decision-making. For example, is there recognition for individual efforts? Is there enough time for social interaction? Was there agreement to an idea, but not to the details? Commend this person's efforts and explore the merits of his or her ideas and actions. As appropriate, recognize his or her enthusiasm and past contributions.

Fig. 4-3: Managing Conflicts by SOCIAL STYLE (Cont.)

4.5 Motivating People

In today's complex and fast-moving business world, employees are confronted with many challenges. One of the most effective ways for leaders to handle arising challenges is to create a productive environment that enables subordinates and the group as a whole to work effectively during both normal and difficult times.

It's only natural for the motivation level of group members to fluctuate due to a variety of causes. However, in the long term one of the most important jobs of a leader is to provide guidance and keep people motivated. Many organizations recognize the ability to coach others as an important core skill set for their supervisors, executives, and managers.

People have different talents and strengths, and they are happiest when utilizing these strengths and spending time on tasks they are good at. Help people make the most of their natural abilities and, to the extent possible, provide your staff with personally meaningful work, which provides opportunity for growth. Also, employees who work in creative environments are more likely to come up with innovative ideas. Though some individuals are more naturally creative than others, most people are capable of some degree of creativity. And creativity can be learned. A leader can foster a department that contributes fresh ideas, whose members are not afraid to think in new ways, and who have the patience to persevere through ambiguity and problems.

Coaching is usually successful when done near in time to the person's actual performance. When coaching your subordinates, attention to the things you shouldn't do is often as important as understanding the things you should do. To be most effective, coaching should be an ongoing process and less of a formal event. Set the stage for your coaching relationships by showing awareness of SOCIAL STYLE preferences.

One study of job performance found that higher Versatility was directly related to effective managerial performance. In particular, this study found that managers with better interpersonal skills were also better coaches, according to their direct reports. Another study evaluated the performance of managers from the perspective of their direct subordinates, senior executives, and the managers themselves. This study found that all three groups cited ineffective communication skills as a top weakness of managers. It also found employees believed that improving their boss's ability to communicate more effectively would have the most beneficial impact on the employee's performance.

Most people understand the value of coaching and how it can help them to develop skills and progress in their careers. However, just as people of different SOCIAL STYLEs accomplish work and communicate in different ways, they also have specific preferences on how to be coached. By understanding these preferences, you can impact people's reactions to your coaching.

The following sections will describe each SOCIAL STYLE's preferences, how they like to be coached and how they respond to coaching.

Driving Style

Initially, people with a Driving Style may be impatient with coaching. Because they have an orientation towards action, listening to another person's guidance might seem like a waste of time or even unnecessary. The value of the process will need to be proven.

Driving Style individuals are good at moving projects forward, so give the person responsibility for managing projects through to completion. Let him or her make decisions about how to complete projects, without undue interference. Because their rush to take action and impatience can cause problems for others, encourage the person to slow down and understand the value that others bring to projects. Inevitably, this will help the person to be more effective.

Driving Style people will become discouraged if they are prevented from making progress. Having to confront barriers can be frustrating for all people, but obstacles perceived as unnecessary or a waste of time will immediately aggravate these individuals. If they believe artificial roadblocks are preventing them from achieving their goals, they may become disengaged. When this happens, these individuals will look for opportunities to either change the course of events or leave the situation altogether. They may try to take control of affairs in order to move things along or get the results they want.

When coaching Driving Style subordinates, make sure you get right to the point. Explain what you hope to accomplish through the feedback, and focus on the most relevant facts and how those are related to department or organization results. Do not take complete control of the conversation, and try not to force correct answers on the person. Make your points in a way that allows the person to respond. Encourage them to make decisions about how to proceed.

As an outcome of coaching, Driving Style people will want options for improving. Be direct and to the point, and show the value of your feedback quickly in the conversation by explaining how it will help them to achieve their goals. Even if your feedback is about some aspect of their performance where they are failing, they would still rather hear it than leave it unaddressed.

Driving Style people will react favorably to coaching, as long as it helps them achieve their goals. They have a strong need for results, so if you frame your advice in terms that will help them succeed, they're more likely to respond positively.

Expressive Style

Expressive Style individuals have a strong internal desire for recognition. By simply taking the time to coach them, you will partly fulfill this need. Their orientation towards spontaneity means they will generally welcome your "in-the-moment" coaching.

People with an Expressive Style are outgoing and big-picture thinkers, so give the person opportunities to work with other people. In particular, allow the person to work in situations where he or she can provide ideas without having to handle a lot of details. Since they can be unprepared and rely on their personalities to get by, challenge the person to monitor his or her behavior and the effects it has on others. Tempering some of their aggressive and outward behavior will help the person be more effective.

Expressive Style individuals can become frustrated if they feel they are being personally rejected, or if their ideas and input are being dismissed. They take things personally, so offhand comments or slights, even if unintentional, can be upsetting for them. When this happens they may actively vent their frustration, either directly to the offending person or to others. Signals that they are upset are usually just as obvious as signs they are motivated and engaged.

When coaching Expressive Style subordinates make sure you keep them involved and solicit their opinions and ideas. This is not difficult since they generally don't hesitate to express themselves. Approach the conversation as an open and free exchange, where the person is providing as much input as you are. These individuals can be very animated, which can be either good or bad. They can dominate discussions or get emotionally carried away. In these cases, you should allow the person to vent or discuss issues as appropriate, but if he or she gets into an unproductive loop, bring the conversation back to a point of focus.

As an outcome of coaching, Expressive Style people want some form of personal motivation for acting on your advice. Your input should include some form of recognition or gain for the person to appropriately inspire them. They also want to hear how their performance is valued in some way, so look for this opportunity. By first meeting this need, you will be better positioned to discuss areas where their performance can be improved.

Expressive Style individuals will respond well to coaching. Even if you have to deliver some difficult feedback, they are more likely to respond positively if you can point out the personal benefits that your advice will have for them.

Amiable Style

As Amiable Style individuals are directed towards relationships, they will typically be open to coaching conversations. They place value on interpersonal communication and will look at your coaching as a way to strengthen their relationship with you.

Amiable Style people are personable and effective collaborators, so provide the person with opportunities to work with others. He or she may be especially effective at organizing the activities of groups. They are sometimes hesitant to state their opinions. Encourage them to take personal risks and directly share their opinions and ideas. By being vocal and open with others, the person will increase his or her effectiveness.

Individuals with an Amiable Style are likely to become frustrated if they feel they are being pushed too hard for change, someone else is unilaterally setting goals or making decisions without their input, or if someone is overly directive or autocratic. In such cases they may not directly confront the person or issue. Instead, they may go along with the course of events, at least until they find a way to escape the situation. You may notice a lack of enthusiasm because they will be significantly less animated than usual, quieter, and will interact less with the person they are discouraged with.

When coaching Amiable Style subordinates, keep these individuals actively engaged in the conversation and process. You may have to ask open-ended questions to draw out their opinions. Do not come across as overly directive or one-sided, or as unilaterally forcing change. If they feel they are being pushed to change in ways they aren't open to, their relationship with you will be detrimentally affected.

The main outcome that an Amiable Style person wants from coaching is to know they can improve and help the organization, and assurance their working relationship with you is solid. It will be helpful if you can frame your advice in terms of the impact it will have on overall effectiveness and cohesion.

Amiable Style people are most likely to respond well to coaching if you are genuine and sincere in your discussion. By showing you understand their work circumstances and care about their professional development, you will meet their need for personal security.

Analytical Style

Analytical Style people want to be "correct" in their work performance. For this reason, they will generally be open to your feedback as long as they believe you are accurate in your assessment of their performance. Take time to prepare for any coaching discussion with an Analytical Style so they will fully consider your feedback.

Analytical Style individuals are methodical and organized. Give the person opportunities to develop processes and procedures related to tasks. They often prefer to work independently, so allow them plenty of time to solve problems and produce work on their own. These people are sometimes overly cautious and slow to act or commit. Encourage the person to be decisive and to commit to activities more quickly when this is reasonable. This will help him or her to be more effective when working with others.

People with an Analytical Style can become discouraged if they believe events are moving too quickly, they are being pressed to make immediate decisions, or important details are being ignored. When this happens they may respond by avoiding people or situations and withholding active contribution to projects. They may become even quieter than usual and will only respond or contribute when necessary. On occasion they will become stubborn and inflexible.

When coaching Analytical Style individuals encourage them to have an active dialogue with you. Listen carefully to their questions and statements, and ask if there is important information you have not taken into account. Let them spend some time thinking about your feedback before following up with them. These individuals may become disengaged from your coaching if they feel you are ignoring important details or facts, relating to them on an overly emotional level, or pressing for immediate decisions.

As an outcome of coaching, Analytical Style individuals want you to take into account their work circumstances and to provide logical feedback that will help them improve their performance. Try to frame your feedback in a way that takes into account history as well as future development. They typically will want time after a coaching conversation to think about what you have said. It may be worthwhile to plan a short follow-up discussion to address any concerns or questions the Analytical Style person may have after having a chance to reflect on your feedback.

Analytical Style people are most likely to respond positively to coaching if you support them in their development. By agreeing to back them in the course of action, they will feel capable of making changes and improving their performance.

The following chart (see Fig. 4-4) summarizes recommendations to motivate people by SOCIAL STYLE.

Analytical Style	Driving Style
• Provide extra support, as needed, to help this person stay on schedule or make more timely decisions • Be patient with this person; give them time to work the details before moving forward • When this person makes a decision, affirm their actions and encourage them to continue to keep things moving • Be business-like, get to the point, but be sure to explain your thinking/logic to them • Provide extra support, as appropriate, to help this person see the big picture or to think creatively • Don't be vague when coaching this person; be specific	• Encourage this person to listen to the input of others and effectively use their strengths to get things done • Keep meetings and interactions business-like, direct, and to the point • Acknowledge this person's need to compete • Don't waste this person's time with too much small talk or with facts and data not needed to get results • Help this person to attend to necessary details while giving him or her latitude to execute his or her own plans

Fig. 4-4: Motivating People by SOCIAL STYLE

Amiable Style	Expressive Style
• Encourage this person to stay focused on the goal • Help this person keep track of timelines and deadlines by asking about them at regularly scheduled intervals • Work cooperatively with this person to create a clear process for achieving complex tasks • Make a conscious effort to make this person feel safe to discuss differences with you around a task or situation • Reinforce this person's ability to create social networks while keeping them focused on the objective	• Help this person examine the advantages and disadvantages of his or her plans before implementing them • Give this person tasks that will bring him or her personal recognition and will allow them to come up with innovative solutions • Don't unnecessarily try to contain this person's high levels of energy • Keep this person moving ahead by publicly acknowledging his or her interim achievements • Give this person room to take reasonable risks • Don't get too serious with this person; allow them to bring some fun and spontaneity into the workplace

Fig. 4-4: Motivating People by SOCIAL STYLE (Cont.)

4.6 Providing Feedback

Effective performance discussions are a critical component of personnel development programs in organizations around the globe. Making them productive for the employee as well as for the entire organization requires ample preparation effort. Giving feedback on technical or functional performance is different from providing information about a person's interpersonal skills. SOCIAL STYLE differences play a key role in how people will respond to each type of feedback. As a leader, you can increase your impact on your people by taking the time to be prepared to discuss specific examples of behavior and performance to back up your evaluation.

As a general rule, it is typically helpful to ask for the person's opinions before discussing your own evaluation. This provides you with a general idea of how the person feels about his or her performance, and is an effective transition into the formal evaluation discussion. Determine the person's professional and personal growth objectives, and how these can be linked to the organization's needs and strategy. Consider any obstacles that may interfere with goal attainment. Finally, conclude the review with clear agreement on overall effectiveness and understanding of future objectives.

One of the most challenging tasks for a manager is to provide coaching to individuals about their failure to accomplish objectives, behavior that is inconsistent with the values of the organization, or some other type of difficult feedback. In the following pages we will provide proven techniques to effectively provide feedback in a way that will promote acceptance and positive action to people of each SOCIAL STYLE.

Driving Style

When conducting a performance discussion with a Driving Style person, keep in mind they are logical, achievement motivated, and do not always listen effectively.

- Prepare to use your meeting time efficiently. Get right to the point; you do not need to spend time on small talk or warming up to the main purpose of the meeting. Plan to focus on the person's ability to achieve broad objectives while also understanding that you will need to review specific behaviors even if the person is not focused on this level of detail.

- Ask open-ended questions as a way to understand the Driving Style person's opinions about their performance. However, with this person you may need to follow up with more pointed and direct questions if the person does not provide adequate input.

- When giving your feedback, find opportunities to point out that your input is intended to help the person succeed; by relating your feedback to increased future effectiveness, you can help the person be more open and accepting of the feedback process.

- These people do not hesitate to share their opinions about feedback, and because they like to maintain control, the person might try to dominate the discussion. Keep in mind this is simply how these people communicate.

- Driving Style individuals prefer to be congratulated in a

direct manner for their specific actions and accomplishments. They are particularly interested in feedback about their ability to achieve goals and outcomes. Though they are not necessarily opposed to public recognition, they generally do not have a prime need for this.

• Though nobody wants to hear they aren't performing up to expectations, it can be especially difficult for Driving Style individuals because they are so focused on results. They may be surprised to hear their technical or functional performance requires improvement. However, these individuals generally want to improve their abilities to meet goals so they will strive to improve in areas where they feel they are capable. Specifics on issues and concrete ideas on how to improve will be appreciated by this Style.

• Most individuals are going to have difficulty accepting tough feedback about their interpersonal skills. Driving Style people typically do not place great importance on getting along well with others, so their difficulties in this area might be completely out of their awareness. It may be surprising for them to hear that their lack of interpersonal ability is affecting the others in the department or organization. As with feedback on their technical skills, explain how their behavior is affecting important processes or outcomes.

• By nature, these individuals control their emotions. Unless they are feeling shock or anger about your feedback, they are likely to appear neutral though concerned. If they accept the feedback, they will want to move quickly into a problem-solving strategy instead of dwelling on the past. They will want to develop a plan for changing their behavior or performance. They prefer to make decisions for themselves, but you should collaborate with them to develop an action plan that will succeed.

- Help the Driving Style person develop a sense of ownership by allowing them to determine broad goals themselves; you can then comment and revise these goals as needed. Clearly indicate the person is accountable for the new goals and has an appropriate level of autonomy to achieve the objectives.

- If appropriate, present the goal as a competitive objective, or a means for the person to help the company achieve an advantage.

Expressive Style

When conducting a performance discussion with an Expressive Style person, keep in mind they are spontaneous, seek recognition, and are not very detail-oriented.

- When you have to give a tough message, approach them in a supportive way that shows you still approve of them, either in terms of some aspect of their performance or of them personally. Tell them the feedback is about their performance and not about them personally.

- When giving your feedback, discuss the behavior or performance that led to the necessity of the meeting, and then focus on how the person can improve in the future. Expressive Style people tend to be oriented toward the future, so frame your feedback as a way for them to improve rather than focusing entirely on criticism of the past. Keep them motivated by showing how improvement will benefit not only the organization or department, but also them personally.

- These individuals show their emotions, so it is likely they will express their feelings about the feedback. If they are not surprised or defensive about the information, they may react with some sadness but will accept the feedback and look for ways to improve. These individuals like to be involved. Instead of telling them exactly what needs to be done, collaborate with them to determine strategies for developing the abilities they need.

- If they are shocked by the feedback or disagree with it, they will openly express their dissatisfaction. The Backup Behavior for Expressive Style people is to attack. They often take criticism personally, so they may be blunt and personal in their response. They might bring up issues that are tangential to the discussion, and can come across as irrational.

- Because they are both emotional and Tell Assertive, they may seek to dominate the conversation. They might vent their feelings about the feedback, and will focus more on their emotions about the information rather than on the logic or rationale of your message. When frustrated, these individuals can be very forceful and loud.

- These individuals are naturally motivated by recognition, so develop goals that allow the person to receive acknowledgment. If possible, design the goal so the process of achieving objectives is exciting and enjoyable. Collaborate with the person as much as possible to develop goals that take into account the person's ideas and opinions; let them brainstorm possibilities, but be prepared to help the person be realistic.

• These individuals prefer frequent interaction and recognition, so there is a certain degree of maintenance involved with Expressive Style people. They have a very social nature and also like to gain personal advantages, so they will usually appreciate public recognition for their accomplishments. Let them know how meaningful their accomplishments are and the benefits they have had, especially on other people and customers.

• Even if your feedback is purely about technical performance and not about interpersonal skills, they may feel personally offended, and this can weaken their motivation. These individuals are concerned about personal recognition and status, and anything that undermines this can be disheartening for them. It will be important to tell them that you are giving feedback about specific aspects of their performance, and this does not influence your overall opinions of them, their potential, or their abilities. Remain optimistic and enthusiastic even when giving tough feedback. Express that together you can develop a strategy for improvement.

• Specific feedback addressing interpersonal skills can be very difficult for these individuals to accept. This is true for all people, but Expressive Style people often pride themselves on their abilities to relate well to others. Their Style Growth Action is to check their behavior, so it is not uncommon for them to offend others or be overbearing and to be unaware of these tendencies. Though it might be difficult to accept this feedback, it is important they hear it. Be sure to emphasize that most of their behavior is seen positively and they have good qualities to build on.

- Regularly follow up with these team members to keep them focused on necessary tasks. They tend to be future-oriented, so they might sometimes stray off course when detailed or time sensitive work is required.

Amiable Style

When conducting a performance review discussion with an Amiable Style person, keep in mind they are friendly, collaborative, and may not fully share their opinions.

- Be genuine with this person and clearly communicate that you have their best interests in mind. Explain to them the performance review will be a two-way discussion, and the two of you will collaborate and move toward mutually agreed-upon goals.

- These individuals are usually comfortable answering open-ended questions as a way to move into more detailed discussions. The person will be most open to your feedback if they trust you and believe the performance evaluation is done for their benefit. But these individuals are likely to take performance information personally, both the good and bad. Reassure them the feedback is about performance and is not a reflection of them personally or of your relationship.

- Amiable Style individuals prefer positive, warm, sincere feedback that serves to strengthen their relationship with you. They particularly like to know they have made accomplishments and contributions to team effectiveness, customer experiences, and the like. Many people appreciate verbal praise when they do a good job, but this form of recognition especially motivates these individuals.

- It is often helpful to discuss areas where they are performing well prior to discussing the difficult topics. When doing this, it is important you are sincere in what you say. Do not avoid the difficult topic, but communicate to the person your feedback is about specific areas and is not a global opinion about them.

- Amiable Style people might feel threatened or intimidated by difficult feedback. If they seem to be holding their true opinions to themselves, make it safe for them to reengage with you. Ask open-ended questions to help them share their thoughts. If they feel very strongly about your feedback, they are likely to respond in an emotional way and may share some of their opinions and feelings. They will take your input personally and might be offended by what you say. These individuals are not usually highly vocal or abrasive, but they can be abrupt when upset. They may try to end the conversation quickly without fully expressing their opinions or searching for an agreeable solution to the problem.

- Though Amiable Style people might take difficult feedback personally, if the message is solely about their technical performance, they are more likely to be receptive. Be sure to clearly state their performance issues can be resolved and they can improve their abilities (assuming this is the case). These individuals aim to please and generally want to do a good job, so they will be open to your specific advice about how to improve their performance.

• It can be very difficult for these individuals to receive feedback about their interpersonal skills. They are especially focused on maintaining good relationships with others, and news that contradicts this can be disheartening. If their issues are with a specific person or are confined to particular circumstances, be sure to point this out and let them know there are concrete steps that can be taken to address the issue. Actively solicit their viewpoints about the situation. To the extent possible, act as their partner when trying to improve interpersonal abilities. Offer to meet with them regularly and help coach them in their efforts.

• When developing goals, be collaborative. When necessary, provide the person with clear instructions or recommendations about specific goals and how to achieve them. The person may be reluctant to initiate activities perceived as risky, either professionally or personally, so give reassurance about the value and purpose of the goal. Ask the person if she is committed to the goal; do not assume silence implies support. Be very clear about specific timeframes or deadlines, but be careful to not come across as unnecessarily demanding or autocratic.

• Because Amiable Style people tend to show a less disciplined use of time and move at a slower pace, you may want to regularly check on their progress. When done in a friendly way, this also helps these individuals to bring up any issues that might otherwise not surface.

Analytical Style

When conducting a performance discussion with an Analytical Style person, keep in mind they are rational, cooperative, and can be slow to act.

- It is often helpful to begin performance reviews with Analytical Style subordinates by acknowledging the quality of their work or some other aspect of their performance. This helps to reassure them they are doing things "right."

- Analytical Style individuals like feedback recognizing the quality of their contributions and the benefits they provide for the team or organization. In addition to verbal feedback, these people like to see it in writing or some other form of citation. They can become slightly uncomfortable when given public recognition, so be careful not to make too much of a show of their achievements.

- If they actively disagree with what you are saying, these individuals can be more vocal and animated. They can be defensive if they believe the feedback is unjust or inaccurate, and they will want to express their opinions. They are often uncomfortable in these types of situations, and this discomfort will be evident in their expressions and mannerisms. They may be non-committal and will be anxious for the conversation to end.

- Even if they are upset, Analytical Style people will be eager to return to a rational and comfortable conversation. You can help bring the conversation back to a more productive state by continuing to approach them in a rational way. Reiterate the reasoning behind your feedback and the evidence that supports your message.

• For Analytical Style people, it may be harder to receive difficult feedback about technical performance than about their interpersonal skills. This is because they often pride themselves on their technical abilities and competence. Provide feedback in a way that helps them maintain their self-confidence. If feasible, let them know their poor performance is only in a specific aspect of their job and it can be corrected. Give them your own ideas on how to improve the situation and let them build on these ideas. Show them you have confidence in their abilities.

• While it is always hard to receive information about poor interpersonal skills, it is possible these individuals will be unaware of the issue and its impacts on others. They may not place much importance on interpersonal relationships at work, or they might even believe they're irrelevant to their jobs. Either way, clearly point out for them the specific issues and the effects that their behavior is having on others. Describe how improvement in this area will benefit the individual and help them to be more effective. Give this feedback in a non-threatening way; it may even be helpful to frame it as a unique problem to solve.

• Collaborate with the person to develop goals, particularly on the details of how to achieve them. The person may want to determine the processes for achieving goals over time, so you may need to plan a follow-up meeting to discuss this. Be clear about the broad nature and outcomes of goals, and provide relevant background information, related details, and supporting information to help the person organize his or her efforts.

- Analytical Style people tend to move at a slower pace, particularly in the early stages of a new project or responsibility. They need to think things through and mentally work through the details and processes before taking action. Try to avoid pressing them for immediate decisions or action. Schedule regular check-ups with them (if appropriate, through email rather than in person), but allow them to work through the details of the discussed goals on their own without unnecessary interruption.

The following chart (see Fig. 4-5) summarizes recommendations on how to provide feedback by SOCIAL STYLE.

Analytical Style

- Take the time to tell this person why you are giving him or her positive feedback and cite specific examples

- The Analytical Style individual does not always need to be praised in front of others; a private word will often do (but public recognition is usually appreciated)

- Congratulate this person for paying attention to important details and for getting (or attempting to get) things right

- This person welcomes positive feedback in writing

- Acknowledge this person's ability to focus on the important details of the task at hand

Driving Style

- Praise this individual for keeping his or her eye on the ball and for getting things done

- Acknowledge this person's ability to set aside "personalities" and superfluous details

- Congratulate this person publicly and privately for his or her accomplishments (results)

- Commend this person's drive and ability to get things done quickly

- Avoid appearing gushy or emotionally "moved" by his or her good performance

- Let this person know there are more challenges for them

Fig. 4-5: Providing Feedback by SOCIAL STYLE

Amiable Style

- Give this person immediate, genuine verbal feedback
- Affirm this person's ability to keep others engaged and motivated
- Be warm and sincere
- Praise this person's ability to organize the work of others and maintain harmony in the workplace
- Publicly and sincerely acknowledge this person's interpersonal skills
- Avoid doing anything, such as rushing, that might indicate you are insincere

Expressive Style

- Make personal contact with this individual (rather than using e-mail or voicemail)
- Show warmth and enthusiasm
- Applaud this person's contribution in public
- Praise this person's sense of fun and spontaneity
- Commend this person for seeing the big picture
- For the Expressive Style individual, it is usually better to err on the side of too much praise than too little

Fig. 4-5: Providing Feedback by SOCIAL STYLE (Cont.)

5 THE VERSATILITY FACTOR IN CUSTOMER RELATIONSHIPS

If you are in a sales or business development role, your knowledge of SOCIAL STYLE and Versatility concepts puts you in a superior position to guide the interplay of your SOCIAL STYLE with those of your customers, and move them toward a mutually productive relationship with you. As a sales professional, you have probably seen all types of sales training programs and you may already have established a methodology that works for you. While most sales techniques focus on the different steps involved in the selling process, we will start our discussion with a focus on individual customers, since it is these people who ultimately decide success or failure.

Unsuccessful sales outcomes can occur when a salesperson fails to help the customer meet their personal needs in addition to their business needs. If you fail to plan or monitor your SOCIAL STYLE interactions, your customer realizes, consciously or subconsciously, that their personal preferences are not being met. Tension builds and both you and the customer may end up in an unproductive, lose-lose interaction.

While SOCIAL STYLE and Versatility concepts can certainly help you improve your interpersonal effectiveness in most sales situations, you should not expect them to work all the time. The support and respect you receive from your customers are key. And research shows that Versatility tends to go up when customers see the salesperson putting forth effort in its four critical categories: Image, Presentation, Competence, and Feedback. As you apply the concepts to improve interactions with your customers, chances are, you too will gain more cooperation, support, and respect, and thereby become a more effective salesperson.

Every interaction with your customers involves two Styles: yours and theirs. As you consider how to adjust your behavior based on their SOCIAL STYLE preferences, keep in mind that your customer perceives you in particular ways based on your Style.

- Salespeople with a Driving Style are seen by their customers as active, forceful, and decisive. These salespeople are direct; they initiate social interaction and they focus their efforts and the efforts of their customers on understanding the facts and making the commitment to buy. Salespeople with a Driving Style can be seen and described by their customers as cool, distant, guarded, pushy, and aloof at times, because they appear to control their feelings and do not reveal the depth of their emotions as they attempt to move toward their goal.

- Salespeople with an Expressive Style tend to be much more willing to make their inner feelings known to their customers. Rather than controlling emotions, salespeople with this style can sometimes appear proactive and impulsive about showing both positive and negative feelings. They can be seen and described by the customers who interact with them as personable, talkative, visionary, creative, exciting, competitive, sometimes overly emotional and inappropriate, and opinionated.

- Salespeople with an Amiable Style also openly display their feelings to their customers. However, they appear less opinionated and generally more agreeable. These salespeople tend to be most sensitive to keeping relationships with their customers on an informal, friendly, and personal basis. They seem very interested in achieving rapport with their customers, sometimes at the expense of gaining the customer's commitment effectively and efficiently. They can be described by their customers as dependable, cooperative, risk averse, reluctant to raise difficult issues, and overly cautious.

- Salespeople with an Analytical Style are typically described by their customers as quiet, logical, and reserved. They tend to be cool toward their customers and may not communicate with them unless there is a specific need to do so. They tend to listen to others, make decisions thoughtfully, and act at a slower pace. Customers usually view them as conscientious, prudent, thorough, overly detailed, rigid, slow to innovate, risk adverse, and overly cautious.

These descriptions tend to be most accurate when a salesperson shows moderate to low levels of Versatility. In other words, the salesperson does not make noticeable attempts to adjust their behavior to meet the SOCIAL STYLE preferences of the customer. Regardless of the salesperson's level of Versatility, the behaviors described here are operating to some extent as described for each Style.

Applying what you know about SOCIAL STYLE and Versatility to the sales process can give you a significant advantage: the ability to predict how your customer will typically react during the sales process and what you can do to help the customer feel comfortable doing business with you. Of course, being able to make these predictions does not mean you will be 100% accurate. You must always stay in tune with the individual differences your customers will express. You will, though, have a reference point for knowing your customer and knowing what you can do for your customer in the sales situation.

The sales process seldom proceeds as a straight line from opening to presentation to close. It is more likely to start and stop, double-back on itself, and change course depending on the complexity of the product or service you are selling, the cost to the customer, the number of people involved in the purchase decision, etc. For purposes of this discussion, the sales process is broken into three stages:

>**1. *Opening:*** At the beginning of the sales call, you introduce yourself and establish initial rapport with the customer. This phase focuses on knowing the customer and establishing the client relationship as well as analyzing and fully understanding the business challenges the customer is facing.

>**2. *Presenting:*** This is the stage during which you probe for the needs of your customers as those needs relate to your product or service. During this stage, you conduct sales calls and meetings where you present relevant information about the features and benefits of the product or service you are selling and how they will help solve the customer's problems. In a continuous sales process, you will be continuously tailoring and adapting the sales approach, clarifying customer requirements, presenting solutions, and handling objections.

>**3. *Closing:*** At this stage, you are trying to gain the customer's

final commitment to your proposal. At this stage, you might get agreement on your request for action, negotiate terms and conditions, and finally close the deal.

These three stages in the sales process are not meant to oversimplify the sales process, but rather to demonstrate how SOCIAL STYLEs can assist you in moving through the process more effectively. Following this chapter, we will illustrate how a salesperson can be more successful in applying the SOCIAL STYLE Model and how Versatility can help resolve, or even head off, unnecessary tension caused by interpersonal friction, which sometimes arises during the selling process.

> Many sales situations have been positively impacted by the proper application of SOCIAL STYLEs. One example is from a large multi-national professional services firm that was in danger of losing a very large client. After an analysis of the new CFO and his team, it became evident the approach the Expressive team took was inappropriate for the new situation with new Styles. The firm adjusted its approach, including the type and content of its recommendations, to better match the analytical preferences of the client. As a result, the client continued with the firm and additional business in excess of $80 million was secured.

5.1 Building Customer Relationships

Customers buy from people and organizations they trust. In part, trust is based on personal comfort with you. Learning how to gain and build trust with each SOCIAL STYLE won't necessarily result in an instant sale, but it will remove one of the roadblocks that would otherwise mean a definite "No." Being aware of your own behavior and your impact on customers is critical for helping them feel comfortable with you. It is a first step toward building trust.

Developing an appropriate and effective strategy for interacting with customers requires knowing both one's own SOCIAL STYLE and that of the customer. To identify a customer's SOCIAL STYLE you need to observe what the customer actually says and does in different situations. This observation will give you clues about the customer's behavioral preferences under different levels of tension. In addition, because people tend to do things that are characteristic of their particular SOCIAL STYLE, you need sufficient observations for a pattern of behavior to reveal itself.

You must be able to accommodate the Style Orientation of customers, no matter how skilled you are at tasks such as account planning or cold calling, or how knowledgeable you are about your industry, organization, and the applications of the products or services you sell. In the business context of typical sales situations, the evaluation of a customer's SOCIAL STYLE should be built from the following three perspectives:

> **1. Observe Attire:** Is he or she dressed formally or informally given the situation? Recall that Analytical and Driving Style individuals are more likely to prefer formal interactions, which may be reflected by dressing on the conservative side. Amiable and Expressive Style individuals are more likely to be somewhat informal in their interactions, which can be reflected in their attire. You should also consider dress in relationship to the culture of the client's organization and industry. If possible, try to learn a bit about the organization's

dress code prior to your meeting. Receptionists and assistants can be valuable sources for this information.

2. Observe Work Environment: If you are in their work environment, glance around for clues to their SOCIAL STYLE. Do they prominently display awards or certificates, or pictures of themselves and others (suggesting an Expressive Style), or do they display "conversation pieces" and "group shot" photos (suggesting an Amiable Style)? Does their work area have an abundance of references and resources for fact checking within easy reach (suggesting an Analytical Style), or are just the bare essentials required to do the job on display (suggesting a Driving Style)? Remember, at this point you are like a detective, collecting clues but not yet reaching any conclusions.

3. Observe "Say-and-Do" Behaviors: As you begin the sales process, get the customer "on stage" so you can begin to observe his or her verbal and nonverbal behaviors. You might, for example, ask an open-ended question, such as, "Before we get started, would you tell me about your present situation?"

Business development involves frequent communication through telephone and email. These virtual communication channels can be challenging and less effective than meeting in person. Not only are they imperfect in terms of understanding customers' needs, but there is also a higher risk of misunderstanding and even conflict. But there exist clear behavioral patterns when communicating through phone and email with customers, revealing their SOCIAL STYLEs.

In the following pages, we will discuss SOCIAL STYLE-specific behavior patterns typical for customers found across all industries.

Driving Style

Customers with a Driving Style are typically more oriented toward results and tasks than they are toward relationships and people. As a result, they may appear uncommunicative, cool, formal, independent, and competitive in relationships with others. A Driving Style customer tends to initiate clear action. However, the personal reasons for such action may not be obvious to you because they seldom see a need to share personal motives or feelings.

Driving Style customers tend to focus on efficiency or productivity and advancing their goals rather than devoting time and attention to casual relationships. Thus, you may feel that you really don't get to know your Driving Style customers on a close, personal basis. In early contacts with a Driving Style customer, you may not consider the situation warm and friendly. In discussions about people, Driving Style customers will seem to display an attitude that suggests they have learned how to work with others only because they must in order to achieve their objectives, not because they enjoy engaging with people on a personal basis. In fact, this individual may appear to treat people as objects rather than individuals. However, these Driving Style customers often can appear very pleasant and even charming…on their terms.

Driving Style people will make their presence known early in a presentation setting. They are likely to ask questions and make comments, and they may even challenge you or your ability to meet their needs. They will focus on the bottom line, at least from their point of view, and they might show impatience if you do not get to your main points quickly. They will typically have neutral nonverbal expressions, with very little smiling, frowning, or other obvious animation. The exception is if they are frustrated, in which case, they may show obvious facial signals.

During phone calls, Driving Style people might be impatient if they feel you are wasting their time. When speaking, these individuals will usually focus exclusively on task-related matters such as priorities and plans. Their emails are usually brief and pointed, and they may not provide much context to help explain their comments and requests.

To deal most effectively with the Driving Style customer, be aware of the following recommendations:

- Plan a sales strategy that will support the Driving Style customer's conclusions and the actions needed to implement those conclusions. Plan ahead for what you are going to say and be efficient so that you don't waste their time.

- These individuals place value on professionalism; they want you to show your abilities and the quality of your services before they will trust you. If you show a lack of confidence in your services or your own skills, these individuals will question your ability to meet their needs.

- They want you to be direct with them and share your opinions, even if your input might be contrary to what they want to hear. But, they will react negatively if you focus too much on your opinions instead of objective facts. Initially, don't try to change their mind with a direct approach. Instead, discover the Driving Style customer's objectives and find ways to support and assist with these objectives without assuming anything or second-guessing what the Driving Style customer really wants. When making decisions, they want you to provide options and then let them decide.

- In your discussions with your Driving Style customer, plan to ask questions about specifics. These customers want to get a job done. Find out what situation or conditions would exist if this individual had their way. Therefore, stick with "what" and "when" questions. Don't get sidetracked in a discussion of "how," "who," or "why" questions. Move directly and quickly to the "what" specifics.

• It's not necessary to discuss what the person wants personally. Instead, focus on an objective they have identified as important. But, be aware that Driving Style customers may be secretive and refuse to share information with sales people, even if it could help meet their own needs.

• Keep the sales relationship businesslike. It is not necessary to build a personal relationship unless the customer indicates that's part of the objective. You should not anticipate friendship as a condition for a good sales relationship.

• Avoid unnecessarily disagreeing with a Driving Style customer on incidental details as this will hinder the sales process; especially avoid starting a debate over minor details or hypothetical implications.

• They want to maintain control in the relationship, but they will value your input as long as you can help them achieve results. When they object to a sales approach, they will be very direct with their opinions and will let you know their specific objections.

• In telephone conversations, speak at a moderate, deliberate pace and get to the point in a business-like manner. When writing emails, they will often not use salutations or include personal comments. Only include attachments if they are necessary. Brief is always better with this SOCIAL STYLE.

Expressive Style

The Expressive Style appears communicative, fun, exciting, warm, approachable, and competitive. Expressive Style customers often involve you and others with their feelings and thoughts. Their actions suggest they want you as a friend, but in the role of a follower and personal supporter of their dreams rather than as someone who might compete with them. These customers consider power and politics important because they can enhance personal recognition and help recruit supporters to the cause. While relationships and people count to them, these relationships may lack depth and be short-lived.

As with Driving Style customers, Expressive Style people will also make their presence known during presentations. They will actively respond to what you say, either with commentary and questions, or with other verbal and nonverbal responses such as laughter and enthusiasm. They will display their level of engagement in your presentation in obvious ways through their reactions and facial expressions. This can range from boredom and hostility to excitement and outward support.

During phone calls, Expressive Style people will typically be very talkative. They will speak more frequently than most others and will also speak loudly. These individuals will often speak about personal matters and will share stories about themselves and others. They often write emails that are wordy and somewhat disorganized. Expressive customers may impulsively send multiple emails rather than a single, organized email. In emails, their comments or requests might be non-specific or unclear.

To deal most effectively with an Expressive Style customer:

- Plan a sales strategy that will provide support for their dreams and intuitions. These individuals want you to support them so they can succeed; help them look good and they will value you.

- Even though they may not work directly with salespeople, they want to share a personal connection with them and want salespeople to share their enthusiasm. Therefore, they like salespeople who are energetic and enthusiastic, and who believe in what they are selling.

- Plan to ask questions about the customer's opinions and future goals. Have this customer tell you what others need to do to achieve objectives. Then, let them tell you what they are personally doing to reach those objectives. Thus, people and their future goals become the subject of this discussion rather than just results in terms of cold, factual, present realities.

- If you do not adequately involve them in your efforts, these individuals may lose confidence in you. It is very important that you solicit their opinions and keep them motivated to work with you.

- The Expressive Style customer tends to form an opinion on almost everything. Look for points of agreement and give this customer credit for their good ideas. Indicate what you can and will do to implement the ideas you agree upon. Ask the customer what you can do personally to help put their ideas into action. Do not argue with these individuals. Find a way to reengage with them by addressing their issues and involving them in the solution.

• Be sure you agree on specifics. Avoid the temptation to proceed on a warm feeling that everything will somehow work out for the best. Take the initiative to formally summarize your discussions in writing. Let the Expressive Style customer know you will provide a summary even if they may want to make a few alterations. Consolidate the new information and move on. This is a subtle but effective way to help your customer stay on track with you and can reduce the amount of time it takes you to move the sale to closure.

• Spend time exploring mutually stimulating ideas and possible solutions. At this point, don't rush a conversation; instead, have a discussion that builds ideas together. Let the customer take as much of the credit for the ideas developed as they care to. Remember, individuals with an Expressive Style are creative, fun, and exciting. As they build their vision and ideas, your task is to help make their dreams a reality!

• They move quickly and are flexible in their use of time. They will rapidly involve you in their priorities and needs, and may change direction quickly. This can be demanding as they may expect you to be quickly available when they need you.

• Avoid disagreeing with an Expressive Style customer on matters of opinion or ideas related to their personal desires. While this person is naturally competitive, they are looking for supporters, so they are likely to see you as one or the other. If you do disagree with these individuals, they are likely to see you as a competitor and feel a strong need to win the argument.

- Expressive Style customers usually make decisions based primarily on intuition and opinion rather than facts. They take into account the opinions of people who matter to them; these people might be experts or important allies within their organizations.

- Talking on the phone is often preferable to using email with Expressive Style individuals because it allows you to maintain a more personal form of contact. When talking or leaving voicemail messages, use your tone of voice and inflection to reciprocate their enthusiasm or feelings. Keep your email messages brief, and do not include unnecessary background information.

Amiable Style

The Amiable Style is the most people-oriented of the SOCIAL STYLEs. To the Amiable Style customer, people count as people rather than just as ways to achieve results or political influence. Avoid competition in relationships with them and instead cooperate as a means of getting things done. Typically, these customers will seek your recommendations and personal support. This connection tends to place a greater responsibility on you before making a recommendation to an Amiable Style individual. They achieve objectives with people through understanding and mutual respect rather than force and authority. These customers will readily accept advice from a friendly, understanding salesperson who treats them as a real individual. They do not seek power over others as an important personal objective.

In a presentation setting, Amiable Style people might not ask many questions or offer much commentary, unless they are particularly excited by your comments. They will often respond to the comments of others or only offer their opinions if they are asked. During the presentation they will usually have pleasant demeanors and facial expressions. This is true even if they are not engaged in your presentation, so be careful not to falsely conclude they are enthused or in agreement with your message.

During phone calls Amiable Style people usually sound enthusiastic, though they may speak in a fairly subdued tone. Since they focus on relationships, they will often discuss people and the effects your product or service will have on others, rather than on the service itself. Their emails will be friendly and personable. They typically use salutations and might include personal messages along with work-related information. They tend to be wordy in their writing, and rather than making direct requests they will considerately ask if you can do something.

To deal effectively with an Amiable Style customer you should:

- Plan a sales strategy that supports this individual's feelings and relationships with others.

- These individuals want to develop a personal relationship with salespeople. However, this relationship needs to be based on trust; if you are insincere they will not want to work with you. They want salespeople to partner with them to meet their needs; they need to feel fully supported by salespeople.

- Take an early initiative to show your personal interest in this person as an individual. Spend the necessary time to deal with the Amiable Style person's personal situation, marital status, family, hobbies, and interests and attempt to find an area of common involvement where you can support this individual in terms of their personal needs. They appreciate people who maintain contact with them, and who do not always wait for particular reasons to check in.

• Support the key relationships Amiable Style customers have with others. Find out who the person feels is important and may influence the purchase decision, even if that person isn't formally involved. Be aware of any source of doubt, fear, or insecurity in the Amiable Style customer.

• If you agree easily on an objective, look for possible areas of early dissatisfaction before taking any joint action. Consider the following checkpoint: "It's great we agree; however, are there any areas where we might possibly disagree in the future?" Encourage personal discussion.

• These individuals generally avoid risks, especially if they believe certain decisions might harm relationships or cause an uncomfortable change to the status quo (e.g., supplier changes). They look for reassurance and guarantees. When making decisions, they want your honest recommendations; they will also rely on the input of others whom they trust.

• Establish a cooperative effort with the Amiable Style customer. The person wants to relate to working with you on a joint basis as a means of achieving their personal objectives. However, this customer may understate personal goals, so you may need to clarify the specifics in terms of *why*, *who*, *how*, and *what* the person expects to achieve. Avoid the temptation to overstate what you can realistically do together to achieve the objective or you will create difficulties in a long-term sales relationship.

• Instead of jumping right in to your message, open with a friendly greeting. Be open to having longer telephone conversations with these individuals. It motivates them to have friendly connections with others, so take time to talk with them. When leaving messages, speak in a conversational style and at a moderate pace.

• Avoid disagreeing with an Amiable Style customer in any way that might be taken personally. If you do have a disagreement, encourage an honest discussion about personal opinions. Expect these customers to be personally offended if you disagree with them too openly or if you speak sharply. If you push your point, you may win the argument but lose the sale!

• If they do not believe that you are sincerely trying to help them or partner with them, these individuals will lose confidence and will not trust you. When objecting to a sales effort, they will usually be polite but distant. They may not tell you directly about their specific issues, and might even make up a reason for their objection that is a cover for their true opinions.

• Do not use email as a substitute for a real conversation. As appropriate and possible, these individuals like to speak in person.

> A salesperson applied their new SOCIAL STYLE knowledge to a prospect they had called on for many years with no success. The salesperson realized that he was Driving Style and the client was Amiable Style. For years the salesperson used his preferred approach when interacting with the client rather than considering the client's desired approach. Following training, the salesperson stopped at the prospect's grocery store and took a new approach focused on building a personal connection. After a one hour meeting during which nothing business-related was discussed, the client told the salesperson that he felt much better about working with him and placed an order for over $ 1 million.

Analytical Style

Customers with an Analytical Style appear uncommunicative, distant, formal, and independent. These customers are cooperative in their actions, as long as they have some freedom to organize their own efforts. Analytical customers tend to be cautious about extending friendships or personal warmth, and initially will be more concerned with how things can get done without the need for personal involvements. Paradoxically, people and friendships may be very important, even though they may not seem to be in initial contacts.

These customers don't want to rush into a relationship until they understand how the relationship can be managed, so no one will get hurt by the degree of involvement or personal demand. This customer also has a "show me" attitude. They tend to be suspicious of power and will avoid becoming involved with others who have power or leverage until they see a system or a predictable pattern in the way power is used.

Customers with an Analytical Style will usually be quiet during presentations, particularly if the audience is large and consists of people who are more Tell Assertive or in positions of higher authority. They often wait until others have stated their opinions or asked questions before speaking themselves. When they do ask questions, their focus is often on a very specific point rather than broader issues. They generally maintain neutral expressions so it can be challenging to determine how engaged they are in your presentation.

Analytical Style people will often be relatively quiet during phone meetings, and will often respond to your statements rather than initiate their own topics. When they do speak, they tend to discuss tasks and information related to work topics, with little discussion of people. They are formal and organized in their communications, and this is reflected in their emails. They sometimes send lengthy messages that contain all the information they think is necessary. When making specific requests, they will typically ask for your assistance rather than being more direct, and they will ask that you follow up with them.

To deal effectively with the Analytical Style customer you need to:

- Show that you will support their principles and thoughtful approach. The goal should be to show that you understand the problem without being too quick with any solution. It is also best not to try to impress them with your social skills, as this can be perceived as form over substance.

- Reinforce deliberate decisions. Analytical Style customers seek assurance their decisions are "right" and their actions can't backfire or clash with other activities. Support this need by contributing to the person's data-gathering efforts.

• Stick with specifics and deliver what you promise. The Analytical Style customer will observe your approach with the critical expectation that you will tend to oversell yourself or overstate what you can or will do. Providing detail and following through can help to counteract their expectation. Also, list the pros and cons of any suggestion or plan you make. Your awareness of the disadvantages of the product or service you sell will tend to build your credibility.

• Take the initiative to demonstrate through actions, rather than words, that you really can help, and then make a specific, organized contribution to the customer's efforts. Do something like preparing a written presentation of recommendations you would like the customer to consider.

• Keep your approach realistic and business-oriented. It should be well thought out, based on common sense, and not too flashy. The Analytical Style customer demonstrates a strong time discipline coupled with a slow pace to action. Therefore, you should allow the customer time to reflect on the situation. Be able to answer questions thoroughly.

• These individuals must be convinced that you are the right partner to meet their needs. They will look for evidence of the quality of your products and services. They also need to feel comfortable that their decisions are based on a comprehensive process, and will not respond positively to salespeople who push too hard. If you move too quickly, their slow actions may appear to be uncooperative, however that's likely due to your impatience.

• If they do not believe you can meet their needs, they may hesitate to tell you this directly. However, if directly asked for their opinions they will usually tell you what their specific concerns are.

• Avoid unnecessary disagreements; never question information presented by this customer that is not important to the success of the sales process. If you disagree over an issue of substance, consider the possibility that you have overlooked something or have not communicated your case clearly and thoroughly enough for your customer. To overcome a disagreement with this customer, be patient and make a business-like and organized presentation of your position. A well-crafted letter or follow-up email might also help.

• When speaking on the phone, do not speak too fast, but get to the point in a business-like manner. Give them time to process your requests or information, and ask if they are clear about what you have said. When leaving voice messages, do not include too many details or instructions. Although this information is important for them, when possible follow up with an email that includes more detailed information.

The following chart (see Fig. 5-1) summarizes recommendations on how to deal with customers by SOCIAL STYLE.

Analytical Style

- Be businesslike
- Be disciplined in using the available time
- Let the relationship develop slowly
- Share your process and agenda for the call
- Let them know you are not seeking a quick decision
- Maintain a slow pace
- Give them time to ask questions
- Proceed in a logical and systematic manner
- Appeal to their orientation toward principles and thinking

Driving Style

- Be businesslike and serious
- Be disciplined in using the time available
- Ask what they want to accomplish in the time available
- Keep on point to the purpose of the meeting
- Let them know you will provide them options to consider
- Don't focus on the relationship unless they initiate the discussion
- Let them know you want to help meet their goals
- Keep the pace moving to avoid creating tension

Fig. 5-1: Dealing with Customers by SOCIAL STYLE

Amiable Style	Expressive Style
• Be casual and less formal	• Be casual yet professional
• Engage in small talk	• Be stimulating in your opening to engage their creativity
• Follow their lead on how to use the time available	
• Listen to identify which relationships are important to them	• Demonstrate excitement about your product or service
• Maintain a low-key, personal, and helpful approach	• Keep the pace fast but take time for off-topic discussions
• Don't rush things unless they suggest faster action	• Reinforce their ideas and opinions
	• Be prepared to redirect the discussion if it wanders too far off track
	• Follow their lead on how to use the available time

Fig. 5-1: Dealing with Customers by SOCIAL STYLE (Cont.)

5.2 Conducting Sales Calls

Effective sales calls are critical to the success of any organization. Salespeople need to be sure to take time to carefully plan, manage, and evaluate each step of the associated processes. Sometimes, even professional sales people fail to adequately prepare for their sales calls, relying instead on their personality, past successes, and product knowledge to guide them through their calls. Too often, the ensuing result is no sale.

It is not just knowing everything you can about the customer's business needs and how your product or service can meet those needs. Knowing your customer's SOCIAL STYLE and adjusting your behaviors to facilitate your interactions are essential to achieving your sales call objective. Planning ahead will result in better organization, clarity, and productivity during the meeting. To effectively engage your customer, let their SOCIAL STYLE be your guide!

Some sales calls are made not to individuals but to purchasing committees or to a primary buyer and their support team. It may not always be possible to make each SOCIAL STYLE totally comfortable during such sales calls—this is not a reasonable expectation for any professional salesperson. However, there are some strategies you can use to strike a balance between competing SOCIAL STYLE needs and achieving the results you require.

Planning ahead is the key. Recognize and identify the SOCIAL STYLE of the different members of your customer's team, and anticipate the different types of responses, questions, and attitudes. Prepare ahead of time to respond to these individuals in a way that will satisfy them without diverting too far from your agenda and sales objective. Provide information ahead of time if this is possible, and even have one-on-one discussions or email exchanges with certain customer team members if you feel this will help.

After the sales call, be sure to follow up with your customers. By doing so, you can get valuable information about the perceived effectiveness of the call and confirm you are still on track to move the sales process to a successful close.

On the following pages we will introduce you to a number of ways to prepare for sales calls with each of the four SOCIAL STYLEs.

Driving Style

Do not schedule a sales call with a Driving Style customer unless it is absolutely necessary. These people usually prefer other means of communicating, such as telephone and email. If you schedule a face-to-face meeting that your customer doesn't feel is necessary, don't be surprised to find them impatient and rushed.

Share your sales call agenda with your customer, in advance if possible. Simultaneously, be ready to change direction if you find your customer has brought a different agenda with them to the sales call. Take a moment to get their input and renegotiate agenda items and time frames with them in a way that allows you both to achieve your objectives.

For a Driving Style customer, provide information in bullet points and data in graphics, such as charts and pie graphs. Avoid lengthy narratives that take time to read, or too many marketing graphics that don't directly support outcomes.

Due to their assertive nature, customers with this SOCIAL STYLE may try to dominate discussions and speak over you. Allowing the customer to dominate the conversation can be frustrating and will decrease the productivity of the sales call. Avoid this situation by ensuring you have agreement on the agenda and move at a suitably fast pace, especially if you have an Analytical or Amiable Style.

Driving Style people can be impatient when talking about specifics. If the sales call entails analyzing and discussing fine details, they may become difficult to deal with and may not interact with you in a meaningful way. To prevent this from happening, don't make analyzing detailed information one of the sales call objectives. Make detailed information available to these customers but don't expect them to focus on it during the sales call.

When asking these customers to do something, such as provide you information that will help you refine your sales offer, be very clear about what you need. Let this customer know you need the information in order to recommend the best options.

Driving Style people generally do not want or need you to check on them after the sales call. Keep your follow-up communication succinct and to the point. Thank them for their time; list the next steps or actions to be taken; and let them know you are available if needed.

Let these customers stay focused on their tasks and deadlines. If they promised you additional information or a decision by a certain date, don't bother them with reminders.

Finally, Driving Style customers are disciplined about time. Always confirm the time available at the beginning of your meeting. Don't expect a one hour call to last that long. Be sure to cover your key items within a shorter amount of time and start to conclude somewhat short of the allotted time. This will ensure the Driving Style person doesn't suddenly end the meeting to move on to their next agenda item.

Expressive Style

Expressive Style customers usually do not mind sales calls, though at times they can be impatient if they are feeling rushed or overwhelmed either by the sales process or by other aspects of their job. When preparing the sales call agenda, try to schedule some time that will be stimulating or personally meaningful for these individuals. This can be accomplished by giving them time to share about themselves (a form of personal recognition), or even through the use of humor.

Plan to engage in lively sales conversations with these individuals as they are vocal and will want to interact with you. Never ask them to wait to the end of your sales presentation to ask questions. Instead, ask them questions and invite them to interact with you from the start; this will help to get them engaged and focused.

For an Expressive Style customer, provide supporting information and materials that have a visual and exciting impact through images and colorful descriptions of your product or service. Materials with testimonials and personal endorsements of your solution are usually highly appreciated by these customers.

If this customer seems insistent on redirecting the sales conversation to other topics, be flexible. Allow them to express themselves and allow them to momentarily wander off the path. Then, gently guide them back to the agenda.

If these individuals feel disengaged or ignored during sales calls, they may become bored. Rather than sitting and listening quietly, they are likely to become agitated. Due to their assertive natures, they may behave in disruptive ways by interrupting you, using sarcastic humor, or otherwise attempting to focus attention on their dissatisfaction with the sales call. This can be frustrating and can decrease the productivity of the sales call. To avoid this situation, move at a faster pace and keep them involved in the sales conversation. Look for hints in your past communications with this person to identify what is exciting and innovative to them, and be prepared to reinforce how your solution can help them achieve their dreams and aspirations.

By agreeing to a general agenda in advance, you can neutralize the potential for counterproductive behavior. Remember their unruly behavior may be a mechanism to insert themselves into the sales conversation if they are feeling left out. Help them get back to a more productive state by appealing to their spontaneity. Ask questions, such as how they feel about the feature or benefit you are discussing. In short, find a way to engage them in the sales conversation.

Expressive Style people are sometimes disorganized in their approach. They are often impatient with details and lengthy discussions about single topics. Keep them enthusiastic and motivated by building on their ideas even if it means temporarily straying from the agenda.

Don't make reviewing or analyzing detailed information one of the sales call objectives. Make detailed information available to these customers but don't make them suffer through it in a sales call. Remember, these customers prefer to see the big picture and to be inspired by how they can make things better in the future.

For the sake of developing a good, long-term relationship, make sure they have practical expectations of what your product or service can provide. Be prepared to show enthusiasm for what your solution can do for this person as well as their organization and let the customer know about well-known individuals or organizations that use your solutions.

Because Expressive Style customers can be less organized than other SOCIAL STYLEs, and because this customer prefers not to deal with details, they generally appreciate it if you take care of the details and manage the process. Provide a summary email that recaps what was covered in the sales call, agreements made, and the next steps in the sales process.

Be friendly in your follow-up communication with this customer. Thank them very much for their time. Be sure to gently remind them of any next step or action they need to take and to let them know you'll check in with them at a specific date in the future. They will generally welcome a follow-up, as long as you don't come across as overly demanding. Recognize their less-disciplined use of time and be patient with them.

Amiable Style

Amiable Style customers actually enjoy sales calls because such meetings give them an opportunity to interact with others. They enjoy mixing casual conversation with business topics; however, this does not mean that they like to waste time. They use the casual conversation as a way of establishing personal relationships, which they inherently value.

When planning the sales call agenda for these customers, if possible, try to include additional time. This may be necessary to account for casual, off-topic discussions. Interacting with others is important to them and will help them be more comfortable with you and more receptive to your sales message.

Before the sales call, if possible, try to anticipate and consider the various issues, concerns, or viewpoints these customers might have. Be prepared to discuss these issues, and be ready to bring them up in the event the customers themselves do not raise them. This is an effective strategy for involving these customers who by nature are less talkative and more hesitant to confront you with their concerns.

For an Amiable Style customer, provide material emphasizing how your solution helps people and their problems. If possible, provide recommendations from other customers. Avoid giving too much information about facts and details, such as overly technical specifications; let this customer know the additional information is at their disposal as the sales process progresses.

Don't expect this customer to make on-the-spot decisions. They like to get the opinions of others and ensure their key relationships will support their decisions.

Because Amiable Style people are naturally cooperative, it can be difficult to recognize when they are frustrated or disengaged from you during the sales call. Some signs this may be the case include them being quieter than usual or making terse or critical statements. In addition, their personal tension can be reflected in their facial expressions and body language. To avoid disengagement, allow the conversation to stray from the agreed-upon agenda. Occasionally ask this customer for their opinion about the topic at hand or some feature of your product or service.

A particularly effective method for keeping these customers engaged in the sales call is to help them to be active contributors and to communicate what is on their mind. This may mean helping them feel safe in stating their concerns or disagreements if they don't seem fully committed to a course of action. Since these individuals are generally noncompetitive, you may need to explicitly ask for their input rather than assume they agree.

Amiable Style customers generally prefer sales calls proceed at a casual pace. Avoid rushing through your sales presentation. Take the time to engage this customer throughout the process and make sure they are comfortable with you and the process.

This customer can seem too agreeable. Be sure to ask questions that uncover their unexpressed feelings and that may later emerge as roadblocks to advancing the sale.

This customer likes to interact with others, so they will likely be less resistant to a sales call with you than other SOCIAL STYLEs; however, their readiness to meet face-to-face with you does not necessarily mean they are ready to buy from you.

Some SOCIAL STYLEs prefer to know their options and the

implications of each. Not so with the Amiable Style. With this customer, provide a specific recommendation you believe offers the best option for them personally. If they need to share your recommendation with others whose opinions they value, don't automatically assume they are stalling or indirectly rejecting your proposal. Getting the input of others is one way this SOCIAL STYLE lowers risk, and thereby gives them permission to move forward.

Because they inherently value relationships, Amiable Style customers will likely want to maintain their business relationship with you, even if they are not interested in buying from you. As a professional salesperson, it can be valuable for you to ask these people for their feedback about sales calls. As long as they trust you, they will give their opinions, and this information can provide insight into how to improve future sales calls with them and others.

Be warm and friendly in your follow-up communication with this customer. Thank them very much for their time. Keep in mind these individuals are motivated by verbal praise, as long as it is sincere. Let them know you'll be checking in with them in the future. They will likely welcome your follow-up as long as you don't come across as being too aggressive.

If you are expecting customers with this SOCIAL STYLE to take some action necessary to move the sale forward after the sales call, keep in mind their less-disciplined use of time and be patient with how their SOCIAL STYLE behaviors can prolong the sales process.

Analytical Style

A good agenda with both adequate detail and timing goes a long way for Analytical Style customers. They tend to focus on time and want to know what the priorities are for a given sales call, so make this clear on the agenda. Try to anticipate their concerns or points of view beforehand so you will be prepared to respond to them during the sales call.

These customers want sales calls to be focused. When planning the sales call, make sure you come prepared with necessary materials and information; otherwise these individuals may feel their time is being wasted and the sales call should be rescheduled.

Be business-like as you move through the agenda at a deliberate pace. At all times, keep in mind this customer is interested in making the right decision and will use the facts and details you provide in making up their mind. Avoid statements that might be interpreted as exaggerations; be as logical and accurate as possible.

These customers can become frustrated if they feel you are wasting time, you are not adequately focused on important matters, or when you try to rely on your personality more than facts and data. When this occurs, they might withdraw and withhold their active involvement in the sales conversation. However, if they feel strongly about a matter, they will share their discontent. They may stubbornly make their points and become entrenched. If this customer seems to withdraw from the sales conversation, make sure you don't move too fast or skip information they feel is important. Explicitly ask for their opinions, since they might otherwise hesitate to state their concerns in a sales call.

Analytical Style customers generally prefer sales calls proceed at a slow to moderate pace. Avoid rushing through your sales presentation. Take the time to engage this customer throughout the process by asking them what their thoughts are as you move through the agenda and allow for enough time to answer detailed questions.

For an Analytical Style customer, provide materials containing facts, full explanations, research data, and graphics such as charts and pie graphs. Avoid relying on marketing materials that don't provide meaningful information to them. Add case examples that realistically show how your solution helped others who have experienced similar business problems. Avoid personal stories meant to have an emotional impact.

Analytical Style customers can be very deliberate and methodical. This affects how they discuss issues during sales calls and ultimately how they make the purchase decision. They can be slow to agree with your assertions and recommendations. When possible, provide them with relevant information well ahead of the sales call. This will give them a chance to review the information in advance and help satisfy their need for supporting details.

Analytical Style people generally do not want or need you to check on them unnecessarily. Keep your follow-up communication with them succinct and to the point. If you have promised to provide them additional information or to take some action after the sales call, do so expeditiously. This will help reassure them of your competence, a trait they highly value in business relationships.

If this customer promised you additional information or to take some action (such as make a decision) by a certain date, let them stay focused on their tasks and deadlines. Keep in mind, however, that even though they are more disciplined about time, they tend to be slower paced, which means that unnecessary reminders may be seen as annoying interruptions. Also, since they don't need strong personal connections in their business relationships, they might prefer if you check with them through email rather than in person or by phone.

The following graph (see Fig. 5-2) summarizes recommendations on how to conduct sales calls by SOCIAL STYLE.

Analytical Style

- Take your time to prepare and organize well to be accurate and precise
- Present relevant information (facts, timeframes, and data)
- Don't rely on testimonials or opinions to make your strongest points
- Present both the pros and cons of your idea to help establish (or maintain) credibility
- Approach the situation as though accepting your idea/action was the next logical step in the process
- If the Analytical Style person seems hesitant or reluctant, ask, "Do you have enough information?"

Driving Style

- Be direct; use your time to be efficient and keep your case short and to the point
- Focus on what will be accomplished by going along with your idea/action
- Provide facts and logic as support, but keep your main points simple. Have the details ready, but don't present them unless requested.
- Look for opportunities to give the Driving Style person choices in how to support you
- To gain commitment, give choices by asking questions like, "Which one do you think is best?"
- Don't beat around the bush and don't be afraid to ask for a decision

Fig. 5-2: Conducting Sales Calls by SOCIAL STYLE

Amiable Style	Expressive Style
• Use a less direct approach, one that does not take on the appearance of confrontation • Take time to be agreeable by presenting your ideas in a less formal, more personal way • Focus on providing assurances that a decision to go along with your ideas/actions is relatively safe • Ask if your idea is acceptable to others who are important to your customer • If the Amiable Style customer seems hesitant, ask, "What other things should we talk about?" • When an Amiable Style customer reaches a decision, "double confirm" to assure that this customer is not just saying "Yes" (acquiescing) just to appease you	• Use your time to be stimulating by presenting the "big picture" of your idea (avoid excessive detail) • Refer to respected others who agree with your idea • Be inspiring, but don't try to outshine this customer • Explain how your idea/action might personally benefit this customer in the future • Press for a decision, but let the Expressive Style customer make it • When you get a commitment, follow up with an e-mail or other reminder of the details • Do what you said you will do in a timely manner

Fig. 5-2: Conducting Sales Calls by SOCIAL STYLE (Cont.)

5.3 Asking Productive Questions

By asking questions in a SOCIAL STYLE-appropriate way, you increase the likelihood of getting information to better position your solution in a way that precisely meets your customers' needs. Asking effective questions requires preparation. Inadequate preparation forces you to ask general questions, which typically yield less useful information. To obtain the information you need, ask questions appropriate for the SOCIAL STYLE needs of the customer. Take into account their SOCIAL STYLE's typical actions toward others, use of time, and approach to decision-making.

People generally do not like answering questions that move them out of their SOCIAL STYLE's comfort zone. To elicit useful information for framing your sales proposal, avoid potentially uncomfortable questions.

The following questioning techniques typically work well with each SOCIAL STYLE.

Driving Style

Get right to the point; do not spend much time on small talk before asking your questions. Review the purpose of the meeting, ask them for any adjustments needed, and then proceed to your questions. In fact, avoid potential time-wasters such as engaging in idle, casual conversation unless this customer initiates it. Ask questions about milestones and timelines to demonstrate that you understand the importance of meeting expectations.

The fact that Driving Style people do not always listen attentively should not be a problem during a fact-finding session. Just be sure to ask open-ended questions so the customer does most of the talking and you do most of the listening. Because they like to maintain control, they will generally be amenable to this approach, which allows them to dominate the discussion.

In general, ask Driving Style customers questions about what results they need to achieve. Their answer(s) will be a central part of later convincing them why they should accept your solution as you explain how your product or service can help them to achieve those goals.

Ask these customers questions specific to their business needs. Good preparation can usually provide questions to get the conversation started, but you will need to listen carefully to their responses to ask appropriate follow-up questions. With this person, you may need to follow up by asking the customer to elaborate on their answer, as they tend to answer questions concisely. Also, because they focus on outcomes rather than processes, you may need to ask additional questions about "how" and "who" to get the process information you need.

Because of their competitive nature, feel free to ask questions about their organization's competition. As appropriate, use this information to frame your sales offer and explain how you can help them beat the competition.

Avoid questions with strong emotional overtones, such as how they feel or how others feel about the business issues at hand. Driving Style people prefer to deal in facts and data, not opinions and feelings. Along the same lines, avoid overly abstract or vague questions. Also, avoid asking the same question in different ways. They do not want to tread the same ground twice and will feel you are wasting their time if each question does not advance the conversation.

Driving Style customers are interested in the here and now. Consequently, avoid asking hypothetical questions about the long term or other circumstances where there are too many unknown variables. Also avoid asking complex, multi-part questions, or questions that require highly detailed answers. While these customers will consider details when they must, they are more interested in talking about the implications and outcomes of facts than about the facts themselves.

Driving Style customers can be especially sensitive to questions about underperformance of parts of their business over which they have some control and to questions about loss of ground or market position against the competition. Asking potentially sensitive, probing questions involves sticking with specifics, being direct, and steering clear of discussions about personalities or dysfunctional working relationships that might have contributed to the problem.

Above all, let these customers feel they have some control over the interaction with you. Expect some direct questions in return but be ready to move on to less-sensitive topics as soon as you have the information you need. Rather than asking leading questions, use open-ended questions that allow them to answer in the way they prefer. Avoid closed-ended questions that can be answered with a simple "yes" or "no" response, or this customer is likely to respond in a few words and expect you to move on.

Expressive Style

Do not begin by asking Expressive Style customers your business-related questions. While these customers like to talk, they also value friendliness and your personal enthusiasm. Take time to engage in some cheerful conversation before getting down to business.

Since these customers often like to diverge from the agenda, be sure to allow enough time for them to take a break from the Q&A to talk about what they want to talk about. Be sociable and support their ideas, if appropriate, and then discreetly steer them back to your questions. Be ready to ask your questions out of order (if you have made a list of questions), since they prefer spontaneity to rigid approaches.

These people like to talk, and their typical failure to check their behavior should not be a problem during a fact-finding session. In fact, they may tell you more than you need to know to put together an effective sales proposal. Asking close-ended questions can be okay since this customer is likely to expand on their answers without being prompted to elaborate.

Because they prefer to take the big picture view of most things, including business problems or situations, get the discovery portion of your conversation started by asking broad questions. These customers will be comfortable speaking in generalities. Listen carefully to their responses and ask follow-up questions, even if you have a well-structured question list to work from.

Ask questions about their hopes and desires regarding their business. Ask how they would like to see things in the future rather than about what factors in the past contributed to the current situation. Their answer(s) will be a central part of later convincing them why they should accept your sales offer. You'll paint a picture that demonstrates how your product or service can help them fulfill those aspirations.

Ask questions that concern their personal role in the business. Because this customer tends to be concerned with personal approval more than others, ask how this person is recognized and rewarded within the business and then identify ways that your product or service can contribute to that reward and recognition.

To get the information you need, you may need to follow up, as they prefer not to deal in details and can easily answer questions at length without ever getting down to specifics. Because they tend to be competitive, feel free to ask questions about their competition. As appropriate, use this information in framing your sales offer to help them triumph over the competition.

Ask for their opinion. While they will consider facts and data when they must, they are more interested in sharing their views and attitudes. For example, you might ask for their opinion about which of the unique benefits of your product or service they find most meaningful.

Avoid asking complex, multi-part questions or questions that require precise, detailed answers. If you require this kind of information to develop an effective sales proposal, ask them to provide you with resources or an introduction to others in the company who might be able to provide the needed information. Also, avoid asking questions in a cut-and-dried manner that suggests you lack enthusiasm or are not personally concerned with this customer's business problem. Instead, be warm and communicative and let this customer know you care. Tell this person what you can and will do to support them.

Sticking to a tightly structured list of questions may stifle this customer's creativity and their need to digress at will from an agenda. If they feel you are there just to get the facts, they will see you as uninterested in supporting them and their ideas.

Avoid questions that focus on the past when a question about the future will elicit the same information. For example, instead of asking how factors in the past have contributed to current business issues, ask how this customer would like to see the business operate in the future.

Expressive Style customers can be especially sensitive to questions they feel are personally challenging or threatening. Such may be the case if they perceive your product or service may not provide any advantages for them personally. Probe to uncover the aspirations of these customers related to your product or service.

Because this customer seems to look for attention and stimulation, be aware they could take control of the conversation and move it in the wrong direction, especially if you broach uncomfortable topics.

Try to stay on target and do not probe further once you get adequate information, as this might lead to the customer expecting more than you can deliver.

Do not allow the session to become tedious or boring by asking too many questions. Closed-ended questions and clarifications are good approaches for returning to the purpose of the sales call if their spontaneity takes them too far off the topic.

Amiable Style

Do not begin by asking an Amiable Style customer questions. While they enjoy interacting with others, they also value friendliness and interpersonal relationships. Take time to engage in casual, friendly conversation before getting down to business. When you do move on to asking questions, continue to be sociable and agreeable or they may interpret your original friendliness as being insincere.

Move slowly through your questions and take time to relate to this customer. When your questions feel like a casual conversation, the information you elicit will be better. Along the same lines, since they prefer to move at a slower pace, be sure to schedule enough time to ask your questions and have an unhurried conversation.

While agendas are always useful, you should be ready to ask your probing questions based on the natural flow of the conversation. The fact that customers with this SOCIAL STYLE like to interact with others can make getting information from them a pleasant experience; however, they do not like to initiate actions or take firm stances. Consequently, do not expect them to take strong positions that you can easily work into your sales proposal.

If this customer has not clearly defined their business needs, simply ask how you can help. Since these customers prefer collaboration and a team approach, ask questions that demonstrate you are on their team. Ask questions about people they consider important to the decision process or who might benefit from your product or service. Their answer(s) will be a central part of later convincing them why they should accept your solution as you paint a picture of how your specific product or service can help them to play a role in helping others.

Ask for their opinion about the business problem that your product or service addresses. While they will consider facts and data when they must, they are more interested in sharing their personal views and feelings about the problem. Also, ask in an indirect way whose counsel they need to seek before deciding to buy. Remember, Amiable Style customers will often want to obtain a consensus from people with whom they have close working relationships before proceeding.

Because this customer tends to focus on people and relationships, you may need to ask specific "what" and "when" questions to get information about outcomes you will need to develop the strongest sales proposal.

Avoid asking your question in a rigid or too business-like way. It is critical to establish rapport with Amiable Style customers, so avoid getting down to business too quickly. If you come across as too business-like, this customer may feel you are indifferent toward them. Take time to be personable.

Avoid asking too many questions or pressing for an answer. In other words, be very careful the conversation does not come across like a prosecutor's cross-examination. Also, avoid asking questions that require highly detailed answers. While they can deal with details when they must, they are generally much more comfortable providing you with access to written resources or referring you to others who might have the information you seek.

Avoid coming across as overly controlling by failing to ask

thoughtful follow-up questions, or by disallowing them to be flexible in their use of time. These customers like to interact one-on-one, as peers. The more you take control of the Q&A session, the more resistant they will be to giving you the answers you need to develop a winning sales proposal.

Amiable Style customers can be especially sensitive to questions they feel are threatening to their personal security. For example, if buying your product or service might impact their current relationships, do not assume this will be acceptable to them. Probe with patience in a casual, personal manner.

Unless the customer trusts and feels comfortable with you, they may be reluctant to let you know that you have hit upon a sensitive area. When this happens, these customers may still act cordial toward you; however, they will be less forthcoming in their answers. They will hide how they really feel, but they will most likely let their peers know after you leave.

Analytical Style

Explain the purpose of the "question and answer" conversation and the process you plan to use during this part of the sales conversation. Working from written questions or an agenda is quite acceptable to the Analytical Style customer. In fact, if appropriate, provide your basic list of questions in advance to give them the time to think about their responses.

It is okay to get right to the point and avoid spending a lot of time on small talk or warming up. In fact, avoid coming across as too personable and avoid too much casual conversation. They don't make decisions based on a personal relationship as much as the details they see as relevant to their issue. Encourage a two-way dialogue by letting the customer know you are interested in fully understanding his or her needs, and that you are willing to give information as well as ask for it.

Avoid appearing too casual in your approach to asking questions. Once you have laid the groundwork for the conversation, you can move directly into asking questions. If you come across as too sociable or too friendly, this customer may conclude that you are not sufficiently serious or business-like.

Analytical Style customers can be especially sensitive to responding to questions where they are not certain of the correct answer. When probing areas where this customer may have only part of the answer to your question, phrase your question in a way that gives them room for uncertainty. They will be much more comfortable in answering such questions when they are prefaced with phrases such as "all else being equal…" or "for the most part…" or "generally speaking…".

Use your questioning time with this customer efficiently but proceed at a moderate pace. Be logical and business-like and be sure to ask questions in a logical order. Since these customers value organization, you might lose credibility if you come across as asking questions in a random order.

The fact that people with this SOCIAL STYLE like to be right and often have difficulty in coming to a quick decision should not be a problem during a fact-finding session. Just be sure to ask specific questions so the customer does most of the talking and you do most of the listening. Because customers with this SOCIAL STYLE are generally uncommunicative, be prepared to ask follow-up questions and to elaborate or provide examples to their initial responses.

In general, ask Analytical Style customers questions that support principles regarding the business problem your product or service addresses. Good preparation can usually provide questions to get the conversation started, but you will need to listen carefully to their responses to ask appropriate follow-up questions. Focus on facts and details rather than personal opinions or feelings. Answers to these questions will likely be a central part of later convincing them why they should accept your sales offer as opposed to other alternatives.

This customer tends to focus on facts and processes rather than on outcomes or the people involved. You may need to ask additional questions about goals and objectives and the people involved to get the information you need to develop the strongest sales proposal.

Ask questions about past records and experience related to the problem your product or service addresses as such things are likely to factor into their decision-making process. Also, ask these customers if they have any questions about the facts and evidence you have provided in advance.

Avoid coming across as needing immediate answers to your questions. This customer prefers to move at a slower pace and needs time to think. In some cases, that may mean scheduling a follow-up meeting. As these people like to deal in facts, try to avoid overly abstract, vague, or hypothetical questions.

The following chart (see Fig. 5-3) summarizes recommendations on how to ask productive questions by SOCIAL STYLE.

Analytical Style

- Take time to ask questions

- Encourage a two-way conversation; give the customer a chance to question you

- Be prepared to answer questions in a specific, accurate, and organized manner

- If you don't have the information, commit to getting it to them and then do it

- Listen to their questions for hints about what is important to this person

- Don't make statements about your solutions that are overly general —accuracy is best

- Present your questions in a logical sequence

Driving Style

- Make the points about your solution in a simple, direct, and efficient manner

- Don't overdo your questions so that it feels like an interrogation

- Expect direct and specific questions

- Let the customer feel they have some control over the discussion

- Be aware of the time

- Begin with open questions that enable the customer to set the direction of the discussion

- Avoid too many questions that can be answered by a yes or no

Fig. 5-3: Asking Productive Questions by SOCIAL STYLE

Amiable Style	Expressive Style
• Avoid using too many closed questions that could cause the customer to feel interrogated • Ask general questions that encourage the customer to talk • Listen for hints about key relationships that are important to the customer • Avoid being too formal and data-oriented with the customer • Recognize the importance they place on feelings and relationships • Be on the lookout for behavior that might indicate the customer is acquiescing rather than agreeing with your comments • Don't promise more than you can deliver	• Start with general questions that encourage the customer to talk • Allow some time for sharing personal topics • If the conversation wanders too far off-topic, use closed questions to return the customer to the purpose of the call • Reinforce the customer's favorable responses about needs that your product or service can meet • Let the customer know about well-known individuals or organizations that use your solutions • Look for hints about what is exciting and innovative to your customer and reinforce how your solutions can help them achieve their dreams and aspirations

Fig. 5-3: Asking Productive Questions by SOCIAL STYLE (Cont.)

5.4 Recognizing Customer Attitudes

Your customer's attitude can have a direct impact on your ability to successfully achieve your sales objective. Early in the sales process, the customer may be indifferent to you, your solution, or your company. Or they might be skeptical of you and your ability to deliver what you promise. Recognizing customer attitudes and adjusting your SOCIAL STYLE behaviors throughout the sales process can give you the competitive advantage needed to win the sale.

Having a great offer is not necessarily enough to make a sale. From prospecting to closing, if customers don't like the way you interact with them, they can put an end to the sales process. To avoid this, you must continuously work to gain acceptance for you and your solution. In addition, customers are not always enthusiastic about buying, even if they have a need for what you are selling. In fact, sometimes they are indifferent to you and what you have to offer. To manage such situations, it is important to recognize when indifference is the problem.

In an ideal situation, the customer maintains an attitude of acceptance throughout the sales process. But such an ideal is rarely encountered. As a professional salesperson, you are more likely to face customer attitudes of indifference and resistance. In fact, during a single sales call, the same customer may frequently move in and out of the attitudes of indifference, resistance, and acceptance. Ultimately, the goal of a salesperson is to overcome indifference and resistance and turn that acceptance into a commitment to do business with you.

You can predict fairly accurately how a customer will display resistance and indifference based on what you know about the individual's SOCIAL STYLE. In general, when customers begin to show resistance, they edge toward their SOCIAL STYLE's Backup

Behavior. As the salesperson, your goal is to prevent the customer from going completely into Backup by adjusting your behavior or asking a question, so you can get the sales process back on track with the customer. If you wait until the customer is in full Backup mode, it's too late—your rapport is gone.

Another caveat: if the customer has a legitimate objection to your product, or truly has no interest or no need, the ideas outlined here can't change that. These ideas help you recognize how different SOCIAL STYLEs express indifference and resistance differently, which will make you more aware of these attitudes.

The following pages lay out how to identify indifference and resistance and how to channel those reactions into a more productive conversation to get your sale back on track.

Driving Style

The Driving Style customer is naturally less communicative with others, so don't automatically assume that lack of communication means indifference. This person may show indifference by not making time for you through actions like allowing your call to divert to voicemail or failing to reply to your email or text message. If this person takes the time to reply, their responses will typically be short with few overt clues as to why they don't care about your solution.

In conversations, this customer's indifference is often displayed with words meant to cut off the sales process and allow them to move on to other tasks such as, "Not a priority right now," or "No need." To overcome indifference, have direct conversations with pointed questions: "Why do you feel...?" "Why hasn't it worked in the past?" Don't be afraid to request more information or ask questions that challenge what the person is trying to achieve: "So what you're saying is...".

Skepticism can arise at any time in the sales process, so look for signs that a Driving Style customer is acting even more rushed than usual. These people can be dismissive and try to usher you out the door with a phrase like, "I appreciate you coming by today." They can also be very direct with their rejection ("This isn't going to work."). This allows you to be direct in return; ask specific questions about areas where this customer seems to be skeptical.

Signs that a Driving Style person has accepted your proposal include taking control of the conversation with very direct questions ("How much is it? When can we implement?") about next steps.

Occasionally, you will run across a Driving Style customer who is unhappy with you or your company. In such situations, it may become impossible to proceed with the sales process until the situation is resolved. As tensions rise, customers with this SOCIAL STYLE become more autocratic. These customers will not hesitate to tell you there is a problem. They will be direct and, potentially, verbally confrontational. Because they feel a need to be in control, they are likely to dominate the conversation, at least initially, and will want to say what is on their mind before giving you a chance to speak.

If they are very upset, Driving Style customers tend to raise their voices. Though they don't often use their hands when talking, in such circumstances they may point fingers or tap on tables when making their arguments. People with Driving Style respect others who stand up to them, particularly when the process results in achieving specific objectives. To help them get past their unhappiness, work with Driving Style customers to identify a particular action you can take to get results.

There is a sales story about a new salesperson who called on a large prospect for the first time. As soon as the salesperson entered the office, the customer began a tirade against the salesperson's company, their former sales representative, and the company's product and service. The new salesperson calmly used active listening skills and paraphrased the comments back to the customer. "So as I understand it, you really disliked the representative who called on you in the past, you think my company is terrible, and that our products and services are worthless, is that correct?" The customer replied with an emphatic "Yes!" The salesperson looked directly at the customer and said, "Great, now that I understand all your concerns, are there any other reasons we can't do business together?" This story is a humorous example of how you can use Versatility skills to get a Driving Style back to a position of engagement and willingness to consider your solutions.

Expressive Style

An Expressive Style customer is naturally communicative. Don't assume they want to buy from you because they want to talk to you. Unlike other SOCIAL STYLEs, people with this SOCIAL STYLE are likely to verbalize their indifference. This customer may display their indifference by avoiding the sales discussion in favor of topics of more interest to them personally.

If you suspect indifference is the problem, show this customer how your solution promotes or advances this person's vision of how things should be. Bring them back to the main topic; summarize for them and refocus ("Is there something we could do that would work better?"). Brainstorm and involve them in finding a better path forward.

When skeptical, these customers may try to make excuses for not moving forward ("We have other priorities right now"). They may also want you to think they do not have authority over the situation. They may be sympathetic to you and blame others or their organization ("We don't have the budget right now"). They have a need to look good personally, so they may shirk responsibility for their own skepticism. Look for signs such as arriving exceptionally late for meetings, moving at an even faster pace than usual, or cutting the sales meeting short.

It can be difficult to tell whether an Expressive Style person has accepted your proposal. They might require a lengthy engagement with you without formal commitment. They may have accepted the proposal if they personalize it and share it with others in the organization. Having the Expressive Style customer make your sale to others is a good sign.

Occasionally, you will run across an Expressive Style customer who is unhappy with you or your company. As tensions rise, customers with this SOCIAL STYLE will verbally attack. They will be blunt and possibly personal in their attack. In some cases, they can come across as irrational and will bring up issues unrelated to the current sales situation. When on the attack, their frustration will be clear from their facial expressions, animated gestures, and lean-forward body posture. They will be louder than usual with a sharp tone of voice, sometimes making an uncomfortable scene for everyone present.

Rather than confronting them directly, which will likely add to their tension, allow the customer to vent their frustration. Then, let them know that you understand their concerns, and help them to separate what happened originally to make them unhappy from the current sales situation. Share your feelings and beliefs in a straightforward but non-confrontational way. The sales story from the Driving Style also applies here as you bring Versatility to bear with a Tell Assertive SOCIAL STYLE.

Amiable Style

Amiable Style customers are oriented toward relationships; don't assume they are interested in buying from you because they treat you with friendliness. They often display indifference by treating others very nicely but dismissively. They may thank you for your efforts, ("It's been a pleasure meeting with you. Let's stay in touch.") or mitigate their personal authority by deferring to others, ("I'm not the right person to talk to."). In this case, bring them back to a state of engagement by helping them relate your solutions to the issue at hand. In a very concrete way, show how your solution helps and how it may impact other stakeholders, specifically how it may improve things for people in the organization. Generally, treat these individuals cautiously and with concern, and avoid confrontation.

Amiable Style people are less direct, so it can be hard to realize they are skeptical. If you are feeling discomfort from them, you may have to give them the words in order to make it safe for them to disclose. For example, you can say, "You seem uncomfortable with this. Am I not meeting your needs in some way?" By making it safe you open them up to share more information. This allows them to express their concerns without feeling like they're damaging the relationship.

Amiable Style people will outwardly display comfort with you when they accept your proposal. This can indicate they trust you. For example, these customers may confide in you and seek your counsel. ("I'm leaning toward you. What advice do you have for next steps?"). They may also express the need to check with others before offering a final commitment.

To enhance commitment with an Amiable Style customer, show visible concern for the customer's business problem and how it affects people. The best approach is to meet in person so you can grow the relationship.

Occasionally, you will run across an Amiable Style customer who is unhappy with you or your company. In such a situation, it becomes impossible to move on with the sales process as intended. As these tensions start to rise, customers with this SOCIAL STYLE will acquiesce to reduce personal tension. At this point, you may be able to close the sale, but by doing so you run the risk of destroying any chance for a long-term business relationship.

When an Amiable Style customer is unhappy, it may not be obvious to all. This is because these individuals often react by keeping their opinions to themselves. To help reduce their tension, openly discuss matters with them in a non-confrontational and conversational manner. Show an understanding for their concerns. Emphasize that disagreements on business issues do not necessarily indicate deteriorating personal relationships. Let your Amiable Style customers know your relationship with them is okay, which will assist them in meeting their need for personal security. Your purpose here is to help the Amiable Style individual to feel safe in proceeding with the sales process.

Analytical Style

Similar to the Driving Style, an Analytical Style customer is naturally less communicative with others, so don't interpret a lack of communication to mean indifference or objection. Typical signs of indifference of Analytical Style people include challenging statements about the usefulness of services, or questioning the evidence to back up your claims. They might also stop asking for information. In this case they are no longer engaged in your proposal, and they can be distant and even uncooperative. Because this SOCIAL STYLE has more disciplined use of time, they might not give you sufficient time to meet with them.

To manage an Analytical Style customer's indifference, make sure you have provided sufficient facts and that you have taken appropriate action to reduce the personal risk associated with engaging with you. Ask them specific, closed-ended questions and rephrase the information they give you ("What you're saying is..." Are you interested in...?"). This will help them reveal more information.

Skepticism can arise at any time in the sales process, so look for signs an Analytical customer is acting even more uncommunicative than usual. When skeptical, Analytical Style customers will often show dismissiveness by stating they have everything they need to make a decision, while subtly telling you not to follow up ("I think I have everything I need. I'll call you."). If this customer's skepticism is growing, they may become increasingly less cooperative and more distant. To overcome, provide back-up information (tables, charts, reports, white papers, etc.) and be patient. This customer's skepticism may dissipate as they ponder the details you have provided.

Once Analytical Style people have accepted a proposal, they will want to move forward. They will begin to discuss procedures and next steps in detail. When they accept a proposal, they will typically shift the types of questions they ask. They may stop asking questions related to details of the proposal and begin asking questions about implementation, strategy, and so forth.

In situations where an Analytical Style customer is unhappy with you or your company, it may become necessary to resolve the situation first before continuing with the sales process. As these tensions rise, customers with this SOCIAL STYLE will withdraw from the sales process. They will not always verbally express there is a problem, but they will show signs of tension and unhappiness by slowing down the process or avoiding speaking with you. While in the heat of a sales negotiation, they are likely to avoid eye contact and display less facial expressiveness and emotion than normal. They may even talk more slowly and lower their voices more than normal when talking about the source of their unhappiness.

To reduce the tension and to get the sales process back on track, affirm for the Analytical Style that you, too, want things done right. Then take the time to discuss the details. Your purpose here is to help the Analytical Style customer become comfortable with the sales process, if not the people, so you can bring the sale to a successful close.

The following chart (see Fig. 5-4) summarizes recommendations on how to deal with indifferent customer attitudes by SOCIAL STYLE.

Analytical Style	Driving Style
• *RECOGNIZE:* The Analytical Style customer may display indifference by asking questions out of curiosity or to collect information, but make no move toward any kind of decision. The customer may remain cooperative, but will tend to show very formal and controlled behavior. This indifferent customer will tend to offer you little or no information to respond to. • *SOLVE:* Probe in a way that will encourage the customer to tell you more. For example: "If I understand you correctly, your current provider has always delivered an acceptable quality level, is that right?"	• *RECOGNIZE:* The Driving Style customer may display indifference by giving you little or no feedback, not listening, or attending to other matters. • *SOLVE:* Probe for the cause of this attitude, using what you know about the Driving Style individual's Style preferences. For example: "Are you concerned about any fall off in productivity if you switch providers?"

Fig. 5-4: Recognizing Customer Indifference by SOCIAL STYLE

Amiable Style

- *RECOGNIZE:* The Amiable Style customer may display indifference by remaining friendly, but asking only "polite" questions about your product or service or wandering off the topic of the sales call. The customer might make statements like, "I just don't know at this time," "I'm not sure right now," or "Maybe later."

- *SOLVE:* Probe to find out more. For example: "What could your current provider do for you that would make your job easier?"

Expressive Style

- *RECOGNIZE:* The Expressive Style customer may display indifference by becoming undisciplined in the use of time. That is, the customer might keep the conversation going, but refuse to stay on the point of the call. Often, too, the Expressive Style customer will simply say he or she is indifferent.

- *SOLVE:* Probe to find out the source of the indifference. For example: "If you could improve your present solution in any way, what would you do?"

Fig. 5-4: Recognizing Customer Indifference by SOCIAL STYLE (Cont.)

CUSTOMER RELATIONSHIPS

The following chart (see Fig. 5-5) summarizes recommendations on how to react to signs of resistance with customers by SOCIAL STYLE.

Analytical Style

- **RECOGNIZE:** The Analytical Style customer might display resistance by stating objections in the form of questions that are difficult to answer or by offering you little or no feedback. They may challenge your research or product specifications. This customer might show very stiff or formal body movements and voice inflections. In general, the resistance is displayed by less assertive and more controlled behaviors, moving toward the Backup Behavior of avoidance.

- **SOLVE:** Probe appropriately to uncover the source of resistance. For example: "That is an interesting question; what would that information resolve for you?"

Driving Style

- **RECOGNIZE:** The Driving Style customer might display resistance by openly stating his or her objection, becoming impatient, or attempting to take charge of or conclude the sales conversation. In general, resistance is displayed by more assertive and more controlled behaviors, moving toward the Backup Behavior of becoming autocratic.

- **SOLVE:** Probe to isolate the specific problem. Phrase your probing questions to relate to the Driving Style's actions toward others, best use of time, and customized approach to decision making. For example: "We've been covering a lot of details about our solution for the past few minutes. Do you want more or should we move on?"

Fig. 5-5: Recognizing Customer Resistance by SOCIAL STYLE

Amiable Style

- **RECOGNIZE:** The Amiable Style customer might display resistance by postponing a decision, expressing doubt or uncertainty in a questioning way, or explaining that he or she wants to talk with someone else about your proposal. In general, the resistance will be displayed by less assertive and more emoting behaviors, moving toward the Backup Behavior of acquiescence (but not commitment).

- **SOLVE:** Probe to uncover the source of resistance in a way that is appropriate to the Amiable Style's preferred action toward others, best use of time, and customized approach to decision making. For example: "Do you have concerns about your colleagues' reactions if you make a decision about using our solution?"

Expressive Style

- **RECOGNIZE:** The Expressive Style customer might display resistance by openly stating what he or she does not like about you, your ideas, or your product or service. The customer might also tend to save the relationship, however, by dismissing the topic of your sales call while still carrying on a lively conversation with you, or making a joke or sarcastic remark about your product or service. Superficially, the sales call appears to be moving forward while in actuality, it is stalled. In general, the resistance is displayed by more assertive and more emoting behaviors, moving toward the Backup Behavior of attack.

- SOLVE: Probe for the source of the problem. For example: "From your comment, it seems you may be feeling that our solution is not a good fit for you. Could you please tell me more about why you feel this way?"

Fig. 5-5: Recognizing Customer Resistance by SOCIAL STYLE (Cont.)

5.5 Gaining Customer Commitment

During the sales process, customers make a variety of decisions, such as whether to allow you to contact them, whether to listen to your sales presentation, whether to interact with you throughout the sales process, and whether your product or service meets their need at a price they are willing to pay. Regardless of whether your customer is making purchases on their own or as part of a committee, individuals will approach decision-making in ways unique to their SOCIAL STYLE.

Getting a customer to commit to your solution can take a considerable amount of time and effort, especially in business-to-business selling. Not surprisingly, this is one of the most challenging aspects of business development. Each SOCIAL STYLE has a unique approach to decision-making that affects how, and whether, they will commit to a proposed solution. Just as different SOCIAL STYLEs reach commitment in unique ways, they also require different types of follow-up once a decision to buy has been made.

Convincing customers to switch from products or services they are currently using to different products can be challenging. People often see change as a threat to the status quo, and they approach change in ways consistent with their SOCIAL STYLE. There are effective ways to communicate the value of change, respond to customer resistance, and help your customer embrace change. The first step in convincing a customer to switch to your products or services is to understand how each SOCIAL STYLE commonly reacts to potential change.

To switch from their current products or services, customers must accept the idea of change. In addition to understanding how people with different SOCIAL STYLEs typically react to change and how you can adjust your behavior to accommodate those SOCIAL

STYLEs, you can apply practices that "change agents" in other situations have found beneficial. Psychologists and human resource specialists have done a significant amount of research on the skills and behaviors of successful change agents.

Here we present advice on how to gain customers' commitment using the SOCIAL STYLE Model.

Driving Style

Driving Style customers like to feel some form of control over decisions. Even if the purchasing process is dictated by corporate policy and procedures, these customers have a strong need to establish their opinions and influence the decision. If they can, these customers make their own decisions, enjoy having power, and don't like being told what they should and should not do. As a salesperson, you should give them options from which to choose.

Driving Style customers give the most consideration to the options with the highest probabilities of getting the result they want; however, because they can accept risks, they are seldom looking for the safest alternative. They are more apt than some other SOCIAL STYLEs to make decisions that have higher risks but also higher potential payoffs. Therefore, they are open for gain-sharing arrangements, including guarantees and penalties.

People with this SOCIAL STYLE like to make decisions quickly, so be aware they may have made up their mind well before you ask for their agreement. If they believe you are wasting their time, they will likely try to take control of the situation so they can bring the conversation to a close and move onto other, more important tasks.

Stay focused on the overall goals to be achieved by the decision. This will help keep your Driving Style customers in a productive and receptive state for making a decision. Don't harm your own cause by allowing the conversation to drift from issues relevant to the decision. If you feel this customer is backing away from a positive purchase decision, attempt to save the sale by offering to get more facts that could either strengthen your case or result in other options.

When dealing with a Driving Style customer, make sure you have provided key facts needed to make a decision in your favor. Provide information about the probability of success or effectiveness of the various options—but only if you can support your estimations with reliable facts. Rather than aggressively offering the solution you feel is the best, enjoy greater success with this customer by providing alternatives and choices from which the customer may select.

Driving Style customers want results and they want to be in control. They will vigorously resist switching to your products or services if they perceive the change will result in their loss of control over familiar processes or will result in delays in achieving desired results. They will be more excited about switching to your products or services if what you are offering gives them more control and better results. Their inclination to act quickly may be an opportunity for you to gain quick acceptance of your products or services, especially if what you are offering represents an expedient solution to the customer's business problems.

The growth action for Driving Style people is to listen, so hearing critical information for making a difficult decision can be challenging for them. These customers will be more open to listening carefully to relevant details when they believe their decision is crucial to accomplishing their goals, and when they trust in your competence.

Be direct in asking for the sale! This customer will be clear when they have agreed to a course of action; they will simply state their commitment. Once a decision to buy is made, they will typically move directly to the next order of business. Follow through on everything you said you would do, when you said you would do it. Failure to do so may result in this person concluding that you are incompetent, which may jeopardize future sales.

Driving Style customers will openly state their objections, whether they are minor or major. If they feel their objection does not have an adequate rebuttal from you, they may attempt to take charge of or conclude the sales process. To overcome major objections, ask questions that focus directly on the reasons for the objection. Listen carefully for ways the objection relates to the most important outcomes the person needs to achieve. Once you have identified the objection, supply additional information that brings new choices to light or shows how choices already on the table can help this customer achieve their desired results.

Expressive Style

Customers with an Expressive Style are naturally assertive and talkative, so they will be very vocal in sharing their opinions as they make up their minds. This is good because it can give you strong clues as to what to emphasize and de-emphasize in the sales process.

During decision-making processes, they may act impulsively without the need to consider all the relevant facts or implications. They can get excited about the impact a decision might have, either for the organization or themselves. Because Expressive Style customers tend to be fast-paced and willing to take risks, if possible, offer them special and immediate incentives for moving forward rapidly.

These customers value the opinions or endorsement of people they consider important or prominent when making a decision—sometimes more than the facts and logic that support the decision. Whenever possible, provide these customers with testimonials from prominent organizations or people who support the decision you want this customer to make.

Expressive Style people are usually obvious in their behavior, so it will be clear whether they have made a decision. They tend to be flexible about decisions; they do not necessarily view a decision as permanently binding. Because of this, they are usually comfortable revisiting a course of action and altering the original decision. Therefore, be sure to follow up with these customers to make sure they are committed to the decision and clear on its implications. And don't ask for their agreement to your sales offer unless it is clear from their behavior they are ready to accept!

The growth action for Expressive Style people is to check, which means they need to make sure their beliefs around the decision are realistic. Making a calm, realistic, and reflective assessment of the issues surrounding a difficult decision can be challenging for them. These customers will be most open to making a difficult purchasing decision if you show them how it will help them achieve personal recognition.

When asking your Expressive Style customer to make a difficult decision, you should seek their input and ideas. Beware of ignoring what may seem to you like exaggerated fears or trepidations. These customers tend to operate in a future time frame, so difficult decisions can be made into a natural opportunity for them to project their hopes and aspirations and to act on them.

Expressive Style customers will respond to change with activity. However, unlike Driving Style customers, there will be a strong emotional component to their reactions. If they favor making the switch you are proposing, they will react with excitement. If what you are proposing makes them uncomfortable, they can come across as unfriendly or even antagonistic. In either case, they will verbalize their feelings about the change, and may do this before seeking to clarify or fully understand your proposal. If these customers do not express themselves directly to you, then they will make their feelings known to others in their organization.

If they support the change, these individuals will want to be actively involved in the effort. They may view it as an exciting occasion, and might look for opportunities for self-promotion or role enlargement within their organization. They will be outwardly enthusiastic and will become your ally in helping their organization to make the switch. Using subjective measures in projects such as their customer or user satisfaction will be highly appreciated.

If this customer does not view your sales proposal favorably, they are likely to be forthright with their dissatisfaction. They may act impulsively and tell you what they are feeling rather than responding in a restrained or analytical way. If they reject your proposal entirely, they might express their dissatisfaction with your offer through the use of sarcasm about you or your proposal. This customer may then attempt to preserve their interpersonal relationship with you by moving on to other topics while carrying on a lively conversation with you. Superficially, the sales call may have the appearance of moving forward but will have stalled in actuality.

To overcome major objections, ask questions related to their opinions or goals. Be sociable and show a personal interest in their answer as you listen attentively to their response. Once you have clearly identified the true objection, take steps to adjust your behavior to this customer's SOCIAL STYLE by showing enthusiasm as you reinforce the unique features, recognition, and personal benefits your solution can provide.

Amiable Style

Expect the Amiable Style customer to be relatively quiet, at least in the short-term, as they contemplate the ramifications of the proposal. Their initial inclination will be to consider how selecting your products or services might affect people. In doing so, this customer tends to use personal opinions, both their own opinions and the opinions of others whom they value, more than facts and data in arriving at decisions. During decision-making processes, they may prefer to hear the viewpoints of others before stating their own, especially people they consider to be key relationships. Therefore, avoid pressing too hard for immediate acceptance of your proposal, as this is an important element of their decision-making process.

These individuals may resist changing products or services if they perceive the change as too threatening to the status quo. These individuals often develop a level of comfort with the people they work with and the processes in place; any change to these things can potentially be risky and disorienting for them. This is not to say that they are incapable of considering change; they are. Allow these customers time to act at a slower pace and to develop a level of comfort with the implications of proposed changes and proceed at a casual pace as you attempt to close the sale. They usually like arrangements with guarantees that provide a safety net in the event of problems with their decision.

If these customers are opposed to switching to your products or services, they may display their resistance in passive ways. Don't mistakenly assume "silence means consent." Pay close attention to the obstacles they say prevent them from making the switch. Rather than explaining their own reasons for not favoring your proposal, they may indicate that they have no control over the situation. They'll blame their inability to accept your proposal on circumstances beyond their control, such as no budget or an obstinate boss. Such words can be cues to you to uncover the real reasons these customers don't support the change.

Socializing is always important for these people, even when you are trying to close a sale; it keeps them enthused and motivated. Avoid saying or doing anything that might make this customer uncomfortable in dealing with you as a salesperson.

When you think you have reached an agreement with this customer, but aren't 100% certain you have their full personal commitment, verify they are committed and ready to proceed. Otherwise, you may find you don't have a sale after all when it's time to sign. Follow up immediately after the sale and do everything you said, when and how you said you would do it. If you fail to do so, this customer may lose trust in you, which will damage your long-term relationship with them.

The growth action for Amiable Style people is to initiate, which means they have difficulties commencing action or moving forward. You can help your customer make a difficult decision by pointing out any impact it may have on them personally and on their relationships with their co-workers and customers. Identify how your product or service can help improve working relationships or customer relationships. Pointing this out to your customer can facilitate their willingness to make the difficult decision.

Rather than objecting outright, Amiable Style customers might display resistance by postponing a decision, expressing doubt or uncertainty in a questioning way, or explaining they want to talk with someone else about your proposal. Their smiles and agreeable demeanor may give you the false impression they view your sales offer favorably, but in reality they may be nowhere near ready to make a commitment. Since they can be hesitant to offer their opinions, ask them to state their opinions on issues that might be bothering them about the decision. However, only use this strategy if you really don't know why they are resisting. Be cautious not to make this customer personally uncomfortable in interacting with you. Move slowly and be casual. Once you have clearly identified the true objection, make specific recommendations, assure this customer there are minimal risks in making the purchase decision, and give your personal commitment to ensure everyone will be happy with the sale.

Analytical Style

Like Amiable Style customers, Analytical Style customers are usually slower paced and do not like to rush into making decisions. Because they tend to act cautiously, they may be reluctant to make decisions they perceive as involving a great deal of risk. Unlike Amiable Style people though, these customers' caution comes from a fear the decision might be the wrong thing to do, or there is not enough good information to make an informed decision. They are usually intent on studying the various options in detail, or at least taking time to think about the issues before committing to a decision.

If these customers believe you are asking them to make a decision too quickly or without taking important information into account, they may try to slow down the decision-making process. When this happens, they can become even less communicative, withhold opinions, and become slow to return phone calls and emails. Consequently, the source of the delay in decision-making may be unclear to you.

Because they want to be right, they like to have flexibility in their decisions in case they want to change something when additional information becomes available. When discussing feasible options, to the extent possible, give them the probabilities that each course of action will result in success (or alternatively, the most likely consequences of each alternative). If appropriate, provide this information in writing as a way of meeting their need for information they can reflect on.

Analytical Style customers can be reluctant to state their opinions or assert firm positions on issues. This can be a problem when making decisions, particularly if they do not fully agree with you. To circumvent this potential problem, specifically ask them to voice any concerns they might have about a decision, and if appropriate, reassure them various viewpoints have been taken into account. Once they have stated their decision, these customers will generally stick by it and want to move forward with the sales process.

Provide customers with an Analytical Style with all relevant facts to make the decision. Remember, these customers prefer to carefully study each option and make decisions based on verifiable information. If they believe they are not taking important information into account, they may try to slow down the decision-making process.

Give the Analytical Style customer time to verify the reliability of your actions and information before asking for an agreement. If you feel that, despite your best efforts, the customer is not responding favorably, bring to light additional information or facts that will meet his or her needs, and make sure this customer agrees with the logic of your claims. Consider providing written guarantees, as this will help assure the Analytical Style customer the decision they make today will be valid in the future. They usually like fixed-price arrangements with guarantees and tend to be suspicious of gain sharing.

Objections don't necessarily mean "no." Some objections are simply customer statements that don't affect the outcome of the sales process. Others are significant objections that indicate the customer doesn't fully or accurately understand your sales offer. The Analytical Style customer might display resistance by stating objections in the form of difficult-to-answer questions or by offering you little or no feedback. They may challenge your research or product specifications.

This customer might show very stiff or formal body movements and voice inflections as they make their objections. In general, they may seem to be avoiding interacting with you in ways that would advance the sale. To overcome major objections, probe appropriately to uncover the true source of the resistance. Ask what information they need to resolve their question or doubts.

The following chart (see Fig. 5-6) summarizes recommendations on how to gain customer commitment by SOCIAL STYLE.

Analytical Style	Driving Style
• Make the close the next logical step in the sales process	• Be direct in asking for their commitment
• Allow them time to decide	• Provide them with several options from which to decide
• Avoid giving too many options which may slow down the decision	• Don't be afraid to ask for their decision
• Probe to see if they are ready to make the decision now	• If they decide unfavorably, ask them what would need to happen for them to reconsider your solution
• If they are not ready, probe to see if they need more information and/or find out when you might expect their decision	• When the agreement is reached, deliver on your commitment in a timely and efficient manner
• When the decision is made, be sure to review the details and make sure everything is specified	• Deliver what you promised
• Deliver on what you promised; don't promise anything you can't deliver	

Fig. 5-6: Gaining Customer Commitment by SOCIAL STYLE

Amiable Style	Expressive Style
• Make the decision request less direct and more conversational • Ask them if they are ready to proceed; if not, ask if they need more time to check with others • Offer to provide additional information for others and even to meet with them if the Amiable Style customer prefers • Don't press for a quick decision or you may get a "yes" that is actually an attempt to avoid a confrontation which they might cancel later • Make sure the customer is comfortable with their decision and their relationship with you • Check back after the sale to let the customer know you are still interested in them and support their decision to do business with you	• Make the decision point an exciting opportunity for personal gain by emphasizing the impact the decision will have on the customer's future or reputation • Don't be afraid to press for a decision but let the customer make it • When you get commitment, follow up with all relevant details in writing • Remember Expressive Style people can often forget or overlook the details, help them out by being clear and precise • Deliver on what you promise and remember failure to do so may be viewed as a personal insult

Fig. 5-6: Gaining Customer Commitment by SOCIAL STYLE (Cont.)

5.6 Negotiating Agreements

Tensions often arise when a sales conversation enters the negotiation phase. Both you and your customer have something to lose if the negotiation breaks down or if one side agrees to terms and conditions they later regret. Similarly, the give-and-take of a sales negotiation can also be a positive experience resulting in a mutually satisfactory agreement.

A sales negotiation typically begins after the customer has indicated he or she is interested in buying from you if you can work out satisfactory terms and conditions. How you open the negotiating session sets the tone for the entire negotiation process.

The following advice will help you prepare to conduct contractual negotiations productively with each of the four SOCIAL STYLEs.

Driving Style

When negotiating, your Driving Style customers will be very direct in their behavior. Since negotiations tend to be the part of the sales conversation where there is the greatest tension, they may move toward their Backup Behavior and take control of situations. Be particularly aware of this type of behavior and watch for signs these customers are feeling a higher-than-normal level of stress, such as raising their voices and becoming more animated than usual.

These customers will usually be forthright and negotiate with you in a direct, business-like manner. They might be verbally confrontational as they push for achieving terms and conditions they have set as goals. These customers are likely to dominate the negotiation session, at least until they have made their objectives clear and are assured you will help them achieve those objectives. They like to be in control and may try to take control of the negotiation session, especially if they feel an alternative to negotiating with you is simply to walk away.

Plan to interact with this customer in a direct, business-like manner. Remember, people with this SOCIAL STYLE are naturally competitive, so be sure to position yourself as being on their team to help them achieve their goals, not as an adversary in the negotiation process. Prepare to negotiate in a clear and logical way, without distraction.

Be prepared to give these customers options so they can feel they are in charge by being the one who decides. Identify in advance where you have flexibility and can offer this customer options and alternatives to such things as timelines, nature of the product or service, or pricing and payment terms. Also, be prepared with facts and proofs that support the need for the terms and conditions you propose. This can be especially important for these customers since they may challenge your position or assumptions.

Driving Style customers will not hesitate to express their opinions about the terms and conditions you propose. They may dominate the negotiation session for a while before allowing you an opportunity to speak again. They may try to take charge of the negotiation session by telling you exactly what must be included in the agreement. This is a way for them to maintain control.

By nature, these individuals control their emotions, so unless they are feeling shock or anger about your proposal they will likely appear neutral throughout a typical negotiation process. Once you reach an agreement on terms and conditions, they will want to move quickly in concluding the negotiation and the sales process instead of exploring the pros and cons of other options. They prefer to make decisions for themselves, but you should collaborate with them to develop an action plan for delivering on the agreed-upon products or services.

If these customers do not like any of the terms and conditions you are offering, you will not have to guess what they think or how they feel. They will tell you. In such situations, be prepared to explain how your proposed terms and conditions will better enable them to achieve their stated objectives. If they strongly disagree with your position or are resistant to what you are saying, they may become outwardly defensive. They will be verbally forceful and will try to assert some sort of control or influence, possibly challenging your information. Though they don't usually show a lot of facial animation, their expressions will often show their frustration.

These individuals will not hesitate to express their opinions. They may dominate the conversation for a while before allowing you an opportunity to speak again. They might try to take charge of the situation by telling you what needs to be done. This is a way for them to maintain control.

Be aware that these individuals enjoy debate. Be direct in bringing up potentially uncomfortable parts of the sales negotiation (such as price), but be careful not to let the discussion turn into a contest they will be motivated to win. These customers can even appear forceful when making their points; however, unless they are obviously frustrated or insistent that you give in to non-negotiable terms, accept this behavior as simply being a part of their SOCIAL STYLE.

If negotiation sessions become particularly intense, these customers can be kept in a more productive state if you show that you understand their point of view, and you communicate with them on a logical basis. Show them how you can help them achieve the results they need. Driving Style individuals are responsive to facts, so if they focus on extraneous issues, bring the negotiation discussion back to the hard data. Reinforce that negotiating terms and conditions is intended to be a means of ensuring that the ultimate purpose of the negotiation is fulfilled.

Expressive Style

When negotiating, expect Expressive Style people to be animated and to share their opinions freely. As tension increases during negotiations, they may move toward their Backup Behavior, which is to attack. These customers will be very direct when negotiating and will at times say things without pausing to consider the implications or your point of view. They may respond defensively if you question or disagree with their counterproposal. Remember, they may have difficulty separating disagreements about their ideas from rejection of them as individuals.

If your customer has an emotional reaction to an element of your offer, they may interrupt you before you have a chance to fully present your offer. They might dominate discussion until they are satisfied they have fully communicated their opinions about your offer. If these customers feel highly stressed during the negotiation, they may display hostility toward you and confront you personally rather than focus on reaching a mutually satisfactory agreement.

From the beginning of the negotiation to the end, be warm and communicative with these customers. Even when you are engaged in an intense negotiation, interact with them in a supportive way that shows you fully support their aspirations, either business objectives or their personal goals. Let them know the purpose of the negotiation is to reach a mutually satisfactory agreement that helps them fulfill those aspirations. Remember, people with this SOCIAL STYLE are naturally competitive, so be sure to position yourself as a teammate, and not as an adversary in the negotiation process.

These individuals will show you how they feel. If they are not defensive about the give-and-take of negotiation, they may react positively to the possibility of the negotiation leading to positive outcomes. Keep in mind that these customers like to be involved, so instead of telling them the terms you would like to include, collaborate with them to identify terms and conditions that will satisfy both of you. This will appeal to their need for recognition and involvement. Even though negotiations can become intense, feel free to use humor to diffuse tension. These customers are oriented toward spontaneity and like to have fun, even in business settings. Humor can help in many situations and is particularly effective with these individuals.

If you do not agree to their terms, choose your words carefully in letting them know. Expressive Style people do not readily distinguish a rejection of their ideas from a personal rejection of them. In such cases they may revert to their Backup Behavior, which is to attack. Consequently, their response may be blunt and personal. They might bring up issues that are tangential to the discussion and can come across as irrational. If this occurs, allow them to play out their emotional reaction before returning to a previous point in the conversation where you were in agreement.

Be prepared for the possibility that this customer may have an emotional response to the specific terms or conditions of your offer. Of course, this does not mean that you should avoid having the discussion, but anticipate possible reactions this customer might have. Help these customers separate their emotions about a negotiation topic from the objective facts. Summarize or restate their opinions in a calm and straightforward way to let them know you understand their concerns and then explain your rationale for your own position.

Because these individuals have the capacity to react in a very emotional way, it is easy to lose control of conversations. If this is happening, listen to what they are saying without responding defensively. Accept the reality of the emotions they are expressing without getting personally involved in it. Do not appear to counter-attack or the situation may rapidly spiral out of control. Once they have adequately expressed their emotions, redirect them to the issues at hand. Remember that Expressive Style people often calm down quickly after they've vented their emotions, so it's possible they will soon be able to discuss the issue more rationally.

Be sure to keep these people involved. When negotiating with them, be sure to ask for their feedback, opinions, and ideas. This is not difficult since they do not hesitate to express themselves. Approach the negotiation as an open and free exchange, where the customer is providing as much input about the potential terms of the agreement as you are. When these customers tell you they need to include a term or condition you find acceptable, be positive and acknowledge their contribution to the process.

Amiable Style

Unlike Driving or Analytical Style customers, these customers are not interested in hearing about a variety of options or examining them in detail. Put forth the best set of terms and conditions you feel this customer will accept, but keep these individuals actively engaged in the negotiation conversation and process. To do this, confirm their agreement at each step of the process by asking if they have any questions or concerns. This is important because you may need to bring to the surface issues you think might be important to them but they may be hesitant to bring up themselves. Asking about questions or concerns provides them with an entry into the conversation and reassures them they can have a positive effect on the outcome of the negotiation session.

With these customers, it is often helpful to begin by talking about terms and conditions upon which you are confident you have their full agreement. This may help put the customer at ease before you move on to discussing issues where there might be less alignment of views. While they normally enjoy talking with others, these customers may become less talkative during negotiation and might not fully share their true opinions. They often display their discomfort nonverbally through their facial expressions, minimal use of hand gestures, and "leaning back" body posture.

Trust is very important for these customers. If they have a good relationship with you, they will be more likely to accept and respond in a positive way to your negotiating points. When presenting the terms and conditions you would like to include in the final agreement, be sure they are aware you are striving to help them achieve a mutually satisfactory agreement.

Amiable Style people display their emotions, therefore their feelings about your message will probably be apparent either through what they say or their nonverbal responses. If they are not surprised by your message they will openly express how they feel about the matter and the conversation will usually be two-sided and collaborative. If they are shocked or disagree with your message, it will be obvious they are unhappy, though they may be less forthcoming than others might be. They may remain relatively quiet and withhold their opinions. Their Backup Behavior is to acquiesce, so they might tacitly agree with what you are saying and privately disagree. If they feel very strongly about your message, they are likely to respond in an emotional way and may share some of their opinions and feelings. These individuals are not usually highly vocal or abrasive, but they can be abrupt when upset. They may try to end the conversation quickly without fully expressing themselves or searching for an agreeable resolution to the issue.

These customers might feel uncomfortable or even threatened by a difficult negotiation process. If you believe they are not fully and openly participating, there may be some issue they are reluctant to mention. If they seem to be holding back, make it safe for them to negotiate with you. An effective way to help these individuals engage in productive negotiation is to ask open-ended questions to help them share their thoughts. Let them know that by negotiating a mutually satisfactory agreement their work situation will improve, and this might include their relationships with others. This approach can help them to overcome their natural hesitancy about initiating ideas or actions.

Since negotiations can become highly demanding the Amiable Style customer may acquiesce or seem to agree. As a result, it may not be immediately obvious to you if these customers disagree with you during the negotiation. At times they may appear to be going along with the terms you put forth even though they may have significant unexpressed concerns. Be aware their feelings are not likely to disappear and may not surface until you attempt to close the sale. If the disagreement is significant, they will later put up obstacles to concluding the negotiation. They may even try to nullify their implicit agreements by citing factors beyond their personal control, such as a committee vetoing the deal or the needs of the organization changing. This allows them to appear to agree with your terms and conditions personally while putting the blame elsewhere.

Do not end the negotiation conversation if you suspect this customer has unresolved questions or concerns. If this is the case, the impacts may linger and remain unaddressed, leading to more difficulty and making them find excuses to cause the sale to fall through later. Before concluding the negotiation, take the time to confirm that the customer is truly in agreement, and is committed to following through on negotiated terms and conditions.

Analytical Style

When negotiating, Analytical Style people might remain relatively quiet or wait for you and others to share their opinions before taking part in the negotiation discussion and offering their own viewpoints. They are most comfortable when they have heard different sides of the debate and information they may not have considered. In addition, they wish to avoid the risk of making the wrong decision. Consequently, they do not like to make quick decisions; they might want you to provide your input on the steps you believe necessary to reach a satisfactory agreement. If they are uneasy about any of the terms or conditions you suggest, they will likely seek ways to avoid making a decision until they can get more information and examine the issues in more depth.

Plan to approach the negotiation session in a straightforward, cooperative, business-like manner. Prepare to present your proposed terms and conditions using a clear and logical approach in such a way that demonstrates your proposal is well thought out and has merit. Be prepared to explain fully the meaning and implications of your proposed terms and conditions. Have ready specific reasons why your suggested terms and conditions are necessary. This is important for Analytical Style people since they will want a sound rationale to help them consider and accept your negotiating points.

Begin the negotiation conversation in a friendly but professional way. Analytical Style people are concerned with both process and making the right decision. State that you would like to put forward the best terms and conditions for discussion and examination that you believe will lead to a productive outcome for both of you.

When negotiating specific issues, take time to summarize the main points and discuss things in a rational way in terms of pros and cons, implications of each decision, and so on. Remember, these customers like to examine all sides of an issue before making a decision. If you do not allow time to do this, they will likely want to postpone concluding the negotiation process until they have had time to think.

These customers will not be interested in negotiating with you if they believe you are ignoring important details or facts, trying to persuade them on an overly emotional level, or pressing for immediate decisions. Avoid glossing over important details or facts, making dramatic, emotional appeals, or pressing for immediate decisions as they value rational thinking and logical approaches.

Encourage these customers to have an active dialogue with you. Listen carefully to their questions and statements, and probe to determine if there are any issues of concern to them that you have not adequately addressed. If necessary, allow meeting breaks and let them spend some time thinking about your proposed terms and conditions before following up with them.

Because these individuals control their emotions, they are unlikely to display very much emotion about the proposition. This is not to say they won't be concerned, but they may not express very much feeling around the message. If they are not surprised or shocked, they are likely to remain calm and may take some time to think about what you tell them. They won't necessarily rush into a problem-solving state of mind, but they might want you to provide your opinion about steps to be taken to address the issue. Even if they are upset, Analytical Style people will be eager to return to a rational and comfortable conversation. You can help bring the conversation back to a more productive state by approaching them in a rational way. Reiterate your reasoning and the evidence that supports your position.

When discussions involve potential points of disagreement, these customers may avoid direct eye contact with you and others more than usual (an indication of their Backup Behavior). They may show their discomfort by frequently shifting their body position in their chairs, leaning back, and holding their arms and hands close to their body. In addition, if the negotiation becomes particularly intense, these individuals may display their discomfort by becoming quieter than usual and by disengaging from the conversation. They may even try to withdraw from the negotiation conversation. However, when they feel strongly about an issue they can be passionate negotiators.

The following graph (see Fig. 5-7) summarizes recommendations on how to negotiate agreements by SOCIAL STYLE.

Analytical Style	Driving Style
• Be well-prepared and organized in your proposal for action	• Be efficient with your time
• Be accurate and don't overstate what you can do	• Keep your proposal short and to the point
• Present the relevant information based on what the customer indicated was important	• Focus on what your product or service will help the customer accomplish
• Be prepared to back up your information with facts, figures, and data	• Provide facts and logic to support your proposal but keep the main points simple
• Don't rely on testimonials or opinions to make your points	• Be prepared to provide more details if requested
• Share both the pros and cons of your recommendation	• Quickly get to the bottom line need and show how you can meet that need
• Let the customer know how you have minimized any risk they would take if they bought from you	

Fig. 5-7: Negotiating Agreements by SOCIAL STYLE

Amiable Style	Expressive Style
• Take time to be agreeable	• Make your proposal stimulating by presenting the big picture of your solution
• Keep the discussion of your proposed solution more casual and informal	• Avoid excessive details
• Watch your pacing; don't try to rush the conversation	• Use third-party testimonials
• Provide personal guarantees and assurances that the decision to buy has little risk	• Give examples of the recognition others have received when they bought your product or service
• Let the customer know why your solution is personally important to them	• Keep the discussion moving forward and avoid letting it get sidetracked on other topics
• Let the customer know why your solution will be acceptable to others who are important to your customer	• Be inspiring but avoid trying to outshine your customer

Fig. 5-7: Negotiating Agreements by SOCIAL STYLE (Cont.)

5.7 Selling to Purchasing Committees

Selling to a purchasing committee, or any situation where there is more than one decision-maker, is seldom a quick and easy process. Purchasing committees are often encountered when selling complex or higher cost products or services, and may require interacting with all committee members. Knowing the structure and decision-making process of the purchasing committee can help you immeasurably.

To convince members of a purchasing committee to buy your product or service, it is important to understand the operation of the committee and their process for making the purchase decision. You should understand who will be making the decision and how the committee members will be involved. Are they "consultants" or do they have a vote? Can the committee chair/leader veto their decision? Knowing the answers to these questions can help you shape your strategy for interacting with the committee as a whole and with individual members. This is important for building support and commitment to buy from you and will affect how you follow up with them afterward.

There are a number of decision-making models that purchasing committees might use. From least participatory to most, some models include:

- ***A leader gathers input from a purchasing committee and then decides***

    This model is often used when a decision-maker needs expert opinions or input to make the best decision. Committee discussion may lead to a better decision, but the committee members don't need to come to agreement about the particular course of action. In this scenario, focus your efforts on interacting with the SOCIAL STYLE of the leader. If this person has an Expressive or Amiable Style it will likely be advantageous to find out the opinions of the committee members, as they are likely to have some influence over the leader's decision.

• Consensus decisions

The word consensus is often thought to mean unanimous agreement, but this is not necessarily the case. Consensus decisions include input from and general acceptance by others. Consensus decisions typically have a very high level of involvement by committee members and can lead to strong, well-supported decisions. While reaching consensus can take time, the process can give you time to interact effectively with each person's SOCIAL STYLE. A consensus decision-making process will require you to determine each committee member's SOCIAL STYLE and adjust your behavior accordingly for each. This is best done by finding opportunities to interact one-on-one with individual committee members, such as following up with more detail after a meeting. When presenting sales information to the full committee, you generally must work the middle ground, being especially careful to control your own SOCIAL STYLE behaviors and to avoid over-compensating your SOCIAL STYLE behaviors for any one committee member's SOCIAL STYLE.

• Consensus with a fallback

This approach is often used because it is an effective way to implement consensus decision-making while allowing for a preset course of action to be taken if the committee is unable to make a decision within an appropriate amount of time. The time allocated for a particular decision often depends on the decision's complexity and importance. The preferred fallback may be to turn the final decision over to the committee leader, who considers the committee's input before deciding. The existence of a fallback plan keeps the committee moving forward without ignoring input from committee members. As long as the committee members seem to be moving toward a decision, you will need to moderate your own SOCIAL STYLE when interacting with the full committee while seeking opportunities to interact one-on-one with individual committee members. However, if you sense the committee is headed toward an impasse, be prepared to shift your focus to an approach that favors the leader's SOCIAL STYLE.

- *Majority rules*

Some purchasing committees might use a "majority rules" voting method for some decisions. While this method is familiar, when used on important decisions it can leave some committee members feeling like they have "lost". Therefore, they are uncommitted to the purchase decision. That can make this method more challenging in sales situations where buy-in is crucial for successful implementation of a product or service. In this scenario, moderate your SOCIAL STYLE and find opportunities to use your knowledge of SOCIAL STYLE in one-on-one situations with committee members. If the committee decides to buy from you, be aware who voted for you and who did not. Follow up in a SOCIAL STYLE-appropriate manner with all committee members, but take any extra steps needed to help win over the naysayers and possibly avoid their active or passive impediment to your efforts.

Regardless of the committee's decision-making model, individual members will approach decision-making in SOCIAL STYLE-unique ways. It may not always be possible to make each SOCIAL STYLE totally comfortable during such selling initiatives. However, there are some strategies you can use to strike a balance between competing SOCIAL STYLE needs and achieving the results you require.

Due to the complexity of the decision process, planning ahead is the key. Recognize and identify the SOCIAL STYLEs of the different members of your customer's team, and anticipate the different types of responses, questions, and attitudes. Prepare ahead of time to respond to these individuals in a way that will satisfy them without diverting too far from your agenda and sales objective. Provide information ahead of time if this is possible, and have one-on-one discussions or email exchanges with certain customer team members if you feel this will help.

Driving Style

Regardless of their formal role on the committee, Driving Style people will want to feel some form of control over the decision. Even if the decision-making process is group-oriented, they will have a strong need to state their opinions and influence the decision. They are likely to offer their opinions ahead of some other committee members and may even try to influence others to their point of view.

These customers are usually comfortable taking risks, which can come across in their approach to making decisions. They are more apt than some of the other SOCIAL STYLEs to support decisions that have higher risks, but only if the risk holds the potential for higher payoffs.

Driving Style individuals are very direct, which can help other committee members stay focused on the task at hand and clarify their roles in the committee's decision-making process. However, these customers like to make decisions quickly, so they may try to rush the process to the frustration of other committee members and the detriment of getting a decision in your favor. If they believe you are wasting their time or if they believe the group is off track, they might try to take control of the sales conversation and decision-making process.

You can keep Driving Style customers in a productive state by maintaining a focus on the overall goals to be achieved by a decision in your favor. If you are making a sales presentation to the committee and sense the sales conversation is drifting away from the relevant issues, try to refocus the committee's attention back to the sales agenda. This will communicate you are in control and will help meet the Driving Style customer's need for results.

If you feel the purchasing committee is taking too much time building a consensus (which is more likely to happen if an Amiable or Analytical Style individual is leading the committee), be aware that Driving Style committee members can become quite frustrated. In such cases, it might be advisable to postpone asking for the final decision so this customer does not feel his/her time is being wasted.

When preparing for a meeting with a purchasing committee, offer all relevant information needed to make the decision. You don't necessarily need to discuss every bit of information; simply have it available for reference. Be ready to discuss and respond to specific questions about your product or services and the impact they will have on the customer's organization. Since your Driving Style customers have a need for results, these individuals will turn their attention to outcomes rather than the processes needed to achieve them.

Driving Style customers will be clear when they have made a decision about the purchase. Whether it's a decision to buy or not to buy, they will simply state their decision. They will typically want to move directly to conclude the sales process or move on to the next order of business—regardless of where other committee members are in the purchase decision process. They usually do not like to revisit decisions, so you probably won't have to engage in any personalized follow-up regarding the decision other than the usual steps you take after winning or losing a sale.

Expressive Style

Expressive Style customers are assertive and talkative by nature, so they will be very vocal with their opinions during any committee decision-making process. While some members will be fairly brief when sharing their thoughts, these individuals may spend quite a bit more time expressing their opinions since they want to be sure others on the committee hear their viewpoints. If they feel strongly about buying or not buying from you, they might try to influence others through their emotional appeals or personal relationships.

These individuals also tend to be fast-paced. During decision-making processes, they may act impulsively without considering all the relevant facts or implications. They can get excited about the impacts decisions will have, either for others in the organization or for themselves, so they can become carried away with their feelings about the decision.

While they are likely to be active contributors to the decision-making process, these individuals are not typically interested in hearing or reading a lot of detail around the different options or the actual implementation process of a solution. You may need to point out the details but avoid dwelling on them if a committee has one or more Expressive Style members.

If they are dissatisfied with the decision, they will not hesitate to express themselves to other members of the committee, both verbally and nonverbally. Their natural Backup Behavior is to attack, so if they feel their position on the purchase decision is being thwarted or challenged by other committee members, they may confront the committee or specific members.

If this occurs during a meeting with a purchasing committee, remain quiet and allow the Expressive Style customer to vent his or her feelings. After the situation has settled down, refocus the committee on the sales agenda. If this customer seems to be against the purchase, find non-challenging ways to bring the person back to the point of considering the positive impacts that your product or service will have for them. You may be able to do this by emphasizing personal benefits or by presenting testimonials of notable, satisfied customers. Your active listening skills will also be important for dealing with this situation with an Expressive Style individual.

Give Expressive Style customers an overview of the different options and sufficient information to make a positive decision. Even though this SOCIAL STYLE does not typically need a great deal of detail, do not gloss over important details if they are important for making the decision in your favor. To achieve agreement from these committee members, point out how the decision to buy will benefit them, the purchasing committee, or the organization as a whole.

Expressive Style customers are usually obvious in their behavior, so it will be clear if they are in favor of buying from you. If they do not back you, they may make this obvious, either in front of the purchasing committee or to you privately.

Expressive Style customers tend to be flexible about decisions and do not necessarily view a decision as permanently binding. That means they are usually comfortable revisiting a course of action and altering their original decision. If they are not initially in favor of buying from you, you may be able to provide them with persuasive

SOCIAL STYLE-appropriate information about personal incentives and testimonials that may help them change their mind.

Once you get a favorable decision, follow up with these individuals to make sure they are clear on the decision and its implications, to reinforce the decision, and to thank them personally (of course).

Amiable Style

When serving on purchasing committees, Amiable Style customers are often more hesitant than other SOCIAL STYLEs to speak forcefully about their opinions or concerns. During the decision-making process, they may prefer to hear others' viewpoints before stating their own.

Because they value relationships with other committee members, they can become uncomfortable and reluctant to state any disagreements openly. They may qualify their statements about the purchase decision in order to maintain a middle ground, or keep open an option to change their position. Observe their body language and gestures when others are stating their opinions to get a reading on whether the Amiable Style customer is comfortable with what others are saying. Look for fewer signs of engagement and fewer head nods or other facial gestures that suggest disapproval. Conversely, don't assume smiles and head nods mean agreement.

These individuals generally do not rush into decisions. This is less about uncertainty and more about a desire to avoid actions they consider risky. Their concern might be that a particular decision will change the status quo to an uncomfortable degree. In particular, they will be cautious when making decisions that have an impact on working relationships, reporting relationships, and especially relationships with customers with whom they have direct contact.

If Amiable Style customers feel a purchase decision will bring about changes that will disrupt the status quo, or in some other way will make them personally uncomfortable, they may try to resist committing to the purchase decision. This resistance can be somewhat passive. For instance, they may bring up questions about your product or service that you—and even other members of the purchasing committee—thought were settled. You can usually avert this behavior by specifically asking if all questions have been answered at each step of the sales conversation, and summarizing the committee's decisions.

Since these customers can be hesitant to offer their opinions, ask them to state their opinions before other committee members express their opinions. Directly ask these people to share their thoughts and concerns. Instead of asking, "Are there any questions?" ask, "What questions do you have?" In this way, you have a better chance of getting their true opinions about your product or service without undue influence from other committee members. However, be careful not to put them on the spot or to make them too uncomfortable. Use this strategy only if it is appropriate and you can do it in a nonthreatening way.

When serving on purchasing committees, Amiable Style customers will be most effective in the decision-making process when they understand why they need to buy your products and services and, especially, the impact it will have on the people in their organization and/or their customers. To move this customer toward making a favorable decision, point out the role he or she can play in making a change that will have a positive impact on people.

As previously mentioned, these customers might appear to be in favor of buying from you, while quietly harboring questions or concerns about your product or service. This is one of the reasons that you should be careful not to mistake smiles and head nods as meaning that they agree with you. To avoid confusion, verify that these customers are committed and ready to proceed with the sale as you move toward asking for a final decision.

These customers generally do not mind revisiting decisions if they have lingering questions. In addition, they can alter their opinions if they feel it is warranted. Be sure to follow up individually with these members of the purchasing committee to ensure they are in full agreement with the purchase decision and to show your personal support of their contribution to the committee's decision.

Analytical Style

Like Amiable Style people, Analytical Style people are usually slower-paced and will resist if they feel they are being rushed into making a purchase decision. They tend to act cautiously and may be reluctant to make decisions they perceive as involving a great deal of risk. However, unlike Amiable Style people, their caution comes from a concern that the decision might be the wrong thing to do or that there is not enough good information to make an informed decision. They are usually intent on studying the various options in detail or at least on taking time to think about the issues before committing to a purchase decision.

If these individuals believe the purchasing committee is making a decision too quickly, they may try to slow down the process. For example, they may insist the committee take the time to analyze printed materials about your product or service or consider other viewpoints before moving forward. You can help manage this behavior by providing them with information before the committee meets to make its decision. This is good meeting protocol with all people, but it is particularly important for these individuals. It allows them time to consider the details of your sales offer and to develop their thoughts and opinions ahead of time.

Analytical Style people can be reluctant to state their opinions or assert firm positions on the purchase decision to other committee members. Because they want to be right, they like to retain flexibility when supporting or rejecting a purchase decision, just in case they learn new information that persuades them to change their minds. How you respond to their lack of a firm commitment depends on the particular decision-making process the committee employs. For example, if the committee is using a consensus-based decision-making model, it is generally acceptable for committee members to state their support for a decision even if they have some minor concerns. This strategy can help them commit to a decision and support it while still communicating they have concerns about the decision. As long as you have the consensus of the committee, do not feel you have to convince the Analytical Style customer fully, as they may be willing to move forward as long as they can express their reservations.

As mentioned previously, provide these individuals with all the information they need to come to a decision. This will help make them comfortable with the process. If they need more specificity and a level of detail that you feel would be off-putting to other committee members, offer to meet or talk with this customer one-on-one to discuss all their questions in detail.

Analytical Style people can be reluctant to express themselves in group settings. This can be a problem when it comes time for the committee to make a decision, whether or not they are in favor of buying from you. Let this customer know you have made available all the information needed to make the purchase decision. If they still seem hesitant to commit, specifically ask them to voice any concerns they might have about a decision, and if appropriate, reassure them everyone on the committee has reviewed the same information.

Once consensus has been reached to buy from you, these committee members will generally support the decision and want to move forward with the new plan. When this occurs, don't feel that you have to revisit any of the details that went into the decision-making process.

6 THE VERSATILITY FACTOR IN TEAMS

Working in teams has become mainstream in the modern workplace. Both individual and organizational successes increasingly rely on effective teamwork. Teams come in many forms: cross-functional teams to achieve strategic initiatives, temporary teams to manage short-term projects, and even cross-organizational teams are common in many industries. Virtual teams are increasingly common, where team members live and work in different locations and may never meet face-to-face.

The one thing all teams have in common is individuals. You are never alone in a team no matter the purpose of the group; you will have to interact with your fellow team members. The SOCIAL STYLE Model can help team members understand each other and how they are likely to interact with one another.

Research has shown the connection between Versatility skills and teams. Managers with high Versatility—the ability to understand others and interact effectively with them—are more effective as team leaders than managers with low Versatility. Further, Versatility was shown to have a high relationship with the ability to work well within a team, effectiveness as a team leader, and the ability to establish effective relationships with others.

People with different SOCIAL STYLEs have different preferences and ways of working. When managed ineffectively, these differences can be the source of dissatisfaction, conflict, and a breakdown in team effectiveness. When managed with skill, team members' SOCIAL STYLE differences can lead to creativity, energy, focus, and better performance.

The way the team handles interpersonal interactions and broad team dynamics is critical. By applying knowledge of individual SOCIAL STYLEs and their team characteristics, the performance of the team can be enhanced. However, when these SOCIAL STYLE characteristics are ignored, team effectiveness can suffer. This can occur in ways that are outside of your immediate awareness, leading to long-term consequences.

Sometimes people work in groups that are not truly teams. We define a team as two or more people working interdependently toward a common purpose through innovative methods. Consider several salespeople working in distinct territories to achieve their individual sales quotas. They may be part of the company's sales group, but they are not a team by our definition. Conversely, if a unique sales opportunity arises and three salespeople work collaboratively to share expertise and achieve a group sale, they have become a team in that situation.

When working in teams, not only do individuals' SOCIAL STYLEs impact performance, their specific roles do too. Positions of authority and the various technical roles people play within a team are important factors that interact with SOCIAL STYLE.

Most teams will consist of a leader and members. The leader may initially play the most important role, but the team members are critical in all phases of the team. In the most effective teams, team leaders and members must contribute in the following ways:

Team Leader	Team Members
• Provide organization and influence during formation	• Gather and internalize initial information about the team and its purpose
• Provide coaching, guidance, support, and opportunities to all team members	• Utilize existing skills and gain new abilities
• Identify and acquire necessary outside resources	• Share information and feelings
• Provide increasing freedom, candor, and flexibility	• Solve problems
• Fine tune and maintain momentum	• Share leadership and participate actively
• Anticipate challenges and manage change with an eye toward the future	• Explore new ideas and stretch their limits

Fig. 6-1: Team Role Contribution

6.1 Teaming Preferences

Each SOCIAL STYLE position has preferred ways they behave toward others, use time, approach decision-making, and deal with stress. By understanding these preferences, you can start to use SOCIAL STYLE awareness to improve team functioning. On the following pages we will review these preferences for each SOCIAL STYLE and analyze the strengths and weaknesses each SOCIAL STYLE brings to a team.

Driving Style

Driving Style people are focused on achieving results and believe action is the best way to succeed. They are typically seen as unconcerned about relationships and people, except as they relate to the overall goal. Other people may consider them to be impersonal, practical, and dominating. They have little tolerance for discussions they consider a waste of time. They prefer getting to the point and staying on target. Though always focused, they may warm up to others after progress has been achieved.

When making a decision, they like to be provided with facts and options. They are likely to choose options they think have a good probability of success, but are willing to take risks. They enjoy having control and making their own decisions. They like to have an agenda and stick to it. Straying from a focus will cause tension.

In times of tension, Driving Style people are likely to attempt to take control. They may say things like, "I'll just do it myself," or they might start making autocratic decisions. These efforts to take control represent their Backup Behavior as a result of the tension they are experiencing.

Driving Style individuals will usually be more outspoken than some of the other team members and will not hesitate to share their opinions. Because they are so focused on action, they can help to move processes forward. Once a decision has been made, they will be ready to move on to the next team task. They want to get results, so when a team drifts from its purpose they can be helpful for re-focusing and getting back on track.

These individuals will generally want to move things along quickly, and this impatience can lead to frustration and tension for other team members who prefer to take more time. When feeling tense, they might go into their backup behavior and try to take control of the team. In these cases, they might try to make decisions unilaterally. This can leave other team members feeling unheard and resentful. In their urgency to get something done, they can come across as negating the value that other members bring to the team.

As a Driving Style person, you will need to be patient with other team members. Give them opportunities to talk during meetings, and listen carefully to what they are saying. Some team members with different SOCIAL STYLEs might need to be prompted to express themselves, so it is usually a good idea to ask questions. Show interest in their points of view, and incorporate their perspectives and talents into team processes and solutions. Team meetings require time to allow all participants to have their input and come to agreements. If you are scheduling meetings, be sure to allow enough time for this, even though you may feel like time is being wasted.

Expressive Style

People with Expressive Style typically focus on spontaneity and recognition. They like to be at the center of activity but don't typically focus on one thing for too long. They generally approach situations in a casual manner and tend to get along well with others who support their ideas. They are frequently big-picture thinkers who prefer not to deal with all the details.

These people like to spend time exploring ideas. They do not like to be rushed to action, but can sometimes change course unexpectedly. They see agendas and timetables as guidelines rather than rules.

Expressive Style people are willing to take risks to achieve big successes. Decisions can be made based on the potential benefits or rewards rather than on facts or logic, and they make decisions quickly. The opinions of others are important factors when making decisions.

In times of tension, these people can become combative or argumentative with others. This Backup Behavior is their way of dealing with the disagreement and maintaining a high-profile role in the situation.

Because they tend to be very outgoing and sociable, these individuals often help build or solidify relationships within teams. They are usually excellent at using humor to relieve group tension. These qualities can help teams be more cohesive, fun, and productive. As big-picture thinkers, they can facilitate the discussion of broader ideas or implications of their work, which helps teams move beyond initial boundaries or ways of approaching problems.

Expressive individuals can be unprepared. They show up for team meetings, but might not have completed their tasks or commitments. This affects team performance and can leave other team members feeling like they are carrying heavier burdens.

Because they seek recognition, these individuals like to be the center of attention and might try to focus the team on their own individual accomplishments. This can distract the team from its focus, and might also frustrate other team members who either feel they also deserve recognition or who don't have as high of a need for personal approval and recognition.

For an Expressive Style to work most effectively on a team, you will need to make sure you don't overwhelm your fellow team members. This can happen if you are too talkative or opinionated. Give others the time to speak and opportunities to share their points of view. Recognize that others have a greater need for data and processes and will move toward decisions at a slower pace. Be open to others and understand they might have information about specific topics you might not necessarily have. During team meetings, you might want to lower your tone of voice since loud talkers can overwhelm some people. Be sure to follow through on your commitments and pay attention to timeframes.

Amiable Style

Amiable Style people are focused on relationships and personal security. They are generally friendly and committed to working with others. They are the most people-oriented of the SOCIAL STYLEs. They enjoy collaborating with others and want a friendly, comfortable workplace. They are open to sharing personal information and tend to take the comments and actions of others personally.

These people tend to work more slowly and with less discipline. They want to allow time for socialization and make sure everyone has a chance to contribute. Other people, even those who are not formally part of the group, can influence their decision process.

Amiable Style people are not risk-takers and want to ensure decisions will not affect personal relationships. The safe choice is often preferred.

Because of their emphasis on maintaining positive relationships, Amiable Style people are likely to give in or acquiesce during times of tension rather than take a firm position. This does not mean the conflict is over. By staying quiet, this person has not agreed to anything.

Due to their natural focus on relationships, Amiable Style people can help team members work together productively. They are very good at creating a sense of camaraderie within teams, and their cheerfulness and enthusiasm can help team members feel optimistic and personable with one another. Their networking abilities are often helpful when teams need to rely on other individuals outside of the immediate team. When conflict arises, they can help mediate between the conflicting parties.

Because they have such a strong need to maintain relationships, these individuals will go along with others in the team to minimize interpersonal conflict. They will be reluctant to state their opinions to the rest of the team. This can pose a problem because the rest of the team may be relying on them for their input and contribution. They like to be personally connected, so they might spend a lot of time interacting on a personal level with others instead of focusing on team business. This can result in others feeling like they are wasting time during team meetings or are not as concerned about performance as they should be.

Most Amiable Style people are easy to interact with, so you will naturally be able to get along with other team members. To be most effective, you should be direct with your input and ideas. Move more quickly when it is appropriate, and don't be afraid to speak your mind or initiate differences of opinion. The team will appreciate your contributions and will have a clear understanding of where you stand. Keep in mind that disagreements are usually expected within work teams, and people can distinguish between work issues and personal disagreements.

Analytical Style

Analytical Style people are focused on information and a desire to make the right decision, from their perspective. Thinking, processing, and careful analysis are important to these individuals. These individuals use time to fully review situations. They do not like to be rushed, believing this will result in mistakes. Therefore, their decision-making is slow-paced and methodical, and they focus on facts and information. Gut instincts or attempted use of influence are seen as negatives. Others therefore see them as reserved, slow moving, and risk averse.

They are cooperative in action, as long as they are not forced to act too quickly and have freedom to organize their own efforts. They appreciate others who support their approach and principles. Follow-through and meeting commitments are important when working with them.

In times of tension, these individuals are likely to avoid making a decision or to leave the situation altogether. The concept of "paralysis by analysis" applies to them. They would rather delay action than make the wrong decision.

Analytical Style people use their organizational skills to influence team processes and help keep teams on track. Their methodical approach to tasks and processes can be helpful, especially for teams that require a great deal of structure in order to achieve their outcomes. These individuals' rational approach to problem-solving is helpful for focusing teams on the most immediate concerns or issues, and can help to divert attention away from interpersonal issues that may keep the team from achieving results. Because they tend to be prepared, they are often very reliable in terms of accomplishing their work, which helps the team continually make progress.

These individuals are sometimes slow to act and can be slow in conversation. They have a tendency to draw out conversations, speaking in more detail than is necessary or wanted by other team members. This can result in others becoming impatient with them and trying to work around them rather than with them. These individuals are also cautious and can be hesitant to take action or move forward, even when the rest of the team is ready. This can result in unnecessary delays. If they disagree with the direction the team is going, they might become disengaged and will not voice their opinions. Alternatively, they may become very stubborn, clinging to their position without being open to other points of view.

When working in teams as an Analytical Style, you can enhance your effectiveness by more directly providing your opinions and input. Determine what your point of view is, and make it. Try to make your main points efficiently, since other team members might not need very much detail or information about the history of an issue. When decisions need to be made by the team, agree to take a course of action even though you might feel you don't have all the necessary information to move forward. When difficult situations come up, do not avoid them. Instead, face these situations with an awareness that this approach will ultimately lead to better outcomes.

6.2 Building Relationships

Each team member has unique ways they prefer to get to know others according to their SOCIAL STYLE. For example, some people try to form relationships immediately after meeting other team members, while others are slower to interact. Understanding different SOCIAL STYLE preferences for establishing relationships is very important. In the following pages we will provide some techniques on how to establish rapport, build relationships, and communicate with people of each SOCIAL STYLE.

Driving Style

To establish rapport with Driving Style team members, make sure that conversations get right to the point. This will support their orientation for taking action and their need for getting results. Clearly explain to them what you believe the team wants to accomplish.

By nature, Driving Style people place less emphasis on personal relationships. Before forming any sort of close bond, they will want you to display your competence. You can establish credibility with these individuals by displaying your competence and contribution to the team. Once you have done this, they will be more open to a closer relationship.

Although they typically make their opinions known, it might occasionally be necessary to solicit their input. These team members are comfortable with specific questions. In particular, open-ended questions and probing questions allow them to emphasize facts and information they consider important. Their answers will tend to be concise and to the point. Be prepared to ask follow-up questions, when necessary, to draw out additional details. They may become impatient with vague or hypothetical questions, since they will view them as lacking focus or unproductive. Be cautious not to come across to these team members as if you are interrogating them.

Signs that Driving Style team members are experiencing tension include increasing impatience, more animation, and verbalizing specific objections to the team. They might attempt to take even more control of the team or discussion. They generally will not be open to listening to other team members while in backup mode.

You can reduce their tension by identifying specific problems that concern them. Pay attention to their need for results, but be willing to stand up to them if necessary. This may be contrary to your own SOCIAL STYLE preferences and uncomfortable for you, but Driving Style people usually respect this form of self-assertion. Offer these individuals options to move the team or the situation forward.

Expressive Style

Expressive Style people are focused on relationships, so they will want to establish some form of relationship with other team members. They will be most open to you if you display some energy and excitement around your roles in the team. Maintaining a healthy sense of humor with these team members will go a long way toward establishing an informal relationship.

To establish rapport with Expressive Style team members, find some ways you can acknowledge your personal approval of them. Show your support for their creativity, aspirations, enthusiasm, or energy for working on the team.

Like Driving Style people, Expressive Style team members will generally make their opinions known. If you need to get information from them, they are generally comfortable with open-ended or hypothetical questions that allow them to express their vision and opinions. They can find closed-ended questions constraining and uncomfortable. When it is necessary to ask a closed-ended question, ask about key facts rather than specific details that would need to be recounted in a precise or logical order.

Tension in Expressive Style team members can manifest itself as emotional outbursts, dominating behaviors, critical statements, and even outright attacks. These people are often very animated, and while in backup mode they can be loud and physically active in their gestures and expressions.

To help alleviate tension with these team members, allow them to vent their frustration, but be careful not to let them get carried away with their emotions. This can result in an unproductive loop. Let them know you understand their concerns, and then move toward a solution that separates the emotion from the facts. If their frustration is directed toward another team member, help them separate the person from the work situation, since Expressive Style people often criticize people on a personal level. Showing appreciation for them and the value they add to the team will also help them come out of their backup behavior. Expressive Style people often cool down as quickly as they heat up. However, do not allow these individuals to use their SOCIAL STYLE as an excuse for inappropriate behavior; hold them accountable so they understand the limits to their expressiveness.

Amiable Style

To establish rapport with Amiable Style team members, it is most important you are genuine. Asking about their family or personal matters will not carry any weight unless you are genuinely interested. As a word of caution, it is generally only appropriate to talk about personal matters if you have already established a solid relationship with your Amiable Style team members.

These individuals are focused on relationships, so they will usually be open to having informal, non-work related interactions. In a team setting, they will work best with you if they are assured you have their interests in mind. If they feel you are simply trying to get work done through them, they might be more hesitant to interact with you.

In team meetings, Amiable Style people may be quieter than some of the others. Get their input by asking them questions. Unlike Driving Style people, closed-ended questions can make Amiable Style team members uncomfortable. Open-ended questions allow them to provide their input, as well as the context around their reasoning. These team members are also typically quite comfortable with hypothetical questions.

Amiable Style team members are likely to become even less assertive as their tension grows. They may acquiesce to the team, simply stating that everything is okay without verbalizing their viewpoints or actively committing to next steps. In meetings, they may avoid eye contact and will sometimes become fidgety and tense.

To help reduce tension, actively discuss any implications that team decisions will have on the people who are involved. Be upfront about the team's needs or commitments and reassure the Amiable Style team members about their concerns. Point out that disagreements on business issues do not necessarily indicate deteriorating personal relationships. Allow them to express themselves by actively giving them the floor to air any grievances and concerns. Make it safe for these team members to disagree, and encourage them to take the risk of expressing their opinions.

Analytical Style

You can establish rapport with Analytical Style team members by initially approaching them in a rational, business-oriented way. You might acknowledge or commend some aspect of their team performance. This helps them meet their need to make sure things are done right. In meetings, approach matters in a logical and organized manner. Being vague or too general can alienate these individuals. Take time in your conversations to share important facts and encourage an organized, logical, two-way dialogue.

Analytical Style team members are generally not focused on relationships, at least not initially. It may take some time to get to know them on a more personal level, although they are generally open to this as long as you aren't overly personal with them. They work best in teams when the focus is on business, but they appreciate when you understand something about their lives.

Like Amiable Style people, Analytical Style team members may be more hesitant to speak during team meetings. They might need to be given time to think, so don't rush them for immediate answers. These individuals might provide the team with unnecessary detail, so be prepared to help them focus. Hypothetical questions may be uncomfortable for them because they might not have thought about the situation or have enough information to answer in a way they feel appropriate.

When feeling tense, Analytical Style team members may become even more quiet and withdrawn than usual. They tend to avoid eye contact and may try to focus their attention on something unrelated to the source of the tension, even trying to physically leave the situation. They may object to certain decisions or postpone action because they are upset with the course of events.

You can help to diffuse tension with these individuals by objectively discussing the issues. Validate their contributions and concerns by stating your understanding, followed by the team's reasoning. Allow them to express their opinions and concerns, being aware this might require some time away from the team for them to process. Oftentimes when Analytical Style people feel their viewpoints have been heard, they will be able to move into a more productive mode.

> What must managers do to create and support an environment of diversity and inclusiveness? Based on a study conducted at one of the world's leading manufacturing companies, the answer was "increase Versatility." The study found that highly versatile managers significantly outperformed less versatile managers on 31 key competencies related to diversity and inclusiveness. So, if you want an organization that gains the maximum benefits of diversity and inclusiveness, teach your managers how to be more versatile.

6.3 Welcoming Team Members

It's natural for teams to shift membership over the course of their existences. Teams are interdependent. Therefore, the loss of one or more members, or the addition of others, will impact the rest of the team. Roles and responsibilities might change, action plans may need to be revised, and operating procedures may need to be adapted.

One thing is certain: integrating new members should not be left to chance. This process requires careful thought and planning. New members form impressions based on how they are initially received by the team. If they are effectively integrated, team productivity increases. If integration is done poorly, productivity and trust may decrease, and conflict may occur.

In the following section we present information about how people of each SOCIAL STYLE are likely to incorporate into a team. We also provide advice on how to welcome new members in a way that will make them feel comfortable and eager to contribute to the team.

Driving Style

Driving Style individuals enjoy fast-paced work environments, so they will be eager to get started with a new team. They will try to focus on the most pressing needs in order to get results. They will want to make a quick contribution and may be perceived by established team members as being overly aggressive. Because they do not focus on relationships, these individuals risk coming across to the team as impersonal, competitive, or even self-serving.

Your team can help new Driving Style members integrate by giving them a clear understanding of their role on the team and the outcomes they are expected to achieve. If possible, allow them to take control of a team function and make relevant decisions. Teams often require decisions to be made by consensus, and this can be a challenge for Driving Style people. Set appropriate expectations about team norms with these individuals early in their integration into the team.

Expressive Style

Because they are naturally outgoing, Expressive Style individuals will generally want to quickly integrate into an existing team. They may try to rapidly make personal connections with other team members, in addition to focusing on the function of the team. Due to their fast pace and personal nature, they may come across to existing team members as undisciplined, unprofessional, and intrusive.

Your team can help new Expressive Style members integrate by giving them a general picture of the team and what it needs to accomplish. Show excitement about their entry in the team, and explain how their contributions can be unique and exciting. If possible, let them make their initial contributions in a creative and public way. If it is comfortable for you, allow yourself to get personally involved with these individuals, since getting to know others personally is important for them.

Amiable Style

Amiable Style people are naturally friendly, so they will be eager to be a part of the team and get to know other members. They generally aim to please and will want to understand how they can contribute to the team's efforts. Because they are slower paced and focus on maintaining relationships, they risk coming across as too agreeable and unwilling to contribute innovative or risky ideas.

To effectively integrate new Amiable Style members, show them how their role within the team will contribute to the goals of the team and how their efforts will be appreciated. Early in their integration, give them opportunities to work closely with other team members. When feasible, allow them to be flexible in how tasks are accomplished and how quickly they are completed. Provide them with opportunities to build social networks that help the team when it needs assistance. Also let them know the expectations the team has around being open and candid in communicating with one another.

Analytical Style

New Analytical Style team members will want to integrate themselves into a team by gaining as much understanding as they can about the team's goals, strategies, and their roles in the team. They will want to make an impact by establishing their credibility or thoroughness within a specified area. Initially, these individuals often show less concern for relationships than some other SOCIAL STYLEs. Due to this, they can come across to existing team members as distant, formal, and unsociable.

Your team can help new Analytical Style members integrate by thoroughly explaining their role, and giving them background information about the team. Give them some time to assimilate information about their role and to get to know the rest of the team. If possible, provide them with tasks they can work on by themselves prior to presenting their information to other team members.

Team Leader Tip: *How to Integrate all SOCIAL STYLEs?*

In addition to the SOCIAL STYLE-specific information presented previously, you can help new team members successfully integrate by establishing a new member integration process. This will ensure all new members start off successfully and have a clear understanding of the team. With new team members you should:

- Explain the team's mission and goals
- Share the history and progress of the team

- Review each team member's role and responsibilities
- Share specific expectations of the new member
- Provide a synopsis of important contacts outside of the team, and how the new member will be introduced to them
- Explain team norms, including communication standards
- Review the team's process for reward and recognition, and for handling disagreements
- Explain the team's operating procedures, including processes for exchanging information, problem solving, and meeting management
- Review the team's process for monitoring and evaluating team and individual performance
- Check for any special requests or needs the new member may have

6.4 Aligning the Team

Your organization may have a specific methodology in place for managing teams or it may leave the details to the individual teams. In either situation, the team exists for a purpose and likely has a set of formal and informal operating procedures. No matter the work phase your particular team is in, there is a series of tasks common to all teams. We will now discuss how SOCIAL STYLE can be applied to establish a common purpose and team roles in order to increase team effectiveness.

Teams become teams for a purpose. The team needs to solve a problem, develop a product, manage a project, or any number of other things. Perhaps because establishing the purpose of the team can seem like the simplest and most obvious task, it is often glossed over. This can have consequences later on, such as confusion among team members, disputes over accountabilities and resources, and misunderstandings about timelines and processes.

When a common purpose has been established, the team should know:

- The group's priorities and goals
- The plan to achieve its goals
- Criteria for success

Involving all members in establishing a purpose and direction for the team is important. In effective teams, all members must own the purpose and plan, and everyone is accountable. Commitment to the plan is more likely if all team members feel their perspectives have been taken into account.

Each SOCIAL STYLE has specific strengths that contribute to this stage. For example, Driving Style members will be interested in developing a timeline and deadlines for progress. Expressive Style people will help to visualize goals and build enthusiasm for other team members. Amiable Style members can be valuable for ensuring the team works well together and there is group agreement on strategy and direction. Finally, Analytical Style members can be helpful for suggesting processes and the measurability of goals and ensuring they are realistic.

When working with a team of individuals, it might be difficult to meet everyone's expectations. However, when formulating team direction and goals, you can apply SOCIAL STYLE to meet different needs in a way that will move the team forward. The following are characteristics you can expect from people of each SOCIAL STYLE when your team is establishing its purpose and goals. This is followed by advice on how to meet the needs of these individuals while maintaining a focus on the overall team's needs.

Driving Style

Instead of a lengthy discussion of a team's purpose, Driving Style team members might simply state it in one sentence. For example, "We need to develop a new technology infrastructure." These individuals are generally focused on specific outcomes but not on the details of how to achieve those goals, which can be reflected in their initial planning. They may not be very interested in discussing the specific process for achieving the outcome, at least not initially. Instead, they may be eager to rush into action. This can leave some team members feeling not only rushed before they are ready, but confused about the purpose and strategy of the team.

Because they are results-focused, getting Driving Style members involved early on is helpful for focusing the team on the outcomes. However, during this stage of team development, it might be necessary to slow them down. Let them know time spent at this stage will save time and energy later on. Developing a common purpose with specific and actionable goals that can be measured will help the team focus and be more efficient.

Expressive Style

Expressive Style individuals like to have a voice in planning, especially since they have a desire to share their opinions and ideas with groups. They tend to speculate on possibilities, with less interest in developing detailed plans. They may be particularly vocal and effective if the team uses any group brainstorming activities at this stage. Their fast approach and big-picture thinking might be frustrating for some team members who will feel the need to focus on details at this stage of the team's development.

Getting these individuals involved during this early stage of team development will help meet their need for approval and recognition. However, you may need to moderate somewhat to prevent them from dominating the process and setting unrealistic goals. Build on their enthusiasm by offering your own ideas and getting quieter team members involved.

Amiable Style

Amiable Style members like the opportunity to be involved in establishing the team's purpose. Due to their orientation towards relationships, they may display particular interest in how the team's activities might impact either themselves or others down the road. And they will be concerned as to how the team itself will work together.

These individuals thrive on group interactions, so involving them will help meet their need for maintaining relationships. Since they have a tendency to quietly go along with groups, you may need to help them get started by specifically asking them for their input during the team planning meeting.

Analytical Style

Because they have a need to be right, Analytical Style members like to be involved in establishing processes. Helping to determine the goals and strategy of the team will appeal to their sense of order and logic. They may show particular interest in establishing detailed and thorough project plans, timelines, or other plans that deal with time and resources. At this early stage, if these individuals spend too much time trying to plan small details or discuss minor steps, other team members might become frustrated by their slow pace.

It is helpful to get these individuals involved early in a team's development by appealing to the opportunity for them to influence the team and its goals. If they do not believe they were included in this critical stage, they may try to slow things down later on, even if the rest of the team is ready to move ahead.

Team Leader Tip: *How to Align the Team?*

If you are the leader of the team, you can help meet the various needs of team members by making this stage of team development a specific event that incorporates the strengths of each SOCIAL STYLE. Facilitate this process by calling a meeting to discuss team strategy and goals. Help each SOCIAL STYLE by incorporating the following techniques:

- ***Driving Style*** - come prepared to discuss options for achieving goals. This will help engage them in the discussion since they particularly like having options to choose from when deciding.

- ***Expressive Style*** - appeal to the spontaneity and enthusiasm of these team members by highlighting opportunities for them to create an exciting vision, and to obtain personal recognition through their team contributions. This will help them focus on team goals and the need to develop plans.

- ***Amiable Style*** - these team members will appreciate the opportunity to develop strategy as a group. You can help them by making sure they are involved in the group discussion, since they might be hesitant to assert themselves.

- ***Analytical Style*** - these team members will appreciate your thorough and organized approach to developing team goals and strategy. You can help them by taking time to focus on the details of the plan, along with clear accountabilities and timelines.

6.5 Roles & Responsibilities

It may seem obvious that every member of a team has a specific role to play. But in reality, individuals actually have two types of roles within a team. The first is their formal role, such as technology expert. The second has more to do with a person's SOCIAL STYLE. In this section we provide techniques for clarifying team roles and for assigning responsibility to team members of each SOCIAL STYLE.

Team roles clarify, in broad terms, what each member will contribute to the achievement of the team's objectives, and how team members will work interdependently to achieve results. When a team is established, every team member should understand what specific part of the plan they will be held accountable for and measured against. This upfront clarification of roles serves many advantages. In particular, it:

- Ensures all members clearly understand what is expected of them personally
- Ensures all members understand what they can depend on others to do
- Eliminates overlaps or duplication of effort
- Minimizes oversights and sets accountabilities
- Builds a sense of team interdependence and shared leadership

The following pages review how a team member's SOCIAL

STYLE will impact how they function within the team. In particular, you will learn how SOCIAL STYLE influences how people take on team responsibilities, regardless of their roles.

Driving Style

When given responsibility for a task, Driving Style team members will generally focus on achieving the task since they are naturally driven by results. They can be enthusiastic about taking on team responsibilities, usually if it helps them achieve a personally important goal. However, due to their Control Responsiveness orientation, their excitement might not always be apparent.

Because they are Tell Assertive, these individuals might sometimes delegate responsibility to others, even when they are not in a position of authority. In part, this arises because of their natural impatience. Be cautious about letting these individuals take control of team tasks or other team members when this is outside the scope of their formal role. If this happens, other members of the team who are working with the individual on tasks might feel like they have lost their independence or personal authority.

When assigning roles and responsibilities to Driving Style people, provide concrete information about the specific outcomes required. Let them know they are in charge and accountable. Instead of telling them exactly how to accomplish the work, provide them with acceptable alternatives or let them decide on their own. Since these team members prefer specific goals, if possible avoid giving them vague assignments with no clear milestones.

Driving Style members are usually not prone to providing detailed or frequent written progress reports. They like to work at a fast pace and use time efficiently, so allow them to stay focused on impending deadlines without unnecessarily checking on them.

Because they tend to be competitive, if possible, avoid requiring these members to collaborate or depend on people over whom they have no influence. This might result in more frustration than accomplishment.

Expressive Style

Because of their orientation for recognition, Expressive Style members are typically enthusiastic about taking on roles and responsibilities. Of all the SOCIAL STYLEs, they are most likely to show outward enthusiasm for team activities and may actively volunteer for assignments. This is especially true if the role will help them become publicly recognized in some way. However, if tasks are repeatedly mundane or do not provide the type of attention these people need, they will lose motivation to work on their assignments.

When working on team assignments with others, Expressive Style members might not meet their obligations in a way others expect. For example, they may show up to meetings unprepared or fail to turn in their work on time. They may fail to communicate often enough with other team members, particularly in written communication. This can be frustrating for other team members. To prevent this, establish clear guidelines around deadlines, accountabilities, and work requirements.

When assigning roles and responsibilities to Expressive Style members, point out the opportunity for them to benefit in some way. Many team responsibilities include some form of recognition or professional development, which will appeal to these individuals. When establishing goals, develop a plan that elicits their ideas and opinions, but be prepared to help them be realistic. Allow some time for fun and avoid developing a plan with so many details that the person feels overwhelmed with minor items that can reduce their commitment.

Regularly follow up with these team members to keep them focused on necessary tasks. They tend to be future-oriented, so they might stray off course when detailed or time sensitive work is required. Try not to ignore their enthusiasm or be impatient with them, since this will impact their motivation and creativity. With these members it is usually helpful if you can make sure having fun is part of the goal.

Amiable Style

Amiable Style team members are naturally cooperative, so they will usually be eager to take on responsibilities. In fact, they are likely to display their enthusiasm about activities. They are most motivated when they can work as part of a group, so any activities or tasks that involve a sub-team will appeal to them. They generally will not respond well to tasks that require them to work in isolation, at least not for long periods of time.

These individuals sometimes struggle with making their opinions known, particularly in team settings. They may be so concerned about going along with the group they may fail to state their opinions or ideas. Encourage these members to assert themselves by explicitly asking for their input.

When assigning roles and responsibilities, Amiable Style team members will appreciate being given either clear instructions or your recommendations. It might be helpful if your assignments are not too risky and include the opportunity to enhance their working relationships with other team members. In addition, they will want to know how their role or task relates to the broader mission of the team. They will generally operate most effectively if there is some flexibility within their roles or projects, so you may need to redefine parameters as you go along.

Because Amiable Style team members tend to show a less disciplined use of time and move at a slower pace, you may want to regularly check on their progress. When done in a friendly way, this helps them bring up any issues with you that might not surface otherwise. When appropriate, allow them to be flexible in how they accomplish tasks. Many people appreciate verbal praise when they do a good job; this form of recognition especially motivates these team members.

Analytical Style

Because they are generally reserved, Analytical Style team members might not show much outward enthusiasm for team projects or tasks. However, they will be motivated by assignments that allow them to display their expertise in some area. This could be either a functional or technical area. Giving them the opportunity to take charge of a specific responsibility will often appeal to their desire to make sure things are done right. They can have difficulty responding to multiple priorities or relying on the input of other team members.

In team settings, Analytical Style team members might withdraw from the rest of the team. When given responsibility for a team task, they might be uncommunicative with other team members who are relying on them for information. Help them stay connected with others by scheduling check-up meetings, and by giving them an appropriate amount of time to complete their work.

When assigning roles and responsibilities to Analytical Style team members, make sure they understand how their contributions are related to the team goals. Provide supporting information if this is necessary, and ask questions to ensure the person clearly understands the scope of their responsibilities. Allow these individuals to voice any concerns about their roles. Once you have agreed to the roles and responsibilities, it might be helpful to put them in writing so they can refer back to them.

Analytical Style people tend to move at a slower pace, particularly in the early stages of a new project or task. This is because they need to think things through and mentally work through the details and processes before taking action. Try to avoid pressing them for immediate decisions or action. Schedule regular checkups with them, but allow them to work through the details of tasks on their own without unnecessary interruption. They might prefer it if you check with them through email rather than in person.

6.6 Team Meetings

You probably have enough experience with meetings to know when they are effective or ineffective. Effective meetings are crucial to the life of teams. They are often one of the few places where team members meet as a whole. It is where they develop a team identity and work interdependently toward their goals.

In order to be successful, team meetings need to be thoughtfully planned, successfully managed, and systematically evaluated. On the following pages, we present information about how each of the SOCIAL STYLEs approaches team meetings and how to increase effectiveness within a team environment.

Driving Style

As Driving Style people are often in a hurry, this can be the case during meetings. They will want to get to the main agenda items quickly. This helps fulfill their need for results. If too much time is spent on issues they do not believe are important, they will become bored with the meeting. As is often the case with this behavior, other team members can feel like they are being rolled over, ignored, or even undervalued.

These individuals will be particularly irritated if they believe the team is scheduling too many meetings. In particular, if the number of meetings becomes burdensome and they perceive meaningful progress is not being made, they are likely to complain. While everyone's time is valuable, these members especially like to use their time efficiently. Related to this, they appreciate it when meetings are scheduled to be as brief as possible.

Help these individuals by creating an agenda that includes specific desired outcomes. This will provide them with a focus. It will also give them assurance that results will be delivered by attending the meeting, and concrete steps are being taken to achieve the overall team objectives. If they try to take over a meeting, try to redirect them by assuring them that the team will focus on important outcomes, but there are good reasons why the discussion is headed in a particular direction. You can be direct with Driving Style people, even if it feels somewhat uncomfortable for you.

To best meet the needs of Driving Style team members, plan to use time efficiently. Make sure you are prepared to focus on what needs to be accomplished. Prepare to clearly state your opinions and look for opportunities to let these individuals make decisions. While considering the team's needs, try to reach decisions quickly when possible. Avoid scheduling unnecessary meetings. Alternatively, invite only team members that are absolutely required, and follow up with others by sending meeting minutes, decisions, or outcomes.

Expressive Style

You can expect Expressive Style team members to be vocal contributors to meetings. They want to share their opinions and ideas with others. This helps fulfill their need for recognition. If they feel ignored or like their opinions are being pushed aside, they will become upset. They may respond by verbally confronting other team members. This can leave others feeling they have been personally attacked.

These individuals are typically sociable, so they like opportunities to meet with others. For this reason, they usually don't mind attending team meetings. They are likely to approach meetings as relatively casual events. For example, they may show up late or be unconcerned with timed agendas. On occasion, their use of humor in meetings can be disruptive and inappropriate. Like most people, they may become frustrated if too many meetings are scheduled, but they are less likely than some other SOCIAL STYLEs to actively oppose meetings.

You can help these individuals be most effective by appealing to their spontaneity. Techniques such as brainstorming will be especially useful for engaging them in meetings. This will provide them with a stage to express themselves and interact with others creatively on tasks. If they become inappropriately confrontational with other team members, try to redirect them by calling their attention to the work at hand. Help them separate the tasks or decisions to be made from the specific members involved.

To best meet the needs of Expressive Style team members, try to prepare for some of the meeting time to be stimulating. This can be accomplished in a number of small ways, such as using humor or giving personal recognition to team members. Plan to describe any personal benefits of team activities to these individuals. After meetings, follow up to make sure they are still engaged in the team and understand any commitments they have made.

Amiable Style

Individuals with Amiable Style will typically act as supportive members of the group during team meetings. They will support the team's decisions, and might provide needed material and information. Though they like being in group settings, they are less likely to be talkative during meetings than some other SOCIAL STYLEs. If they feel disregarded or unappreciated by other team members, especially the team leader, they may respond by going along with whatever decisions are being made. However, their silence does not signal consent. This can leave others feeling like these team members are in line with everyone else, when in fact they are not.

Because they are so focused on relationships, they typically welcome the opportunity to meet with the team. They will approach meetings as an opportunity to strengthen relationships with other team members. This is often shown by giving verbal support for others' positions and by encouraging others. They usually will not mind attending multiple team meetings, as long as the meetings are not entirely focused on tasks. They will be uncomfortable if meetings constantly involve conflict or other forms of tension.

You can help Amiable Style members by involving them in group activities. This is a natural advantage to having them as team members, since many tasks will involve other people. Working closely with other team members will appeal to their orientation for relationships. Like Expressive Style people, these individuals will also react favorably to group activities. If these members appear to be acquiescing to group decisions without stating their opinions or objections, involve them by explicitly asking for their input. Regularly asking for an individual's input is always a good idea, but it is especially effective for involving these members.

To best meet the needs of Amiable Style team members, interact with them in a friendly and personable manner. Try to consider their viewpoints and concerns ahead of time, and prepare to discuss these, even if they do not bring them to the surface themselves. Ask open-ended questions to help them open up and share with the team, such as, "What are we missing? What concerns are we not addressing?" or "Who else needs to be involved?" After meetings, follow up with these individuals to confirm any action plans and make sure they are committed.

Analytical Style

Analytical Style team members will generally approach meetings as an opportunity to ensure that processes are comprehensive enough to accomplish team goals. They will try to accomplish this by influencing key decisions and procedures. This helps fulfill their need to be right. Like Amiable Style members, they are less likely to speak up during meetings than other SOCIAL STYLEs. They will often wait for others to state their opinions before giving their own input. They will become uncomfortable if they believe important information is not being addressed, or worse, is being disregarded.

Analytical Style people are usually comfortable working independently on tasks, so they may not approach meetings as sociably as some other SOCIAL STYLEs. They will be more patient during meetings than Driving Style members, but they will want meetings to be focused. They generally will not mind attending a lot of meetings, as long as they believe the meetings are relevant and necessary to achieve the team's goals. They will react unfavorably if they have to attend so many meetings that they are unable to complete their own work.

Analytical Style team members will be especially appreciative of detailed agendas. They tend to be focused on time and schedules, so they may pay particular attention to the timeframes developed around agenda items. If these individuals appear to be withdrawing from the team, attempt to re-engage them by surfacing issues important to them. Allow them the time to discuss their viewpoints. When possible, support them by agreeing their ideas are valid, and offer to back them up in a course of action.

To best meet the needs of Analytical Style team members, come to meetings prepared with necessary materials and information and make certain other team members have followed through on their commitments. If it is your responsibility, plan to present this information to the group. Take time to understand and present the pros and cons of different ideas. Since these individuals do not focus too much on feelings, address them in a straightforward way during meetings.

Team Leader Tip: *How to Plan a Meeting to Meet the Needs of All SOCIAL STYLEs?*

As the team leader, it may not always be possible to fully please everyone during team meetings, nor is this a reasonable expectation. However, there are strategies you can use to strike a balance between meeting everyone's needs and achieving the results you need.

Developing an organized agenda, complete with desired outcomes, timeframes, and participant responsibilities, will help your Driving and Analytical Style team members. This will satisfy Driving Style members' need for results, and having an organized process will appeal to Analytical Style members. Infusing a bit of humor and fun into meetings will help keep Expressive and Amiable Style members engaged. Keep these individuals involved by utilizing problem-solving strategies such as brainstorming.

If appropriate, try to schedule meetings with subgroups of the team to discuss specific issues. This will ensure progress is made without needlessly taking up the time of team members who are not required for specific aspects of the project.

6.7 Decision-Making

Making decisions within teams is not always a neat and clean process. Many teams struggle with this fundamental aspect of team performance. The truth is, it often takes longer for teams to make decisions than would be the case if decisions were made unilaterally. However, the extra time is usually worthwhile because everyone understands and supports the decision. This ultimately leads to faster execution of decisions.

Team decision-making will be most effective if:

- Team goals and priorities are clear
- Team members understand their levels of responsibility for making decisions
- The team has an effective process for making decisions

Regardless of the decision-making process your team uses, individual members will approach decision-making in unique ways. Here we describe how SOCIAL STYLE impacts team decision-making, and how to interact with people of each SOCIAL STYLE to create effective decisions.

Driving Style

Driving Style people are usually comfortable taking risks, and this can come across in their approach to making decisions. They are more likely than some of the other SOCIAL STYLEs to support decisions that have higher risks, but also higher payoffs. They like to make decisions quickly, so a lengthy process for establishing group consensus might try their patience. If they believe the group is taking too long, or is focused on extraneous details, they may try to assert themselves in order to move the group along. Once a decision is made, these members will generally move directly to the next order of business. They typically do not like to revisit issues once a decision has been made.

Staying focused on the primary outcomes of a decision will help meet these members' needs and may also prevent them from trying to dominate the decision-making process. You can help them by providing all relevant information needed to make a decision, but not in too much detail. Provide an overview of the different sides of an issue, as well as the implications of any decisions.

Expressive Style

Expressive Style people also tend to be fast paced. When making decisions, they may act impulsively without considering all the relevant facts or implications. Because they are future oriented, they may get excited about the impacts of decisions made, either for the team or themselves. They will usually want to be involved in the decision-making process, and can be quite forceful in asserting their opinions. However, they will not be interested in a lot of details around implementing decisions. If they feel left out, they will become impatient and might try to involve themselves in any way they can. They tend to be somewhat malleable in regard to decisions. They are usually comfortable revisiting a course of action and altering their original decisions.

By pointing out how the outcome of decisions will benefit Expressive Style team members, or the team as a whole, your team will engage these individuals in the decision-making process. When possible and necessary, involve them in making decisions. If they do not need to be involved, explain the reasoning and advise them of decisions.

Amiable Style

Amiable Style people tend to be slower paced and usually don't rush into decisions. They are more risk averse than other SOCIAL STYLEs, and may be hesitant to agree to risky courses of action. They operate in the present time frame and will want assurance that decisions will not change the status quo to an uncomfortable degree. In particular, they will want to be clear on any impact decisions will have on working relationships, reporting relationships, and lines of communication. If they feel a decision is too disruptive to the status quo, they may try to resist. This resistance can be somewhat passive; for instance by resurfacing the issue down the road. These members generally do not mind revisiting decisions, and can alter their opinions if they feel it is warranted.

Amiable Style team members will be most effective in the decision-making process when they understand why a decision needs to be made, and especially the implications of a decision. Because they like to avoid conflict, help them state their opinions to the team. Point out any opportunities for them to contribute as a result of a decision. Verify they are ready to proceed before finalizing a decision.

Analytical Style

Like Amiable Style people, Analytical Style team members are usually slower paced and do not like to rush into making decisions. They tend to act cautiously, so they may be reluctant to make decisions that involve a great deal of risk. When making decisions, these individuals will usually consider the past as a way of framing what should happen in the future. They will want to make sure decisions take into account what has happened in the past. If they believe decisions are being made too quickly, or important information isn't taken into account, they may try to slow down the team. They will do this by withholding their opinions, or by insisting that the team consider other viewpoints before moving forward. Once a decision has been made, these members will generally support it and want to move forward.

Analytical Style team members will be most effective in the decision-making process if they have been provided with all the information they believe is necessary for making a decision. They are most effective when they can obtain this information prior to a decision-making meeting. Encourage these individuals to voice any concerns they might have about a decision, and reassure them the team has taken various viewpoints into account.

Team Leader Tip: *How to Get Consensus?*

It may look like achieving consensus with different SOCIAL STYLEs will be difficult because they have different needs and perspectives. However, it is usually not as difficult as you may believe. When proposing a decision, be sure it presents an action-oriented outcome with clear accountabilities. This will help satisfy Driving Style members. Keep Expressive Style people involved throughout the process, in particular by making sure they contribute to any solutions. Likewise, keep Amiable Style individuals involved and be sure they are comfortable with the direction the team is headed. During the problem-solving process, provide all available information to Analytical Style members so they will feel well prepared to recommend a course of action and support the decision.

6.8 Motivation & Engagement

Many teams exist permanently, while other teams only stay together for a planned amount of time. Regardless of the life span of your team, its members may fluctuate in terms of their motivation to participate. This is only natural. However, this can become a serious problem in the long term if team members become actively disengaged. At best, they won't meaningfully contribute to the team. At worst, they might cause the team to become dysfunctional and unproductive. By recognizing signs that team members are becoming unmotivated, you can help them get back on track. Here we describe these signs and offer advice on how to help team members of each SOCIAL STYLE remain engaged with your team, both in day-to-day activities and in the long term.

Driving Style

You will know Driving Style team members are engaged with the team when they are actively asserting themselves and offering input. This will be noticeable because they will be speaking to the team during meetings and making direct eye contact. They will readily share their opinions, and will listen to the input of other members. They will want to help the team achieve its goals, and will be very active in this pursuit.

These individuals tend to become upset when they feel their time is being wasted, and this will be particularly true if they believe the team is not making progress. If they sense the team is stalling, especially because of inadequate leadership or disruptive members, they may become disengaged from the team. Disengagement looks different for Driving Style people than it does for some other SOCIAL STYLEs. These individuals like to take action, so if they are disconnected they will look for opportunities to either change the course of the team or leave altogether. They may try to take control, either to move things along or to get the results they want.

During typical day-to-day tasks, make sure team meetings get right to the point for Driving Style teammates. If you are presenting information, explain what you want to accomplish. This will support their orientation for taking action and their need for results. If they become disengaged, refocus the discussion on the most important points and how those are related to the team goals.

If a Driving Style team member becomes seriously disengaged from the team, more dramatic measures may need to be taken to get them back on track. Because they respond to direct feedback, it may be necessary to confront them about their lack of commitment. Let them know the impact they have on team performance, and seek their reasons for disengaging. Though it may feel uncomfortable, speaking very directly and openly with these team members is necessary.

Expressive Style

For Expressive Style people, signs of engagement are usually obvious. They will be enthusiastic with the team and will display animated hand gestures and facial expressions, in particular smiling and laughing. During team meetings, these people will generally be quite talkative, but will also listen well.

These team members are likely to become disengaged if they feel the team is rejecting them personally, dismissing their ideas, or pressing for too much detail in their tasks. Consequently, they may become upset and begin to vent feelings rather than engage with the team in a productive manner. This might be directed to a single member or the whole team. Signs that they are upset will usually be just as obvious as signals they are engaged.

To keep Expressive Style people engaged during day-to-day tasks, find some ways to show your personal approval of them. Show your support for their team enthusiasm or energy. Give them attention without letting them take total control. If they begin to vent emotions, allow them to do this as much as is appropriate, but be cautious about letting them get emotionally carried away.

If these individuals become more seriously disengaged from the team, it will be necessary to speak with them about the source of their dissatisfaction. You can be direct with these team members, but expect them to be emotional when they describe their feelings. Once they have made their feelings known, try to reengage them by stressing the important role they play. If possible, respond to their concerns by making changes that will help these members have a larger or different role in the team.

Amiable Style

When engaged, Amiable Style team members are lively and personable, and will share their opinions with the team. Like Expressive Style people, they will display their enthusiasm, though they will not be as talkative. They are active listeners and will communicate to other team members they have heard what was said.

These individuals are likely to disengage if they feel the team is pushing too hard for change, unilaterally setting goals without their input, or becoming too directive or autocratic. They are not likely to confront the team, and may simply go along with whatever is recommended. In these situations, they will become less animated, quieter, and may avoid eye contact more than normal. They will be eager to end the team discussion.

On a daily basis, you can usually stay engaged with Amiable Style people by showing the team is open to their input. During team meetings it might be necessary to ask open-ended questions to draw out their opinions, or review the topics you have discussed and ask for their opinions about those areas. If they become disengaged, you or someone else on the team will need to make it safe for them to share their feelings and concerns.

If these members become seriously disengaged from the team, it will be necessary to discover the source of their dissatisfaction. This can be a challenge with these individuals since they are not always open to voicing their concerns. You will need to draw out their feelings in a non-threatening way. Let them know you have noticed they are not contributing to the team as much as they had previously, and ask for their feelings about this. It may take some time for them to open up, but once they make their feelings known, you can assure them you will respond appropriately.

Analytical Style

Analytical Style team members will display engagement by listening attentively and conversing freely with the team. They may become more animated and talkative than usual, and will share their opinions. They will be openly supportive of the team and will accomplish work that moves the team toward its objectives.

These individuals may disengage if they feel the team is ignoring important details, trying to engage them on an emotional level, or pressing for immediate decisions. They may not actively contribute to the team, and might avoid meetings and deadlines. During meetings they will be more quiet than usual, and may not contribute to discussion except in response to direct questions. In some situations they may use sarcasm as a signal they are displeased.

In day-to-day interactions, the team can stay engaged with Analytical Style members by sharing important facts and taking into account information provided by these individuals. Encourage them to share their thoughts, and listen carefully to their questions and statements. Ask if there is any important information the team has not taken into account. If they become disengaged, try to assure them their input is valuable and the team will support them to conduct their work.

If they become seriously disengaged from the team, it can be a challenge to bring these members back to a point of meaningful contribution. They are unlikely to seek out other team members to express their discontent. You can confront them about their dissatisfaction, but do this in a straightforward way that avoids emotion or blame. Ask them to express their concerns, and if appropriate, let them know that you will support them in making any necessary changes to their roles or to specific issues with the team.

Team Leader Tip: *Reward and Recognition*

Just as they display enthusiasm and motivation differently, people of each SOCIAL STYLE respond to reward and recognition differently.

- **Driving Style** people like to be recognized for their ability to achieve specific goals and objectives. While not necessarily opposed to public recognition, they generally do not crave this.

- **Expressive Style** people enjoy recognition. They have a very social nature and also like to gain personal benefits, so they appreciate public recognition for their accomplishments.

- **Amiable Style** people particularly like to be recognized for accomplishments that contribute to team effectiveness. They usually appreciate public recognition as long as it is appropriate and genuine.

- **Analytical Style** people especially like praise that recognizes the quality of their contributions and the benefits these have on the team. They can become slightly uncomfortable when given public recognition, so be careful not to overdo this.

6.9 Changing Team Direction

Change in team strategy and priorities is inevitable. This presents both a problem and a challenge for teams. If change is not managed successfully, team productivity can suffer. Team members who are overly stressed by change cannot give their full energy or attention to their work.

Whenever there is a change effort there will be resistance. However, from resistance comes resilience. Resistance brings a feeling of security. Team members find comfort and stability based on where the team and organization have been in the past. Resilience implies a feeling of uncertainty. The team is suddenly moving in a new direction, and the future is uncertain.

Most people deal with change in predictable patterns. By understanding and recognizing this pattern, you will be able to help your team effectively work through the change process.

People of different SOCIAL STYLEs will react differently. It is important to recognize signs of resistance within team members so their concerns can be appropriately addressed. Here we discuss how people of each SOCIAL STYLE typically respond to change, and how to help these team members effectively adjust to changing circumstances.

Driving Style

Driving Style people tend to work in the present time frame. Therefore, when change happens they might see it as a challenge to be dealt with, and usually the faster the better. They like to have control over outcomes, so they will want to take some form of immediate action in response to the change in strategy.

When feeling resistant to change, Driving Style team members will generally show some form of active opposition. They may be outwardly opposed to the sudden change in course, and might vocalize this opposition to the team or individuals they believe are responsible.

To move these team members into a more productive state, the team should help them see the benefits in the new strategy. Stress the opportunities and challenges in the new direction. If options are available, present these and involve these team members in making decisions and setting goals.

Expressive Style

Expressive Style people tend to work in the future time frame, and they have less concern for routine than some other SOCIAL STYLEs. When the organization or team changes its strategy, these individuals will want to be involved in the change effort. They may see change as an exciting opportunity, and might look for opportunities for self-promotion or role enlargement.

When feeling resistant to change, these team members are likely to be very vocal with their opinions. They may act impulsively, venting their feelings before thinking through the situation in a rational way. If they feel a specific person or group is responsible, they might express their dissatisfaction in a highly emotional way.

Time is a necessary ingredient for helping Expressive Style people become more resilient to change. If they need to vent, allow them to do this but do not allow them to dominate or influence the rest of the team. Bring them to a less emotional state by presenting the rationale for change, and highlight any ways they might benefit from the new situation.

Amiable Style

Amiable Style people tend to work in the present time frame, but they are more hesitant to change than Driving Style people. When a team changes direction, they will be inclined to support that change, but might not be outwardly active in their support. They might look for opportunities to develop new or better working relationships with other team members.

When opposed to change, Amiable Style team members display their resistance in passive ways. They might be quietly hostile toward those they feel are responsible, and may reduce their performance. In some circumstances they might play the role of victim, indicating they feel they have no control over their situation.

To help these team members move into a state of resilience, clearly explain the reasons for the change. If possible, try not to press too hard for immediate changes in their work or circumstances. Instead, institute change gradually and involve them in implementing it. Point out any opportunities in the new situation for them to contribute.

Analytical Style

Analytical Style people tend to work in a historical time frame, and they are cautious to take action. Therefore, when an organization or team suddenly changes direction, these team members may be slower to embrace the change than others. They might look for opportunities to influence the change. For example, they may want to be involved in designing new strategies or processes.

Similar to Amiable Style individuals, these team members may show resistance in less obvious ways than others. They may procrastinate with their work or commitments, or they may try to withhold important information. In a more active way, they might make demands on the team, such as insisting changes be implemented in a specific way they think is right.

To help Analytical Style members move into a state of resilience, show them the rationale and reasoning that went into the decision to make a change. They often prefer to be alone with information before acting, so give them time to process the change and its implications. Point out any opportunities for them to influence the way in which the change is implemented, or to contribute within their area of expertise.

Team Leader Tip: *How to Be a Change Agent?*

As the team leader, you will be called on to champion successful change within your team. A significant amount of research has been done on the skills and behaviors of successful change agents. Effective change agents:

- **Establish a common purpose** - Identify problems that are central to team or business success, and take action only after careful analysis. Clarify team members' roles and responsibilities, and set and renegotiate priorities.

- **Understand team capabilities** - Recognize you and your team's skill strengths and weaknesses. Invest time in developing and coaching your team, and recognize when to ask for help from others.

- **Welcome change** - Change is a way of life and is filled with opportunity and lessons, so be proactive about it. Draw lessons from past change initiatives, and be versatile in your perceptions of change.

- **Establish team norms** - Lead by example and demonstrate courage to take risks. When dealing with change, be patient and understanding with your team.

- **Communicate** - Keep an open flow of information and create opportunities for input and feedback. Generate a strategy of cooperative networking, build supportive relationships with others in the organization, and be able to influence others. Effectively manage conflict.

- **Recognize and reward** - Encourage your team members in their efforts to make change. Celebrate your team's achievements and share recognition unselfishly.

- **Establish team operating procedure** - Approach change as a manageable process. Build procedures and processes to address and minimize ambiguity.

- **Evaluate** - Follow up on changes and hold yourself accountable for the effectiveness of changes.

6.10 Virtual Teams

Technology and the global economy have made it possible for teams to operate virtually, where members work in different regions and the majority of meetings are conducted via the Internet or teleconference. Most of the communication outside of meetings is through email or telephone, and in some teams the members never meet in person.

Virtual teams run a higher risk of misunderstanding and conflict. By their nature, they may be slower and possibly less effective due to lack of face-to-face communication and the potential for failing to share necessary information with one another. There are fewer opportunities for team members to socialize or get to know one another. This makes it very difficult to gain a clear understanding of one another or to assess the individual team members' SOCIAL STYLE.

As a member of a virtual team, there are steps you can take to determine the SOCIAL STYLEs of other team members, even if you have not observed them in person (although with technology like Skype, this is now becoming possible). But even without this technology, you can learn more about other team members through such tools as emails and SMS. Research has shown that email communication Styles are highly related to SOCIAL STYLE.

Here we provide tips for understanding other SOCIAL STYLEs when working virtually, as well as advice for communicating effectively with your virtual team.

Driving Style

During virtual meetings, Driving Style members are likely to make their presence known. They will not hesitate to talk and will typically focus on task-related matters such as plans, priorities, and deadlines.

When not meeting with the whole virtual team, these individuals are generally comfortable working alone on their tasks. However, if they are in charge of team functions that involve other members, they may actively seek them out, sometimes to the point of intrusiveness.

Driving Style team members are likely to write brief, pointed emails. Their statements will be direct and might not provide much context. For example, they might ask you to do something without explaining why it needs to be done or how the task fits with the broader work of the team. They might wait until the last minute to communicate their needs, which can frustrate other team members.

When communicating virtually with Driving Style people, try to get to the main points right away. Focus on key facts, options, and any impacts on the team's goals. When sending emails to these individuals, include attachments only if necessary. They can become impatient with too much detail. When leaving voicemails, get to the point quickly and directly to avoid being perceived as wasting the person's time.

Outside of formal team meetings, give Driving Style members the freedom to pursue their team goals. They generally do not like being checked on, so keep this to a minimum when possible. However, you can ask them for regularly scheduled updates to review their status on projects. They are most productive when they are appropriately challenged and busy, so give them tasks that keep them active. Make sure they understand the roles and importance of other team members in order to prevent them from dominating events.

Expressive Style

During virtual team meetings, Expressive Style people are likely to be among the most talkative. They will attempt to be personable with the team, often sharing stories about themselves and encouraging others to do the same. They tend to focus on people rather than tasks, which will be reflected in the issues they discuss. When not meeting with the whole team, they will seek out personal connections with other team members. They are likely to be heavy users of the telephone in order to meet this need. These individuals prefer to work with others; solitary work environments can be uncomfortable for them.

Expressive Style team members are likely to write wordy and somewhat disorganized emails. Their requests might be non-specific or unclear. For example, they might leave out necessary details such as timeframes or accountabilities. These individuals might write multiple emails because they left out information, or because they impulsively send messages as ideas arise.

When communicating virtually with Expressive Style people, be clear but try not to load your message with too many facts or details. Keep it brief and don't include unnecessary background information. Be personable with these individuals, since they will be more likely to work cooperatively with you if they feel like they share some kind of personal bond. It might be preferable to use voicemail rather than email because you will be able to establish a more personal interaction.

Outside of formal team activities, Expressive Style team members will often crave being connected with the team. For a virtual team, schedule events where the team can meet in person when possible. These individuals will usually work better with people whom they've met and with whom they have shared experiences. Check in with them regularly, not only to review their activities, but also to stay personally connected. Whenever possible, give them projects where they can interact frequently with other team members.

Amiable Style

During virtual team meetings, Amiable Style people will generally be less talkative than Driving or Expressive Style people. They will participate in meetings, but will fill in the spaces between more talkative members. They focus on relationships, so the topics they choose to discuss will often be centered on people rather than tasks. Outside of formal meetings, they will want to interact with other team members and will show curiosity about those they have not met in person. These people like to work in teams, and this will come across in their interactions through telephone and email.

Amiable Style team members tend to be very friendly in their communications. For example, they will usually address others with a warm greeting and they don't hesitate to use emoticons or exclamation marks. They will often ask how you are, or include some reference to your well-being. They tend to be wordy in their writing, and rather than making direct requests they will considerately ask if you can do something.

Amiable Style people respond well to friendly and personable people, so keep this in mind when communicating virtually with them. It is helpful if you do not rely too much on email. Have phone conversations when you can, in order to maintain a personal relationship. Make your key points in a conversational style.

Outside of team meetings, Amiable Style team members like to stay personally connected with others, though they may be more subdued than Expressive Style people. These individuals will be particularly eager to have face-to-face interactions with the team, particularly in casual circumstances, so look for opportunities to schedule team social functions. These team members will usually want to discuss project plans to make sure they are on track, so it is generally all right to check with them frequently. When possible, provide them with tasks where they will interact with others and support the team.

Analytical Style

During virtual team meetings, Analytical Style people will often be quiet, particularly if there are other team members who are more Tell Assertive. When they do speak, they will focus on tasks and information related to work topics, with very little discussion of people. When not meeting virtually with the rest of the team, these individuals will be comfortable working on their own. They will seek out other team members if they feel it is necessary in order to complete their work.

Analytical Style team members are typically formal and organized in their communications. They sometimes send lengthy emails that contain all the information they think is important. Other team members might find it difficult to understand the key points, not to mention unnecessary. When making specific requests, they will typically ask for assistance and will also ask for you to follow up with them.

When communicating virtually with Analytical Style team members, try to be precise and well structured. Clearly state any actions you want them to take, why they are necessary, and timeframes. Give them time to respond. Include background information or other contextual information.

Outside of formal team events, give these individuals time to accomplish their work without needlessly interrupting them. When you do check in with them, be sure to schedule the meeting well in advance. These individuals are comfortable working alone, so they may not require much interaction with the team. When possible, give them opportunities to showcase their work to the team, as this will help them make their contributions known to other team members.

Team Leader Tip: *How to Lead Virtual Team Meetings?*

As the team leader, it is your job to ensure virtual meetings are effective. Use the following strategies to help keep your team focused and efficient.

Conference Calls and Webinars:

- Send an agenda ahead of time, along with background information. Try to send it at least 24 hours in advance. After the meeting, write the agenda for the next meeting.

- Before critical conference calls, contact team members and verify the agenda. Check if there are any issues that need your attention before the call.

- Set a team norm that participants are to be actively engaged and focused on the purpose of the meeting during the calls, not attempting to multi-task. Research shows this is not really possible and both tasks suffer from it.

- If new members are attending, circulate a short background of them ahead of time. Be sure to introduce them during the call.

- In agendas or materials, use numbers instead of bullets. Numbers are easier to reference.

- Have participants turn on their webcams if feasible so team members can see and hear one another. This appeals to the Expressive and Amiable Styles by being more personal and it allows Analytical and Driving Styles to observe reactions of their fellow team members to their statements or questions.

Emails:

- Before sending an email, ask yourself, "How could this email be misunderstood or misinterpreted?" Others misinterpret most emails because your intended tone does not come across in this medium.

- Carefully consider who to CC. Do not overload people with unnecessary email.

- If you are CC'd, consider whether you need to respond.

- When working with international team members, do not use idioms (e.g. "We're in the ballpark").

- Use numbers for all key points, especially those you want answered.

- If two emails and responses have occurred on one topic without resolving the issue, then use the telephone.

Using E-Mail and Voicemail to Communicate:

Email and voicemail provide fewer cues about a person's "Say and Do" behaviors. You will need to put more thought into the process when you communicate via e-mail or voicemail to ensure your message is properly interpreted and supports your working relationships with your direct reports.

The following graph (see Fig. 6-2) summarizes recommendations on how to communicate in virtual settings by SOCIAL STYLE.

Analytical Style	Driving Style
For emails and voicemails: Be precise and well structured, and focus on tasks. Explain the logic of your thoughts, and clearly state any expected action and why it is the appropriate next step. Avoid setting an unnecessarily tight deadline—give time to think and act, but include parameters and timeframes. **For voicemails only:** • Don't speak too fast—get to the point in a business-like manner. • Avoid loading voicemails with facts and details; voicemail is less capable of conveying the underlying structure of your message—which might be interpreted as rambling. **For emails only:** • To appear organized and systematic, include data and supporting facts in attachments.	**For emails and voicemails:** Be business-like, get to the point, and avoid unnecessary side comments. Focus on the key facts, the options, and the impact they have on accomplishing the goal. Summarize choices and let this person decide what he or she needs to do next. **For voicemails only:** • Speak at a moderate, deliberate pace and get to the point in a business-like manner. • Carefully plan what you are going to say and stick to it to ensure that you don't inadvertently waste this person's time. **For emails only:** • Include attachments only if they are necessary for performing a task or making a speedy decision.

Fig. 6-2: Communication in Virtual Teams

Amiable Style	Expressive Style
For emails and voicemails:	**For emails and voicemails:**
Open with a personal note; be clear and keep a friendly tone. As appropriate, mention how you or others feel about the message's content and say something positive about your working relationship like, "It was nice meeting with you."	Make your point, but take time to acknowledge this person's contribution. Be clear and avoid loading your message with facts and details. Don't be afraid to use adjectives with a bit of exaggeration (e.g., "scary deadline").
For voicemails only:	**For voicemails only:**
• It may be preferable to use voicemail because you can use tone of voice and inflection to convey a sense of friendliness and personal warmth.	• It may be preferable to use voicemail because you can use tone of voice, a faster speaking pace, and inflection to convey a sense of excitement or enthusiasm.
• Make your key points in a conversational style, speaking in a moderate to slow pace.	• In voicemail messages to the Expressive Style person, you can use your tone of voice and inflection to reciprocate the enthusiasm of this direct report.
For emails only:	**For emails only:**
• Don't try to make the email a substitute for a real conversation, and if you use email, make your point in a casual writing style. If appropriate, it's okay to use emoticons.	• Keep the message brief and avoid unnecessary background or "nice to know" information in the message and attachments.

Fig. 6-2: Communication in Virtual Teams (Cont.)

6.11 International Teams

According to the United Nations Conference on Trade and Development (UNCTAD), the number of transnational corporations (TNC) increased to almost 80,000 in 2007, with about 800,000 affiliates abroad and more than 80 million employees in total. With the number of individuals and teams working across borders increasing, it has never been more important to ensure that people are able to use SOCIAL STYLE awareness and the Versatility Factor effectively with colleagues from other cultures.

As anyone who has ever worked in a culture outside of their own can attest, there are unique challenges involved. Language differences create the most obvious barrier to communication. However, even for teams that speak a common business language, challenges are common due to the subtleties that can only be understood by native speakers.

Beyond language, other issues arise. Every country has its own unique cultural customs, traditions, expectations for interacting with others, and standards for greeting friends and associates, among others. The question is, how much do these cultural customs affect human behavior? Do Style behaviors differ across countries? Culturally, China is dramatically different from Germany, but is SOCIAL STYLE meaningfully different across these societies? Would a Chinese person working in Germany be able to identify the SOCIAL STYLE of their German colleagues, and would their colleagues recognize their SOCIAL STYLE?

These questions have been answered by research exploring SOCIAL STYLE across countries that has generated country-specific norms. Here we're using the term "norms" as a statistical concept; it is a shortened term for "normative scores" and is a way of comparing people based on their SOCIAL STYLE. It is similar to the relative numeric measures business schools use to determine where a person stands compared to everyone else who took the same exam. For SOCIAL STYLEs, this is accomplished by creating percentiles that make it possible for people to understand their behavior relative to others. In fact, norms are the basis for determining which SOCIAL STYLE a person is (e.g., D1 Analytical vs. C2 Analytical), according the country-specific reference norm used (see Appendix A for the complete list of available norms).

SOCIAL STYLE across Borders

Our research shows that SOCIAL STYLE is a global concept; it exists across nationalities. However, different cultures display SOCIAL STYLE behaviors in unique ways. For example, in China, Assertiveness behaviors are generally more direct than in Western societies. When we compare China with the U.S. and Germany, the Chinese average is more Tell Assertive than the averages for the U.S. and Germany. This does not mean that Ask Assertiveness does not exist in China; it is simply displayed differently. Therefore, we developed norms for China that adjust for their cultural attributes. This provides a more meaningful measure of SOCIAL STYLE for people in China because they are being measured relative to others within their culture.

So, how different are countries from one another on their SOCIAL STYLE behaviors? It turns out the differences are typically only moderate. However, though slight, the differences are important and have meaningful implications. First, a person can profile differently when using different country norms. A Chinese person might profile as Driving when scored against the U.S. norm, but would profile as Analytical using the Chinese norm. Second, understanding SOCIAL STYLE differences across countries can be invaluable for helping people who work across borders. Westerners working in China will benefit greatly by understanding the differences in Assertiveness behavior and recognizing how they themselves are perceived as a result.

The map on the following page (see Fig. 6-3) shows a selected set of countries, denoted by their flags, plotted on the average of their Assertiveness and Responsiveness scores. These averages are derived from the rating scale values contributed by respondents from the respective countries. The averages are an aggregate of all available data from each country. It is important to recognize that these are averages from large groups of people; individuals' scores vary and all SOCIAL STYLEs are represented in all countries. Also, the dark blue lines are simply to provide perspective; they are not SOCIAL STYLE borders. The countries tend to cluster very near one another. This is what we would expect. If some countries were dramatically different from one another, we would be concerned about the validity of measuring SOCIAL STYLE across countries since this could indicate problems with the measurement system. This clearly isn't the case, indicating that SOCIAL STYLE is valid across countries.

This analysis indicates that SOCIAL STYLE behaviors appear fairly similar across countries. Taking a closer look, we've zoomed in on the same data, showing differences at two decimal places on the rating scale (see Fig. 6-4). The differences across countries are becoming more obvious. For example, it's clear that China is more Tell Assertive than the other nations, while Japan is the most Ask Assertive of the group.

Taking an even closer look at relevant sub-sets of countries (i.e. Europe) will enable multinational companies and/or trainers to shape team development initiatives according to their actual international composition (see Fig. 6-5).

TEAMS

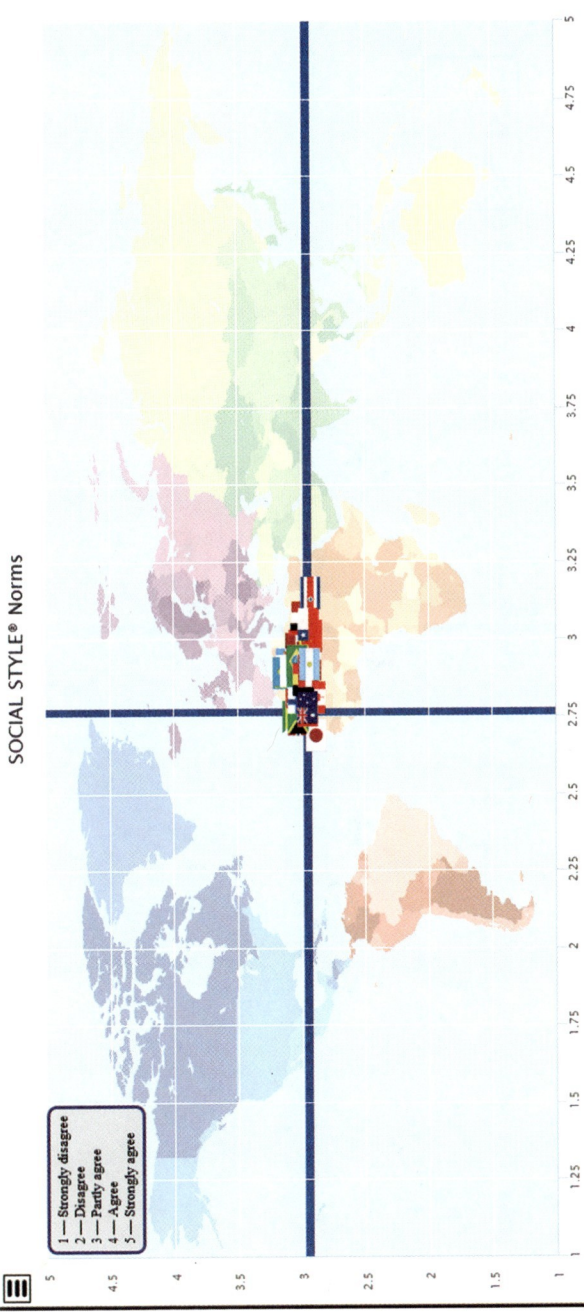

Fig. 6-3: Spread of International Norms

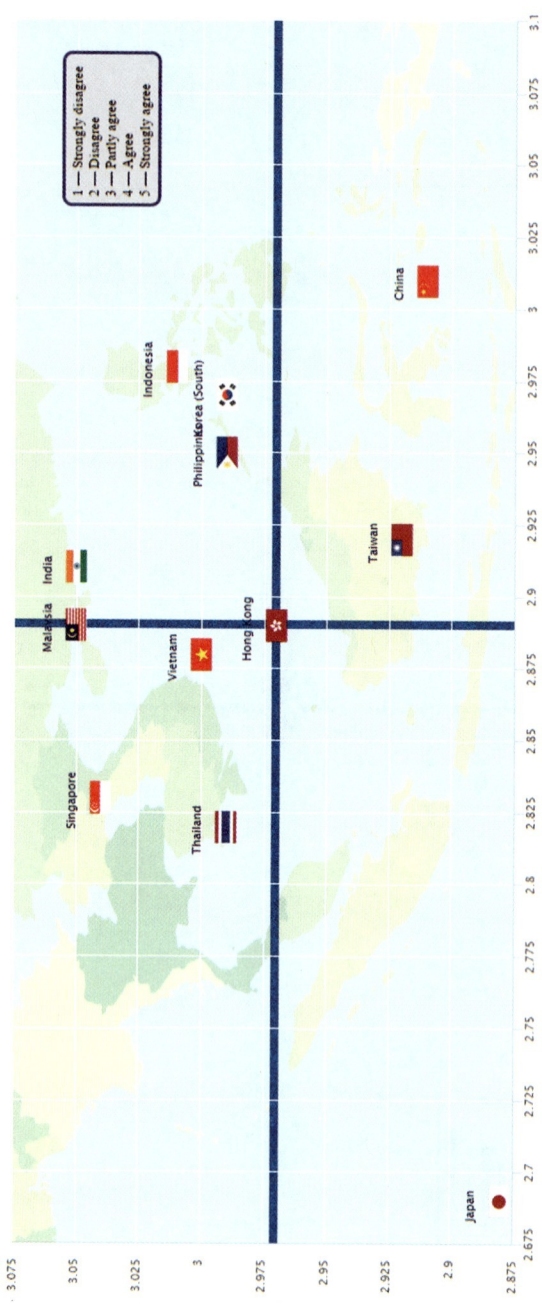

Fig. 6-4: Spread of International Norms (Asia Pacific)

TEAMS

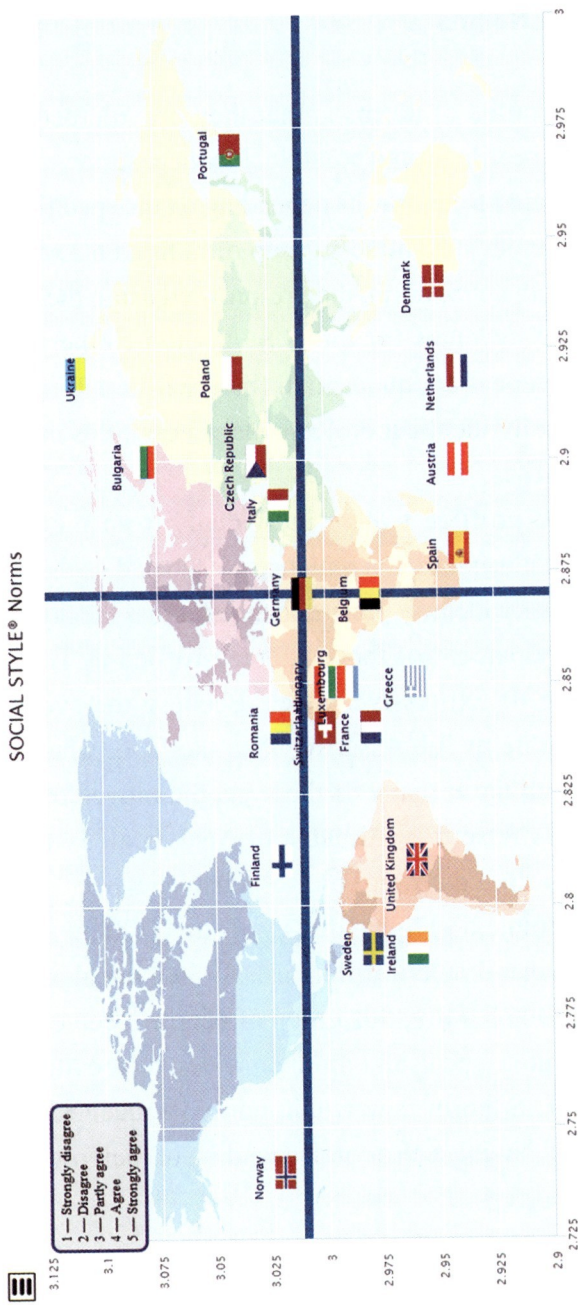

Fig. 6-5: Spread of Norms – Europe

The Effect of Norms

One of the benefits of norms is that they provide people with the most accurate profile results possible. Identical survey responses can result in different profile results depending on the specific norm used. As an example, let's examine a group of individuals who were first profiled using the U.S. norm, then re-profiled using the Dutch norm. Below are the averages for the U.S. and the Netherlands. While absolute differences are quite small (barely over 0.15 on Assertiveness and virtually identical on Responsiveness), this can still affect individual profiles.

First, we profiled twelve individuals from the Netherlands using the U.S. norm. For convenience we labeled each person using a number to easily identify profile changes across the norms (see Fig. 6-6A/B). Fifty percent of these people profiled as Tell Assertive, either Driving or Expressive Styles. Because the average for the Netherlands is more Tell Assertive than the U.S., when re-profiled using the Dutch norm many of these people moved to the left and profiled as Ask Assertive, Amiable or Analytical. Two individuals (3 and 7) even shifted upward on Responsiveness.

This example highlights that even small differences in norms can result in rather dramatic differences for individual profile results. By using the Dutch norm, this group of people received results that were most accurate and useful for them within their culture. Had they relied on the U.S. norm they would not have received the insights that come from having a clear understanding of their own and others' behavior.

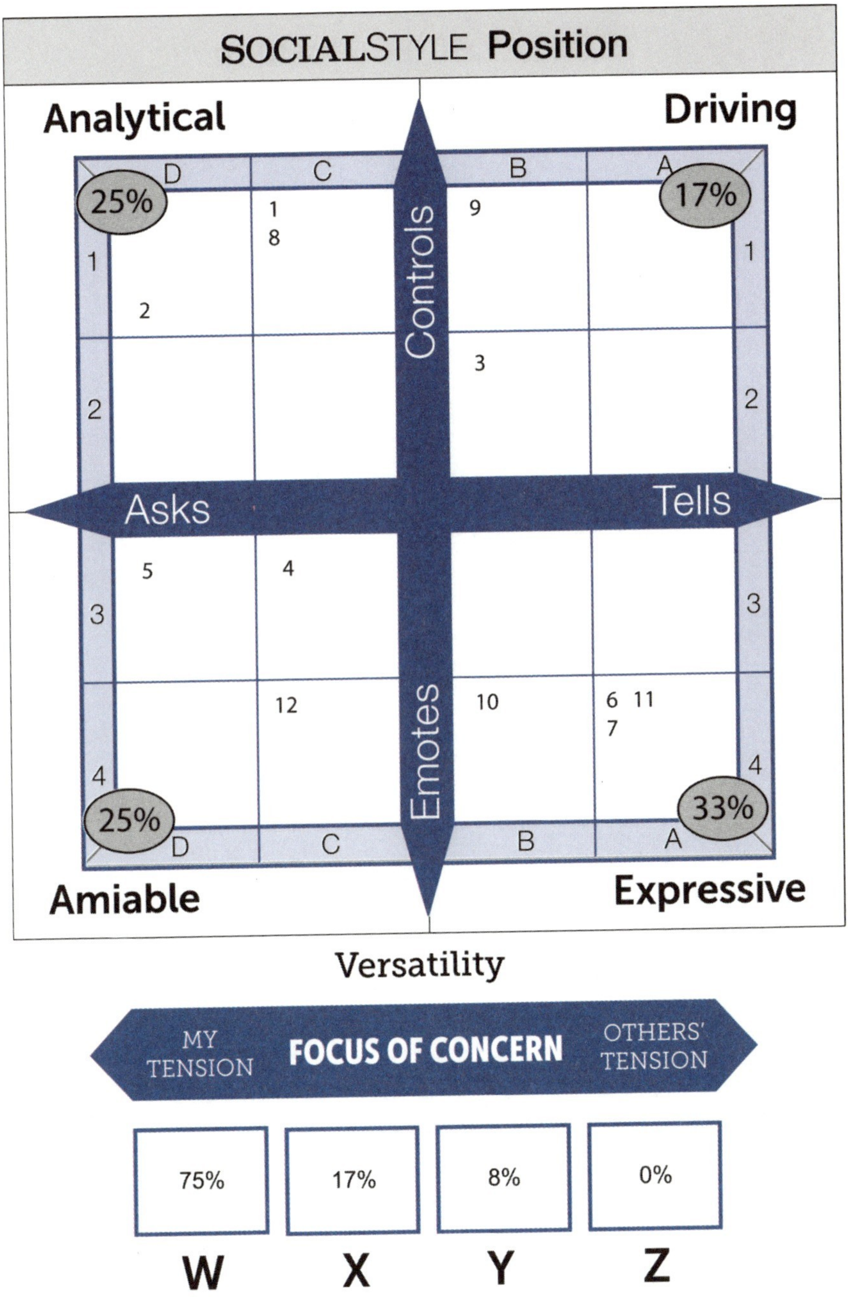

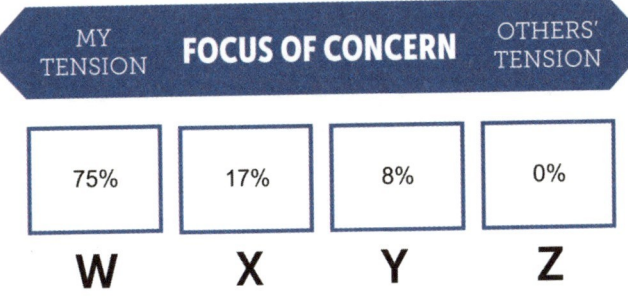

Fig. 6-6A: Impact using Different Norms (United States Norm)

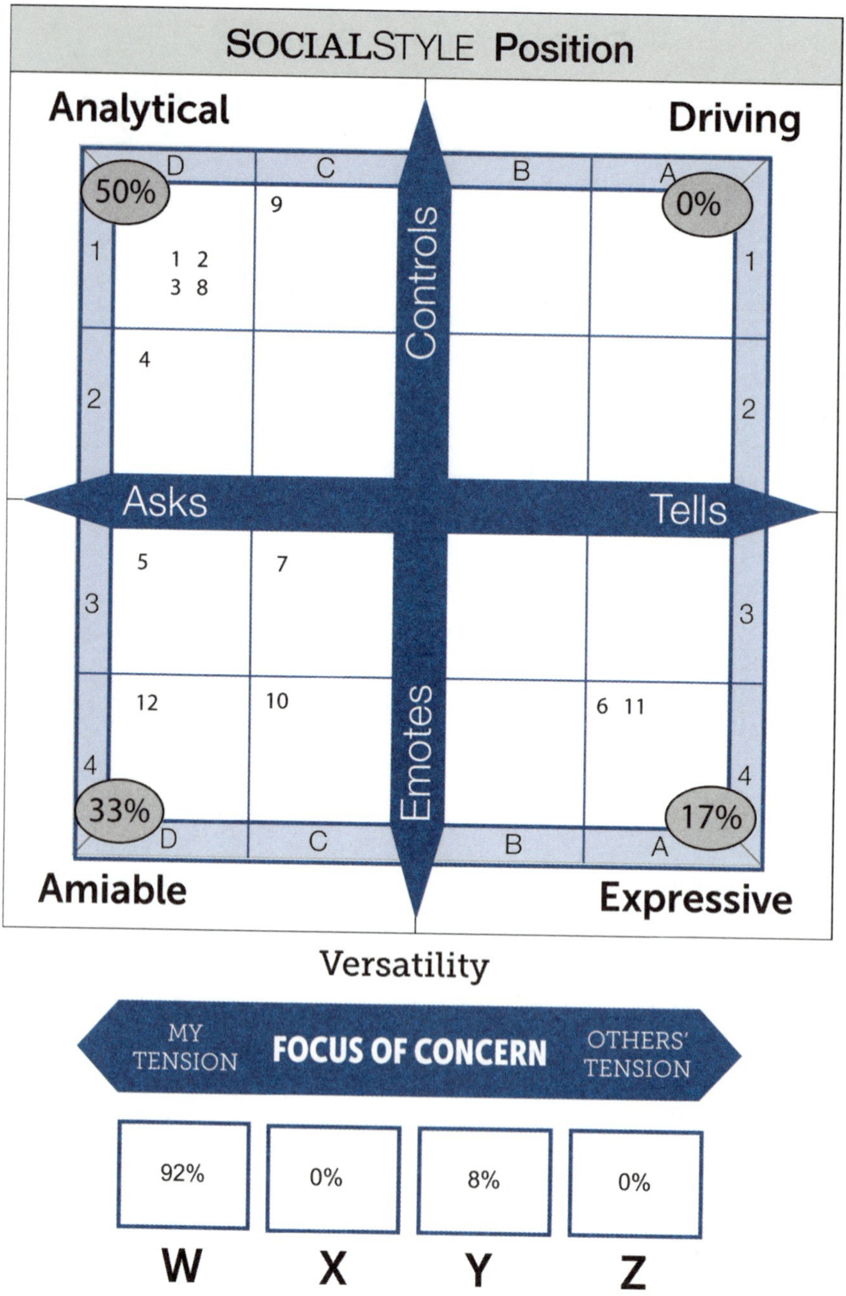

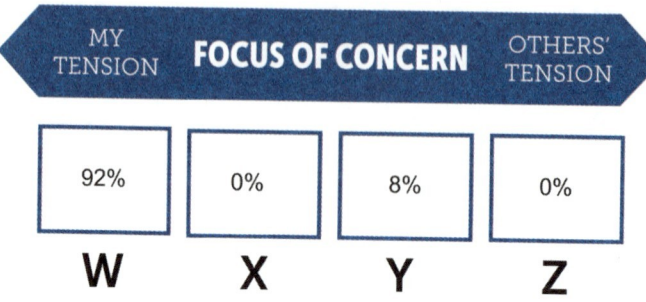

Fig. 6-6B: Impact using Different Norms (Dutch Norm)

The Effect of Norms when Working across Cultures

Another benefit of norms is that they help people recognize important differences across cultures and account for those differences when working with individuals from other countries. The "cultural competence" of organizations and their members is becoming critical in modern times, and many companies now provide education and training in this area.

Culture represents, "the values, norms, and traditions that affect how individuals of a particular group perceive, think, interact, behave, and make judgments about their world." Referring to one of the most comprehensive studies of how values in the workplace are influenced by culture conducted by Professor Geert Hofstede, national cultures can be distinguished according to the dimensions Power Distance (PDI), Individualism vs. Collectivism (IDV), Masculinity vs. Femininity (MAS), Uncertainty Avoidance (UAI), and Long-Term Orientation (LTO).

Two aspects of cultural awareness are especially important for people utilizing the Versatility Factor. First, it is crucial to be aware of oneself and how people in other cultures can interpret behavior. Self-reflection and self-monitoring of behavior are fundamental to working cross-culturally. Second, it is important to recognize the SOCIAL STYLE of others within the context of their cultures, and respond appropriately to that behavior. Country-specific norms are invaluable for assisting people with these activities.

Building on the previous example, let's add Germany to the norms map and describe how this information can be used for someone working internationally. The U.S. and the Netherlands are approximately the same on the Responsiveness scale, and are more emoting than Germany. Therefore, a German working with people from these nations should expect that those individuals might be more comfortable with expressing their emotions, sharing information about themselves, and being outgoing. This knowledge allows them to be prepared for this behavior and not surprised by it.

They should also be aware of their own SOCIAL STYLE and behavior, and how American and Dutch colleagues might interpret this. If they happen to be Analytical or Driving according to German norms, then they may come across as particularly controlled with these colleagues. By recognizing this, they can adjust their behavior slightly to show more of their feelings and share more of themselves, when appropriate. On the Assertiveness scale, Germany essentially straddles the middle ground between the U.S. and the Netherlands. This means that their American colleagues might naturally come across as slightly more asking than what they are used to at home, while the opposite will be true with their Dutch colleagues.

We want to emphasize again that these differences in average scores are not tremendous. However, they do exist and can help when working with people from other nations. The most important thing to remember is while these maps can be helpful, it is more important to treat each person as an individual, no matter where they come from. Wherever you travel in the world, you will encounter people of all SOCIAL STYLEs.

7 THE VERSATILITY FACTOR IN A BROADER WORLD OF RELATIONSHIPS

One of the most common reactions from people learning about SOCIAL STYLE is they quickly see the ubiquitous application of SOCIAL STYLEs in many other areas of their lives beyond their workplace. As these learners connect the dots related to how Styles impact their lives, they also come to realize effective use of Styles is critical in many areas in relationships.

Over the past several decades, many different studies around the importance of effectively using SOCIAL STYLEs have been conducted. Here are some examples across many areas of application outside the business context:

- In 2010, TRACOM worked with educators to deploy a learning curriculum addressing issues related to self-worth and bullying in elementary schools. Called *Kid's Style*, this course translated to a 3rd and 4th grade level and helps students gain insights into their SOCIAL STYLE and the SOCIAL STYLE of others, to see worth in themselves and others, and to reduce negative judgments about others who simply approach things differently. The results show a meaningful reduction in inappropriate behaviors and conflict within the school environment.

• TRACOM helped Sigma Chi, a preeminent international fraternity, to develop the leadership skills of its members. Using SOCIAL STYLEs, Sigma Chi helped participants bring to life their professed ideals of building a common bond among people through sharing belief systems of different temperaments, talents, and convictions. Results show that 85% of participants felt SOCIAL STYLEs changed their lives for the better and increased their leadership abilities in their post-graduate roles.

• In a study conducted at one of America's leading graduate business schools on factors impacting career success three years after graduation, former students reported the curriculum on human behavior using SOCIAL STYLEs gave them the greatest advantage in their work. Basically the graduates shared that everyone coming into the workplace at their level had a high degree of technical and intellectual competence, but they had a distinct advantage in understanding how to work effectively with others of similar and dissimilar Styles. This allowed them to have a higher level of trust and cooperation within their teams and with co-workers and clients.

• A number of studies on physicians and patient healing rates indicate that doctors who demonstrate a high level of interpersonal skill have patients who are more satisfied, more committed to making changes, and spent less time in the hospital than the patients of doctors with lower levels of interpersonal skills.

There are many other stories and examples that demonstrate the impact SOCIAL STYLEs have made for people in their career. But what about one's personal life, especially around how SOCIAL STYLE comes into play at home and within the family?

7.1 SOCIAL STYLE and Versatility at Home

When we leave work at the end of the day and return to our private lives, we carry our SOCIAL STYLEs with us. We don't leave it at the office or change our core behaviors as most of us think we do.

When we interact with casual acquaintances or participate in community activities, we behave very much the way we do at work. For example, a person with a Driving Style who volunteers to help set up a marathon for charity would probably begin to influence or even lead the charge of the entire event. On the other hand, the person with Analytical Style who volunteers for the same committee might prefer to help out by setting up key processes or creating a more efficient and faster way to keep track of the pledges or register participants. Expressive Styles would likely bring their enthusiasm and creativity to the projects and seek ways to build excitement and commitment within the community, while Amiable Styles might prefer to serve on an important committee with their friends or support participants during the event.

In a community setting, though, there's generally less tension than at work and less need to use backup SOCIAL STYLE behaviors. Although organizing a Red Cross fund drive can be demanding, it also has a recreational aspect, and since we participate in such activities by choice, the tension is not as great as it often is at work. While there is basically no difference between the behaviors we use at work and those we use in the community, in recreational situations we tend to use our SOCIAL STYLE in a more relaxed, positive manner.

While many people tend to think their SOCIAL STYLE is something they can put on or take off like a coat, research shows our workplace behaviors are also typical of how we behave at home. For many people this is at odds with their own views of how they act in the various parts of their life. There is not a workshop that we have conducted where several participants haven't told us they act differently at home and with friends than they do at work.

To some extent, they are right; but the perception they are talking about is not so much a difference in their SOCIAL STYLE as a difference in how they demonstrate behaviors related to Versatility. When participants in a workshop get their results, we frequently hear several say, "But I know this is not the way my family sees me." Again, in some ways, they are correct. But research has continued to show our SOCIAL STYLE behaviors are what we fall back on within our homes and among our friends. As we shared earlier, our typical SOCIAL STYLE behaviors were actually learned at home when we were in our formative years. Those years formed the core responses to others that we show in all parts of our lives to a greater or lesser extent depending on the tension we are experiencing.

One of the reasons those individuals who are closest to us have difficulty defining our SOCIAL STYLE is due to the fact they are not impartial, objective observers. Our personal relationships are much more intricate than those we experience in the workplace. Within our closest relationships perceptions can easily be blurred as a result of key factors like shared values, beliefs, attitudes, and emotional and sexual involvement. With SOCIAL STYLE, others are only discussing what they can describe about what you say and do. In these intimate relationships, shared religious beliefs may do more to hold a relationship together than the concern with those observed behaviors that reflect your SOCIAL STYLE. People living together accept the values that hold the relationship intact and very often are inattentive to specific behaviors or accepting of behavior because a marriage or close friendship is more valued than personal habit patterns.

In these deeply personal relationships, people become involved with the total personality of others—like their beliefs and values—and establish emotional ties which change their perspectives of the other person. With SOCIAL STYLE, the focus is on observable behaviors, what they tell us about the other person, and how to best interact with them. With SOCIAL STYLE there is no focus on someone's beliefs, values, or overall personality. SOCIAL STYLE is about habit patterns—not beliefs, values, or attitudes—and these habits have a major influence on personal relationships.

Understand that our skills that allow us to observe behaviors objectively are much more challenged within our close personal relationships than in our everyday social interactions with our workplace colleagues. In close relationships, we get used to our significant others and friends and develop interdependent behavior patterns. We frequently don't see the obvious in terms of behaviors or actions that fall outside the norm.

How many of us have done something to our appearance, hairstyle, or other actions we consider obvious only to have these changes missed or overlooked by those closest to us? This is a reflection of just how habitual we are in our most intimate relationships. It is often only changes with shock value that get noticed, while more moderate changes are likely to go unnoticed for days or weeks. Have you ever heard someone say, "There is something different about your hair. What did you do?" Only to have the other person respond with "I had six inches cut off and changed from brown hair to blonde two weeks ago! Thanks for noticing." Obviously not enough shock value here to get an immediate response.

Cultural stereotypes that are part of our traditional ideas about home and family also get in the way of objective observations of SOCIAL STYLE. We often find that men in our workshops want to think they have Driving Styles because they associate that type of behavior with authority, confidence, control, and "masculine" behavior. Women, on the other hand, often want to be thought of as warm, supportive, and caring—characteristics of the Amiable Style traditionally thought of as "feminine." Although traditional male/female family roles have started to change, these stereotypes still exist and do cloud perceptions of SOCIAL STYLE at home. Despite cultural dictates, our research has shown these stereotypes do not hold true. Both males and females are observed in all of the SOCIAL STYLEs; gender doesn't dictate Style.

Because of the intimate nature of the relationships in our private lives, to a certain degree we do behave differently at home than we do at work or in casual social situations. However, this difference is not a matter of a difference in SOCIAL STYLE, but in the degree of Versatility we show. Most of us learn intuitively that we can't show our backup SOCIAL STYLEs—nonproductive, exaggerated behavior—too quickly to our bosses, clients, or even to our co-workers and casual friends. If we did, we would jeopardize relationships essential to maintaining our positions. If we attack our boss or get autocratic with him, we are likely to find ourselves without a promotion or looking for another job. So, while we're careful not to show our discomfort at work, the compromises we make to adjust to work relationships produce tension.

It's not uncommon to carry it home if sufficient tension is built up during the day. When that happens, backup SOCIAL STYLEs can surface rather quickly. Ironically, we tend to take out our frustrations on the people who mean the most to us because of the "safety" implicit in an intimate relationship. The tendency is for us to believe this person has accepted me as I am, so I don't have to put effort into trying to please them.

Think about the situation where a spouse with either an Analytical or Amiable Style arrives home after a stressful day at the office. The other spouse is also under stress due to a pressing deadline at work and a conflict develops about whether or not to go out for dinner. The first spouse has been under tension all day without a chance to withdraw (their preferred behavior for reducing tension). Rather than showing versatility and discussing the matter, they attempt to ignore the situation by logging onto a social media site and avoiding the conflict altogether, hoping it goes away. The other spouse, especially if they have a more tell assertive SOCIAL STYLE, confronts the situation directly and wants it resolved so they can reduce their tension. Neither person feels the need to be versatile like they might in a similar situation at work. This is a typical conflict that arises between two people whose preferred way of doing things can clash due to a lack of Versatility.

Other sources of conflict experienced in close personal relationships can manifest themselves during holidays and, very often, a vacation—a time when people are looking for personal pleasure and relaxation or have different traditions from each other. How can we understand this phenomenon? During holidays or on vacation, people often unconsciously cease their attempts to be versatile. The focus seems to be a strong desire to "do my own thing" during time away from their daily routines. But, when what comes naturally to one person does not to another, tension mounts. Unless a person recognizes this and chooses to be more versatile since they can only control their own behavior, their closest relationships can get damaged. If they choose to become more versatile, they will find everyone can get their needs met in a way that does not lead to damaged relationships.

7.2 SOCIAL STYLEs in the Family

Family members and close friends usually don't consciously observe behavior. But whenever people share a meaningful relationship, SOCIAL STYLEs—even if not identified in our terms—become very predictable. Certain people are counted on to behave in certain ways, not just by the immediate family, but also the extended family and close friends.

Different SOCIAL STYLEs within the home can generate a lot of different outcomes in terms of positive and negative results. Who hasn't seen siblings have conflict, even if they share the same SOCIAL STYLE? They each try to get their needs met, and with the Tell Assertive SOCIAL STYLEs this can lead to lots of shouting and screaming. At other times they appear to have a fun and nurturing relationship and can come across as protective of one another. The chances these siblings will view their childhood interactions more positively than negatively is very high as the closeness of their relationship continues to evolve through their formative, teen, and early adult years.

Most of our behavioral preferences are formed early in life, usually by the age of five, and are reinforced by parents, teachers, siblings, and peers. Because people learn to behave the way they do by imitating and satisfying those around them, they have quite an emotional investment in their SOCIAL STYLEs. For this reason, it's important not to tamper with or to try to change another person's SOCIAL STYLE; in most cases, your efforts will be met with resistance and resentment.

This is especially true with children, who will develop behavioral patterns that help them feel comfortable in the presence of their parents or other significant people, whether or not their parents consciously try to influence the child to have a certain SOCIAL

STYLE. If parents have two different SOCIAL STYLEs and fail to understand each other's approaches, the child can be in for a frustrating experience. However, when parents with different Styles show a wide range of appropriate responses, for example, providing appropriate discipline or patient understanding when needed, the child will benefit from relating to each parent in a different way. In fact, the healthiest family is often the one that includes and accepts all SOCIAL STYLEs without making any value judgments about them. If parents label one SOCIAL STYLE good and another bad, they will certainly create discomfort (if not more serious developmental problems) for the child with the "bad" SOCIAL STYLE.

We find it's the first-born child who is most influenced by the preferred behaviors of their parents and will adopt one of their Styles. Other children are likely to be more influenced by their siblings or the social environments they encounter, rather than just the SOCIAL STYLEs of their parents. This is likely influenced by the fact they can learn through their siblings which behaviors are reinforced positively or negatively in the family. For example, if an older sister has a strong Driving Style and the younger child notices this creates a lot of tension for the parents, the younger sibling is likely to try other behaviors that seem to get more approval. This is how we learn our preferred behaviors. When we experience tension we respond to it; if the response we tried is positively reinforced, it is likely we will use it again in similar circumstances until it becomes a habitual behavior. This is why the second child in a family almost always develops a SOCIAL STYLE preference different from their older sibling. This is what allows them to get the attention they need. The SOCIAL STYLE patterns attempted by a trial and error approach eventually lead to finding our comfort zone from which we evolve our SOCIAL STYLE.

Once SOCIAL STYLE patterns develop, they remain set until

the teenage years when we once again begin to experiment with different behaviors in the process of discovering ourselves. Once we reach the early twenties, the experimenting will end, and we will probably settle back into the same SOCIAL STYLE patterns we developed as a child.

The point is, of course, that SOCIAL STYLE patterns are deeply ingrained. Even if we don't recognize it, SOCIAL STYLEs are present at home and among our friends, and style differences do exist within these groups. If we acknowledge and adjust to these differences, we can use these contrasts to broaden the value of our relationships.

Does it make sense to apply what you know about SOCIAL STYLE with your friends and family? Our personal experience is: absolutely! The skills developed by using SOCIAL STYLE and Versatility at work can also be used to improve our most meaningful relationships. The four key steps to this are known as the PRO Strategy Model.

- **First, Know Yourself.** Understand the key behaviors of your SOCIAL STYLE and what impact it might have on friends and family.

- **Second, Control Yourself.** If our SOCIAL STYLE preference has elements that are likely to cause tension in others, it's important to know how to manage these tendencies to be less controlling, less spontaneous, less rigid, or less indecisive. Knowing this about ourselves makes it possible to understand how others react to us without becoming overly defensive.

- **Third, Know Others.** This comes from using the "say" and "do" behaviors of our friends and family to come to understand their SOCIAL STYLE. Once we know this we can better know how their behavioral tendencies might cause tension for us and how we can avoid causing undue tension for them.

- **Fourth, Do Something for Others.** This is where the skills of Versatility come into play and can lead to much more comfortable and intimate relationships.

Intimate relationships are difficult; because of our fear over how this important person might react, there is a tendency to avoid being in conflict. Remember, we all desire the approval of those closest to us and we don't want to risk a negative outcome. If we learn how to best communicate around these issues rather than avoid them, the result can be a much deeper and more intimate relationship. All it takes is the courage to be Versatile.

Our search for deeper meaning in our close relationships involves risk. No one wants to deal with the emotional response of an Expressive Style by challenging their vision or spontaneity. Who wants to risk offending an Amiable Style friend by being too direct and hurting their feelings? No one wants to share emotions or ideas with an Analytical Style if one can expect a critical and dismissive response. Finally, who wants to face a Driving Style's "don't challenge me" response? There is a tendency to become evasive rather than direct and candid.

In close relationships, lack of candid and honest feedback stifles constructive communication and prevents growth, regardless of SOCIAL STYLE differences or similarities. As one withholds feedback or avoids conflict, tension will continue to grow within him. Like steam coming from a teapot, the pressure must be released and a person will react so negatively that he will create a much worse impact on their relationship than if he had the courage to communicate earlier. To avoid this, practice Versatility, particularly the use of feedback, to alter a defensive cycle of communication. Practicing the skills of good communication allows you to reach interpersonal understanding and reduce the likelihood of barriers developing in the future.

7.3 Do Opposites Attract?

It's been our experience that when people are choosing a partner, opposite SOCIAL STYLEs—or at least different SOCIAL STYLEs—frequently do attract. In the past, this subject has been the source of much scientific debate, with psychiatrists and psychologists typically holding opposing points of view. Some psychiatrists tend to advocate partnerships built on complementary needs, in which each person brings different qualities to a relationship, thus forming a mutually supportive bond. Behavioral psychologists, however, have maintained people with similar value systems and backgrounds have fewer sources of conflict and are likely to make relationship adjustments more easily. Essentially, we agree with the latter point of view. When we say that different SOCIAL STYLEs attract, we're only talking in terms of the behavioral patterns rather than in terms of the deeper need levels.

Obviously, a relationship between partners with different SOCIAL STYLEs presents many opportunities for the individual partners' behavior to grate on each other. Why does this attraction occur? It's our guess that most of us envy the qualities and characteristics of SOCIAL STYLEs that differ from our own. Also, such relationships can produce complementary interactions, simply because of the natural differences. For example, a person with an Analytical Style is generally reserved in social settings. This individual will often participate in a wider variety of social experiences than he would normally if he has a partner who has an Expressive

Style and tends to seek involvement with people.

The partner with Expressive Style can also add excitement to the relationship by stimulating activity that wouldn't occur with the more reclusive approach. The Expressive Style partner of an Analytical Style person might, for instance, mention that it would be fun to fly to Vancouver and see the spring flowers "sometime." However, unless the Analytical Style partner grabbed the idea and implemented the vacation, that "sometime" might never come—or if it did, the spring flowers would have given way to fall colors. In short, the partner with Expressive behavior will often enliven the pair's existence by leading the more cautious partner into being more spontaneous. By the same token, the more detailed person's preference for facts and logic can temper the risks involved with impulsive behavior.

In another example of complementary interaction, an individual with a Driving Style with a highly competitive desire to win might possibly turn every card game into tournament play if a partner with Amiable Style behavior didn't point out the game really should be played for fun and many people don't care to play a competitive game. In this situation, the Amiable Style person's sensitivity to others can have a modifying influence on the partnership, and the couple can have a more pleasant and relaxed social life. Although unlikely to admit it, the partner with the Driving Style probably admires the Amiable Style partner's ability to bring warmth, openness, and supportiveness to social situations. In turn, because the person with the Driving Style appears to be in charge, confident, and able to get results without worrying about relationships, the Amiable Style person can rely on these qualities in some social dealings.

Still, the seeds of eventual irritation and discomfort are inherent in our choices of partners. It is important to recognize the tendency to be fascinated by behavioral differences and to select partners with qualities we feel are lacking in ourselves can eventually give way to

SOCIAL STYLE-related conflict unless common experience, beliefs, and values support the relationship. It seems that over time more effort goes into trying to change the other partner's SOCIAL STYLE than into finding ways to accommodate each other's preferences.

It is true that differing SOCIAL STYLEs do contribute interest and excitement to close relationships, but it is just as true that contrasting SOCIAL STYLEs can be the source of many interpersonal tensions and family problems (see Chapter 2.4 "Toxic Relationships"). It is not hard to imagine a person with one SOCIAL STYLE might be disappointed with how their partner of a different SOCIAL STYLE carries through on their idea of what it means to "do something together." An Amiable Style individual might interpret this as a chance to have one-on-one time together only to find that their Expressive Style partner thinks they should include friends and other family members. The Driving Style might see the chance to "do something together" as a project that needs to be done efficiently and quickly, while their partner with a more emotive SOCIAL STYLE might see it as a chance to talk about personal issues and share their feelings. An Analytical Style person might interpret "do something together" as a chance to spend quiet time with their partner at a play or movies while their below-the-line partner views it as a chance to engage with others in a very social setting.

SOCIAL STYLE differences are frequently the cause of the conflicted relationships couples experience. Dr. David Merrill referred to these types of relationships as fascination/discomfort relationships, rather than the more common view of love/hate relationships. Dr. Merrill found that people are often attracted to behaviors opposite of their own. Yet, as one becomes closer to a person with different behavioral preferences, the attraction gives way to the discomfort that arises as each partner manages interpersonal tension differently. This tendency results in a lot of effort going into getting the other partner to change their SOCIAL STYLE rather than into learning to manage these differences. These differences must be dealt with if an intimate relationship is to be truly intimate, mutually productive, and survive all the stresses that are a natural part of daily living. This is where the Versatility Factor comes into play!

There are, of course, those relationships in which two people with the same SOCIAL STYLE are attracted to each other. Such relationships seem to be rare, however, and while at first glance they might appear preferable to those that include SOCIAL STYLE differences, they, too, can have drawbacks. While same SOCIAL STYLEs arrive at behavioral compatibility easily, the relationship can suffer from the lack of contrasts and can readily slip into boredom. The key to overcoming this in a close relationship is through common experiences and shared values and beliefs.

While similar SOCIAL STYLE relationships might have some positive elements, they can also suffer from the weaknesses of that SOCIAL STYLE. For examples, two Analytical Styles who have a misunderstanding may both retreat into silence and avoid each other for several days to avoid the tension they feel. If they don't learn to appropriately respond in this situation, their resentment with each other can build and damage their relationship. This then requires a great deal of effort just to recover the relationship to its prior level. Even when two partners' SOCIAL STYLE are the same, it's important to recognize that SOCIAL STYLE exists in intimate relationships, that it has both positive and negative aspects, and that it must be understood and dealt with if such a relationship is to succeed. It is equally important to remember that although two people may share a SOCIAL STYLE, they are both individuals and not clones of one another.

SOCIAL STYLE is not the only deterrent to having a successful intimate relationship. It's also essential for partners to be sexually compatible and to have common interests, beliefs, and value systems.

When partners have little in common, SOCIAL STYLE differences often become key sources of irritation in the relationship. And if that's the case, there's not much point in trying to resolve SOCIAL STYLE conflicts when deeper problems are at the root of the trouble. It is these underlying values and beliefs that become more relevant the longer partners interact in close relationships.

It's been our observation that discomfort in a relationship is often caused by differences in SOCIAL STYLE—the way people manage their tension levels—rather than in beliefs and attitudes. And when partners share strong beliefs and values, there is solid motivation for learning to deal with those conflicts and for becoming more versatile.

If it's true that many conflicts in the home result from differences in SOCIAL STYLE, rather than from deeper psychological problems, how can home life be made more fulfilling? We believe a great many of the conflicts couples experience can be resolved with counseling that focuses on understanding SOCIAL STYLE and SOCIAL STYLE differences, rather than in-depth therapy. Certainly there are situations that require a great deal more than learning to understand behavioral habits and deal with them objectively. But many people look for deeper reasons for their conflicts than may be necessary to resolve misunderstandings.

It might be as simple as learning positive ways to avoid "bucket-dumping," which occurs when we allow the stresses of our day outside of our personal relationship to intrude into this arena. All of us need to release our tension, but rather than taking it out on those who are closest to us, we need to learn to release the tension in other ways. Activities such as listening to music, exercising, or meditation can significantly reduce the tension.

In addition to finding constructive ways to release tension, it's important to recognize the difference between belief and behavior.

Of course, ways in which people behave can also be a reflection of their beliefs. But we should recognize this is not always the case, and we should try to determine whether we are observing values in action or just SOCIAL STYLE-related behavior that leads us to misinterpret another person's actions.

If the differences between partners are the result of SOCIAL STYLE differences versus differences in values, they can be worked out through compromise and understanding. But, once again, because people tend to interpret and read into behaviors in terms of values, they usually don't want to change their own habit patterns and are much more apt to suggest the other partner do the changing. For instance, at one point or another, the person who exhibits Driving behavior might say to a partner, "You shouldn't be so impulsive and outgoing—it's childish." And, the reply to this statement might be, "Well, you shouldn't be so cold and self-centered. You're always so busy pushing people around you never pay any attention to how they feel." Such criticisms start a vicious circle of defensiveness that must be broken so the relationship won't end in alienation, if it survives at all.

Here's the point we're trying to make: People's SOCIAL STYLE should be left alone. There's no profit in tampering with SOCIAL STYLE to resolve conflict. All SOCIAL STYLEs have both positive and negative aspects, and if you did succeed in changing someone's SOCIAL STYLE (although this is highly unlikely), you would only be faced with a new and unfamiliar set of negative characteristics to deal with (those of the new SOCIAL STYLE). Rather than trying to modify one person's behavior to match another's, we are convinced that successful relationships grow out of adjustments to one another's behavioral preferences through understanding, tolerance, and mutual caring. This is the core of the Versatility Factor!

Partners might have difficulties in identifying each other's SOCIAL STYLE, simply because the emotional investment in their relationship makes objective observations of SOCIAL STYLE difficult. Arguing about each other's SOCIAL STYLE will only become self-defeating, so it is a good idea to get some input from outsiders—other than very close friends—to obtain an accurate picture of the way each partner behaves with people in general. We don't recommend using close friends because they are unlikely to be much more objective than the partner, and are also apt to support preconceived ideas about the relationship.

Yes, people are different, not just at work, but also at home. And this difference not only makes their lives richer, it's probably what attracted them to each other in the first place. Complementary interactions are part of the strength of any close relationship. Where there are differences, there are difficulties, but dealing with these differences can well be worth the price.

7.4 Social Media

In today's world, social media platforms like Facebook, YouTube, WeChat, LinkedIn, Instagram, FaceTime, Skype, and Twitter play a significant role in communicating and interacting with friends and colleagues as well as customers and the public.

Research shows people approach social media from two distinct perspectives, depending on whether a particular outlet is geared toward making personal or professional connections. According to The Mindset Divide, users of personal social media outlets like Facebook are mainly driven to socialize, keep in touch with others, share content, and be entertained. The same users approach professional social networks like LinkedIn with different motivations; they're driven by a desire to keep up with professional contacts, maintain a professional identity, search for career opportunities, and make new contacts in their industry. Considering SOCIAL STYLE preferences can make the differences even more distinct, as people of different SOCIAL STYLEs approach their personal and career interactions in different ways, regardless of the outlet. People of different SOCIAL STYLEs are likely to act in different ways when interacting with others via social media.

Given these findings, it is easy to see why people use different social networks in different ways, as they are reaching out to accomplish different goals. In the context of these general preferences, we can anticipate the most likely ways people of each SOCIAL STYLE approach both personal and professional networks online.

Driving Style people are likely to have an agenda in mind when they log on to a personal or professional social media outlet. Whether it is to check private messages, search for a contact to make a connection, or check in on a discussion, these people are likely to get in and out quickly, scanning updates and posts rather than reading in detail. On personal social networks, Driving Style people are less likely to broadcast opinions and long stories to their connections, but will not hesitate to add their input to a discussion. In fact, they run the risk of being misinterpreted due to their brief remarks.

Like their Driving Style counterparts, Analytical Style people are likely to have a clear purpose in mind when logging on to a social network. They may spend more time searching or dissecting information than others, and though they are typically not very talkative, the format of social media can appeal to their preference for commenting with the ability to think things through before stating their opinions. Because of this they might get particular satisfaction out of engaging in online discussions since they can take the time to write their thoughts, instead of stating them verbally. When they have something to say, they are likely to include details or links supporting their opinions. However, they will almost always think twice before making public posts.

Amiable Style people are likely most interested in cultivating relationships on social networks. They will treat social media in a similar way as the rest of their lives, seeing the opportunity to establish a large network of friends and contacts. Even on a career-centric network like LinkedIn, they are genuinely interested in the lives and well-being of their contacts. These people are less likely to browse information without becoming involved, as their Analytical Style colleagues may, and will spend a good amount of time engaging in conversation and interacting with groups. Amiable Style people can view social-media interactions as just as significant as in-person interactions, with the same impacts on relationships.

People with an Expressive Style are likely most interested in using social networks as a way to expand their relationships and share what is going on in their lives on a very personal level. They will treat social media in a similar way as the rest of their lives. They see the opportunity to establish a large network of friends and contacts while sharing their accomplishments, ideas, and major life events. Even on a career-centric network like LinkedIn, they are likely to disclose more about their lives and accomplishments than other styles. These people are less likely to just read a friend's social postings and are much more likely to add their comments and their own stories to the message chain. Like the Analytical Style, Expressive Style people will spend a good amount of time engaging in conversation and interacting within groups where they want their opinions, stories, ideas, and accomplishment shared. Expressive Style people can use social-media interactions as an easy replacement for in-person interactions.

With the constant evolution of technology, many new challenges and opportunities for displaying our SOCIAL STYLEs will emerge. In the early 2000's, email was the dominant technology, which has now given way to texting, Snapchat, Twitter, and other easy to use applications. And while earlier in the 21st century Social Media focused only on what we "say" in a text format, technology has now placed video streaming in our hands and we are able to now focus on what people "say and do." With that, we can apply what we know about SOCIAL STYLE in new and interesting ways.

8 FINAL THOUGHTS

No matter what the reason you had for reading this book, by now you have come to understand how different we are as individuals and how we prefer to be treated when interacting with others. You have learned about the concepts of SOCIAL STYLEs and how the Model can provide you with a robust framework to speed up your personal development and communication skills. You've learned the advantages you can gain in building high-performing relationships through the Versatility Factor.

Self-awareness is the first step towards improvement, but knowing our own SOCIAL STYLE and the associated behavioral weaknesses will help us to better control our behavior. Carefully observing the people you are dealing with and knowing their SOCIAL STYLE will enable you to adapt your own approach to the preferences of others, which is the ultimate goal of all management, leadership, or selling theories.

At times it is difficult to behave with high Versatility. Like in sports or the arts, some people are more naturally talented than others. None of us can be perfect all the time, particularly when we're operating under a lot of stress. During these difficult times we often lose control of the behaviors we would normally like to engage in and revert back to our more natural and basic behaviors.

As with any other competence we try to master, the Four Stages of Learning apply to increasing consistency in our Versatility behavior. The SOCIAL STYLE Model provides the context and an application road map showing how to progress from the learning stage *Unconscious Incompetence* via *Conscious Incompetence* and *Conscious Competence* to the target stage of *Unconscious Competence*, where Versatility has become natural and can be demonstrated while executing other tasks.

Like in sports or the arts, achieving high levels of mastery in Versatility not only requires constant training, it also presupposes significant effort and perseverance as well as fearlessness when it comes to failure. None of the world's top athletes are able to succeed without the help of a coach. This means in our case that a trainer can introduce you to the underlying principles of SOCIAL STYLE and equip you with the secrets you need to broaden your behavior portfolio. You may discover that enlisting a colleague who is also familiar with SOCIAL STYLE to coach you will be key to helping you embed new Versatility behaviors so you can make the Versatility Factor work to your benefit and the benefit of others.

Now that we have described the concepts of SOCIAL STYLE and Versatility, we can explain how they differ from other current psychological theories. We identified the dimensions of the SOCIAL STYLE Model—Assertiveness, Responsiveness, and Versatility—through empirical measurement methods. As we have mentioned, other researchers have discovered similar scales; in fact, there is strong agreement about the two dimensions making up SOCIAL STYLEs. This remains true even though methods vary greatly for collecting information about how people interact. There are, however, several distinctions between the SOCIAL STYLE Model and that of other personality concepts.

The first distinction is one of source and type of measurement. The SOCIAL STYLE Model is based upon socially reported measurement. And, it is based on others' impressions of a person, not someone's self-impressions. This is in contrast to most personality profiling techniques (e.g. Insights, DiSC, or MBTI), which ask people to report about themselves. These self-report sources of data are useful only for providing feedback about how one sees oneself. However, when people report about themselves, their perceptions are often significantly different from those of others who see them acting out behavior.

The second major distinction is that this concept is limited to objective, observable behavior. That is, SOCIAL STYLE and Versatility, as we define it, are concerned only with the "is", not the why, the cause, or the motivation of behavior. The focus is on what our behavior is likely to do to someone else, how that may work to our advantage or disadvantage, and what we can do to negotiate an interpersonal relationship so that both parties achieve mutually satisfactory goals.

The final major distinction is that SOCIAL STYLEs are nonjudgmental; there is no good or bad, right or wrong SOCIAL STYLE or formula for success. Never is it suggested that you imitate someone else's SOCIAL STYLE for succeeding. In fact, our research suggests there is little we can do to change our core SOCIAL STYLE behavior. We can try to enhance our Versatility and make our actions work more effectively by adding something to our customary habit patterns, but we don't need to eliminate or change existing behavior.

This nonjudgmental approach allows us to concentrate on understanding our own behavior instead of trying to figure out other people's motivations or the deeper aspects of ourselves. SOCIAL STYLE training helps us to improve perception, delay making value judgments about good and bad or mature and immature behavior, and learn to accept and work with each person's differences. Attaining this understanding pays off in improved communication skills, because the emphasis is shifted to learning to reduce defensiveness in relationships by doing something about how we appear to others. This approach of teaching us to be less defensive in our own actions allows us to focus on working with others instead of trying to manipulate them by capitalizing on their defensiveness.

The true value of SOCIAL STYLEs lies in the fact that it recognizes the individual preferences of the people we are dealing with. No matter what business you are working in, whether you are a manager, a team member, or a salesperson, the SOCIAL STYLE Model provides you with a globally used tool for adjusting your behavior based on situational and personal differences. Accepting the fact that we all have different personalities but share common patterns of behavior (the SOCIAL STYLEs), there exist at least four best approaches for dealing most effectively with other people. Whatever strategies or methodologies you follow in your organization, using the SOCIAL STYLE Model as the overarching framework will enable you to interact more successfully with others, internally and externally. It is the foundation of gaining the advantages from the Versatility Factor!

From recent research, we know that observing the behaviors of others plays a key role in the development of our minds as well in the evolution of human development as a whole. Against this background, our vision is to make the world a better place by enhancing the way people all over the world work together to solve the challenges they face. We are convinced that understanding the concepts of SOCIAL STYLE and attempting to use Versatility skills can ultimately increase our overall effectiveness.

So, let's try to communicate more effectively, utilize the Versatility Factor, and enhance our interpersonal relationships one person at a time!

CHAPTER NOTES

Chapter 1

1. Loehlin, J. C. (1992). Genes and environment in personality development. Newbury Park, CA: Sage.

Chapter 2

1. Dr. David W. Merrill was the founder of Reed, Merrill, Brunson and Associates (RMBA) and Personnel Predictions and Research, Inc. (PPR). Both companies were joined to form TRACOM in 1976.

2. Dr. James W. Taylor at that time was staff psychologist at Martin Corporation (later Lockheed Martin) in Denver.

3. The original research uncovered three other scales that were combined, originally called the STAR scale and renamed to Versatility.

4. American Educational Research Association; American Psychological Association, and National Council on Measurement in Education, 1999

5. Shrout, P. E., & Fleiss, J. L. (1979). Intraclass correlations: Uses in assessing rater reliability. *Psychological Bulletin, 86,* 420-428.

6. Meyer, G. J., Finn, S. E., Eyde, L. D., Kay, G. G., Moreland, K. L., Dies, R. R., Eisman, E. J., Kubiszyn, T. W., & Reed, G. M. (2001). Psychological testing and psychological assessment: A review of evidence and issues. *American Psychologist 56 (2),* 128-165.

Chapter 4

1. TRACOM: Managerial Success Study, 2005

2. TRACOM: Managerial Performance Evaluation Research, 2007

Chapter 5

1. This resource is adapted, in part, from materials from Interaction Associates, LLC, Mastering Meetings.

Chapter 8

1. The theory was developed at the Gordon Training International by its employee Noel Burch in the 1970s.

# REFERENCES & SUGGESTED READINGS

American Educational Research Association, American Psychological Association, National Council on Measurement in Education. (1999). Standards for educational & psychological testing. Washington, D.C.: American Educational Research Association.

ASTD's annual review of trends in workplace learning and performance. Alexandria, VA: American Society for Training and Development.

Bar-On, R. (2000). Emotional and social intelligence: Insights from the Emotional Quotient Inventory (EQ-I). In R. Bar-On and J.D.A. Parker (Eds.), *Handbook of Emotional Intelligence*. San Francisco: Jossey-Bass.

Bar-On, R. (1997). The Emotional Intelligence Inventory (EQ–i): Technical manual. Toronto: Multi-Health Systems.

BPM Forum and Success Factors. (2007). Performance & talent management trend survey 2007. [White paper]. Palo Alto, CA.

Charter, R. A. (2003). A breakdown of reliability coefficients by test type and reliability method, and the clinical implications of low reliability. *Journal of General Psychology*, July, 2003.

Cherniss, C. & Goleman, D. (2002). *The emotionally intelligent workplace: How to select for, measure, and improve emotional intelligence in individuals, groups, and organizations.* San Francisco: Jossey-Bass.

Cicchetti, D. V. (1994). Guidelines, criteria, and rules of thumb for evaluating normed and standardized assessment instruments in psychology. *Psychological Assessment, 6*, 284-290.

Cohen, J. (1988). *Statistical power analysis for the behavioral sciences (2nd ed.).* Hillsdale, NJ: Erlbaum.

Cohen, J. (1990). Things I have learned (so far). *American Psychologist, 45(12)*, 1304-1312.

Connelly, B. S. & Ones, D. S. (2010). An other perspective on personality: Meta-analytic integration of observers' accuracy and predictive validity. *Psychological Bulletin, 136(6)*, 1092-1122.

Conner, D.R. (1993). *Managing at the Speed of Change.* New York: Villard Books.

Conway, J., & Huffcutt, A. (1997). Psychometric properties of multisource performance ratings: A metaanalysis of subordinate, supervisor, peer, and self-ratings. *Human Performance, 10(4)*, 331-360.

Crocker, L. & Algina, J. (1986). *Introduction to classical & modern test theory.* Belmont, CA: Wadsworth Group.

Cronbach, L. J. (1951). Coefficient alpha and the internal structure of tests. *Psychometrika, 16*, 297-334.

Cross, P. (1977). Not can but will college teaching be improved? *New Directions for Higher Education, 17*, 1–15.

Dancey, C., & Reidy, J. (2004). *Statistics without math for psychology: Using SPSS for Windows.* London: Prentice Hall.

Darwin, C. R. (1872). *The expression of the emotions in man and animals.* London: John Murray.

Davidson, Richard J. & Begley, Sharon (2012). *The Emotional Life of Your Brain: How Its Unique Patterns Affect the Way You Think, Feel and Live – an How You Can Change Them.* New York, NY, Plume Publishing.

Dunning, D., Heath, C., & Suls, J. (2004). Flawed self-assessment: Implications for health, education, and the workplace. *Psychological Science in the Public Interest, 5*, 69-106.

Eberle, B. (1984). *Help! In solving problems creatively at home and school.* Carthage, IL: Good Apple, Inc.

Firari, F. (2007). *Email in style, improving corporate email communications with employees at remote locations: A quantitative study.* Doctoral dissertation, Capella University.

Fredrickson, Barbara (2009). *Positivity: Top-Notch Research Reveals the Upward Spiral That Will Change Your Life.* New York, NY. Harmony Books.

Gardner, H. (1983). *Frames of mind: The theory of multiple intelligences.* New York: Basic Books.

Gilbert, Daniel (2006). *Stumbling on Happiness.* New York, NY. Vintage Books.

Goleman, D. (1995). *Emotional intelligence.* New York: Bantam Books.

Goleman, D. (1998). *Working with emotional intelligence.* New York: Bantam Books.

Goleman, D. (1998). What makes a leader? *Harvard Business Review, 76(1)*, 93-102.

Goleman, D. (2006). *Social intelligence: The new science of human relationships.* New York: Bantam.

Goleman, D., Boyatzis, R.E., & McKee, A. (2002). *Primal leadership: Learning to lead with emotional intelligence.* Cambridge, MA: Harvard Business School Press.

Grant, Ph.D, Adam M. (2013). *Give and Take: Why Helping Others Drives Our Success.* New York, NY, Penguin Books.

Harvard Business Review Press (2015). *The Harvard Business Review's 10 Must Reads on Emotional Intelligence.* Watertown, MA, Harvard Business Review Press.

Heath, C., & Heath, D. (2010). *Switch: How to change things when change is hard.* New York: Random House, Inc.

Herbert, W. (2010). *On second thought: Outsmarting your mind's hard-wired habits.* New York: Broadway Paperbacks.

Hofstede, Geert; Minkov, Michael (2010). Cultures and Organizations: Software of the Mind.

http://www.psychologicalscience.org/index.php/news/releases/being-facedwith-gender-stereotypes-makes-women-less-likely-to-take-financial-risks.html

Inscape Publishing. (2008). *Everything DiSC® Classic Validation Report*. Inscape Publishing, Inc.

Ibarra, Herminia (2015). *Act Like a Leader, Think Like a Leader*, Watertown, MA, Harvard Business Review Press.

James, L. R., Demaree, R. G., & Wolf, G. (1984). Estimating within-group interrater reliability with and without response bias. *Journal of Applied Psychology, 69*, 85-98.

Joseph, D. L. & Newman, D. A. (2010). Emotional intelligence: An integrative meta-analysis and cascading model. *Journal of Applied Psychology, 95(1)*, 54-78.

Judge, T. A., Colbert, A. E., & Ilies, R. (2004). Intelligence and leadership: A quantitative review and test of theoretical propositions. *Journal of Applied Psychology, 89*, 542-552.

Kahneman, Daniel (2011). *Thinking, Fast and Slow*. New York, NY, Farrar, Straus and Giroux.

Kirkpatrick, D.L. (1994). *Evaluating Training Programs: The Four Levels*. San Francisco, CA: Berrett-Koehler.

Kraiger, K. & Crane, E. (2009). The relationship among three measures of workplace interpersonal effectiveness. [Whitepaper]. Fort Collins, CO: The Center for Organization Effectiveness at Colorado State University.

Kraiger, K. & Kirkpatrick, S. (2010). An empirical evaluation of three popular training programs to improve interpersonal skills. *Journal of Psychological Issues in Organizational Culture, 1(1)*, 60-73.

Kruger, J., Epley, N., & Parker, J. (2005). Egocentrism over e-mail: Can we communicate as well as we think? *Journal of Personality and Social Psychology, 89*, 925-936.

LinkedIn, (2012). The Mindset Divide: Revealing how emotions differ between personal and professional networks.

Lockwood, T. (2008). *Voice and language. Call centres: Maximising performance training manual. Fenman Professional Training Resources.* Retrieved January 6, 2009.

Loehlin, J. C. (1992). *Genes and environment in personality development.* Newbury Park, CA: Sage.

Luthans, F., Avolio, B., Avey, J. B., & Norman, S. M. (2007). Psychological capital: Measurement and relationship with performance and job satisfaction. *Personnel Psychology, 60*, 541–572.

Lyubomirsky, Sonja (2007). *The How of Happiness: A New Approach To Getting the Life You Want.* New York, NY. Penguin Books.

McClelland, D. C. (1973). Testing for competence rather than intelligence. *American Psychologist, 28*, 1-14.

McGonigal, Kelly (2012). *The Neuroscience of Change: A Compassion-Based Program for Personal Transformation, Audio CD.* Louisville, CO, Sounds True, Inc.

Mabe, P.A. III, & West, S.G. (1982). Validity of self-evaluation of ability: A review and meta-analysis. *Journal of Applied Psychology, 67*, 280–286.

McKinley, J. (2013). *Want to change the world? Be resilient.* Harvard Business Review Blog Network.

Mehrabian, A. (1971). *Silent messages.* Belmont, CA: Wadsworth.

Merrill, D. W. & Reid, R. H. (1984). *Personal styles & effective performance.* Boca Raton, FL: CRC Press.

Messick, S. (1989). Validity. In R. L. Linn (Ed.), *Educational measurement (3rd ed., pp. 13-103).* New York: MacMillan.

Meyer, G. J., Finn, S. E., Eyde, L. D., Kay, G. G., Moreland, K. L., Dies, R. R., Eisman, E. J., Kubiszyn, T. W., & Reed, G. M. (2001). Psychological testing and psychological assessment: A review of evidence and issues. *American Psychologist 56 (2)*, 128-165.

Mulqueen, C., Kahn, A. and Kirkpatrick, J.S. (2012), Manager's Interpersonal Skills and Their Role in Achieving Organizational Diversity and Inclusiveness. *Journal of Psychology Issues in Organizational Culture, 3*: 48-58. doi: 10.1002/jpoc.21062

Nicholson-Kluth, H. (2004). *Predicting the effectiveness of first line supervisors in law enforcement with the use of social styles concepts.* Unpublished master's thesis, Regis University, Denver, Colorado.

O'Boyle, E. H., Humphrey, R. H., Pollack, J. M., Hawver, T. H., & Story, P. A. (2011). The relation between emotional intelligence and job performance: A meta-analysis. *Journal of Organizational Behavior, 32*, 788-818.

Oh, I., Wang, G. & Mount, M. (2011). Validity of observer ratings of the five-factor model of personality traits: A meta-analysis. *Journal of Applied Psychology. 96(4)*, 762-773.

Petrides, K. V. (2009). Technical manual for the Trait Emotional Intelligence Questionnaires (TEIQue). London: London Psychometric Laboratory.

Petrides, K. V., Pita, R., & Kokkinaki, F. (2007). The location of trait emotional intelligence in personality factor space. *British Journal of Psychology, 98*, 273-289.

Prinz, Wolfgang (2012). *Open Minds.* The Social Making of Agency and Intentionality, The MIT Press.

Randstad Corporation (2008). The world of work 2008. [White paper]. Randstad North America.

Rivera, R. & Paradise, A. (2006). State of the industry in leading enterprises.

Reivich, Karan & Shatte, Andrew (2003). *The Resilience Factor: Seven Essential Skills for Overcoming Life's Inevitable Obstacles.* New York, NY. Harmony Books

Roberts, B. W. & DelVecchio, W. F. (2000). The rank-order consistency of personality traits from childhood to old age: A quantitative review of longitudinal studies. *Psychological Bulletin, 126(1)*, 3-25.

Rock, David (2009). *Your Brain at Work*, New York, NY. HarperCollins Publishers.

Sawyer, K. (2013). *Zig zag: The surprising path to greater creativity.* San Francisco, CA: Jossey-Bass.

Salovey, P. & Mayer, J. D. (1990). Emotional intelligence. *Imagination, Cognition and Personality, 9(3)*, 185-211.

Schaubhut, N. A., Herk, N. A., & Thompson, R. C. (2009). MBTI® Form M Manual Supplement. CPP, Inc.

Seligman, Martin. D. P.(2011) *Flourish: A Visionary New Understanding of Happiness and Well-being.* New York, NY. Atria Books.

Shrout, P. E., & Fleiss, J. L. (1979). Intraclass correlations: Uses in assessing rater reliability. *Psychological Bulletin, 86,* 420-428.

Simba Information (2006). Corporate training market 2006: Forecast and analysis. Stamford, CT

Siu, O., Hui, C., Phillips, D. R., Lin, L., Wong, T., & Shi, K. (2009). A study of resiliency among Chinese health care workers: Capacity to cope with workplace stress. *Journal Of Research In Personality, 43(5),* 770–776. doi:10.1016/j.jrp.2009.06.008.

Spencer, L.M., Jr., & Spencer, S. M. (1993). *Competence at work.* New York: Wiley.

Sternberg, R. J. (1996). *Successful intelligence: How practical and creative intelligence determine success in life.* New York: Simon and Schuster.

Stokes, P. D. (2005). *Creativity from constraints: The psychology of breakthrough.* New York, NY: Springer Publishing Company, Inc.

Thorndike, E. L. (1920). Intelligence and its uses. *Harper's Magazine, 140,* 227-235.

TRACOM Corporation (2012). SOCIAL STYLE & Versatility Technical Report: Development, Reliability and Validity. Centennial, CO.

TRACOM Corporation (2005). Documenting the Relationship Between Versatility and Job Performance in Managers. Centennial, CO.

TRACOM Corporation (2005). Managerial Success Study. Centennial, CO.

Tubbs, S., & Moss, S. (2006). *Human communication: Principles and contexts*. New York, NY: McGraw Hill.

Viswesvaran, C. & Ones, D. S. (2000). Measurement error in "Big Five factors" personality assessment: Reliability generalization across studies and measures. *Educational and Psychological Measurement, 60(2)*, 224-235.

Walters, A. E., Stuhlmacher, A. F., and Meyer, L. L. (1998). Gender and negotiator competitiveness: A meta-analysis. *Organizational behavior and human decision processes, 76*, 1–29.

Wechsler, D. (1940). Nonintellective factors in general intelligence. *Psychological Bulletin, 37*, 444-445.

Youssef, C. M., & Luthans, F. (2007). Positive organizational behavior in the workplace: The impact of hope, optimism, and resilience. *Journal of Management, 33*, 774–800.

Zenger, John & Folkman, Joseph (2009). *The Extraordinary Leader.* McGraw Hill Education; 2nd edition.

Zenger, T. R. (1992). Why do employers only reward extreme performance? Examining the relationships among performance, pay, and turnover. *Administrative Science Quarterly, 37*, 198–219.

 **APPENDIX**

Appendix A
Multi-Rater SOCIAL STYLE & Enhanced Versatility Profile

The Profile Report that learners receive is the result of responses to a questionnaire that is completed by the learner and his or her reference group. In addition to the learner, at least three people need to complete the questionnaire in order for a Profile Report to be produced. A minimum of three raters is necessary in order to maintain rater confidentiality and to produce reliable results. There is no maximum limit to the number of raters who can respond to a questionnaire, though learners should be encouraged to invite only people who work with them and know them well.

Questionnaire Description

The questionnaire consists of 88 behavioral statements. Individuals respond to each statement by indicating their agreement on a 5-point scale ranging from "strongly disagree" to "strongly agree" (see Fig. A-1).

APPENDIX A

Item	Strongly Disagree	Disagree	Partly Agree Partly Disagree	Agree	Strongly Agree
1. Approaches new situations with a positive outlook.	○	○	○	○	○
2. Generates creative solutions to problems.	○	○	○	○	○
3. Takes action without hesitation.	○	○	○	○	○
4. Cares about others' problems.	○	○	○	○	○
5. Builds good relationships with co-workers.	○	○	○	○	○
6. Effectively presents ideas to groups.	○	○	○	○	○
7. Concentrates on the logic and reasoning behind decisions.	○	○	○	○	○
8. Smiles a lot.	○	○	○	○	○
9. Does not hesitate to let others know what he or she is thinking.	○	○	○	○	○
10. Listens to others without interrupting the speaker.	○	○	○	○	○

Fig. A-1: Sample Questionnaire Items

Each item on the questionnaire is related to a specific behavioral scale. In particular, the questionnaire measures two scales that determine SOCIAL STYLE (Assertiveness and Responsiveness) and four scales that measure Versatility (Image, Presentation, Competence, and Feedback). Each scale has the following number of items that measure it:

- Assertiveness: 15 items
- Responsiveness: 20 items
- Image: 4 items
- Presentation: 5 items
- Competence: 26 items
- Feedback: 18 items

Profile Description

The Multi-Rater SOCIAL STYLE & Enhanced Versatility Profile consists of two sections:

1. SOCIAL STYLE
2. Versatility

These two sections are distributed to learners at separate times appropriate for the teaching points associated with each.

Debriefing the SOCIAL STYLE section of the Profile Report is a generally straightforward process. Most people have little difficulty accepting and understanding their SOCIAL STYLE. On the other hand, Versatility can be more difficult. Unlike SOCIAL STYLE, a result on Versatility implies an evaluative judgment, and it can be difficult for people to accept their results.

SOCIAL STYLE

Besides providing basic information for report interpretation, the Profile Reports show a graphic depiction of the full SOCIAL STYLE Model, complete with all 16 sub-quadrants (see Fig. A-2). A learner's SOCIAL STYLE is displayed, as seen by *Others* and *Self*.

It is important to stress that one should focus on the *Others* position since this is how a rater group perceives our behavior. Our research has shown that more than 50% of the population perceives their own behavior differently than their reference groups!

This Model provides narrative descriptions for the learner's specific SOCIAL STYLE. This narrative is based on the Others sub-quadrant position. The narrative is divided into three topic areas:

- Others Describe Your Behavior
- Your Behavioral Pluses
- Your Behavioral Minuses

There are 16 sub-quadrants on the Model, but only 12 possible narratives. This is because some SOCIAL STYLE sub-quadrants

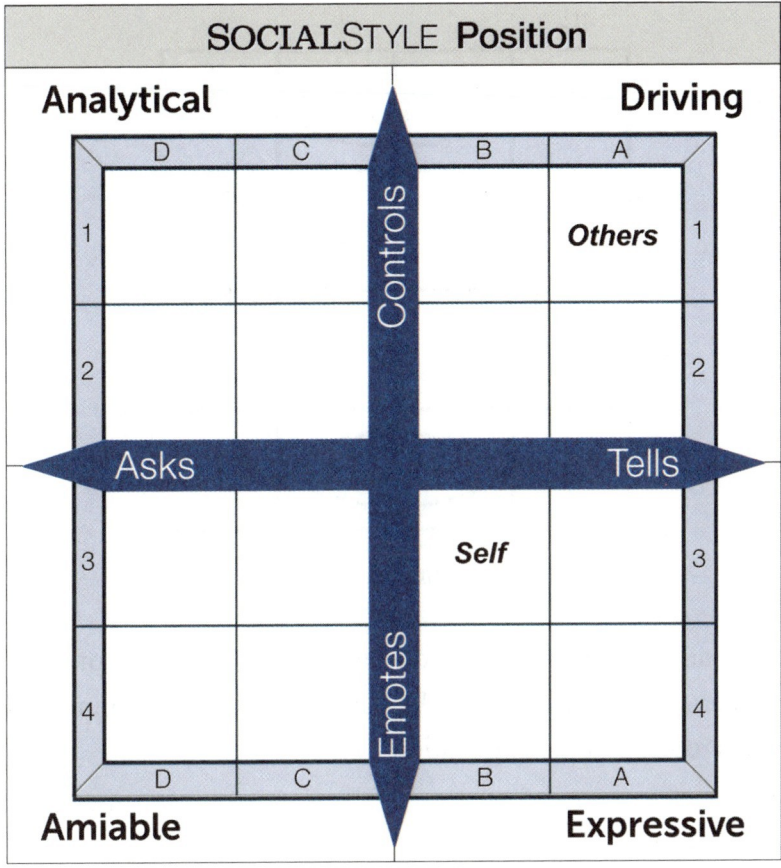

Fig. A-2: SOCIAL STYLE Position (Example)

share narratives due to similarity in their behavioral Profiles. Sub-quadrants that share narratives are: A2/A3, B4/C4, D2/D3, and B1/C1 (see Fig. A-3).

The narratives are generalizations about the behavioral characteristics of people with a particular sub-quadrant position. They do not describe any individual precisely. Expect that a few people might challenge the accuracy of this information as not being a perfect fit. This is true because all individuals are unique, and a simple description of behavior cannot totally characterize them.

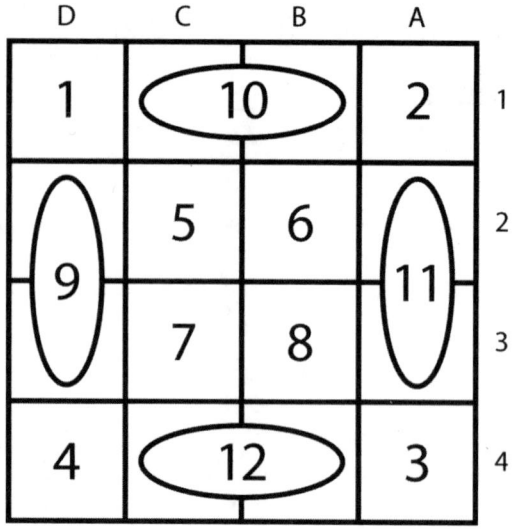

Fig. A-3: SOCIAL STYLE Narratives

In addition, reports provide summary descriptions of each of the other three SOCIAL STYLEs and several key reminders for learners to support the application.

Versatility

The Versatility section provides a general description of the learner's overall Versatility, and a summarizing graph that displays the learner's results in all four sources of Versatility, as well as Versatility overall (see Fig. A-4).

As in the SOCIAL STYLE section, *Others* is the most important data point. Each component of Versatility adds a percentage to the overall Versatility score. Because Competence and Feedback contain more items on the questionnaire, they account for a larger percentage of the Versatility score.

Narrative descriptions of each of the four Versatility sources are provided with four possible narratives, one for each 25th percentile "W", "X", "Y", and "Z". Unlike the overall Versatility, there are only three narratives used for each Versatility category (see fig. A-5). The X and Y quadrants are very similar in their behavioral profiles. Therefore, these narratives are identical.

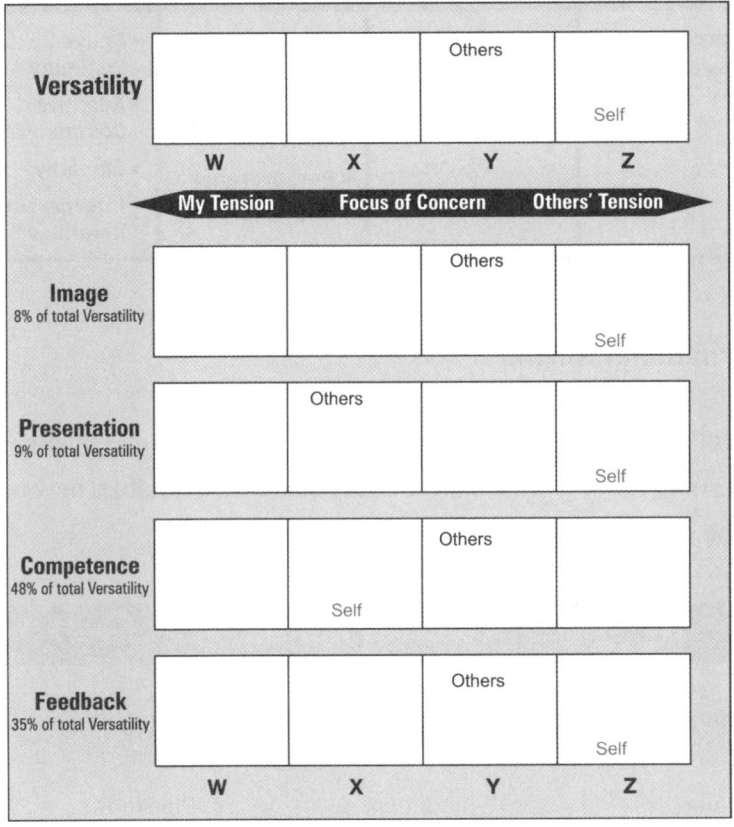

Fig. A-4: Versatility Scores (Example)

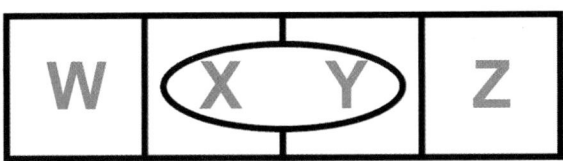

Fig. A-5: Versatility Narratives

Each narrative explains what is measured and gives the learner information about his or her standing in that area. The specific behavior categories measured are shown in the following table.

IMAGE	PRESENTATION	COMPETENCE	FEEDBACK
• Appropriateness of Dress	• Effectiveness of Group Communication	• Conscientiousness • Flexibility • Innovation • Perseverance • Optimism	• Active Listening • Adaptive Communication • Empathy • Interpersonal Relations

International Norms

The following country and region-specific norms are available as of 2014. With more representative data becoming available, new norms will be developed.

COUNTRY NORMS		
Argentina	India	Portugal
Australia	Indonesia	Puerto Rico
Austria	Ireland	Romania
Belgium	Israel	Russia
Brazil	Italy	Saudi Arabia
Bulgaria	Jamaica	Singapore

APPENDIX A

Canada (English-Speaking)	Japan	Slovakia
Canada (French-Speaking)	Jordan	South Africa
Chile	Kazakhstan	Spain
China	Korea (South)	Sweden
Columbia	Lebanon	Switzerland
Costa Rica	Luxembourg	Taiwan
Czech Republic	Malaysia	Thailand
Denmark	Mexico	Trinidad and Tobago
Egypt	Netherlands	Turkey
El Salvador	New Zealand	Ukraine
Finland	Nigeria	United Arab Emirates
France	Norway	United Kingdom
Germany	Pakistan	United States
Greece	Peru	Venezuela
Hong Kong	Philippines	Vietnam
Hungary	Poland	Zimbabwe

REGIONAL NORMS	COUNTRIES INCLUDED IN REGIONAL NORMS		
Africa (Eastern)	Burundi Comoros Djibouti Eritrea Ethiopia Kenya	Madagascar Malawi Mauritius Mozambique Rwanda Seychelles	Somalia Uganda Tanzania Zambia Zimbabwe
Africa (Middle)	Angola Cameroon Central African Republic	Chad Congo (Brazzaville) Congo (Kinshasa)	Equatorial Guinea Gabon Sao Tome and Principe
Africa (Northern)	Egypt Morocco	Algeria Libya	Sudan Tunisia
Africa (Southern)	South Africa Botswana	Lesotho Namibia	Swaziland
Africa (Western)	Benin Burkina Faso Cape Verde Cote d'Ivoire Gambia Ghana	Guinea Guinea-Bissau Liberia Mali Mauritania	Niger Nigeria Senegal Sierra Leone Togo
America (Central) and Mexico	Belize Costa Rica El Salvador	Guatemala Honduras Mexico	Nicaragua Panama
America (North)	Canada (English-Speaking)	United States	
America (South)	Argentina Brazil Chile Colombia	Peru Venezuela Bolivia Ecuador	Guyana Paraguay Suriname Uruguay
Asia (Central)	Kazakhstan Kyrgyzstan	Tajikistan Turkmenistan	Uzbekistan

REGIONAL NORMS	COUNTRIES INCLUDED IN REGIONAL NORMS		
Asia (East)	China Hong Kong Japan	Korea South Macau Mongolia	Taiwan Korea North
Asia (South Central)	India Maldives Sri Lanka	Pakistan Bangladesh Bhutan	Nepal Afghanistan
Asia (Southeast)	Brunei Cambodia Indonesia Laos	Malaysia Philippines Singapore Thailand	Vietnam Burma East Timor
Caribbean	Antigua and Barbuda Bahamas Barbados Cuba Dominica	Dominican Republic Grenada Haiti Jamaica St Kitts & Nevis	St Lucia St Vincent and Grenadines Trinidad and Tobago
Europe (Eastern)	Belarus Bulgaria Czech Republic Hungary	Moldova Poland Romania	Russia Slovakia Ukraine
Europe (Northern)	Denmark Estonia Finland Iceland	Ireland Latvia Lithuania	Norway Sweden United Kingdom
Europe (Southern)	Albania Croatia Greece Italy Portugal Spain	Serbia Montenegro Andorra Bosnia and Herzegovina Holy See	Kosovo Macedonia Malta San Marino Slovenia
Europe (Western)	Austria Belgium France	Germany Netherlands Switzerland	Lichtenstein Luxembourg Monaco

REGIONAL NORMS	COUNTRIES INCLUDED IN REGIONAL NORMS		
Middle East	Armenia Azerbaijan Bahrain Cyprus Georgia Iran Iraq	Israel Jordan Kuwait Lebanon Oman Qatar Saudi Arabia	Turkey United Arab Emirates Yemen Palestinian Territories Syria
Oceania	Australia Fiji Kiribati Marshall Islands Micronesia	Nauru New Zealand Palau Papua New Guinea Samoa	Solomon Islands Tonga Tuvalu Vanuatu

Questionnaires and Profiles are available in the following languages:

1. English (US)
2. English (International)
3. Bulgarian
4. Chinese (Simplified)
5. French (Canadian)
6. French (European)
7. German
8. Greek
9. Italian
10. Japanese
11. Korean
12. Portuguese (Brazilian)
13. Romanian
14. Russian
15. Spanish (European)
16. Spanish (Mexican)
17. Spanish (Latin American)
18. Swedish
19. Thai
20. Turkish

Appendix B
SOCIAL STYLE and Versatility by Job Function

The following section discusses the distribution of SOCIAL STYLE in 24 common job functions as well as the relative average Versatility for those job functions. Please keep in mind that some job functions dominate specific industries while others are broadly dispersed across various industries. For example, the Teaching Job Function is the dominant job within the Education industry, whereas professionals who identify as Marketing Job Function could be found in all industries. Percentages are rounded to the closest whole number for convenience.

SOCIAL STYLE & Versatility – Teaching
Versatility Ranking by Job Function – 1st

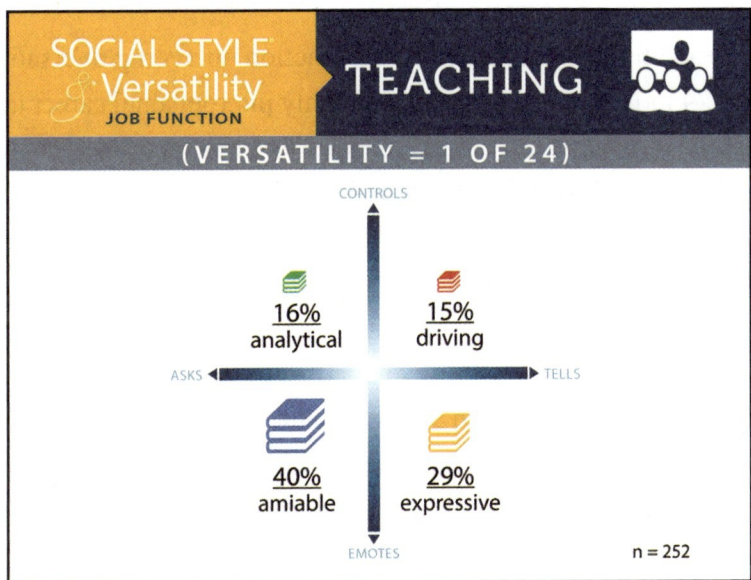

The Teaching job function includes traditional K-12, higher education, and adult education. The Amiable Style is the most common within education, and at 40.1%, Amiable Style people are more concentrated in teaching than in any other job function that has been researched. Many people in teaching are drawn to this career because they have a desire to impact their students and to have personal relationships with students and peers. This Style—along with the Expressive Style, which represents 28.5% of the teaching population—looks to make personal connections and have an influence upon others. Most people can recall a teacher who had a positive effect in their own life, and oftentimes these contributions were based on creating a personal connection rather than simply conveying technical expertise. But this shouldn't discount the Analytical Style and Driving Style people in teaching. Although the Analytical and Driving Styles are under-represented among teachers, with 15.9% and 15.1% respectively, these two Styles also bring an array of benefits to the world of teaching through their thoroughness, accuracy, timeliness, and exploration of data.

Teaching is the top-ranked job function on average Versatility, among 24 industries with data. This highly interpersonal career takes a great deal of Versatility skills in order to be successful. So which came first? Are those who are naturally Versatile drawn to this career or do those who are interested in Teaching learn to become highly Versatile out of necessity? Probably a little bit of both! This high performance is likely the result of both the people who are drawn to the education field and skills developed on the job. Primary and high school teachers often need to develop connections with students from a wide range of backgrounds and certainly different behavioral profiles. They receive both advance and on-the-job training in these skills. An increasing national emphasis on evaluating teacher performance likely will help teachers understand the importance of building effective connections.

SOCIAL STYLE & Versatility – Healthcare Professionals
Versatility Ranking by Job Function – 2nd

Working in a healthcare job function can be a highly demanding job that requires a wide range of skills. Because the term Healthcare professional is an umbrella term for a large number of jobs in the healthcare job field, there are various occupations that can require different skills. Such jobs can range from doctors and nurses to pharmacists, medical technicians, and administration. Almost all job functions as a Healthcare practitioner require a high degree of knowledge and technical expertise gained from formal education, as well as excellent customer service skills. While there is a little something for almost every Style, the Analytical Style makes up the largest percentage and the Driving Style is the most underrepresented in this job function. Analytical people (30.6%) are skilled at developing and following procedures. Their scrupulous tendencies help save lives in medical care. Expressive Style people (26.1%) can bring a sense of optimism and humor to customers who may otherwise struggle with worry and nervousness—think Robin Williams as Patch Adams. Amiable Style people (25.8%) are natural caregivers, helping patients feel at ease through their empathy and willingness to help. Driving Style people (18.4%) can rally employees and provide quick direction in emergency situations.

Healthcare professionals rank 2nd of 24 for highest average Versatility. This isn't surprising considering the high degree of human interaction combined with accuracy and stress that can be found in this job function. When people's lives are on the line, losing your cool with your co-workers or patients isn't going to improve the effectiveness of your job. Versatility is a key factor for smooth collaboration, teamwork, enhanced communication, and flexibility. While a person's Versatility can understandably falter under extreme pressure, high Versatility is practically a requirement among healthcare practitioners in order to be most effective in their job.

SOCIAL STYLE & Versatility – Consultant
Versatility Ranking by Job Function – 3rd

According to our research, consultants are most typically Expressive Style people (31.5%) followed closely by Analytical Style people at 28.4%. Driving Style people also make up a good proportion of consultants (23.3%), however Amiable Style people only make up 16.9% of this job function. Expressive Style people are drawn to positions with a great deal of autonomy and flexibility, and since many consultancies are often created by experienced professionals who wish to continue in their current roles while achieving some career independence, this is a natural fit. The Analytical Style is drawn to consulting positions because this type of job allows them to exercise their precise knowledge of a particular subject, while being able to work independently for a large portion of their time.

Analytical consultants can become true knowledge-leaders in their field, possessing a wealth of knowledge that in-house employees performing the same tasks do not have. This can enhance a consulting company's reputation among potential clients.

The consulting function ranks 3rd for highest average Versatility among all job functions. Success in this highly interactive field requires a great deal of Versatility practice, which is likely the reason these individuals are so well versed in the different skills necessary to have high Versatility. In order to become a reputable Consultant and maintain a steady clientele, you must practice and maintain all of the major components of Versatility.

SOCIAL STYLE & Versatility – Executive
Versatility Ranking by Job Function – 4th

An executive job function includes those who operate as directors, vice presidents, general managers, and CEOs. These people have

usually climbed the ladder, either through extensive education or job experience, and have paid their dues to reach the top tier of their company. Typically, we think of an executive as someone who is older and has gained a great deal of knowledge not only through pursuing education, but also through years of experience in their job, but a recent shift has come under way. Many large companies now have CEOs under the age of 35, but many times this is because these young men and women founded the business venture and appointed themselves in the executive role. According to our research, Expressive Style people make up the largest percentage of Executives with 35.9%, followed by Driving Style people at 30.2%. Analytical Style people represent 20.2% of this population and Amiable Style people make up 10.3%. The Expressive Style person appears communicative, fun, exciting, approachable, and competitive. They are generally motivated by personal approval and what greater gain of personal approval is there than to join the ranks of becoming CEO? A Driving Style person is typically more oriented toward results and tasks and is very effective with their time and getting things done. Driving Style people do not like being told what to do, which is quite possibly why they strive to become an executive.

As Versatility is a major component of workplace success, it's not surprising that the Executive job function ranks among the highest in average Versatility at position #4. An executive's ability to work with a wide range of audiences is critical. This typically includes managing teams, customers, suppliers, investors, etc. Versatility skills, more so than technical expertise or Style-based behaviors, will lead to success.

SOCIAL STYLE & Versatility – Outside Sales Representatives
Versatility Ranking by Job Function – 5th

Outside sales representatives are those who primarily work outside of the four walls of the office, and seek clients through direct contact and meetings. Depending on what is being sold, these people are typically encouraged to be very outgoing, energetic, knowledgeable, and relationship driven. Naturally, Expressive Style and Amiable Style individuals make an easy fit for these positions. Expressive Style people are more concentrated in an Outside Sales position than in any other occupation surveyed (37.7%). The second closest Style is Amiable with 23.7%. Driving Style (18.4%) and Analytical Style (20.2%) people are less common but still can bring certain behavioral preferences that appeal to some buyers. An Analytical Style's thoroughness can be highly effective when helping customers evaluate products. And a Driving Style's directness can be refreshing, as many people don't like to be schmoozed when trying to make purchases.

Due to the highly interactive nature of the job, it's no surprise that outside sales representatives rank in the top five for highest average Versatility. A good Sales representative needs to adapt to many different people's Styles and how they prefer to be treated in order to get the sale. These people need to know how to moderate themselves with their prospects in order to be successful in their job. Versatility is exactly that. It is understanding Style and learning to assess others' Styles, which allows you to identify the preferences of others and modify your behavior to make others more comfortable.

SOCIAL STYLE & Versatility – Human Resources
Versatility Ranking by Job Function – 6th

Those who have a career in human resources (HR) are at the core of their company's culture, effectiveness, and overall well-being. These individuals are typically in charge of managing interoffice conflict, hiring new employees, assessing and providing training and development, and promoting equal opportunity and diversity programs. It is no wonder that Amiable Style (31.5%) and Expressive Style

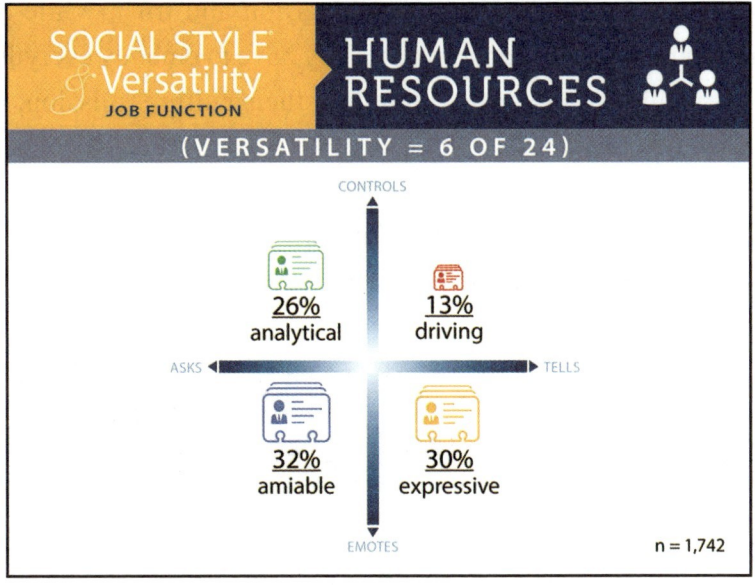

(29.5%) people make up the majority of those with a career in HR. Analytical Style people make up a quarter of HR professionals represented. Their thoughtfulness and diligence allow them to make carefully analyzed decisions and they are able to not allow their personal relationships interfere with their HR role. Driving Style people are underrepresented in this career field (13.3%). Driving Style people do not typically pursue a career in HR, as they are more driven by results and tasks and less focused on relationships and feelings. Driving Style people have little tolerance for actions they deem a waste of time. They prefer getting to the point and staying on target.

Like many of the other careers ranked highly for average Versatility, this is a greatly interpersonal career where, in order to succeed, one must be regarded highly in all four components of Versatility; Image, Presentation, Competence, and Feedback. These people are the face of their company. When someone is interviewing for a position, these individuals will be the interviewees' first impression of the company. When someone has a problem, these people must instill a sense of compassion and trust, while also remaining unbiased and thorough. They have to embody everything the company aspires to be, including their culture, mission, and vision.

SOCIAL STYLE & Versatility – Training
Versatility Ranking by Job Function – **7th**

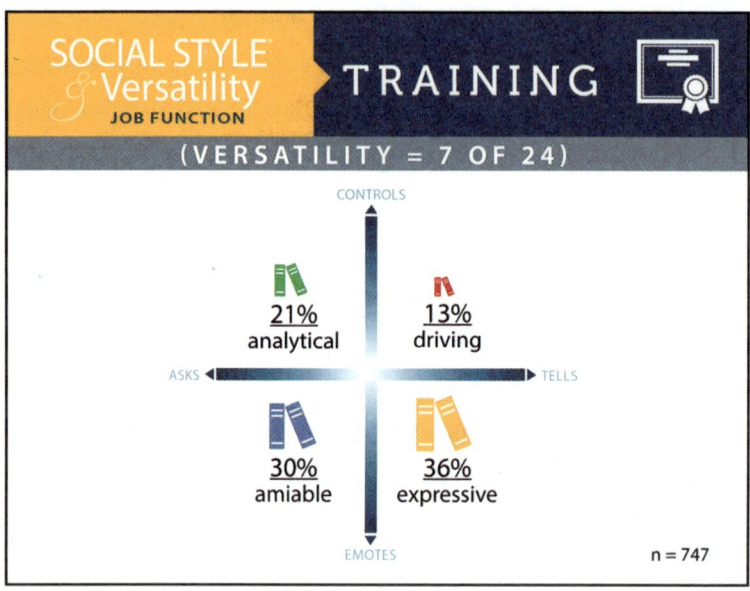

In order to be a good trainer you must feel comfortable being the center of attention and having all eyes on you. You will be the focus of everyone's attention and should feel comfortable in front of an audience. This is likely why the Expressive Style is drawn to this career path. To others, the Expressive Style person appears communicative, fun, exciting, and approachable. The Expressive Style person is naturally comfortable with sharing their feelings aloud with others, so it's a natural transition to share what they know with others as well. Their need is for personal approval, and what better way to gain this recognition than through training and facilitation. Amiable Style people also make up a large percentage of this role. The Amiable Style is the most "people oriented" of the four Styles. The Amiable Style person prefers cooperating or collaborating with others to competing with them. Those who are an Amiable Style might see training and facilitation as a suitable career as it allows them to form many connections and friendships at one time. A career in training or facilitation requires a lot of knowledge in a particular subject area. You must be so well-versed in the subject matter you are training or facilitating that you feel comfortable enough to teach it to others. An Analytical Style's meticulousness comes in handy when training occurs. The Analytical Style will be careful not to miss a certain detail. Although the Driving Style is less represented here than in any other career, they still make up nearly 12.9% of this job function. A Driving Style would make a good choice for a facilitator or trainer because they remain timely in their delivery and they will not stray off course from the subject matter.

Although training and facilitation can be in many different forms and on many different subject matters, it's still important for those in the training industry to be highly versatile to get their message across. One major reason that those who have high Versatility are also the most successful is because it is what people respond well to. Just the same that nobody is inspired or motivated by an arrogant boss, a trainer or facilitator who doesn't know how to adapt to different behavioral Styles will not be well-received.

SOCIAL STYLE & Versatility – Manager
Versatility Ranking by Job Function – 8th

A manager's role can vary widely depending on what type of organization you manage. Whether you're a store manager for a major

retail outlet, construction manager, a branch manager, or a regional manager, you most likely got to where you are through hard work, dedication, and experience. The Analytical Style (28.9%) person makes up the largest percentage of managers. People with this Style are well-suited for management positions because of their need for evidence to be tangible, realistic, and convincing—not someone's opinion. They are likely not going to be swayed by interoffice politics and will stray away from making close personal relationships at work. These individuals are more concerned with how to do things without the need for personal involvements. Expressive Style people are nearly tied for the largest percentage, but trail ever so slightly behind Analytical. Expressive Style people are naturally competitive so they may seek out these roles as means of advancement. This Style is less concerned with details and more focused on the big picture and end goal. Driving Style people also follow closely behind the Expressive Style people, at nearly 25.6%. A natural fit for the Driving Style, these people tend to initiate clear action and focus on efficiency or productivity. These people appreciate assistance that can help with achieving objectives and prefer "what" and "when" questions as opposed to "how", "why", or "who".

Managers are ranked 8th for highest average Versatility. Our research tells us that individuals with high Versatility are 27% more effective in managing conflicts, 26% better at influencing others, and 19% better at listening. Someone with all of these enhanced skills would be a favorite to be promoted to Manager. As a Manager, having enhanced Versatility is crucial to the success of your company. Your technical abilities and intelligence can only go so far. To ever become a manager you must have Versatility skills. Although underrepresented, Amiable Style people also make great managers, if they are highly versatile of course. This is because an Amiable Style person's "growth action" is to initiate. There is a skill that doesn't come naturally for Amiable Style people, but with practice they can become just as proficient as any other Style. Again, any SOCIAL STYLE can be successful in any job function with high Versatility.

SOCIAL STYLE & Versatility – Marketing
Versatility Ranking by Job Function – 9th

Those who work in a career in marketing are the brains behind promotions, advertisements, events, social media, publications, and buyer research. The marketing profession is heavily dominated by Expressive Style (33.9%) people, who are known to be highly energetic in social settings, very creative, and spontaneous. Expressive Style people have a distinct ability to generate excitement and buzz, and they are often in the know on popular trends among target consumer groups. Amiable Style people make up the second largest Style, trailing behind at 24.8%. Amiable employees' need to make and nurture personal connections, and a career in marketing, particularly in roles involving events and tradeshows, these

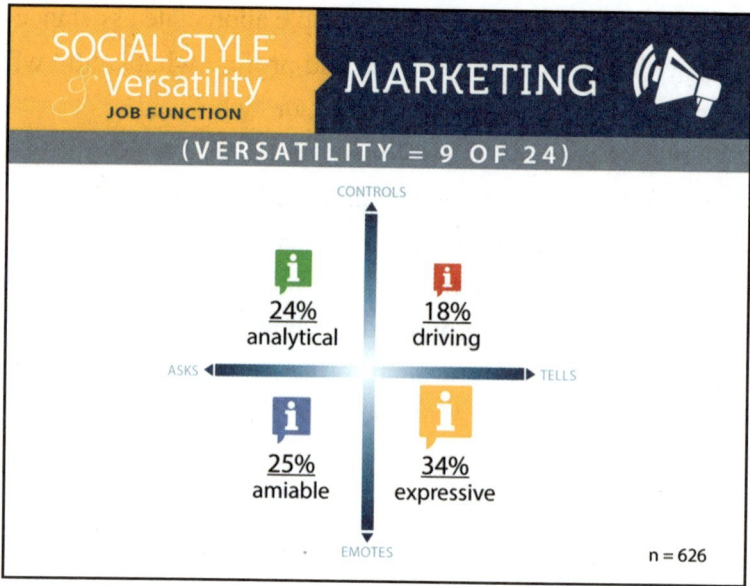

people are also highly in-tune with the people-side of things. They bring a fresh eye when examining and analyzing buyer behavior and shopping patterns. Analytical Style people are also heavily involved in marketing at 23.6%. These people are naturally inclined to the science and analysis side of marketing. These people will likely be the ones involved in creating surveys, monitoring the statistical software, monitoring ROIs, etc.

Marketers' main goal is to appeal to people. These people have learned to do this through understanding people and their behaviors and in what ways people want to be treated (and sold to). Minus the selling aspect, this is practically the definition of Versatility. Understanding Style allows you to identify the preferences of others and modify your behavior to make others more comfortable. Although underrepresented, Driving Style people can be highly successful marketers as well, they just have to master their growth action, to listen. Being a marketer has a lot to do with not only asking the right questions, but also listening. A lot of listening.

SOCIAL STYLE & Versatility – Finance & Accounting
Versatility Ranking by Job Function – 10th

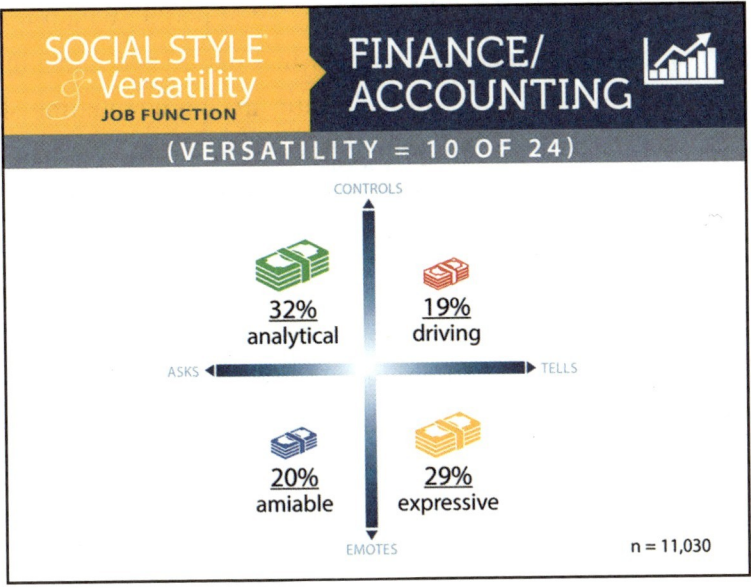

It's probably not shocking that those in finance and accounting careers are most highly represented by the Analytical Style. These jobs can be characterized by number-crunching and a thoughtful attention to detail. Working with finances can be just as complex as working on engineering-related tasks, which is a strong draw for Analytical Style people. What might be more surprising is that the Expressive Style people make up the second largest percentage at 28.6%. Expressive Style people are likely drawn to the fast-paced lifestyle of a finance career. Expressive Style people are needed in situations where time is sensitive and matters are urgent. Even in a career in finance, there are still many front-facing, interactive jobs that make a perfect fit for the Expressive Style bunch.

Contrary to popular belief, working in the accounting industry requires effective communication, teamwork, and patience. Job roles in the accounting industry are very dependent on each other, which requires collaboration and working efficiently and effectively with others of various Styles. Both the Amiable Style, which makes up 20.2% of this job function, and Driving Style people which makes up 19.1%, can have lucrative careers in finance and accounting. Driving Style people can bring their hard-driving negotiating skills to bear when arranging complex agreements with investors, and conversely, the Amiable Style people are effective at creating lasting relationships, an important role when seeking investors.

The average Versatility for the finance and accounting occupation falls in the top half of all tracked functions at #10 of 24. As this occupation has a tendency to involve many individual contributors, it's understandable that these skills are not as consistently developed.

SOCIAL STYLE & Versatility – General Manager
Versatility Ranking by Job Function – 11th

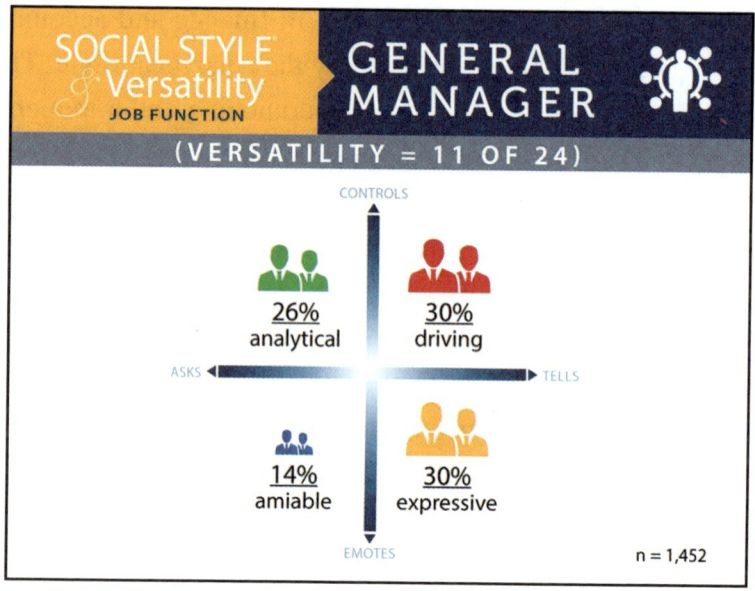

The job role of General Manager (GM) is similar in both SOCIAL STYLE distribution and Versatility. In the role of a General Manager, both the percentages of Driving Style and Expressive Style people are nearly tied and they are likely attracted to similar aspects of this position. Both the Driving and Expressive Style people like to not only influence and motivate others, but like to be viewed as influencers too. Expressive Style people consider power and politics important because they can enhance personal recognition and help recruit supporters to the cause. These individuals feel a strong need to defend personal positions they have taken, so co-workers are advised to use caution when challenging them. The Driving Style likes to initiate clear action and focus on efficiency or productivity. Although they are known to seem uninterested in relationships and social matters, they can also appear very pleasant and even charming, especially if it can help them achieve their end goals. The Analytical Style people come in at a close third making up 26% of this population. Analytical Style people are suspicious of people with power, but what better way to combat this suspicion than to be the person in power? They are likely drawn to General Manager roles because of their thoughtful and practical manner and their need to be right. They seek assurance that their decisions are "right" and based on accurate data. This Style of person also has a "show me" attitude, which works well in the role of GM.

Although this group is nearing the middle of the pack on the Versatility scale, Versatility is a highly important skill, especially for a GM. So, why does a manager (ranked 8th) have higher Versatility than a General Manager? Recent research tells us that those who feel they are experts can become less open-minded and versatile. GMs need to practice challenging themselves to avoid getting in a rigid pattern of thinking. While still fairly high in Versatility, there is room for growth for GMs to get more in-tune with focusing on adapting to the behavioral styles of their employees rather than expecting their employees to adapt to them. Those who can master this skill and take the time to appeal to their employees will have a more loyal company with less turnover and higher productivity. Although they have the lowest percentage among Styles with this job function, Amiable Style people make great GMs because of their focus on relationships, but the trick is to not get too caught up and focused on relationships and pleasing everyone. Those who are Amiable Style GMs are likely very highly Versatile as their growth action is to initiate—a must to obtain a role as GM.

SOCIAL STYLE & Versatility – Project Manager
Versatility Ranking by Job Function – 12th

Project managers have an eye for detail and are very thoughtful and thorough in their planning. It is important that they look over every miniscule facet of a project and not miss a beat. Naturally, the

Analytical Style person is a good fit for this job function. The Analytical Style person has a strong time discipline coupled with a slow pace to action. He or she moves with deliberateness and takes time to review all facts and available data. Although project managers need to be very precise in their planning, it is also important to be able to see the end goal and big picture and move swiftly toward that goal. This is the draw to this career for an Expressive Style, the second highest percentage among the Styles. But the Driving Style person remains a close third, and their directness and ability to focus efforts on goals and objectives that need done now are a huge asset for them in this career. These individuals are not reluctant to challenge the ideas of others and certainly are not afraid to take risks.

Project managers are not only in charge of the completion of a job or project, they are in charge of a team of people and must work to ensure the effectiveness and productiveness of their team. While project managers are typically known for having a higher Versatility, their emphasis on the project can sometimes get in the way of their behavior towards others. They might resort to something we call "backup behavior" in times of stress. Each SOCIAL STYLE has a fundamental need, and the backup behaviors of that Style are activated subconsciously when someone's interpersonal tension rises due to feeling threatened or dissatisfied with outcomes or marginalized in social settings. For example, an Analytical Style person might resort to backup behaviors when they feel rushed. These backup behaviors can include becoming withdrawn from the situation and not asserting themselves where they need to. The Amiable Style population is the smallest among Project managers, but the Amiable Styles who have taken on this job role are most likely to be highly Versatile as they would need to put their fears aside and initiate a lot of direction when working as a Project manager. Project management falls in the middle of the pack for average Versatility.

SOCIAL STYLE & Versatility – Protective Services
Versatility Ranking by Job Function – 13th

Protective services include jobs like police officers, detectives, firemen, and the National Guard. This career is heavy with the Analytical Style population and, in fact, has the largest Analytical Style percentage of any other job function. This might be surprising as Analytical Style people like to avoid risk, and there seems to be a great deal of risk in a career as a police officer or fire fighter, but there is also a great deal of reward for someone who appreciates caution and carefulness when making decisions. Analytical Style people thrive in the roles of detectives or researchers as this allows them to use their natural behaviors—like attention to detail and slow pace, as a strength to solve major crimes. Driving Style people make up the second largest percentage in this career. This might seem less surprising as the Driving Style is seen by others as active, forceful, and determined. People with a Driving Style are direct. They initiate social interaction and they focus their efforts and the efforts of others on the goals and objectives they wish to get accomplish.

Those in protective service roles are right in the middle for average Versatility. This might have something to do with the young age of many of the men and women in this profession. You can become a police officer at the age of 18 without a college degree. There is no current research that those who are older are more Versatile, but since we know that having a high Versatility is gained through practice and experience, we can assume that those who are older might be more aware of their own Style as well as the Styles of others, making them more Versatile. While this task is typically seen as very Versatile, due to the stressful nature of the job, people might not always be thinking about adapting themselves to the different Styles around them. While collaboration is still an important aspect of this career, when there is a fire burning a building down, these individuals are more focused on getting the job done well than adjusting their Style for the needs of others. Although not as highly represented, Amiable Style people make a good fit for this role as they prefer cooperating and collaborating with others rather than competing with them. Amiable Style people are most motivated when they can work as part of a group—something that many police officers, firefighters, and members of the National Guard do. Finally, consider that the primary objective for these workers is protection and safety. There are likely times that quick, decisive action outweighs the need for building relationships or developing consensus.

SOCIAL STYLE & Versatility – Legal
Versatility Ranking by Job Function – 14th

Those who have a legal job function include those in the roles of lawyers, paralegals, judges and district attorneys. The Analytical

Style makes up the largest percentage of this population at 36.3%. These individuals are drawn to these careers due to their value of precision, clarity and detail. They must remain focused on the facts and not be swayed by unverifiable knowledge. The Analytical Style person needs evidence to be tangible, realistic, and convincing. Tied for second, the Expressive and Driving Styles are also common in legal professions. Innate Expressive Style behaviors go hand in hand with being a lawyer. Expressive Style giveaways include fast-paced speech and also large quantities of speaking. These individuals like to make their presence known and are direct with their eye contact. They are facially animated and use a great deal of hand motions. The Driving Style also has a faster, louder pace of speech but is more controlled in their facial expressions. These people use facts and data to make decisions and use this as their means to influence others.

The legal job function is in the middle of overall Versatility. This is probably due to the greater emphasis on facts and procedure than on interpersonal aspects. It would still benefit people in these jobs to develop their individual Versatility skills to maximize their performance.

SOCIAL STYLE & Versatility – Customer Services
Versatility Ranking by Job Function – 15th

A career in customer service is a natural fit for those who enjoy a lot of interaction, which is why the Expressive Style makes up 32.9% of the people in this career. This Style is seen as casual and approachable. They work well in customer service roles because they can rapidly get into a social interaction and they appreciate social exchanges. These people are also able to change course rapidly. Amiable Style people make up 27.7% of this population and as the most people-focused of any of the other Styles, these individuals are highly sought after for customer service roles. To this Style, people count as people rather than as a way to achieve results or recognition. They are not risk-takers and attempt to reduce risk by ensuring actions will not damage ongoing personal relationships. Although ranked third, the Analytical Style still makes up a large percentage of this job function. They work well in this job function because of their ability to listen without interruption and their ability to separate facts from opinions.

Customer service can either make or break the reputation of a company. Jobs in customer service are typically characterized by individuals with less experience, knowledge, and education, yet they are the focal point of a consumer's perception about any business. Many customer service interactions are due to a previous negative customer experience; an ability to defuse conflict is critical. While average Versatility for customer service overall is in the bottom half of job functions, some organizations have identified these skills as critical strategic differentiators.

SOCIAL STYLE & Versatility – Information Systems and Technology
Versatility Ranking by Job Function – 16th

A career in information systems and technology (IS/IT) is a highly technical job dedicated to developing and supporting operating systems, digital programs, hardware, and communication platforms. And as one would expect, they are dominated by the Analytical Style. At this point, it is probably pretty obvious why an Analytical Style might be drawn to this type of job. The Analytical Style person appreciates job roles that support his or her tactical principles and thoughtful approach. Their precision to their work is what allows them to be naturally good in roles involving technology, where even slight errors could send an entire information system crashing down. The Driving Style makes up the second largest percentage of people in IS/IT. The Driving Style person is typically more drawn to careers where the emphasis is task

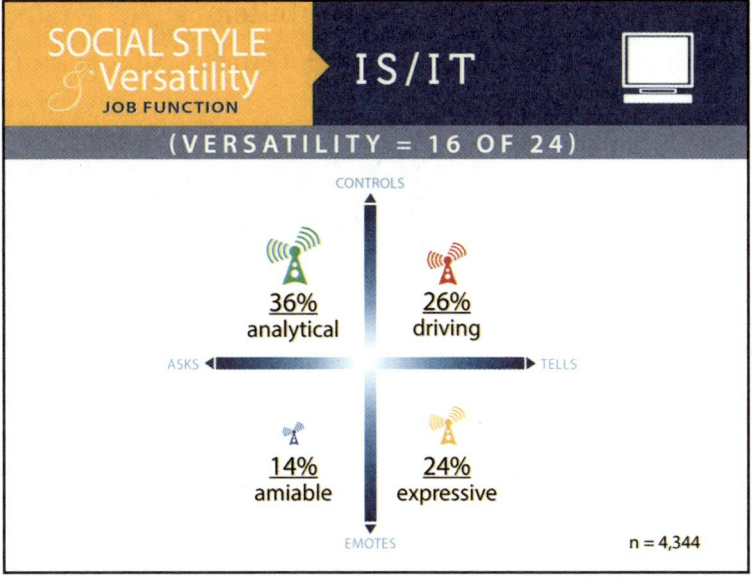

focused rather than people focused. People of this Style tend to initiate clear action and focus on efficiency and assignment completion rather than using time on developing interpersonal relationships with co-workers. This isn't to say that they don't form friends in the office; these bonds will just naturally form over time, as this Style of person isn't going to go out of their way to form these bonds. Expressive Style people make up 24% of this population. These individuals are likely drawn to careers where they are able to utilize their creative side, for example designing a new user interface.

Historically Versatility in IS/IT jobs has been low, currently ranking 16 of 24. But as technology has changed, some organizations are recognizing that these workers need strong relationship skills to go along with their technical expertise. This can be particularly important as IS/IT workers move from individual engineer roles into positions with broader responsibilities.

SOCIAL STYLE & Versatility – Bank Teller
Versatility Ranking by Job Function – 17th

Expressive Style people (32.6% of population) are drawn to the type of customer-facing positions that can be found in retail banking, which provide opportunities to meet and interact with a large number of people each day. Their ability to switch to a different task at the drop of a hat and immediately engage in active conversation makes them a preferable choice for this position. Amiable Style people are also often found in this job function, making up 31.6% of this career. Similar to customer service personnel, they are naturally good at this job because of their people focused tendencies. As an Analytical Style person, (22.6% of this job function) a career as a bank teller takes advantage of a knack for carefulness and meticulousness, while also supplying them a job that allows them to have quick bursts of short interactions that typically are never too lengthy.

Considering the highly interactive nature of a bank teller, one might be surprised that this career has a lower-than average Versatility. When a person becomes a bank teller, it is typically their first job in a professional setting. You can enter into this career without a college degree (although many people do have college degrees, and enter management trainee positions that begin as a bank teller). These people may be inexperienced in the proper behaviors of a professional setting, nor have they learned to adjust their behaviors to appeal to different SOCIAL STYLEs. But considering the customer-facing nature of this position, residing in the bottom third of average Versatility rankings tells us that many banks need to focus on training that would optimize their tellers' interactions with customers and each other.

SOCIAL STYLE & Versatility – Research & Development
Versatility Ranking by Job Function – **18th**

As the name indicates, research and development professionals are heavily involved with research and analysis, so it's no surprise that at nearly 35.5%, this group is largely made up of Analytical Style people. Analytical Style people make a natural selection for this job type because of their data-driven and methodical tendencies. The Expressive Style, who represents 26.2% of this job market, has a natural inclination to spontaneity and creativity. These folks use their whimsical ideas to try new things and can oftentimes produce incredible and innovative products and services. Driving Style individuals are third, representing 21.9% of the people in this career. These individuals are driven to these jobs because they are big picture thinkers with a goal in mind, determined to find the means to achieve it. These people are not reluctant to challenge the ideas of others and are certainly not afraid to take risks, allowing for many product enhancements.

Many people assume that those in research and development roles are highly independent workers, who need their alone time and quite space for creative inspiration. Even the managers of these people think that, which is why they likely have lower Versatility. Their upper management does not take the time to train them in interpersonal skills because it is assumed that they do not need them due to the independent nature of their work. What many people, and management, don't realize is that collaboration is the key to many of the world's most innovative inventions. Having the ability to work effectively with different Styles is important for individuals and organizations.

SOCIAL STYLE & Versatility – Purchasing
Versatility Ranking by Job Function – 19th

People in this career are responsible for negotiating, buying and

selling, investing, and initiating contractual agreements with other organizations. The Analytical Style (34.8%) is attracted to these careers because of its process orientation. Their preference to focus on data is valuable in these roles. The competitive nature of the Expressive Style person (26.1%) is a good match in this career, as competition can be fierce when negotiating new contracts, bidding for new jobs, etc. Driving Style people (23.7%) are the third largest Style in this job function. This Style's cool and controlled emotions and behaviors are important for this job. These individuals enjoy having power and making their own decisions. This Style of person is likely to choose alternatives with good probabilities of success, but they are not risk averse. They may occasionally select a less-likely-to-succeed alternative. While the Driving Style individual can accept risks, this person may be considering facts in addition to what is presented.

Purchasing professionals are most likely measured on objective statistical and financial measures, so demonstrating interpersonal skills is not necessarily a priority. They rank in the bottom third for Versatility. But as organizations seek to build more collaborative and longer-term supplier partnerships, Versatility skills can help achieve those goals.

SOCIAL STYLE & Versatility – Administrative/Clerical Assistant

Versatility Ranking by Job Function – 20th

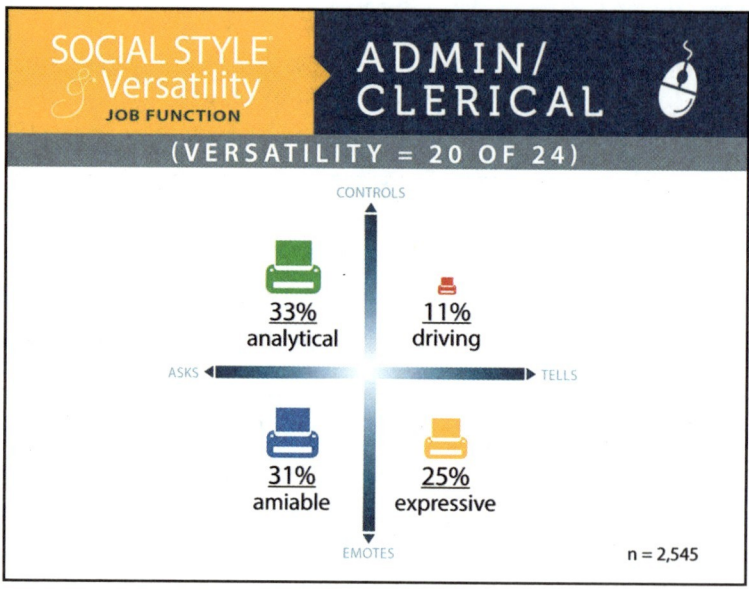

The most important aspect of a career as an administrative/clerical assistant is organization. If you are not an organized person, or don't learn to be one quickly, your days as an administrative assistant are numbered. Tasks of this job function include: managing calendars, taking phone calls, planning and coordinating travel for the various members of an organization, coordinating meetings and events, and much more. (Technology has reduced the number of people in these roles.) This job role is perfect for the task-focused Analytical Style person (32.8%). The Amiable Style person is also drawn to this role and represents 31.3% of the population. The Amiable Style person is also drawn to the "people" aspect of this job. Because they care about people and their relationships, they will be more apt to being aware of people's personal needs when managing events and calendars. The Expressive Style person makes up about a quarter of the people in this job role. Their friendly, approachable, and animated behavior is a huge draw for tasks that include answering phones and hosting events and meetings.

The low average Versatility in this job is likely based on the lack of investment many organizations make in it. Administrative personnel are among the lowest compensated employees and typically have less formal education and training. Given the influence they have on other staff such as executives and managers, building Versatility skills is a smart investment.

SOCIAL STYLE & Versatility – Engineering
Versatility Ranking by Job Function – 21st

Engineering is a career that requires a strict attention to detail, careful organization, and exhaustive calculations and planning. There are many different kinds of engineers with many different tasks, but most require specific technical education or experience. It's no surprise that the Analytical Style comes in first here, at 38%. Engineering careers also have a high percentage of Driving Style professionals (29%). Both of these Styles are task focused and less emotive than the other Styles. They are more focused on getting the job done than on people. A major difference between these two Styles is their risk-taking. The Analytical Style tends to avoid risks, and he or she may continue to display caution and deliberateness until they are fully comfortable with the amount of certainty in making decisions. The

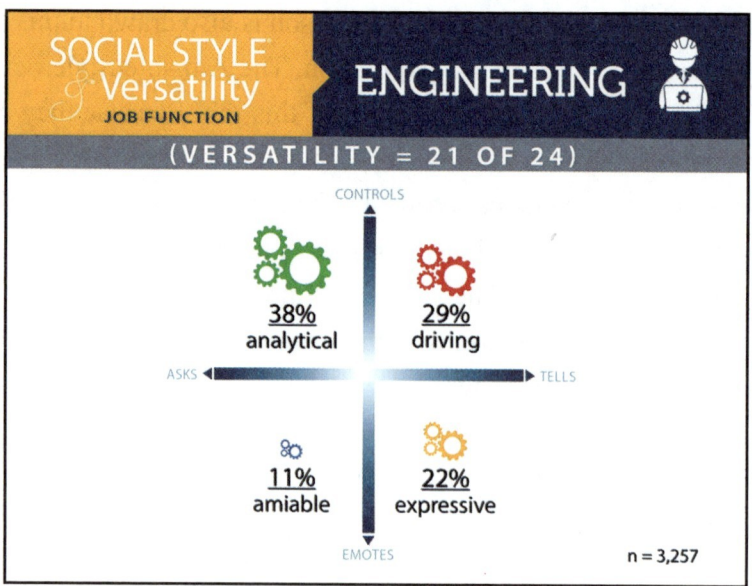

Driving Style person is likely to choose alternatives with good probabilities of success, but they are not risk averse. These two traits help to offset each other in times when risk is not wise, but in other times a decision must be made even without all of the details.

Technical skill has long been seen as the most important driver of professional competence and upward career growth, but the low average Versatility among this group is a concern. This is because, more than ever before, people in any position with a technical skill set need more than traditional competence to succeed. To achieve lasting results in the collaborative era, engineers need to be able to communicate effectively with people around them, including peers, supervisors, subordinates, and customers. Based on these low levels of Versatility, the disconnect between interpersonal skills and technical ability is apparent and must be addressed.

SOCIAL STYLE & Versatility – Construction
Versatility Ranking by Job Function – 22nd

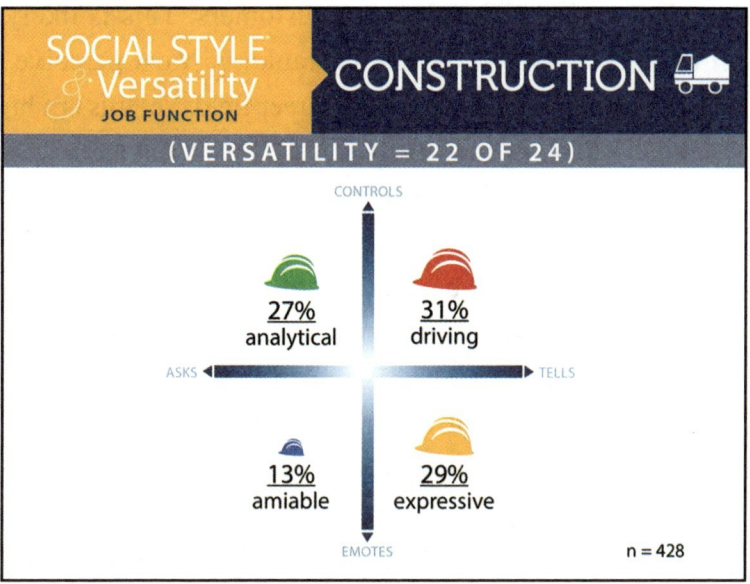

The Driving Style makes up the largest percentage of those with a career in construction, and at 31.3% this is the largest percentage of Driving Style people than in any other job function. While the engineers might be designing our roads, buildings, and bridges, those who work in construction are the ones to assemble the parts. The Driving Style is drawn to this type of career because of their directness and big picture thinking. These people tend to initiate clear action and focus on efficiency or productivity. When they initiate social interaction it is to focus their efforts and the efforts of others on the goals and objectives they wish to accomplish. They prefer getting to the point and staying on target and are driven by deadlines and schedules. The Expressive Style person comes in second, making up 29% of those in construction. These people are drawn to these careers because they are proficient in moving quickly and also changing course rapidly.

A construction career doesn't typically involve a great deal of customer interaction. Most construction personnel will never even speak to their company's clients or customers. This is likely the reason for their very low Versatility ranking. Most perceive that people skills are not important in this career field. Yet this is a highly collaborative career where teamwork is not only valued but required to complete the job. With deepened understanding of SOCIAL STYLEs and how to more effectively work with one another, construction jobs would be completed at a quicker rate due to fewer mistakes and lower turnover.

SOCIAL STYLE & Versatility – Manufacturing
Versatility Ranking by Job Function – 23rd

Careers in manufacturing are characterized by working in factories with extreme specialization. The Analytical, Driving, and Expressive

Styles are all nearly tied for percentages in manufacturing careers. This is probably due to the varying tasks and job roles that can all be assigned within a manufacturing career. Only the Amiable Style is underrepresented in this career, making up just 11.7%. A possible reason why there are fewer Amiable Style people in manufacturing might be that there are fewer opportunities for customer-facing roles than in other industries, which are a natural attraction for these individuals. Contact with customers is often limited to high-level managers and salespeople. However, the mix of Styles shows that there are unique roles in which each Style is able to thrive.

Manufacturing careers rank near the very bottom of average Versatility, ranking 23rd out of 24 job functions profiled in our research. This is likely due to the unique atmosphere and culture of working in manufacturing facilities. Historically, many manufacturing companies have operated under a command and control leadership hierarchy, where interpersonal skills have not been highly valued. This, of course, is changing now that organizations are realizing the payoffs and benefits of Versatility. For example, modern manufacturing plants now rely not only on top-notch technical abilities, but also workers' skills at team problem-solving, customer awareness, and personal innovativeness. In today's highly competitive environment, manufacturers can differentiate themselves from competitors by increasing employees' Versatility and team skills.

SOCIAL STYLE & Versatility – Installation & Repair
Versatility Ranking by Job Function – 24th

As we have become highly dependent on our appliances, we have also become very reliant on the people who install and repair them. The Analytical Style people make up the largest percentage of people in these careers at 37.3%. The methodological tasks and slower pace

of work are huge draws for this Style. The Driving and Expressive Styles are nearly tied for second at approximately 26%. The appeal of the job for the Driving Style people is the autonomy and task-central focus. The Expressive Style enjoys the opportunity to meet and work with new people regularly.

Installation and repair is the lowest ranked job function by Versatility. These individuals often do not always have the opportunity for long interactions and thus not as much opportunity to practice the skills that lead to a heightened Versatility. But similar to a career in manufacturing, the job would be enhanced through the expansion of Versatility training. Because of review sites like Angie's List, simply completing a task is no longer enough. People will review work based not only on the task assigned, but someone's ability to appeal to the customer's behavioral Style. The need for soft skills is on the rise in these types of careers as competitors become more customer satisfaction oriented, and trained to be more aware of the client's behavioral preferences.

Appendix C
SOCIAL STYLE and Versatility by Industry

The following section discusses the distribution of SOCIAL STYLEs in selected industries as well as the relative average Versatility for those industries. Please keep in mind that some job functions dominate specific industries while others are broadly dispersed across various industries. For example, the education industry is dominated by teachers, so the data are quite similar. Conversely, the consumer products industry is made up of people in wide-ranging job functions.

SOCIAL STYLE & Versatility – Education Industry
Versatility Ranking by Industry – 1st

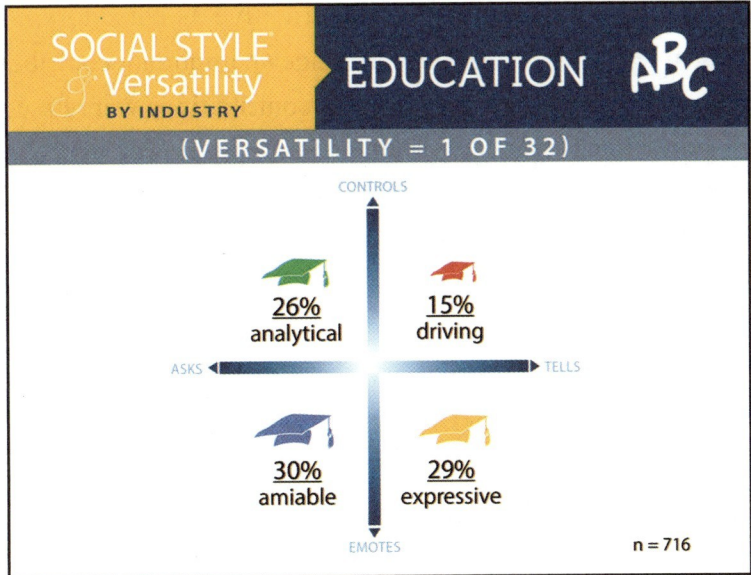

The education industry includes traditional K-12, higher education, adult education, and people in both direct educational roles and administration. The Amiable Style is the most common within education and at 29.7% Amiable Style people are more concentrated here than in any other industry that has been researched. Interestingly, Expressive Style and Analytical Style people are also common within education. Only the Driving Style (15.4%) is under-represented in education.

Given the education field's natural tendency to have ongoing personal relationships, it's not surprising that Amiable Style people are drawn to this industry. This SOCIAL STYLE—along with the Expressive Style—looks to make personal connections and have an influence upon others. The quest-for-knowledge and research aspects of education can appeal to the Analytical Style, which is also well represented inside educational organizations.

While all SOCIAL STYLEs bring benefits to the world of education, the Amiable and Expressive Style are especially skilled at building connections that can be effective as educators. Most people can remember a teacher who made an important contribution in their own life, and oftentimes these contributions were based on creating a personal connection rather than simply conveying technical expertise. In the world of higher education, the Analytical Style educator can be successful through research and publishing, which are likely to be enhanced by this SOCIAL STYLE's emphasis on accuracy and exploration of data.

The education industry is the top-ranked industry on average Versatility, besting 32 other industries with comparable data. This high performance is likely the result of both the people drawn to the education field and skills developed on the job. Primary and high school teachers often need to develop connections with students from a wide range of backgrounds and certainly different behavioral profiles. They receive both advance and on-the-job training in these skills. An increasing emphasis on evaluating teacher performance likely will help teachers understand the importance of building effective connections.

Amiable, Expressive, and Analytical Styles can bring their unique behavioral skills to improving the educational environment and creating a culture for learning. Even with a relatively small percentage of people in the education field, Driving Style people can contribute to success in education, particularly as new teaching techniques and school formats are tested and evaluated.

(Based on a sample size of 716 participants)

SOCIAL STYLE & Versatility – Healthcare Industry
Versatility Ranking by Industry – 2nd

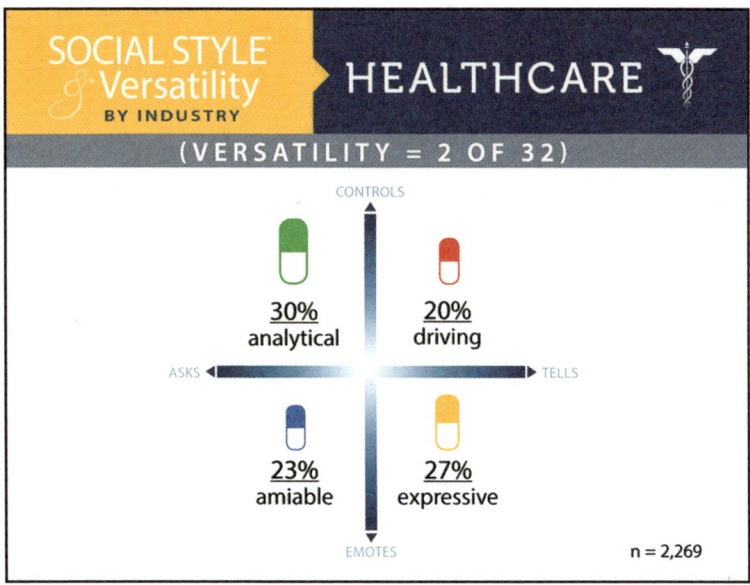

Though slightly weighted towards the Analytical Style, the healthcare industry contains nearly equal numbers of people in each SOCIAL STYLE. Healthcare professions run the gamut from emergency-room surgeons to administrative specialists in records departments.

The wide range of occupations in this industry makes room for people of all SOCIAL STYLEs.

Because there are such a variety of job roles in this industry, healthcare occupations can require a high degree of knowledge and technical expertise gained from formal education, as well as excellent customer service skills, often within the same role. Thus, there is something for every SOCIAL STYLE. For example, many Analytical Style people are drawn to scientific and research roles, while many Amiable Style people will find a natural fit in roles where they can help others and care for them.

Each SOCIAL STYLE brings unique strengths to the healthcare field. Analytical people are skilled at developing and following procedures, which can literally help save lives in medical care. Amiable Style people are natural caregivers, helping patients feel at ease through their empathy and willingness to help. Expressive Style people can bring a sense of optimism and humor to customers who may otherwise struggle with worry and nervousness. Driving Style people can rally employees and provide quick direction in emergency situations.

When compared with other industries, the healthcare industry has one of the highest average Versatility scores, ranking second out of 32 industries profiled in our research. This is not surprising, considering the high level of internal teamwork, not to mention customer interaction, which is commonplace in this field. Many people in this industry are highly attuned to the needs and preferences of others and skillfully put this into practice in their daily work lives.

Healthcare is one of the unique industries where all SOCIAL STYLEs are almost equally represented; in fact, it is the most balanced of all the industries. What is most striking is this industry also has one of the highest Versatility scores of all the industries studied. This shows that this field has learned not only the value, but the necessity, of effective interpersonal skills and teamwork.

(Based on a sample size of 2,269 participants)

SOCIAL STYLE & Versatility – Telecommunication Industry
Versatility Ranking by Industry – 3rd

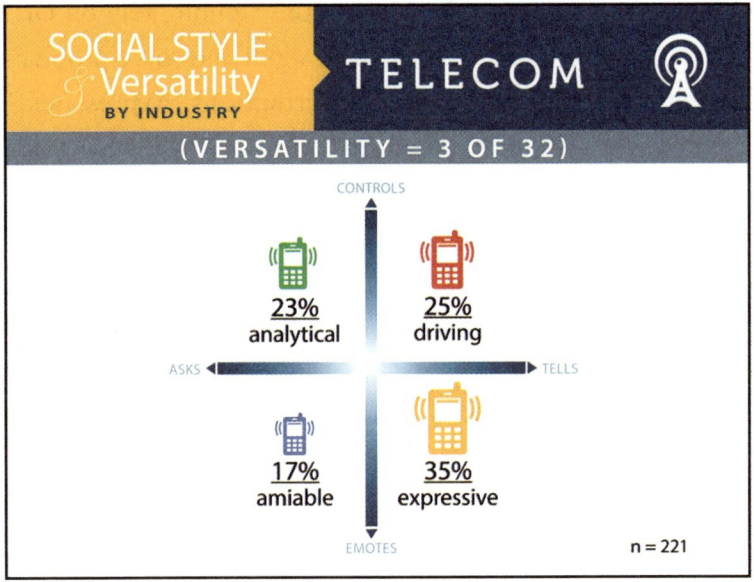

The telecommunications industry predates the Internet age and cellular technology, providing the main form of communication for individuals and businesses for many years. Even with the modern shift toward satellite and Internet communications technology, telecom companies still thrive on business and government clients. The Expressive Style is most highly represented in this industry, representing the largest percentage of Expressive Styles among any other industry, coming in at 34.5% of all surveyed employees.

The assertive nature of Expressive and Driving Style individuals can attract them to the fast-paced telecommunications industry. Telecom projects are often large and complex, giving Driving Style people opportunities to lead teams with tight deadlines. The customer service orientation of the industry can appeal to Expressive Style people, as it affords opportunities to converse with a wide range of people each day.

There are many segments of the telecom industry in which Driving and Expressive Style employees can contribute their strengths. Telecom utility companies, for example, rely on Driving Style leaders and technicians to troubleshoot and solve problems as quickly as possible during service interruptions. Expressive Style individuals can also add value to telecom sales teams by adding excitement to otherwise undifferentiated services or products.

Average Versatility scores in the telecom industry rank third of 32 profiled industries, putting the industry in the top 10%. This is an asset in an industry with such a heavy focus on customer service. Even though average scores are high, telecom companies can still gain strategic advantages by enhancing their employees' Versatility. Our research consistently proves people of all SOCIAL STYLEs can contribute to company success in their own way in any industry, and telecom is no exception. For example, Amiable Style customer-service employees are good at calming customers down over the phone, and can salvage damaged customer relationships by providing excellent service under pressure. The Analytical Style's penchant for engineering comes into play heavily in telecom R&D departments.

(Based on a sample size of 221 participants)

SOCIAL STYLE & Versatility – Media Industry
Versatility Ranking by Industry – 4th

Of the 32 industries researched, the media industry has the most even distribution of SOCIAL STYLEs with the largest percentage being the Expressive Style at 27.1% and the smallest percentage belonging

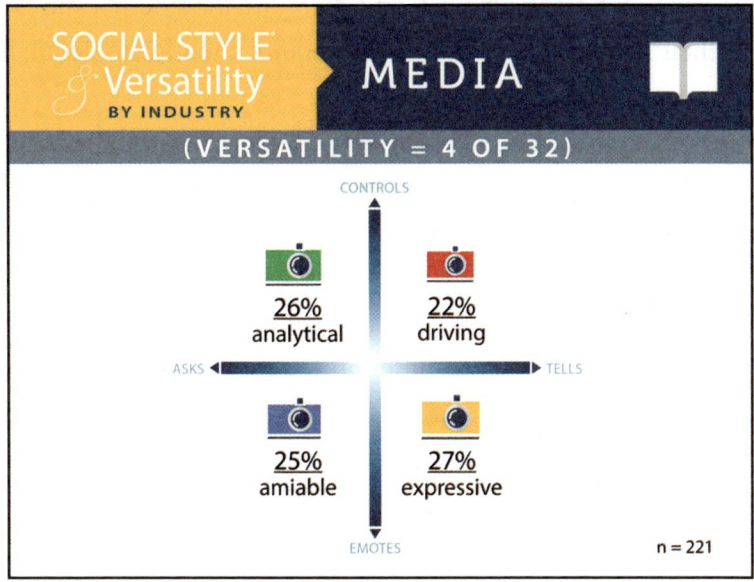

to the Driving Style at 22.2%. Like many of the other industries, this industry is comprised of a variety of roles and responsibilities creating a diverse group of skills needed to cover the broad range of duties.

Due to the creative tasks associated with this industry, it's not surprising that Expressive Style people are drawn to these roles. Such positions can include journalists, writers, designers, creative directors, and radio personalities. In addition to the Expressive Style person, such roles might be well suited for Amiable and Driving Style people. There are also roles that involve more technical, task-oriented, and complex skills. These roles can include computer-animation specialists, directors, producers, editors, and publishers.

There is really a job for everyone and every SOCIAL STYLE in this industry, which explains the evenly distributed percentages of SOCIAL STYLEs. Expressive and Amiable Styles can lend their creative and personable touches to produce an entertaining magazine, a script for a funny sitcom, or be the headlining personality on a talk show. Those who are Driving and Analytical Style people could utilize their strengths in positions that require attention to detail, hard work, and vision for completion.

Another important strength that characterizes this industry is the high Versatility people in this type of business display. Coming in at number four of 32 profiled industries, it's evident those who work in media know how to work well with others, especially those with a different SOCIAL STYLE than their own. This is not surprising considering the high level of internal teamwork needed to make a finished product. Whether that be an animated movie or a radio talk show, there are a lot of moving pieces requiring reliance on others. This evokes trust, dedication, encouragement, and understanding, along with other related Versatility skills. While there is always room for improvement, the people of this industry are contributing to create a harmonious workforce.

It seems to be a trend that those industries where almost all SOCIAL STYLEs are equally represented also have among the highest Versatility scores. As a driver of innovation, the media industry is well versed in the value and necessity of effective interpersonal skills and teamwork, but one of the characteristics of high Versatility is the ever-present aspiration to improve. While fourth in Versatility is good, there is still room for improvement.

(Based on a sample size of 221 participants)

SOCIAL STYLE & Versatility – Legal Industry
Versatility Ranking by Industry – 5th

Research shows the Analytical Style is more drawn to the legal industry than any other SOCIAL STYLE, with Expressive Style a close second at 29.1%. This may sound counterintuitive at first, since Analytical and Expressive Style people fall on the opposite ends of

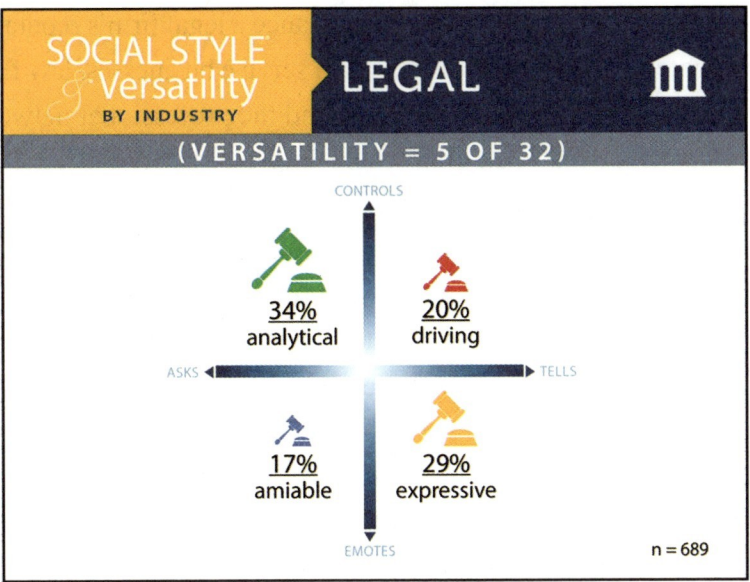

both the Assertiveness and Responsiveness scales. However, digging deeper into the daily challenges that attorneys face can provide insight into why this dichotomy holds true.

Analytical Style people are driven by a need to be right. Since certain legal jobs involve meticulous analysis of clients' situations, contracts, IP protection, estate plans, or business to make sure everything is "right," this is a natural fit for Analytical Styles. The legal field covers a wide range of practice areas, which allow Analytical Style people to exercise their precise knowledge of a particular subject and work independently for a large portion of their time. Expressive Style people are naturally drawn to positions with a great deal of personal liberty, especially in the area of personal expression. Since experienced professionals who wish to continue in their current roles while achieving career independence often create law firms, this is a natural fit for experienced Expressive Styles.

Analytical Style attorneys can become true knowledge-leaders in their field, possessing a wealth of knowledge that others performing the same tasks do not have. This can enhance a legal firm's reputation among potential clients. As professional service businesses, law firms rely to a great extent on relationships and the professional networks they establish. This is an area where Expressive Style people can bring their unique strengths to bear.

The legal industry is among the top third in Versatility scores, ranking number five of 32 industries profiled in our research. This shows that employees in this industry are highly attuned to the needs and preferences of others, and they have the ability to effectively work with others in a wide variety of situations.

Although the Analytical Style is most highly represented, research shows all SOCIAL STYLEs are represented at some level, proving that each SOCIAL STYLE's distinct strengths and perspectives can be useful in different areas. For example, Amiable Style attorneys can be adept at negotiating agreements or in determining the underlying organizational source of a client's problem, rather than focusing on symptoms.

(Based on a sample size of 689 participants)

SOCIAL STYLE & Versatility – Accounting Industry
Versatility Ranking by Industry – 6th

Within the Accounting industry, the Analytical Style represents the largest percentage of employees with 30.7%, followed by Expressive Style with 29.0%, Amiable Style with 24.2% and Driving Style with 16.1%. This sequence of represented Styles is the same for two other related industries: banking and finance, and insurance. Although it's important to note the percentages were not the exact same across all three industries, just the order of the Styles ranging from highest percentage to lowest.

Many jobs in the accounting industry require number crunching

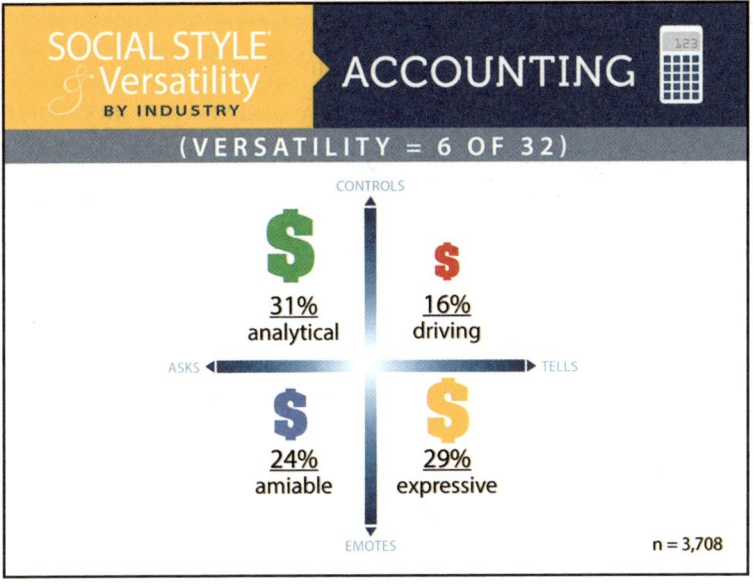

and a thoughtful attention to detail. Those of the Analytical Style typically make perfect accountants, but working in the accounting industry isn't solely about being an accountant. There are a number of other jobs that include roles in administration, management, sales, and consulting. These types of roles are what likely attract many of the Expressive Style people to this industry. These roles are all involved in a fast-paced work environment and require a great deal of creative thinking and problem solving.

    The dedicated and focused work ethic of the Analytical Style person fits perfectly in a field where accuracy and attention to detail are required. Analytical Style accountants ensure the job is done correctly and thoroughly. They don't rush to finish; they strive for perfection even if that means going the extra mile, and their strengths fit hand in hand within the accounting industry. As mentioned previously, the accountants, while a huge and lucrative piece of the puzzle, couldn't do it alone. Expressive Style people comprise a close second in this field because their strengths are needed in situations where time is sensitive and matters are urgent.

Contrary to popular belief, working in the accounting industry requires effective communication, teamwork, and patience. Job roles in the accounting industry are very dependent on each other, which requires collaboration and working efficiently and effectively with others of various SOCIAL STYLEs. This takes a great deal of Versatility, which is likely why this industry is rated sixth out of 32 industries.

(Based on a sample size of 3,708 participants)

SOCIAL STYLE & Versatility – Consulting Industry
Versatility Ranking by Industry – 7th

Research shows the Analytical Style is drawn to the consulting industry more than any other SOCIAL STYLE, with Expressive Style a close second at 29.2%. This may sound counterintuitive at first, since Analytical and Expressive Style people fall on the opposite ends of both the Assertiveness and Responsiveness scales. However, digging deeper into the daily challenges that consulting businesses face can provide insight into why this dichotomy holds true.

Analytical Style people are driven by a need to be right. Since a consultant's job may be to meticulously analyze a segment of a client's business and make sure that everything is "right," this is a natural fit for Analytical Styles. Consultant positions allow Analytical Style people to exercise their precise knowledge of a particular subject, while being able to work independently for a large portion of their time. Expressive Style people are naturally drawn to positions with a great deal of personal liberty, especially in the area of personal expression. Since experienced professionals who wish to continue in their current roles while achieving career independence often create consultancies, this is a natural fit for experienced Expressive Styles.

Analytical consultants can become true knowledge-leaders in their field, possessing a wealth of knowledge that in-house employees performing the same tasks do not have. This can enhance a consulting company's reputation among potential clients. As service businesses, consultancies rely to a great extent on relationships and the professional networks of salespeople and managers. This is an area where Expressive Style people can bring their unique strengths to bear.

The consulting industry is among the top third in Versatility scores, ranking number seven of 32 industries profiled in our research. This shows that employees in this industry are highly attuned to the needs and preferences of others, and they have the ability to effectively work with others in a wide variety of situations.

Although the Analytical Style is most highly represented, research shows all SOCIAL STYLEs are represented at some level, proving that each SOCIAL STYLE's distinct strengths and perspectives can be useful in different areas. For example, Amiable Style consultants can be adept at determining the underlying organizational source of a client's problem, rather than focusing on symptoms. Consulting companies are known for their investment in developing both the functional and interpersonal skills of their employees.

(Based on a sample size of 3,054 participants)

SOCIAL STYLE & Versatility – Government Industry
Versatility Ranking by Industry – 8th

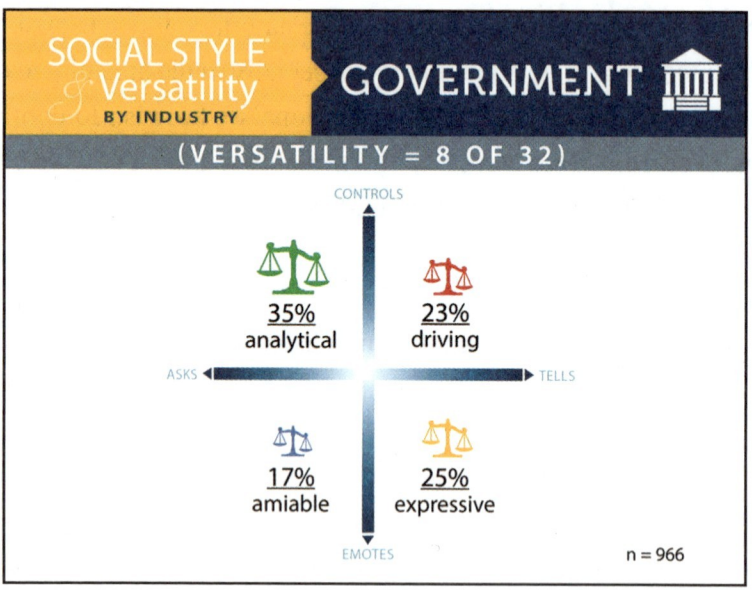

SOCIAL STYLE and Versatility come into play in the public sector just as much as in the private sector, and effective interpersonal skills can be even more important in government agencies that deal with a wide range of diverse individuals on a regular basis. Government agencies exist to serve myriad purposes, from providing citizen-facing services such as vehicle licensing, to ensuring national defense. Although people of different SOCIAL STYLEs may be specifically drawn to different agencies, people of all SOCIAL

STYLEs can find ways to contribute their unique strengths.

Government agencies operate within strict regulatory guidelines and are accountable to many more stakeholders than private businesses. This requires immaculate precision and strict attention to detail on the part of government employees, which creates a natural draw for Analytical Style people. This industry has the highest percentage of Analytical Styles compared to 32 other industries. It is likely that Analytical Style people are even more highly represented in certain agencies than others, such as the Internal Revenue Service, which processes taxes for individuals and businesses in the United States.

Analytical Style people are skilled at navigating complex systems of regulation and at creating and following detailed processes for ensuring reliable output. Government agencies rely on their Analytical Style employees to provide the most reliable services to citizens possible, even at the expense of speed or efficiency.

The Government sector ranks eighth in terms of average Versatility scores among the industries profiled in our research, revealing that employees in this industry are well versed in effective communication and collaboration with a diverse range of people. Employees with high Versatility can leave lasting impressions on customers and other stakeholders through excellent customer-service skills and the ability to cultivate long-term relationships.

People of all SOCIAL STYLEs can find a place in the government sector in which their distinct strengths can shine. For example, even though the Amiable Style is represented in smaller numbers than others, these people can make excellent liaisons between agencies and their most valuable stakeholders. As another example, Driving Style people can ensure emergency and disaster response agencies provide service as quickly and efficiently as possible.

(Based on a sample size of 966 participants)

SOCIAL STYLE & Versatility – Entertainment and Leisure Industry
Versatility Ranking by Industry – 9th

The Expressive Style dominates the entertainment and leisure industry with 32.9% of surveyed employees. This makes sense in both settings, as both entertainment and leisure companies are focused on creating memorable customer experiences. The Analytical Style comes in second place at 26.1%. Much like other industries we have profiled, this industry features a range of front-facing and back-of-house roles, making this unlikely combination the perfect fit.

Expressive Style individuals are natural entertainers, whether they seek an official outlet such as an acting career or whether it comes out in their daily interactions with others. Any job role that involves being on center stage is a natural draw for this SOCIAL STYLE. Although customers often do not realize it, entertainment experiences rely on extremely complex planning and coordination of numerous details. The complex puzzle involved in crafting the perfect customer experience can be deeply rewarding for Analytical Style people, who gain the benefit of seeing their work put into practice in final productions.

Creating an excellent customer experience relies on both outgoing customer service staff and great attention to detail. Expressive Styles serve as excellent company ambassadors to customers enjoying an entertainment experience—they can get people excited and capture attention with their general flair for entertainment. Analytical Styles have the right kind of mind to ensure each of the myriad of supporting details is in place to create a flawless experience.

The entertainment and leisure industry is among the top third in Versatility scores, ranking number 10 of 32 industries profiled in our research. This shows employees in this industry are highly attuned to the needs and preferences of others, and they have the ability to effectively work with others in a wide variety of situations. Although the Expressive Style is most highly represented, research shows all SOCIAL STYLEs are represented at some level, proving each SOCIAL STYLE's distinct strengths and perspectives can be useful in different areas. For example, Amiable Style people can help to smooth relations with guests who have undergone a negative customer service experience.

(Based on a sample size of 716 participants)

SOCIAL STYLE & Versatility – Hospitality Industry
Versatility Ranking by Industry **– 10th**

The hospitality industry primarily includes hotels and lodging with operations including service staff, food operations, and even cleaning and maintenance. Tell Assertive people from the Driving and

Expressive SOCIAL STYLEs make up nearly two-thirds of workers in the hospitality industry. The Expressive Style is measured at 36.7% and Driving 26.1%. The Amiable Style represents just 11.9% of these employees. These numbers are similar to the related entertainment and leisure industry data.

The goal in this industry is typically to meet or exceed customer expectations, so Versatility skills are more important than Style distribution. Creating an excellent customer experience relies on recognizing the priorities and preferences of guests and then taking the appropriate steps in response. So, it's not a surprise that the hospitality industry ranks in the top 10 for average Versatility.

(Based on a sample size of 218 participants)

SOCIAL STYLE & Versatility – Pharmaceuticals Industry
Versatility Ranking by Industry – **11th**

The distribution of SOCIAL STYLEs in the pharmaceutical industry

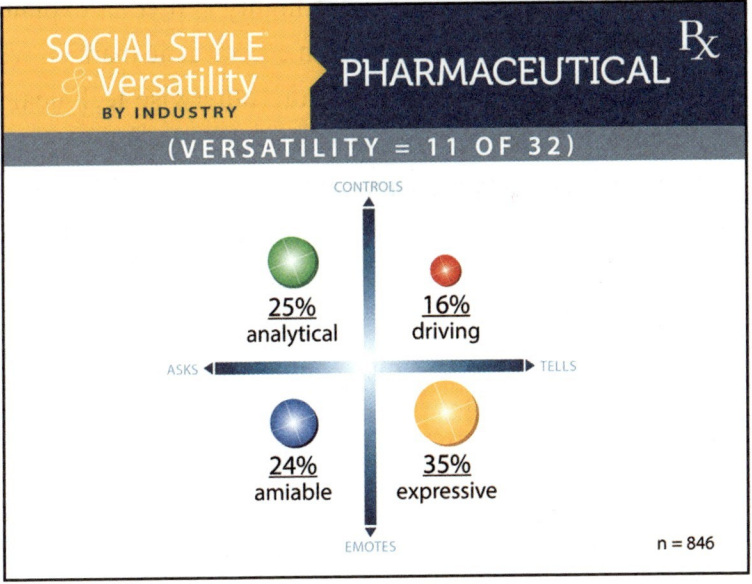

proves there is a place for all SOCIAL STYLEs in different job roles. The Expressive Style is represented much higher than any other SOCIAL STYLE, while the Driving Style is less represented here than in most other industries.

While there are multitudes of job roles within the pharmaceutical industry, this industry relies heavily on marketing, specifically mass-market advertising, to spread the word about new medications and services. It also employs many people in sales who have the job of convincing their customers their products are the most effective. Expressive Style people are naturally drawn to these types of roles, as this kind of work can provide them great freedom in expressing their ideas and creativity through highly visible output. Other roles provide natural fits for other SOCIAL STYLEs. For instance, there are many scientists and researchers in this industry, and it is likely many of these people have an Analytical Style.

In addition, advertising and direct marketing to medical practitioners play a large role in the success of new pharmaceutical products. Expressive Style people are highly skilled at explaining the big-picture benefits of products in an enthusiastic manner, which can help differentiate their products from otherwise technical and unexciting presentations.

The pharmaceutical industry ranks 11th out of 32 industries profiled in our research, reaching the top third in Versatility. This shows many people in this industry possess strong interpersonal skills and display Versatility in their interactions with others. However, there is always room for improvement, especially in a highly competitive industry like pharmaceuticals. Moving into the top ranks of Versatility can give an organization a distinct advantage against others in the same industry.

Although the Expressive Style is most highly represented, research shows all SOCIAL STYLEs have distinct strengths and perspectives and can be successful regardless of the industry. For example, Driving Style people's focus on achieving goals and meeting deadlines can be invaluable in such a competitive industry, while Amiable Style individual's ability to establish cohesive teams can go even further towards achieving milestones.

(Based on a sample size of 846 participants)

SOCIAL STYLE & Versatility – Business Services Industry
Versatility Ranking by Industry – 12th

The business services industry is home to a wide range of companies, from carpet cleaners to printer maintenance providers. As such, this industry requires a mix of customer service and precise attention to detail, which explains the unusual preponderance of Analytical Styles.

Some positions in this industry require frequent interactions with customers, while other positions require detail-oriented work

that is done methodically and independently. The opportunity to troubleshoot and solve unique challenges on their own is highly appealing to Analytical Style people. On the flip side, Expressive Style people delight in the opportunity to work in varied settings and interact with a large number of people.

Thoroughness marks the work of Analytical Style people, and such diligence can make or break a company's valuable relationships in the business services industry. Whether on the front line, in the ranks of management, or serving in a specialist's position, Analytical Style individuals can drive a company's reputation for providing reliable service. Likewise, Expressive Style people are skilled at interacting with customers and making them feel important. These individuals are likely to be the "face" of many companies in this industry, possibly in a sales or customer relations role.

Compared to other industries, business services ranks 12th out of 32 industries for Versatility scores. This shows many people in this industry possess decent interpersonal skills and awareness of others' needs and preferences, but there is still room for improvement. Moving from the median range to the top third in terms of Versatility can give an organization a distinct advantage against competitors in the same industry.

The combination of Analytical and Expressive Style dominating an industry is somewhat unique. It leaves a lot of opportunities for the other SOCIAL STYLEs to find ways to succeed by relying on their unique abilities and characteristics. For example, Driving Style people can complete work quickly and efficiently, minimizing the impact on clients' normal routines, while Amiable Style people can develop strong and lasting relationships with customers, ensuring repeat business.

(Based on a sample size of 1,270 participants)

SOCIAL STYLE & Versatility – Computers and Technology Industry

Versatility Ranking by Industry – 13th

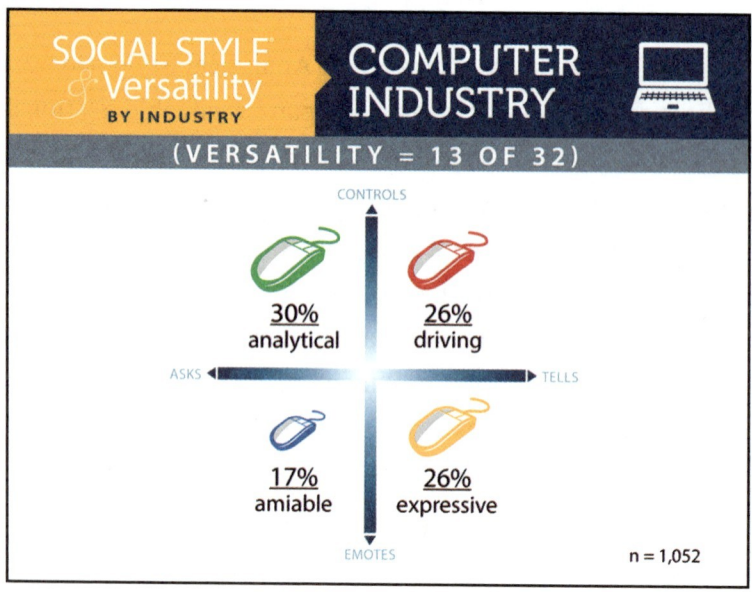

The computers and technology industry contains numerous segments in both the product and service categories, but all of them share the same focus on highly technical, engineering-driven competencies. It's no surprise the Analytical Style comes in first here, at 30.3%. As with other highly technical industries, the computer industry has a high percentage of Driving Styles. Because the computer industry includes organizations focused on customer service as well as those focused on engineering, the Expressive Style is represented highly here, too.

There are different elements of computer-industry segments that appeal to each of the four SOCIAL STYLEs. Analytical Style people, for example, can be strongly drawn to engineering-related positions, such as R&D for new computer technologies. Driving Style people can be drawn to fast-paced and quickly changing industries, and the computer industry has always been one of them. Expressive and Amiable Style people can be drawn to positions that allow for frequent interaction with customers, which the service segment of this industry provides in abundance.

Given there are so many diverse roles in this industry, each SOCIAL STYLE can add its own unique strengths to different functions within their organization.

Versatility scores in the computer industry rank toward the middle of the 32 industries profiled in our research, coming in 13th place. This indicates people in this industry possess strong skills in understanding others' needs and preferences in their interactions, but there is still room for improvement. Moving from the middle range to the top third in terms of Versatility can give an organization a distinct advantage against others in the same industry.

(Based on a sample size of 1,052 participants)

SOCIAL STYLE & Versatility – Marketing and Advertising Industry

Versatility Ranking by Industry – 14th

The marketing and advertising industry covers a wide range of businesses from advertising agencies to direct sales service providers. Expressive Style people make up the largest portion of the workforce here, coming in at 35.0%, while Amiable Style individuals make up the second largest portion with 26.9% of the workforce. This industry has the lowest percentage of Driving Style and is tied for the highest percentage of Expressive Styles compared to any other. This is to be expected in an industry defined by artistic expression and skillful relationship management.

There are things about every facet of marketing that can appeal to the Expressive and Amiable Styles. Advertising can provide exciting creative outlets for Expressive Styles, for example, while consultative sales can satisfy Amiable Style employees' need to make and nurture personal connections. The same things that attract these SOCIAL STYLEs to marketing occupations in other industries can attract them to organizations whose main line of business is marketing.

The marketing industry thrives on the exact skill sets Expressive and Amiable Style people bring to the table. Expressive Style people have a distinct ability to generate excitement and buzz, and they are often in the know on popular trends among target consumer groups. Amiable Style individuals are careful communicators who value the feelings and needs of others highly. This lends itself well to positions in sales, and can also provide insightful perspective for crafting compelling advertising messages.

The marketing and advertising industry Versatility scores rank slightly better than average, coming in at number 14 of 32 industries profiled in our research. This shows that employees in this industry are highly attuned to the needs and preferences of others and they have the ability to effectively work with others in a wide variety of situations, but there is still much room for improvement.

Although the Expressive Style is most highly represented, research shows all SOCIAL STYLEs are represented at some level, proving that each SOCIAL STYLE's distinct strengths and perspectives can be useful in different areas. For example, Driving Style designers are strong in setting goals and meeting deadlines, which can help project teams to stay within clients' time frames.

(Based on a sample size of 260 participants)

SOCIAL STYLE & Versatility – Transportation Industry
Versatility Ranking by Industry – 15th

The transportation industry includes a wide variety of job roles filled by a diverse range of people, whether they serve as drivers, pilots

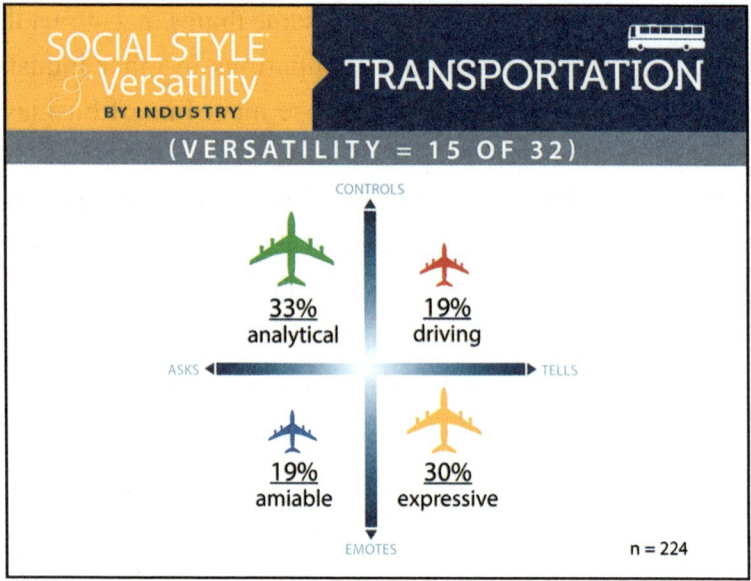

and engineers, back-office support, or customer-service personnel. This diversity of roles makes room for people of all SOCIAL STYLEs, although research shows the Analytical and Expressive Styles are most highly represented.

Specific jobs in the industry can hold different appeals for different people. Analytical Style people, for example, can be drawn to the solitary nature of work as a truck driver or train engineer, while Expressive Style people may be more at home in customer-facing roles. A breakdown of SOCIAL STYLE by job title may reveal these two SOCIAL STYLEs are mainly concentrated in different roles.

Each SOCIAL STYLE lends its unique strengths in different ways, and high Versatility can make everyone more effective when working with each other. Expressive Style people can be an asset in roles requiring frequent interaction with customers, co-workers, and others. Analytical Style people can add value through their strict attention to correctness and skill in drafting detailed plans.

The transportation industry ranks directly in the middle of the

32 industries profiled in our research on average Versatility, coming in 15th place. This rank reveals the industry is generally more skilled in working effectively with a diverse range of people, while at the same time reveals an opportunity for improvement. Any transportation company that can boost its employees' average Versatility can gain a distinct advantage over competitors.

Driving and Amiable Style people can add value to transportation companies through their unique strengths, although they are represented in smaller numbers than the other SOCIAL STYLEs. Driving Style people can add value as traffic controllers or supply-chain managers, for example, by leveraging their penchant for efficiency. Amiable Style employees can boost team spirit in difficult times through their supportive nature.

(Based on a sample size of 224 participants)

SOCIAL STYLE & Versatility – Nonprofit Organizations
Versatility Ranking by Industry – 16th

The Analytical Style is most highly represented in the nonprofit sector, with almost equal proportions of the Expressive and Amiable Styles not far behind. Nonprofit organizations are often service-oriented, and as such they require a strong mix of customer-service employees and detail-oriented planners. Even though they operate somewhat differently than for-profit companies, nonprofit organizations still include a diverse range of job functions in which people of all SOCIAL STYLEs can excel.

The nature of nonprofit work supersedes considerations of personal Styles. Working to improve people's lives, sustain the environment, or achieve political change can connect with people of all SOCIAL STYLEs, regardless of their specific job-role preferences. However, there are different aspects of nonprofit work that

appeal to individual SOCIAL STYLEs. The Analytical Style can be drawn to the precise planning and organization required to provide services to the public. The Expressive and Amiable Styles, on the other hand, can be drawn in by the opportunity to meet people face-to-face and help them change their lives.

The Analytical Style's penchant for planning can ensure services run successfully, which takes on greater importance when the people's welfare or other meaningful objectives are on the line. Expressive Style individuals are uniquely suited to make people's day as they provide nonprofit services. Nonprofits often serve downtrodden or hurting individuals, and Expressive Styles' outgoing and perky dispositions can lighten moods in addition to meeting needs.

The nonprofit industry ranks 16th place in average Versatility scores among the 32 industries profiled in our research. This reveals that people working in the nonprofit sector are fairly well versed in communicating and collaborating with a diverse range of people. Non-profit employees can continue to refine their skills even further with advanced Versatility training. In the nonprofit sector, increased Versatility can mean more than just customer retention; it can mean deeper impacts in the lives of target need groups.

Research proves people of all SOCIAL STYLEs can make valuable contributions in any industry, based on their distinct strengths. For example, even though the Driving Style is represented in smaller numbers than other SOCIAL STYLEs in nonprofit organizations, the urgency and determination of the Driving Style can be a real asset in emergency situations, which can arise in nonprofit hospitals and rescue operations.

(Based on a sample size of 449 participants)

SOCIAL STYLE & Versatility – Consumer Products Industry
Versatility Ranking by Industry – **17th**

The consumer products industry features an interesting distribution of SOCIAL STYLEs. The Expressive Style outweighs all others at

33.3%, and the remaining SOCIAL STYLEs are represented fairly evenly between 20%-25% each. This industry relies on sales and R&D for success, which can provide insight into why the different SOCIAL STYLEs are distributed in this way.

Success in consumer products relies to a great extent on sales, and specifically on the ability to stir up excitement and word-of-mouth advertising for products. The excitement of speaking with new people about hot new items can appeal to Expressive Style people, as can the ability to share their personal opinions about new products and trends.

The distribution of SOCIAL STYLE shows that all SOCIAL STYLEs contribute their unique strengths to the success of consumer products companies. Expressive Style people fuel the sales efforts of these organizations, which often make up a large part of their strategic growth plans. Analytical Style people can lend their focus and precision to Research & Development efforts. Driving Style people can help to ensure that R&D tasks remain on schedule and sales quotas are consistently met.

Versatility scores in the consumer products industry rank in the median range compared to the 32 other industries profiled in our research, coming in 17th place. This indicates people in this industry possess strong skills in understanding others' needs and preferences in their interactions, but there is still room for improvement. Moving from the median range to the top third in terms of Versatility can give an organization a distinct advantage against others in the same industry.

Although the Expressive Style is most highly represented, research shows all SOCIAL STYLEs are represented at a significant level, proving each SOCIAL STYLE's distinct strengths and perspectives can be useful in different areas. For example, Amiable Style people are uniquely suited to design consumer products with which people can form emotional connections.

(Based on a sample size of 1,125 participants)

SOCIAL STYLE & Versatility – Banking & Finance Industry
Versatility Ranking by Industry – 18th

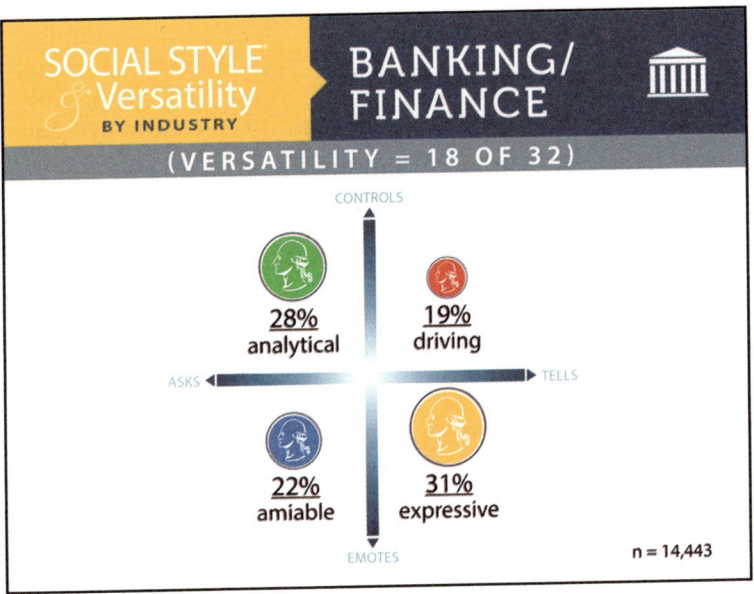

The banking and finance industry is dominated by the Expressive and Analytical Styles (31.0% and 27.8% respectfully). Given the unique mixture of job roles and responsibilities in this industry, this is no surprise. The Amiable Style makes a strong showing here as well, coming in at 22.4%, while the Driving Style is represented much less than in other industries.

Working with finances can be just as complex as working on engineering-related tasks, which is a strong draw for Analytical Style people. Positions in research or money management can be attractive to these people. Expressive Style people are drawn to the type of customer-facing positions found in the retail banking industry, which provides opportunities to meet and interact with a large number of people each day.

Many customer-facing banking positions require the people skills of Expressive Styles and the detail-orientation of Analytical Styles at the same time. Both of these SOCIAL STYLEs can contribute their strengths to customer service roles in banking, although each may have to work a bit harder on the other SOCIAL STYLE's competencies. Analytical Style individuals can contribute their precise research and information-gathering skills to finance positions such as analysts, stock traders, and fund managers.

Versatility scores in the banking/finance industry rank in the middle range of the 32 industries profiled in our research, coming in 18th place. This shows that people in this industry possess strong skills in understanding others' needs and preferences in their interactions, but there is still room for improvement. Moving from the median range to the top third in terms of Versatility can give an organization a distinct advantage against others in the same industry.

Although the Expressive Style is most highly represented, research shows all SOCIAL STYLEs are represented at some level, proving that each SOCIAL STYLE's distinct strengths and perspectives can be useful in different areas. For example, Driving Style people can bring their hard-driving negotiating skills to bear when arranging complex agreements with investors.

(Based on a sample size of 14,443 participants)

SOCIAL STYLE & Versatility – Insurance Industry
Versatility Ranking by Industry – **19th**

As with the banking and finance industry, as well as the accounting industry, the insurance industry's first and second largest percentages of SOCIAL STYLEs come from the Analytical Style and the

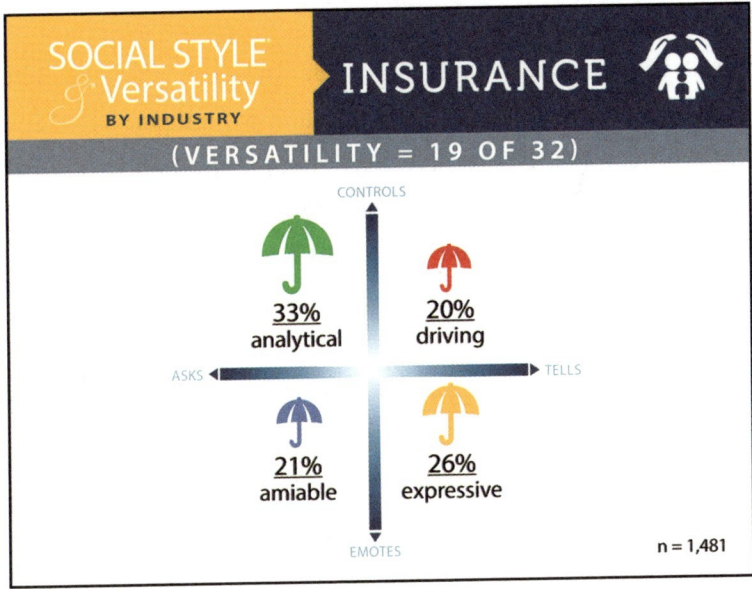

Expressive Style, making up 33.0% and 26.2% of this industry, respectively. With a multitude of job roles inside the Insurance industry, it is no surprise that all SOCIAL STYLEs are represented. What's also interesting is the percentages of Amiable Styles come in third and the percentages of Driving Style come in last, which is also true with the Banking and Finance Industry as well as the Accounting Industry.

Working in the insurance industry can be a very complex and tactical job, making it an easy fit for someone with an Analytical Style. While there is much behind the scenes, analytical work involved, insurance also offers a broad variety of other jobs, ranging from information technology to managerial positions to sales and customer support. Such roles in sales and customer service require people who enjoy working in a fast-paced environment and thrive with constant interaction, hence the high percentage of Expressive Styles.

With many investigative and systematic jobs found in insurance, the strengths an Analytical Style person brings to this industry are countless. Even in customer-facing roles, Analytical Style individuals can contribute their precise knowledge and patient persistence when pursuing objectives. Expressive Style people are handy at working in the fast-paced environment of this industry. In sales roles they are exceptional at explaining the important big picture information and feel comfortable building relationships with clients.

One of the earliest applied uses of SOCIAL STYLE was in the life insurance industry. Companies wanted to determine what distinguished top performers from others. Research showed it was Versatility, the ability to build effective working relationships. You can see how the ability to understand the preferences and priorities of different customers is critical in selling life insurance. Today, as a whole, the insurance industry ranks 19th out of 32 total industries. One of the reasons for the slightly lower-than average Versatility ranking might be due to the highly saturated landscape of the insurance industry. Competition is steep; due to the fast-paced nature of the game, acting with Versatility to peers might not always be on the top of the list. While they're certainly not the lowest ranked, there is still opportunity for improvement. In a highly competitive environment, a company with very high Versatility would be a valuable differentiating factor amongst the other Insurance companies.

Although the Analytical Style is most highly represented, research shows all of the SOCIAL STYLEs are equitably represented in this industry. For example, Driving Style people are needed in roles such as management and sales, which require quick, fact-based actions and a high level of discipline.

(Based on a sample size of 1,481 participants)

SOCIAL STYLE & Versatility – Chemicals Industry
Versatility Ranking by Industry – 20th

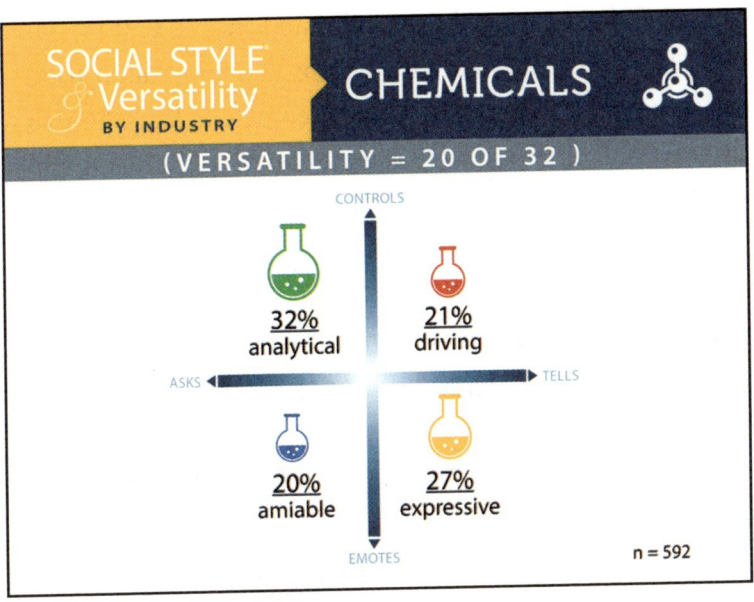

The chemicals industry is characterized by companies that produce, export, and import chemicals used for industrial or manufacturing purposes. Chemicals are used to create most of the products we use daily. Job functions in the chemical industry include those of scientists and chemists, logistical personnel, researchers, and engineers.

The Analytical Style comprises 32.4% of the industry. Their knowledge-driven and curious nature draws them to these roles. The Expressive Style encompasses 27.1% of this industry, and the Driving and Amiable Styles represent 20.9% and 19.6% respectively. The Expressive Style people are likely drawn to careers that allow them to express themselves creatively and work with groups. The Driving Style person is likely drawn to procedural careers that give them control and independence. The Amiable Style person is likely fulfilling roles that allow them to further their relationships with co-workers and work interactively in group settings.

With an average Versatility rank of 20th out of 32 industries, this industry has considerable room for improvement. As a highly integrated and continuously consolidated industry, these workers probably have more internal interactions than other industries. With the development of Versatility skills, people can learn how to work effectively with others as well as control behaviors that might clash with other people.

(Based on a sample size of 592 participants)

SOCIAL STYLE & Versatility – Defense Industry
Versatility Ranking by Industry – 21st

The defense industry is characterized both by those who work directly for the military and those who provide weapons, aircraft, and other technology for the military. The Analytical Style comprises the vast majority of this industry at 40.6%. This is the single highest percentage of Analytical Style people in any industry. Likely drawn to careers in engineering, mechanics, contracting, and computer science, there are numerous jobs to appeal to this task-central and methodical Style. Expressive Style people make up the second largest Style in the defense industry at 23.1%. These fast moving, big picture thinkers are likely drawn to careers in negotiating contractual agreements, project management and PR. The Driving Style makes up 19.3% of this industry while the Amiable Style makes up only 17.0%.

This industry ranks 21st of 32 industries in terms of average Versatility. This middle-of-the-road ranking can be understood when analyzing the great variety of careers that can be found in this industry. While some job functions can be highly interactive like negotiating contracts with clients and conducting meetings with clients to determine needs, other tasks within this industry are highly autonomous. But Versatility enhancement is important not just for those who have highly communicative job functions, but also those who appear to work independently as well. As knowledge sharing becomes more incremental to the success of a product, project, or business entity, the ability for everyone to put their heads together will determine which companies survive.

(Based on a sample size of 212 participants)

SOCIAL STYLE & Versatility – Retail Industry
Versatility Ranking by Industry – **22nd**

The retail industry is one of the most customer-facing industries we have surveyed, but there is such a variety of job roles that the distribution of SOCIAL STYLEs is fairly even. Not surprisingly, Expressive Style individuals make up the majority of retail employees, with the Analytical Style coming in second. While these SOCIAL

STYLEs are opposite of one another, the way retail businesses operate makes individuals with these SOCIAL STYLEs a likely fit in different roles.

Expressive Style people are naturally drawn to the customer-facing nature of the retail industry. The opportunity to meet new people every day and socialize with customers can be irresistible to Expressive individuals. Since retail relies tremendously on increasingly sophisticated processes and strategies for managing inventory and accounting for customer preferences, there are also plenty of job roles that appeal to Analytical Style people.

Staffing a retail storefront with Expressive individuals can be a valuable asset, especially in outlets that rely on personalized and engaging customer interactions. Retail personnel who bring excitement and energy to customer interactions can encourage buying decisions by their very attitudes. While Analytical Style people would be obvious assets behind the scenes to work in areas such as inventory management and accounting, they can also be skilled in customer-facing roles. For example, some businesses rely on their sales staff to be experts in their product lines and to be able to answer very detailed questions from customers. Many customers prefer the sort of objective and non-pushy approach that Analytical Style people bring to the table.

The average Versatility score of the retail industry places it in 22nd place, the bottom third compared to the 32 other industries profiled in our research. This shows there is quite a bit of room for improvement, especially considering the relationship-based industry that retail is. Moving from the bottom of the pack to the upper echelons in terms of Versatility can give an organization a distinct advantage against competitors in the same industry. This is particularly true for retail, which relies heavily on interpersonal effectiveness to enhance customer experiences.

In an industry as broad as retail, there are many opportunities for people to succeed through their natural strengths and SOCIAL STYLE characteristics. For example, Amiable Style people are adept at smoothing relations with customers who have undergone a negative customer-service experience. Their personal commitment to help customers can be invaluable. Driving Style people are also highly valued by customers, particularly when time and efficiency are priorities, because they can meet customer needs quickly and without unnecessary distraction.

(Based on a sample size of 1,130 participants)

SOCIAL STYLE & Versatility – Automotive Industry
Versatility Ranking by Industry – 23rd

The automotive industry is heavily weighted to Tell Assertive SOCIAL STYLE employees. Expressive Style people are most common, comprising 35.4% of this industry. Driving Style people

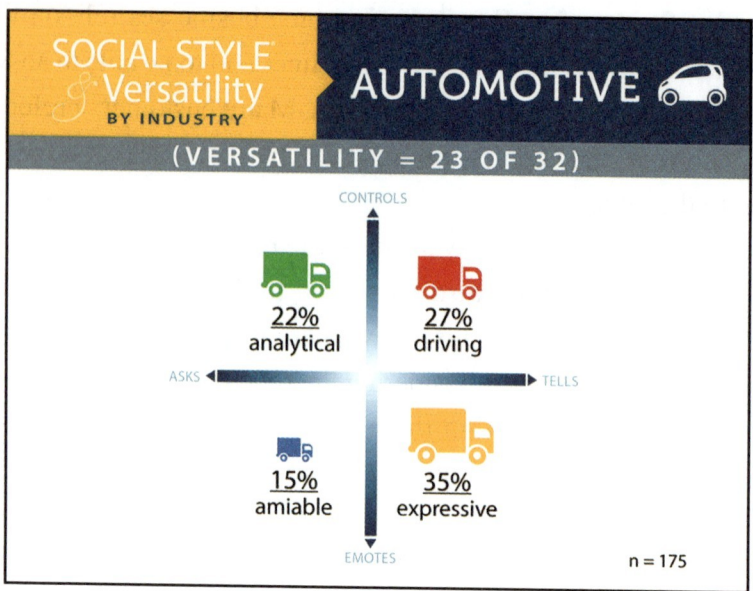

make up an additional 27.4% of this industry with Analytical Style people at 21.8% and Amiable Style people only 15.4%.

The broad range of jobs in this industry offer opportunities for any of the Styles. You can see where sales positions in this industry would be appealing to Expressive Style people. Certainly product development, manufacturing, or logistics would both appeal to and take advantage of the Expressive Style person's skill set.

Ranking 23rd of 32 industries, the automotive industry is in the bottom third for average Versatility. Learning to understand people's behaviors and patterns of communication allows you to better understand your clients' needs. These skills are obviously extremely helpful in sales situations such as understanding priorities and overcoming objections. But Versatility skills are also important in such an integrated industry where development, engineering, manufacturing, marketing, and finance must work collaboratively for success.

(Based on a sample size of 175 participants)

SOCIAL STYLE & Versatility – Construction Industry
Versatility Ranking by Industry – 24th

The construction industry involves more than just the people we see in hard hats and florescent colored gear building bridges, highways, houses, and commercial buildings. Yes, these people of course comprise a large part of this industry, but those who work in construction also include behind the scenes people. These people are the ones involved in project management, architecture, contractual bidding, and heavy equipment operations, training, and rentals. The knowledge-driven tendencies of the Analytical Style make an obvious fit for this industry and they make up the largest segment of this industry at 31.3%. The wide variety of job functions allows for a great deal of personal creativity and expression as well as big picture thinking and constant new challenges and tasks. The Expressive Style is naturally inclined to such an industry, making up the second largest portion at 28.3%. The Driving Style and Amiable Style make up

21.7% and 18.7% of this industry respectively.

    The Construction industry ranks 24th among the 32 other industries in terms of average Versatility. We can understand the lower levels of Versatility among those working in this industry; due to the dangers that can be associated with this industry, the need for safety and abruptness might get in the way of appealing to the behavioral preferences of others in times of crisis. Still, efficient communication and clarity when working with others is the key to a harmonious work atmosphere. As the opportunity for mistakes is large when working with so many different pieces and people, Versatility is necessary to eliminate error, ensure optimum levels of efficiency, and establish safety protocols.

(Based on a sample size of 198 participants)

SOCIAL STYLE & Versatility – Utilities Industry
Versatility Ranking by Industry – 25th

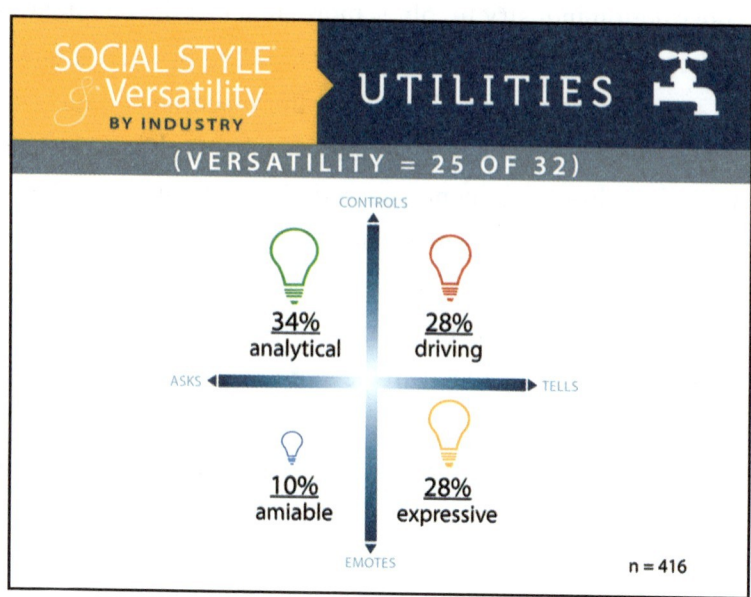

The utilities industry is filled with a wide range of job roles, and thus a diverse range of individuals. This is true whether a utility company focuses on residential, commercial, or government contracts. The Analytical Style is most highly represented here, with the Amiable Style showing in smaller numbers than most other industries.

Research finds Analytical Style people can be drawn to engineering-related positions, as this SOCIAL STYLE is most highly represented in all engineering-focused industries TRACOM has profiled. The trend holds true for employees in this industry—the complex and technical nature of engineering or technical service falls right within an Analytical person's comfort zone. Expressive Style people may be more drawn to the customer service and sales roles in the industry, which are of vital importance to utility companies. This isn't to say that Expressive Style people aren't engineers; according to our data, of the people who profiled as engineers, Expressive Style people make up 21.6% of this demographic.

All SOCIAL STYLEs bring their unique strengths to the table in the electrical industry. In addition to the strengths illustrated above, the unique traits of both Analytical and Expressive Style employees are important to utility companies providing on-site service. On-site technicians require the mix of technical competency and people skills displayed by these two SOCIAL STYLEs.

The utilities industry ranks 25th of the 32 industries included in our research on Versatility, placing it in the bottom third. This is not necessarily a bad thing in an industry focused on safety and reliability of service as the main driver of customer retention, but there is always room for improvement. A workforce with high Versatility can overcome the pressures of service interruptions, for example, using a time of crisis to build stronger customer relationships.

Our research shows people of all SOCIAL STYLEs can succeed in any industry, and this holds true for utility companies. For example, even though only 10.1% of employees in the industry display the Amiable Style, these individuals can be a valuable asset due to their strengths in building relationships and collaborating with coworkers and external stakeholders.

(Based on a sample size of 416 participants)

SOCIAL STYLE & Versatility – Publishing Industry
Versatility Ranking by Industry – 26th

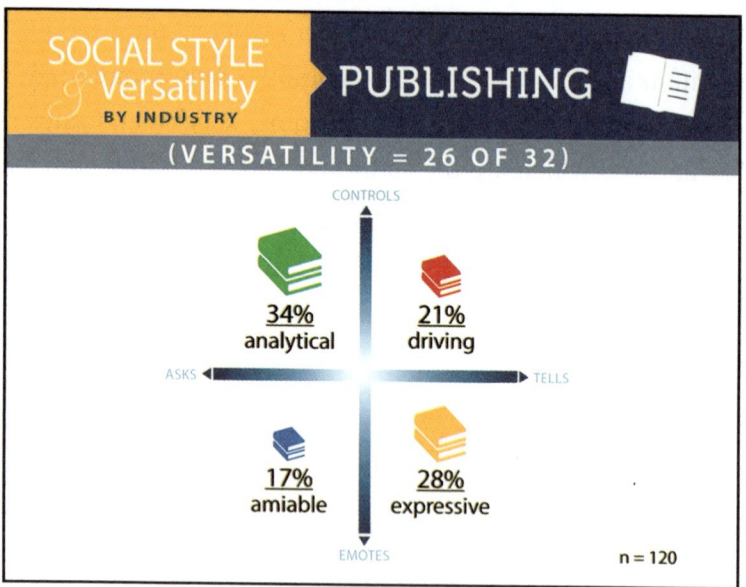

While the publishing industry is a subset of the media industry, there are some interesting differences. Media is among the most balanced in terms of SOCIAL STYLE, with no single Style accounting for less than 22% or more than 27%. But the Publishing industry features a much higher percentage of Analytical Style (34.2%) than others and the Amiable Style only makes up 16.7%. This is likely because the publishing subcategory includes more traditional printed publications while the media industry includes broadcast and web/mobile media as well as print.

Significantly the Versatility scores are quite different as well. Where media ranks 4th of 32 industries for average Versatility, publishing is 26th. There is research that shows that Versatility abilities are closely related to other workplace skills such as effectively managing change and overall performance. So, given the challenges and contraction the publishing industry has experienced over the past two decades, it's interesting to consider whether the lack of Versatility here was the precursor or result. Perhaps those with high Versatility were best able to anticipate and drive change in their organizations to create multi-faceted "media" organizations.

(Based on a sample size of 221 participants)

SOCIAL STYLE & Versatility – Aerospace Industry
Versatility Ranking by Industry – 27th

The aerospace industry is one of the most technologically sophisticated and innovative industries in the world, employing tens of thousands of engineers and scientists. Not surprisingly, the Analytical Style is highly represented in this industry, along with Driving Style people, which is often the case in highly technical industries. The percentage of Amiable Styles is among the lowest compared to any other industry.

Many job roles in the aerospace industry require an immaculate attention to detail. People involved in manufacturing aeronautic or space vehicles, for example, understand that people's lives rely on their accuracy and precision. This environment is a natural draw for Analytical Style people, as it gives them an opportunity to make meaningful contributions that directly rely on their unique characteristics and strengths.

The strengths an Analytical Style person brings to this industry

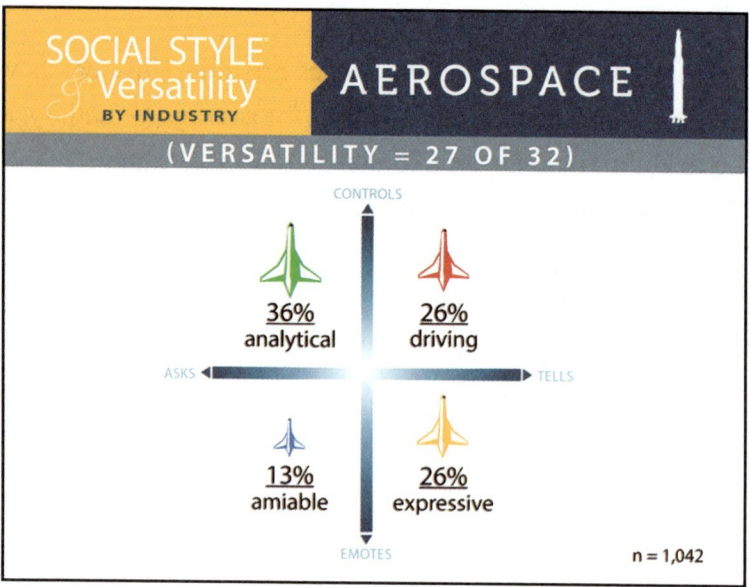

mirror the attraction mentioned above; namely, the ability to focus on small details, follow detailed technical and project plans, and a patient persistence when pursuing objectives. Driving Style individuals also add a great deal of value here as well, since complex engineering projects require people to keep things on schedule and moving forward.

Compared to the other industries, the aerospace industry ranks 27th on average Versatility score. There are several possible reasons for this. First, aerospace is often a very fast-paced and results-driven work environment, which may push people beyond their natural comfort levels to the point where they operate in Backup mode and do not act with high Versatility. Second, because many people may work on teams that are dominated by Analytical and Driving Style people, it is possible that "group-think" occurs, whereby different ways of working, solving problems, and interacting are not encouraged. Both of these scenarios discourage people from showing Versatility since there would be minimal reward for this. Whatever the reasons may be, the data reveal an opportunity for companies in this industry to differentiate themselves from competitors by increasing employee Versatility.

While Analytical and Driving Style people are highly represented in aerospace, all SOCIAL STYLEs are present and can be successful. For example, Expressive and Amiable Style people can rely on their unique strengths, such as developing strong teams that are able to meet goals, and forcing teams to consider the big picture and larger priorities when they are mired in the details.

(Based on a sample size of 1,042 participants)

SOCIAL STYLE & Versatility – Manufacturing Industry
Versatility Ranking by Industry – 28th

There are a variety of companies and job roles within the manufacturing industry, which is why there is a roughly even mix of SOCIAL

STYLEs in this industry. A possible reason there are fewer Amiable Style people in manufacturing might be because there are fewer opportunities for customer-facing roles than in other industries, which is a natural attraction for these individuals. Contact with customers is often limited to high-level managers and salespeople. However, the mix of SOCIAL STYLEs shows there are unique roles in which each SOCIAL STYLE is able to thrive.

With such a variety of functions and roles, there is a fit for every SOCIAL STYLE in manufacturing. Analytical Style individuals often prefer to work on technical matters, and manufacturing jobs frequently afford this opportunity. Driving Style individuals are attracted to the fast pace of the industry and the opportunity to achieve results, while many Expressive Style people are likely found in roles that require team or customer interaction, such as marketing and sales.

The Analytical Style's precise attention to detail and penchant for engineering-related job roles makes them an asset in the manufacturing industry, which relies more on automated production technology than ever before. Driving Style people can help manufacturing companies meet quotas and consistently follow regulations by leveraging their efficient and logical leadership style. In addition to these two SOCIAL STYLEs, Amiable and Expressive Style employees can contribute in meaningful ways.

The manufacturing industry is in the bottom third of average Versatility scores, ranking 29th out of 32 industries profiled in our research. This is likely due to the unique atmosphere and culture of many companies within this industry. Historically, many manufacturing companies have operated under a command and control leadership hierarchy, where interpersonal skills have not been highly valued. This is changing now that organizations are realizing the payoffs and benefits of Versatility. For example, modern manufacturing plants now rely not only on top-notch technical abilities, but also on workers' skills at team problem solving, customer awareness, and personal innovativeness. In today's highly competitive environment, manufacturers can differentiate themselves from competitors by increasing employee Versatility and team skills.

Manufacturing is well represented by all SOCIAL STYLEs, proving there are job roles that appeal to all SOCIAL STYLEs and people of all SOCIAL STYLEs are successful in this industry. Though the Amiable Style is less common, it is not hard to find jobs that fit these individuals within manufacturing. For example, Amiable Style people can make skilled liaisons between employers and labor unions, and might often serve in human resources roles in this industry.

(Based on a sample size of 2,925 participants)

SOCIAL STYLE & Versatility – Electronics Industry
Versatility Ranking by Industry – 29th

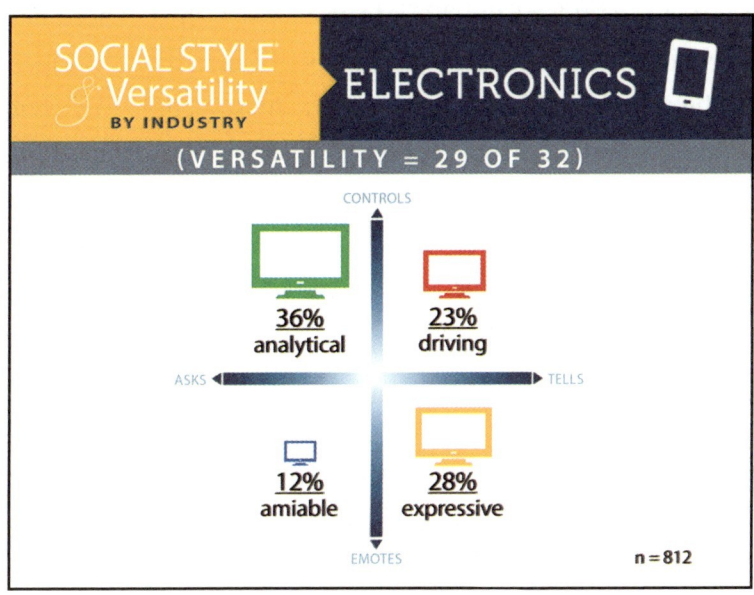

As we have grown highly dependent on our electronic devices, this industry has expanded to include many different job functions. Those who work in the electronics industry range in job roles, but some of the most common job functions that come to mind include computer science and engineering. Think of the people designing your latest iPhone or Galaxy device, Fitbit, Bluetooth speaker, or GoPro. Just as in any other industry that is highly technical, the Analytical Style makes up a large chunk at 36.2%. This isn't to say that the other Styles aren't as successful in a technical setting, because they can be! It just means that because of the procedural tendencies of the Analytical Style, they are more characteristically drawn to a high-tech vocation. Expressive Style people make up 28.1% of this industry. They likely favor the more outwardly present roles such as promotion and marketing, although their creative nature can be a help in designing and engineering new products. Driving Style comprises 23.4% and Amiable Style 12.3% of this industry.

The Electronics industry has one of the lowest average Versatilities, ranking 29th of the 32 industries researched. These people are more focused on universal appeal as well as form and function, but furthering Versatility skills can allow these people to develop a greater understanding of their buyer and what appeals to their different target markets. Additionally, the importance of effective collaboration is a huge competitive advantage in the electronics industry, and those who have mastered the art of effective interoffice relationships are those who will lead the pack.

(Based on a sample size of 812 participants)

SOCIAL STYLE & Versatility – Energy Industry
Versatility Ranking by Industry – 30th

Organizations in the energy industry are similar in many ways to the

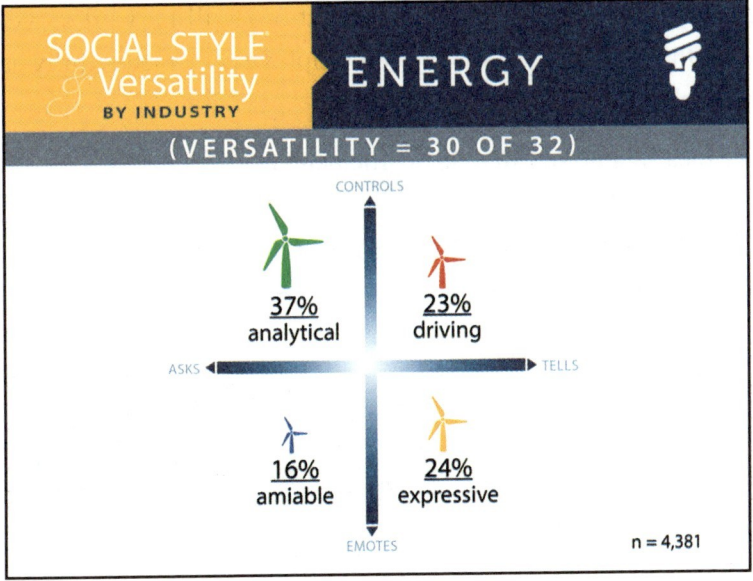

extractive industry. This includes many operational similarities as well as SOCIAL STYLE distribution and Versatility scores. Energy companies have a somewhat more diverse range of jobs compared to the extractive industry. This would typically include broader distribution, retail operations, and marketing positions. Similarly, the Analytical Style is the largest representation of SOCIAL STYLE with 36.6% of employees having that Style. The Driving Style is measured at 23.2% and Expressive Style at 23.9%. The Amiable Style represents only 16.3% in this industry.

Although the Analytical Style is most highly represented, research shows all SOCIAL STYLEs are represented at some level, proving each SOCIAL STYLE's distinct strengths and perspectives can be useful in different areas. For example, Amiable Style people can make skilled liaisons between employers and labor unions in this industry.

The energy industry ranks 30th in Versatility scores, compared to all 32 industries profiled in our research. As new technologies influence both energy production and distribution, the competitive landscape is changing. These organizations will be well served to develop the Versatility skills of their employees to successfully adapt to those changes.

(Based on a sample size of 4,381 participants)

SOCIAL STYLE & Versatility – Extractive Industry
Versatility Ranking by Industry – 31st

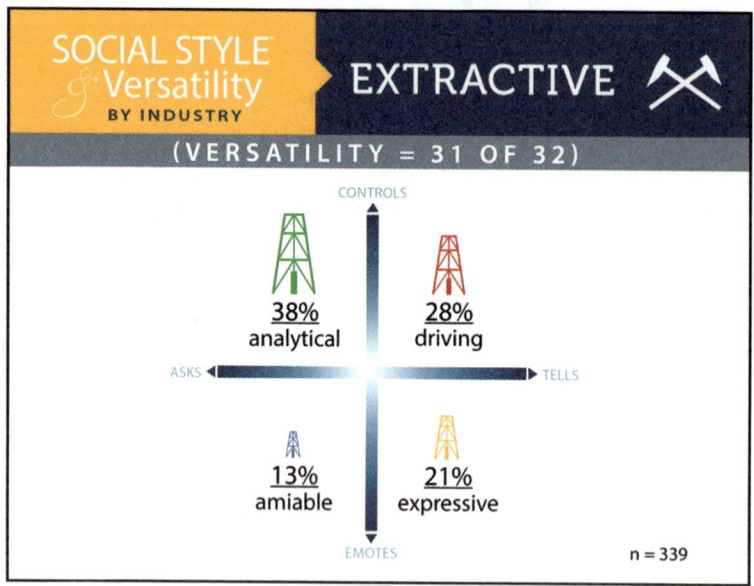

Organizations in the extractive industry (mining, oil, gas, etc.) are skilled and knowledgeable technicians. As in other industries with similar technical expertise requirements (energy, engineering, IS/IT), the Analytical Style makes up the largest portion of the workforce here. The Analytical Style represents 37.8% of employees in this industry, with the Driving Style at 28.0% and Expressive Style at 20.9%. The Amiable Style represents only 13.3% in this industry.

This distribution is not surprising given the emphasis on technical skills and an emphasis on efficient procedures and safe operations. Engineering plays a large role in extractive organizations, and Analytical Style people are often attracted to engineering-related occupations. The complex challenges of assembling and disassembling rigs, distributing large machinery across continents, and maintaining safety systems can be quite appealing to an Analytical Style person. The high compensation for entry-level employees can attract Driving Style individuals who are ambitious and eager to achieve financial goals quickly, as can the fast-paced and energetic environment of extractive work places.

The no-nonsense work ethic of Analytical and Driving Style people fits perfectly in an environment where accuracy and compliance with complex regulations can determine success or failure. Analytical Style supervisors and R&D employees can help keep employees safe and machinery running smoothly, while Driving Style extractive employees possess the sense of urgency and tenacity required to succeed on the front line.

The extractive industry ranks 31st in Versatility scores, compared to the total 32 industries profiled in our research. This is one spot lower than the closely related energy industry.

(Based on a sample size of 329 participants)

SOCIAL STYLE & Versatility – Research and Development Industry
Versatility Ranking by Industry – 32nd

As expected, organizations in the research and development field are heavily populated with Analytical SOCIAL STYLE people. Most of their staff are heavily involved with research and analysis, so it's no surprise that at nearly 38.4%, this group is largely made up of Analytical Style people. Analytical Style people make a natural selection for this job type because of their data-driven and methodical tendencies. The Expressive Style represents 26.6% of this job

market and has a natural inclination to spontaneity and creativity. These folks use their ideation skills to try new things and can oftentimes produce incredible and innovative products and services. Driving Style individuals are third, representing 19.2% of the people in this industry. These individuals are driven to these jobs because they are big picture thinkers, with a goal in mind, determined to find the means to achieve it. These people are not reluctant to challenge the ideas of others and are certainly not afraid to take risks, allowing for many product enhancements. The Amiable Style makes up just 15.8% of the population.

Of the 32 industries evaluated, research and development has the lowest average Versatility. This is likely due to a more solitary work environment or the more long-term project horizon than other industries. But as development processes become more team-based, including more virtual teams, it's important that even the Analytical researchers develop collaboration skills. This will allow for faster and more creative development efforts.

(Based on a sample size of 146 participants)